Reading for Reform

Reading for Reform

THE SOCIAL WORK OF LITERATURE IN THE PROGRESSIVE ERA

Laura R. Fisher

UNIVERSITY OF MINNESOTA PRESS
Minneapolis London

A different version of chapter 1 was published as "Writing Immigrant Aid: The Settlement House and the Problem of Representation," *MELUS: Multi-Ethnic Literature of the United States* 37, no. 2 (Summer 2012): 83–107. Another version of chapter 1 was published as "The Settlement House as Contact Zone," in *Contact Spaces of American Culture: Globalizing Local Phenomena* (Berlin, Vienna, London: LIT Verlag, 2012), 133–48. A different version of chapter 3 was published as "Head and Hands Together: Booker T. Washington's Vocational Realism," *American Literature* 87, no. 3 (December 2015): 709–37.

Copyright 2019 by the Regents of the University of Minnesota

All rights reserved. No part of this publication may be reproduced, stored in a retrieval system, or transmitted, in any form or by any means, electronic, mechanical, photocopying, recording, or otherwise, without the prior written permission of the publisher.

Published by the University of Minnesota Press
111 Third Avenue South, Suite 290
Minneapolis, MN 55401-2520
http://www.upress.umn.edu

The University of Minnesota is an equal-opportunity educator and employer.

Library of Congress Cataloging-in-Publication Data
Names: Fisher, Laura R., author.
Title: Reading for reform : the social work of literature in the Progressive Era / Laura R. Fisher.
Description: Minneapolis: University of Minnesota Press, 2019. | Includes bibliographical references and index. |
Identifiers: LCCN 2018024548 (print) | ISBN 978-1-5179-0382-4 (hc) | ISBN 978-1-5179-0383-1 (pb)
Subjects: LCSH: American literature—20th century—History and criticism. | Literature and society—United States—History—20th century. | Books and reading—Social aspects—United States—History—20th century. | Social problems—United States—History—20th century.
Classification: LCC PS223 .F57 2019 (print) | DDC 310.9/0052—dc23
LC record available at https://lccn.loc.gov/2018024548

To the memory of Alfred Joel Fisher (1942–2016)

Contents

Introduction: The Politics of Proximity   1

1. Sites of Contact: The Settlement House   31

2. The Problem with Comparison: The Working Girls' Club   75

3. Correlation and Conformity: From the African American College to the Harlem Renaissance   125

4. Forms of Mediation: Undercover Literature   177

Coda: Twenty-first Century Afterlives   227

Acknowledgments   235

Notes   239

Index   291

Introduction

THE POLITICS OF PROXIMITY

In November 1890, the *Far and Near* literary journal made its modest debut in New York City. Founded by members of the Association of Working Girls' Societies of America, *Far and Near* grew out of the first national meeting of a social uplift organization that would reach its peak popularity around the turn of the century and then fade just as quickly into relative obscurity. The opening editorial of *Far and Near* was something of a manifesto, charged with simultaneously summarizing the mission of the working girls' club movement, its periodical, and its institutional commitment to friendship across the boundaries of class and station:

> [The clubs] begin with nearness. A few girls who are already near each other in location wish to gain opportunities to grow nearer in sympathy, in mutual comprehension, and in aim, and the first Club is formed. From this the suggestion passes to other girls, who in their turn unite in a Society, and the idea constantly spreads from the near to the far. The office of this paper is to bring those who are far apart near to one another. We are glad to have the circle of Clubs widen indefinitely, but we hope that the twelve yearly issues of *Far and Near* will, like the spokes of a wheel, unite all its parts to a common center.[1]

Far and Near arose to meet a number of institutional and cultural demands. Its editors aimed to consolidate what was still, in 1890, a loosely knit network of working girls' societies scattered across the Northeast and Midwest, and they felt that a periodical would help congeal these disparate clubs into a unified movement equal to the energy of the dawning Progressive Era. The journal was also designed as a forum where club members—office and factory workers on the one hand, middle- and leisure-class women on the other—could share ideas and, just as important, rehearse lessons in well-mannered self-expression and composition that were central to the clubs' pedagogy of uplift. In the four years of the paper's existence, *Far and Near* upheld the reformist mission of the club movement: each issue contained practical guidance in fashion, speech, and manners; summarized the goings-on in clubs from Iowa to Rhode Island; and more generally offered literary and intellectual fare.

But what does it mean to begin with nearness and expand to include the far? At a basic level, this language seeks to account for the particular way working girls' clubs were formed, in contrast to the more famous mainstream, middle-class club movement. Women of the same class and community (those who share a "nearness" in status) wished to develop more diverse and potentially ameliorative friendships, and they understood this institutionalized effort to "grow nearer in sympathy" to women who were geographically proximate but socially remote—say, New Yorkers living in a neighborhood three miles away, in conditions scarcely imaginable—as a form of social praxis.[2] Just as important, this discourse of distance and proximity betrays a larger faith in the transformative power of print culture. If the institution of the club brought the near to the far, then print did exactly the opposite: its systems of distribution brought the far to the near. Scattered women united into a movement by becoming a national network of readers. The resulting intimacy of a club composed of affluent and wage-earning members, and the so-called nearness that the periodical made possible, combined to produce a uniquely relational method of imagining and implementing social reform. And yet this approach to the problem of social distance, one that draws equally on the dynamics of cross-class friendship and the forms and practices of literary expression, constituted the guiding social ethic of a whole cohort of contemporary reform institutions that, like the working girls' club, were premised on the existence of asymmetrical social relations while also nominally working to repair them.[3]

Beyond articulating the mission of the working girls' club within the broader landscape of education and uplift, *Far and Near*'s opening editorial expresses a distinctly reformist vision of the value literature was thought to hold as a medium of cross-class affiliation and repair. This vision of what we might call the social work of literature reverberated far beyond the periodical's own limited circulation, and indeed well beyond the context of the club movement. The idea that literature held a special power to shape the U.S. social order gained new meaning around the turn of the twentieth century, as reform institutions from the settlement house to the African American college generated their own nuanced institutional vocabularies to describe the unequal but still friendly relations that obtained between reform's benefactors and its beneficiaries. This vocabulary circulated widely across the axes of reform and literary culture, shaping the work of minor and canonical American authors alike. Writers from Edith Wharton and Booker T. Washington to Dorothy Richardson found in the relations of reform the kind of social complexity that provided a crucial model for their interrogation of inequality and literary cultivation of realist precision, historical texture, and ethical sensibility. Indeed, the social details that Henry James famously claimed were missing in "the texture of American life" and therefore in its national literature were richly available both to participants in the uneasy interpersonal transactions of reform culture and to its observers.[4] Both within reform's pedagogical contexts and within literary representation more broadly, tropes describing patron–client relations structured ways of writing and speaking about social problems and their amelioration, as writers located in Progressive reform culture a vital new vocabulary for describing a socially asymmetrical world.

Reading for Reform: The Social Work of Literature in the Progressive Era explores the unexpected collaboration between modern U.S. literature and the culture of social reform. I argue that organizations devoted to educating and uplifting the socially disadvantaged functioned as vibrant literary institutions from the 1880s until the Harlem Renaissance, infusing U.S. literature across modes and genres with a reformist ethos. Yet this is not the story we are accustomed to telling about the development of Progressive reform or about the fate of literary practice in the era of "art for art's sake."[5] This book thus proceeds along two tracks simultaneously. I document the way reformers, guided by the belief that access to literary culture would transform the "culturally impoverished" and bring about wide-ranging social change, made literature central to the reformist mission of their institutions, generating flourishing amateur literary cultures that have been lost to literary history. These literary scenes brimmed with oppositional energy as participants pushed back against philanthropy's many indignities. At the same time, I uncover the way more established authors absorbed these institutional practices and vocabularies into the thematic preoccupations and rhetorical structures of their work. As foundational institutions of modern U.S. literature and important sites of social and racial formation, Progressive reform organizations influenced how diverse authors wrote about issues of race, class, gender, and work.

The terms "reform," "uplift," and "institution" suffer from a diminished reputation in popular contemporary usage. To many, they smack of political conservatism and social disciplinarity, bringing to mind *Wall Street Journal* editorials on tax reform or the carceral apparatus of the prison.[6] "Reform" conjures the incremental work that politicians perform within well-established and not particularly creative institutional contexts such as health care, immigration, and marriage. Scholarly accounts of late nineteenth- and early twentieth-century social reform generally situate their subject within the context of legislative campaigns, the genesis of state welfare programs, the development of social science, or the professionalization of social work. Many monographs on the history of the settlement house movement—Progressive reform's signal institution—advertise their subject as just such an origin story, bearing titles like *Spearheads for Reform* and *Professionalism and Social Change*.[7] These accounts figure the settlement house as a social laboratory that transformed well-intentioned reformers into politicians and public intellectuals, subordinating the experiences of the working class—typically immigrant men, women, and children who attended settlements—to a historical narrative of professionalization. This scholarly narrative relegates reformist literary clubs, periodicals, and aesthetic pedagogies to the status of minor background props, if it mentions them at all, and it overlooks reform agencies as sites in which literature was institutionalized at the dawn of the twentieth century.

This book turns to the rich interplay between reform institutions and U.S. literature to excavate an alternative historical trajectory in which reform culture was, instead, a nexus of experiments in the form and social utility of literature. Reformers of the Progressive Era—a period that I define loosely as spanning from 1890 to World War I but whose philosophical tentacles extend further in both directions—mobilized in reaction to a volatile social landscape transformed by industrial capitalism, the end of Reconstruction in the South, mass immigration, the surge of women into the U.S. workforce, violent labor relations, and urbanization. In these years of dramatic change and flux, Progressives rushed to devise new institutional forms for ameliorating the social ills that ailed the nation and that had transformed their cities and towns. They pursued structural solutions to socioeconomic maladjustments, passing waves of groundbreaking legislation around issues such as urban housing (the New York State Tenement House Act of 1901), public health (the Pure Food and Drug Act of 1906), the "social evil" of prostitution (the 1910 White Slave Traffic Act, or Mann Act), banking (the 1913 Federal Reserve Act), and labor (the 1916 Adamson Act, which established eight hours as a workday for railway employees, and, beginning in 1916, a succession of child labor laws). Within this broader context of Progressivism, women activists developed a relatively autonomous and nonpartisan reformist culture anchored in suffrage, temperance, and settlement reform.

Americans had been forming reform organizations long before the Progressive Era. Women founded the first benevolent societies to support so-called worthy poor members of their own sex in the 1790s, and by 1835 Alexis de Tocqueville had described with astonishment the sheer number and variety of voluntary associations to be found across the nation. "Americans of all ages, all stations in life, and all types of dispositions are forever forming associations," he writes in *Democracy in America*. "There are not only commercial and industrial associations in which all take part, but others of a thousand different types—religious, moral, serious, futile, very general and very limited, immensely large and very minute.... If they want to proclaim a truth or propagate some feeling by the encouragement of a great example, they form an association."[8] Antislavery and temperance organizations had multiplied by the antebellum period, as had moral reform associations dedicated to regulating or eliminating prostitution; organizations for suffrage and dress reform; Indian rights organizations; asylums, prisons, and reformatories; and uncountable societies devoted to education and self-improvement. The Civil War is considered a key turning point in nineteenth-century reform culture both because it marked the end of the powerfully networked abolitionist movement and because officers in the U.S. Sanitary Commission introduced the scientific-management method to reform work during the war, hiring paid agents to organize and provide aid to injured Union soldiers. From the 1870s onward, social reform organizations became increasingly efficient and professionalized, turning away from the sentimental benevolence of the past. Progressive reform was also dramatically more secular than its predecessors. Turn-of-the-century activists decentered the church as a primary agent of social change, instead forging institutional alliances with universities and new corporate philanthropies.[9]

The move toward structural and legal redress of "social destitution" helped earn reformers the generational title of *Progressive*. Progressive reformers connected their efforts toward social amelioration to municipal, state, and federal governmental powers, and they mobilized their expertise within burgeoning social scientific disciplines that bolstered their movements. But the thinkers I address in this book were also keenly interested in the literary, spatial, and interpersonal contexts of contemporary social problems. This latter model of reform, I argue, took shape around the ideal of personal, direct contact—an expansive ideal that includes the contact beneficiaries made with literary culture, with the privileged human bearers of that culture, and indeed with forms of labor explicitly intended to substitute for liberal culture. Following Susan M. Ryan, I understand reform in conceptually supple terms, as "a nexus of social movements, including their various persuasive texts and performances, [which] cannot be neatly distinguished from benevolence, charity, or, for that matter, radicalism." Thus, even as reform movements were undeniably becoming more professional and bureaucratic by the beginning of the twentieth century, the term "reform" continued to hold a rich variety of meanings that "shifted, expanded, and contracted, often depending on the social and political commitments of the author."[10] The uplift organizations addressed here gained political resonance even though their cultural activities did not always support a strict definition of reform as legislative process.

In what follows, I examine the intersections of reform and literature within three important institutions: the settlement house, the working girls' club, and the African American college. Others might as easily have been selected from the array of organizations that flourished during this period, including social purity groups, the National Consumers League, trade unions, the Young Men's Christian Association (YMCA), the National Association of Colored Women, the Charity Organization Society, the National Association for the Advancement of Colored People (NAACP), suffrage and temperance associations, and more. These organizations emerged at the end of the nineteenth century as part of a broader wave of cultural institution building that included the consolidation of public libraries, research universities, museums, and corporate philanthropic foundations, creating a rich institutional network with overlapping sociopolitical affiliations and a common crop of funders, organizers, and volunteers. By the 1880s, museums and concert halls had been established in every major American city as well as in several midsized cities. The exponential growth of such organizations across the nation registers the end point of the incorporation of America in the decades following the Civil War.[11] Notwithstanding the fact that cultural organizations abounded by 1900, the institutional network of individual donors and supporters remained relatively small, reflecting the concentration of immense wealth in the hands of a powerful economic elite. As Amanda Claybaugh observes of an earlier historical period, reformers and philanthropists typically committed their energy to more than one social movement at a time. The boards of trustees serving museums, libraries, and universities often substantially overlapped with those of reform organizations.[12] The large corporate philanthropic foundations that emerged around the turn of the century particularly embraced the settlement movement as a Progressive cause, with the Rockefeller Foundation, the Russell Sage Foundation, the Phelps-Stokes Fund, and the Carnegie Corporation all generously supporting settlements in the urban Northeast.[13] In the sphere of black higher education, these same corporate philanthropies used their monopoly power to shape the pedagogical methods and curricula of black colleges and universities.

The fact that a limited pool of wealthy philanthropists supported a wide range of social and cultural endeavors is not notable in itself: as Thorstein Veblen details in *The Theory of the Leisure Class*, philanthropy had become a veritable class obligation for U.S. elites by the late nineteenth century. What is notable, however, is the fact that a small number of benefactors offered such dramatically unequal provisions for literary and cultural access to the different populations of beneficiaries they served. Over the course of several case studies into African American, Jewish immigrant, and white working-class female literary communities whose conditions of possibility were forged through decidedly uneven philanthropic allocations, I build an argument that takes these disparate pathways of cultural access as a crucial lens onto U.S. literary history. Consider, for example, Andrew Carnegie. The industrialist's various philanthropic trusts supported over a dozen New York City settlement houses and numerous black colleges in the South, in addition to thousands of public libraries across the nation.[14] A 1903 *New York Times* article cited Carnegie's enthusiasm for the project of Americanizing immigrants through culture, quoting him as he left the annual meeting of a Jewish settlement house. "Ladies and gentlemen," he announced, "language makes race. Show me the man who speaks English, reads Shakespeare and Bobby Burns, and I'll show you a man who has absorbed the American principles."[15] Yet while Carnegie's various philanthropic entities worked tirelessly to disseminate literature within white immigrant communities in the urban North, they did much less to build up the life of arts and letters among African Americans living in the rural South. Carnegie contributed $20,000 to build a library at the Tuskegee Institute in Alabama in 1900 and donated an even more significant endowment of $600,000 in 1903, yet black Tuskegee students would not find in that institution a comparable devotion to the reformist power of Shakespeare or Burns. In fact, the philanthropists who almost single-handedly supported the school pushed to ensure that the only books used in Tuskegee classrooms would be "practical" ones offering information that dovetailed with lessons in brick making, sewing, farming, and so on. By allocating funds in this way, philanthropists and the educators and reformers who sometimes begrudgingly collaborated with them produced a new social purpose for the literary: as an adjunct to racialized manual labor.[16]

As an investment in disadvantaged communities and in literary culture itself, philanthropy demanded uneven returns. This book insists that we can learn a great deal about the social life of literature in the United States by tracking how the dissemination of philanthropic moneys to particular identitarian groups mapped onto and helped engender nascent ideas of what literature meant and whom it was meant for. As we shall see, the same small circle of philanthropists and reformers supported different literary projects in distinctly unequal measure. Far from being an accident or contradiction, I argue, these divergent ways of conceiving literature's utility as an instrument of social reform reflect inequalities at the very heart of modernity in the United States. In each chapter I explore how ongoing tension between gratitude and defiance, dependency and self-reliance, conformity and self-determination translated into debates over social and literary autonomy.

The reform institutions addressed in this study were committed to modifying existing racial, ethnic, gender, and class formations by facilitating the upward mobility of marginalized groups. They had explicitly social mandates: to Americanize immigrants and their first-generation offspring at the settlement house; to elevate, refine, and individuate white female wage earners at the working girls' club; to educate and uplift the first generations of African American college students along competing ideological lines at vocational schools and liberal arts institutions; and in the case of undercover writers, to expose in print the dark reality of urban-industrial capitalism by spending time "down and out" as manual laborers. Because the mandate of individual and collective uplift took shape around literary forms and practices, and because so many American authors responded to those mandates in their writing, I situate these sites of reform as *literary institutions*.

"Institution" is a notoriously slippery and abstract concept within literary studies. As Mark McGurl, Jeffrey Williams, Lisi Schoenbach, Lawrence Rainey, Caroline Levine, and James F. English have defined it, "institution" refers both to real, concrete entities (*Atlantic Monthly*,

Farrar and Giroux, the Colored Reading Society of Philadelphia, the Pulitzer Prize) and to established ideas and practices (literature, Shakespeare, modernism).[17] Institutions can serve as concrete patrons of literary practice, as McGurl suggests of the postwar university, for instance, while functioning in a more impalpable way as social technologies that regulate and codify human behavior toward specific ends. In both these senses, the institution mediates between literature and those who produce and consume it, forming a constitutive part of the cultural field that, as Pierre Bourdieu has argued, inserts itself between producers and their work.[18]

The argument of *Reading for Reform* is indebted to vital work on social institutions by Bourdieu and Michel Foucault, both of whom put relationships of power at the center of inquiry. Defining the concept of the institution in broad terms, as "all the field of the nondiscursive social," Foucault examines modern institutions as vehicles of surveillance and sites in which disciplinary power "becomes embodied in techniques, and equips itself with instruments and eventually even violent means of material intervention."[19] I take as a given Foucault's and Bourdieu's foundational insights: that institutions help people recognize themselves as social subjects, enabling them to experience and internalize the unwritten laws of their world. I draw attention throughout this book to the disciplinary violence of Progressive reform, which is, in my telling, as frequently conservative as it is radical. One way of understanding the specific historical resonance of that violence is to consider a dynamic that Barbara Cruikshank calls the "will to empower." Settlement houses, working girls' clubs, and African American vocational colleges regulated the actions of the individuals who attended them, but they did so only after first securing their "capacity to act as a certain kind of citizen with certain aims." The fact that Progressive reform functioned by instilling the will to empower explains how these institutions could be both voluntary and coercive at once: reformers' efforts to foster the subjectivity and cultural enrichment of underprivileged clients always constituted a relation of power, no matter how good their intentions nor how worthy the outcome.[20] But I also bring critical attention to the creative and often unexpected ways in which reform institutions produced historically contingent understandings of literature's meaning and use value as a core part of their social mission. A perspective attuned to the social uses of literature helps explain how settlements, clubs, and colleges were able to gain the status of literary institutions in their day without necessarily courting the economies of prestige that structured the work of, say, a publishing house or a periodical. Each institution gained its particular position within the larger social and cultural field by forging connections with disempowered groups.[21]

The archives of social reform agencies help connect the specific and the general senses of literary institutions. Meeting minutes, mission statements, fund-raising materials, and letters—the workaday documents that keep bureaucracies alive and that tell their stories—richly describe the institutional practices and positions that characterize turn-of-the-century reform culture. For the most part, these administrative materials hew closely to their "institutional frames," to adopt Lisa Gitelman's cunning expression, detailing reform culture's daily operating tasks and larger social objectives in what amounts to a bureaucratic paper trail.[22] But when these documents are taken as a whole and read across the entire field of Progressive reform activity, as I do in this book, they reveal certain stunning cross-institutional commonalities that illuminate the literary and social politics of the Progressive Era.

To bring the far near, uplift organizations consistently sought to bring representatives of high culture into close contact with underprivileged clients, an ethos I describe as their *politics of proximity*. This ethos encompasses beneficiaries' personal contact with literary objects and practices as well as their proximity to individuals whose education and knowledge made them ready stand-ins for "culture" writ large. The reformist concept of proximity has qualities in common with Charles Taylor's notion of "fullness." Taylor's spatial metaphor describes a person's sense of having been empowered or uplifted as a result of having situated him- or herself "in 'contact' with" or close to a "place of power," which he defines as an object or idea that makes life feel "fuller, richer, deeper, more worthwhile, more admirable" simply through proximity. According to Taylor, the feeling of fullness emerges in the presence of material, consecrated locations and structures—religious sites, historically significant landmarks, valued art objects—but a person might equally experience fullness in proximity to abstract ideas or literary-aesthetic concepts that reflect socially consecrated values.[23]

More than an abstract and transhistorical idea, however, the concept of a politics of proximity emerges directly from late nineteenth- and early twentieth-century reform culture's unique patterns of affiliation and assumes a number of social forms. In each chapter, I examine the politics of proximity within the methods and practices of one institution: in the settlement's literary curriculum, spatial organization, and code of friendship; in the working girls' club's pedagogy of cross-class comparison between wealthy ladies and working-class "girls"; in the African American college's tethering of racial uplift alternately to contact with or distance from the book; and in undercover literature's literary-reformist methods. Novelist and settlement worker Vida Scudder described proximity as reform's deepest motive and most useful method. "The inner life" of the settlement house, Scudder writes, "springs from the growing impulse among people to draw closer together ... the deep desire of many to whom a great deal of the beauty and wisdom of the world has been taught, to come nearer to the people who are doing the world's real work—to live right among them, and, so far as may be, under the same conditions."[24] In a similar vein, undercover author Cornelia Stratton Parker argued that labor reform depended on cross-class contact—or, as she put it, getting "within eyesight and earshot of the other."[25] In the work of diverse reformers and writers, proximity becomes a mechanism for resolving social problems and a force capable of revitalizing literary expression. Levine explains that particular institutional techniques disseminate quickly and coherently across different organizations "because these forms afford portability," suggesting that "techniques of organizing bodies or objects ... travel from one institution to another, from one time to another, precisely because they can break with any single context; they are useful ways of imposing order that can crop up wherever and whenever they are needed."[26] Thus, even as individual reform agencies met the larger goal of proximity in idiosyncratic ways that aligned with their religious, political, and academic orientation, the imperative of contact marks the point of their institutional coherence. The concept of proximity gives shape to social, political, and aesthetic experience around the turn of the twentieth century.

Reform institutions developed specific methodologies for bridging the actually existing and merely imagined social gulfs that characterized these years of rapid industrialization and urbanization. Crucially, these historical practices exist in dynamic relation to specific literary works, movements, and archives, and so I read them within and across texts of modern U.S. literature. What I find is that the politics of proximity drive the antiauthoritarian Yiddish theater and the antisentimental style of reformist memoir; they animate Nella Larsen's critique of uplift, Anzia Yezierska's defense of beauty, and Edith Wharton's discourse of similitude and difference. The speeches and writing of Booker T. Washington and W. E. B. Du Bois and the once-flourishing subgenre of undercover literature are all structured in different ways by their authors' approach to proximity. When we put reform institutions at the center of U.S. literary history, we see that wildly diverse authors make the promise and perils of proximity a medium for telling stories about race, class, gender, and social aspiration.

Proximity also provides a critical hinge between the historical and literary arguments I forward in this book. In this sense, *Reading for Reform* does not just propose a new way of understanding U.S. literature, but also produces a portable method for reading literature and history together. Reading for proximity joins close reading, distant reading, and surface reading as a critical method grounded in the spatiality of literary encounter, yet its analytical purchase derives from the historical practices of education and uplift that mediated literature for diverse constituencies around the turn of the century.[27] The reform logic of proximity becomes a powerful way to read across genres of U.S. literature without merely reading for themes or plumbing literature for examples of a historical event.[28]

To gain some purchase on how this reform logic functions and what its critical affordances are, let me briefly outline some key ways that reading for proximity engages the gender, class, and race relations of the era. Many reformers and authors argued that proximity galvanized social and economic change in the lives of disadvantaged subjects by transforming their habitus, a concept Bourdieu devised to describe individuals' reflexive, subjective dispositions, shaped by the class conditions of their upbringing and guiding their patterns of consumption, social interaction, and taste. To Bourdieu, habitus is a collection of "schemes of perception, appreciation and action."[29] It is structured by objective, material factors in an individual's upbringing, and it adapts throughout the course of one's life to become an unconscious, wholly comfortable way of being in the world. Reformers did not wish their beneficiaries to crudely imitate certain behaviors and boast artificial cultural tastes; rather, they hoped that beneficiaries would internalize those norms until they became a "habitual state," seamlessly "turned into second nature."[30] Progressive reformers like Grace Hoadley Dodge and Booker T. Washington encouraged the individuals who attended their institutions to model themselves on the cultural objects, practices, and persons they identified with the good life, arguing that such aspirations were not simply imposed from above but, rather, were voluntary and self-willed.[31] In this sense, reformist proximity was often injurious in its uneven conception of which individuals, objects, and practices should hold the power to transform others. And as the following chapters elucidate, one need not look far to find reform's beneficiaries pushing back against these hegemonic ideals.

Yet the politics of proximity did not function in a strictly top-down manner. In fact, when we read for proximity, we can see that reform institutions developed a working definition of upward mobility that departs from a strictly individualist, rags-to-riches model. They grounded upward mobility in the mutual relationship between benefactor and beneficiary: a shopgirl's social ascent was inextricable from the worldly education of her privileged mentor, or a box maker's newfound taste for sonnets was said to alleviate a settlement worker's neurasthenic symptoms. This reform logic of asymmetrical but still reciprocal influence reflects what Bruce Robbins calls the "hidden sociability" of upward mobility narratives. In contrast to the myth of the self-made man or woman popularly associated with Benjamin Franklin or Horatio Alger tales, the emotional core of upward mobility narratives lies in the relationship between a protagonist and his or her "patron, mentor, or benefactor," who functions as a mediating figure. Progressive reform institutions appropriated the language of individualism only to redefine social mobility as a relational process that shaped the subjectivity of benefactors and beneficiaries in equal measure. These relations formed a kind of privatized politics operating within the intimate, voluntarist structure of uplift organizations.³²

One word we might use to describe such a model of relational selfhood, of course, is "pragmatism." The activists, thinkers, and writers in this study cannot all properly be defined as capital-*P* Pragmatists, but the politics of proximity nonetheless reflect turn-of-the-century intellectual tendencies to conceive of the modern self as a social being and to regard subjectivity as inevitably relational in nature.³³ From one angle, the argument I have been sketching about reformist proximity bolsters James Livingston's claim that artists and intellectuals saw the powerful social and economic changes that accompanied the transition from proprietary to corporate capitalism as "sources of a new, *social* self," a self whose boundaries were broadened "by association with others in managing the 'collective property' of culture," including parks, libraries, museums, and literature.³⁴ The reconstructions of subjectivity that reform institutions encouraged chime with an emergent philosophy of pragmatism. On a more official level, the alliance between pragmatism and social reform was struck most publicly in the close association between Hull-House founder Jane Addams and John Dewey at the University of Chicago. Drawing on her firsthand experience in Chicago's Nineteenth Ward, Addams wrote that the critical task of reformers and educators was "to take actual conditions and to make them the basis for a large and generous method of education."³⁵ Heeding the pragmatic appeal to experiment, applied knowledge, and instrumentalism, the settlement movement helped nurture a culture of firsthand experience in the United States by facilitating new modalities of contact and interaction across borders of class and ethnicity. When affluent white reformers "settled" in immigrant, working-class communities, those community institutions became critical laboratories of firsthand experience, generating pragmatic forms of knowledge about contemporary social problems that reformers claimed could not be understood by reading books alone.

Yet the pragmatic call to "connect learning with industrial pursuits" resonated differently within the Jim Crow order.³⁶ As an analytic, the politics of proximity index broader crises in the racial economy of firsthand experience under Jim Crow. The idea of proximity was at the heart of ongoing debates over the literary and intellectual entitlements of African American citizens, debates waged within the institution of the black college between advocates of industrial training and those in favor of a liberal arts education. Booker T. Washington's doctrine of "learning by doing" was closely attuned to the currents of Progressive educational reformers, and African American education was shaped in large part by his racialized discourse of far and near: even though he became a prolific author, Washington decried books as distant and irrelevant objects, as a force that blinded black students to their immediate surroundings and probable status as future laborers in an agrarian economy. "I have found, too, that it is the visible, the tangible, that goes a long ways in softening prejudices," Washington wrote in his 1901 autobiography *Up from Slavery*. "The actual sight of a first-class house that a Negro has built is ten times more potent than pages of discussion about a house that he ought to build." Though people who had received a liberal arts education might be able to quote "a phrase or a sentiment from Shakespeare, Milton, Cicero, or some other great writer," he claimed that this very "book knowledge" rendered them powerless when faced with practical challenges in the here and now.[37] Washington's white supporters in the world of philanthropy and reform embraced industrial education as a distinctly modern expression of the authority of firsthand experience. School reformer and Birmingham, Alabama, superintendent of education J. H. Phillips exemplifies the tendentious politics of "the immediate" within Jim Crow in his claim that "the negro school should be made an instrument for the elevation of the negro laborer, by training him for the immediate work of the shop, the field, and the household." Similarly, white philanthropist and reformer William H. Baldwin Jr. praised the Tuskegee Institute on the grounds that the school "educated [black students] for their environment and not out of it."[38]

When Washington's reformist rivals—most famously Du Bois, but also members of his own faculty—sought to improve black students' access to literary and intellectual materials, to bring them into closer and more sustained contact with books, they were laboring to direct students *away* from the unequal immediate surroundings and desultory local conditions of Jim Crow. I show how this fight against the tyranny of the proximate put advocates of a liberal arts education for black students at odds with the pragmatic ethos of the Progressive Era. Indeed, African American intellectuals and authors pointedly adopted the discourse of industrial modernity to deliver their critiques of social reform. The euphemism "Tuskegee Machine" circulated widely, for instance, and Larsen's *Quicksand* begins with the protagonist's tirade against educational uplift as a "cruel . . . machine" of conformity. Claude McKay too wrote of his "machine-like existence" as a Tuskegee student.[39] This language of automation and mass production captures the extent to which institutions of higher education for black students were anchored in white supremacy: this embeddedness was the very mark of their modernity. In the 1920s, when thousands of African American students demanded that their institutions implement curricular reforms and loosen the stringent social codes that were in place, their protests crystallized a broader demand for immediate access to the intellectual fruits of modernity. I argue, then, that higher education was a key domain through which black intellectuals and writers challenged the principles of pragmatism and debated the modernist doctrine of autonomy in the late nineteenth and early twentieth centuries.

In addition to elucidating the racial dynamics of the era, the politics of proximity at work in reform sites illuminate the class stratification of modern U.S. life. Reformist contact gave rise to a host of what Robbins calls "class-related feelings," from anger, envy, and condescension to pity, gratitude, and admiration.[40] These class-related feelings are everywhere in the institutional and imaginative literature of reform, but they are often submerged and flattened under the title "friend." If we take their word for it, the reformers and educators I follow here wished to cultivate new forms of friendship across axes of difference. These tenuous friendships, they claimed, could serve as engines — as well as proof — of social change. Jane Addams argued that the changing dynamics of social democracy thrust into view the awkward and untenable relation that existed between citizens who were able to make charitable donations and those who were compelled to accept them. Reflecting on the crucial intersection of affect and class position, Addams contended that the vast gulf between helpful neighbor and visiting philanthropist in modern U.S. cities represented the "absolute clashing of two ethical standards." In times of need, she explained, residents of working-class neighborhoods reciprocally exchange tokens of relief with "emotional kindness," whereas distant and detached charitable agents dispense aid to beneficiaries with the kind of "guarded care" that breeds resentment. Yet Addams also perceived some value in that cross-class discord. In her telling, the charitable relation involves "incredibly painful difficulties" on both sides, but "the perplexing experiences of the actual administration [of charity] have a genuine value of their own" in that they formulate the "emotional incentive" that must precede a true industrial democracy.[41] In other words, the reformism of "painful" friendship between rich and poor precedes and makes possible broader structural reforms.[42]

Addams is perhaps the most eloquent writer to broach patronage and unequal power relations in her prose, those thorny issues that both defined and complicated the relationships people formed in the context of reform work. Hull-House was the Progressive Era's preeminent reform institution by any measure, but its importance as a center of liberal politics and civic improvement—not to mention as a site of queer kinship—has obscured the trickier interpersonal dynamics that prevailed within contemporary reform sites.[43] Relatively few social reformers actually conducted their agencies according to Addams's example, and they should not be evaluated solely against the standard of a "public philosopher," a reputation Addams still holds today.[44] Within the settlement movement, for instance, Jewish philanthropists directed a number of important organizations and rose to eminent positions within the larger network of Progressivism. Prominent reformers such as Lillian Wald, Henry Moskowitz, Julia Richman, and Jacob Schiff were certainly eager to support the eastern European Jewish newcomers who flooded U.S. cities around the turn of the century. They too worried about their charitable relation with poorer, greener brethren. But the texture of their concern over the "clashing of two ethical standards" necessarily differed from the concerns of the white Protestant Addams, since they were powerfully motivated to protect their own perilous social standing as assimilated Jewish Americans. Addams's wish for a more egalitarian democracy does not adequately capture the cross-class but intracultural exchanges that marked the nation's many Jewish settlement houses. The personal interactions between Jewish reformers and immigrant beneficiaries—tender but strained, sympathetic and disciplinary, often caught between kinship and disavowal—remain the foremost affective legacy of Jewish reform culture.

The desire to conceptualize the connection between privileged benefactor and underprivileged beneficiary as *friendship*, and thereby to smooth over the ineluctable reality of class hierarchy, was a primary motivator in Progressive reform's philosophical arsenal. For some reformers, this intense focus on philanthropic friendship may also have helped deflect attention away from the same-sex intimacies that took root among unmarried women at settlement houses and the dawning moral panic over what Scott Herring calls "settlement perversion."[45] But we can also understand this turn to friendship as, in large part, a self-periodizing gesture. The Associated Charities adopted the slogan "Not alms, but a friend" in the late 1870s, and the expression maintained currency in social service circles for years afterward as a way of distinguishing a modern scientific philanthropy based on organized personal contact ("a friend") from its comparatively more disorganized and sentimental predecessors (mere "alms"). As Du Bois's citation of this expression in both *The Philadelphia Negro* and *The Souls of Black Folk* suggests, friendship remained central to the reformist zeitgeist into the twentieth century, unimpeded by the ascendency of professionalism and expertise as Progressive values.[46]

Literary-reformist accounts of friendship between donor and client scarcely resemble the expressions of passionate homosocial amity that Sharon Marcus finds characteristic of late nineteenth-century culture, which defined female friendship as a "luxury good that expressed freedom from instrumental relationships."[47] Novelists were among the first to take note of the instrumental nature of these bonds. Henry James critiques reformist friendship in *Princess Casamassima* (1886), satirizing two elite female characters who desire friendly proximity to the urban poor. The Princess and Lady Aurora experience "the same mysterious longing . . . to know the *people,* and know them intimately—the toilers and strugglers and sufferers," believing them to be "the most interesting portion of society."[48] Francesca Sawaya points out that the pursuit of cross-class friendship in James's novel swiftly bleeds into commodification and objectification.[49] And in William Dean Howells's *A Hazard of New Fortunes*

(1889), the wealthy Margaret Vance enters into the "ludicrous" profession of welfare work because her extensive reading about "very common people" had "enlarged the bounds of her imagination," inspiring in her "the vague obligation . . . to be helpful" to economically and merely socially impoverished women alike. But the philanthropic character's primary purpose in the novel is to raise the unanswered question of whether the "poor wretch and the radiant girl [can] really belong to the same system of things."[50] The urge to cultivate or reject cross-class intimacy—and the sense that this intimacy heralds larger social exigencies—appears in the work of a critical mass of novelists active in the late nineteenth and early twentieth centuries, not only authors I examine in this study (Wharton, Yezierska, and Washington) but also those I engage only briefly (Howells and James, as well as Sinclair Lewis, Charles Chesnutt, William James, Charlotte Perkins Gilman, Stephen Crane, and Jack London). What their work collectively illustrates is that the politics of proximity traveled back and forth between clubroom, committee notebook, and U.S. fiction.

While the promise of real fellowship helped elide the taint of charity by distinguishing a friend's support from a patron's philanthropic relation to a client, the reality of these relationships was much more dissonant. Reformist friendship was, in fact, a class fiction that served not to dissolve but actually to support and entrench social distinctions.[51] Examining friendship as a crucial part of the reformist imaginary brings the affective dimension of class relations into view and affords a revitalized sense of how class identities were made and remade in the modern United States. In each chapter, I explore how authors and reform participants theorized, instrumentalized, and even at times weaponized the cross-class affiliations that reform institutions made possible. I navigate the troublesome politics of this scenario as they play out in the factory, in the boardroom, and on the page, for if reform institutions enabled some journeys of cross-cultural understanding, bourgeois self-exploration, and social mobility, they more assuredly generated normalizing judgments and imposed coercive standards of value and behavior that accorded with a fundamentally white, middle-class, Protestant model. And yet I turn to reform culture's alloy of domination and creativity in the belief that social and political complicity "is a privileged vantage point for understanding historical and social complexity," as Stephanie Foote has brilliantly articulated.⁵²

THE SOCIAL WORK OF AMERICAN LITERATURE

A major goal of this book is to particularize the way we think about literature at the historical moment of the Progressive Era, in which "literature" constitutes not only a body of texts but also a set of historically contingent practices and collective values. As I have suggested, putting social reform institutions at the center of literary history reveals a whole constellation of nascent ideas about and instrumentalities for the literary in the decades under investigation here. Nancy Bentley identifies the turn of the twentieth century as a transformative moment in the relationship between culture and civic governance—as, in fact, a "plausible origin" for the now-commonplace tendency to look to aesthetic culture as a resource for critically reflecting on social and political matters.⁵³ As agencies that conjoined culture and civil governance in innovative ways, Progressive reform sites did much to secure this understanding of aesthetics. The heightened traffic between Progressive reform institutions and literature could not help but influence the social purpose of literature more broadly—its meaning, its circulation, its effects.

Let me briefly review some of the conclusions scholars have drawn about earlier conjunctions of literature and reform so that we can better understand the particular social and historical associations that literature had accrued by the turn of the century. We know that during the antebellum era, for example, the phenomenal success of Harriet Beecher Stowe's *Uncle Tom's Cabin* helped raise the prestige of the novel form and institutionalize sentimentalism as a primary aesthetic strategy and thematic concern of American writing. Following Stowe, U.S. reform fiction typically combined the affective and the pragmatic, enjoining readers to identify and sympathize with marginalized populations while also delineating a concrete course of ameliorative social action.⁵⁴ We know, too, that the idea of the novel as a public instrument capable of enacting social reform was of relatively recent vintage; after all, as Glenn Hendler observes, "it was not until 1836 that the American Temperance Union voted to approve the use of fiction to further the cause."[55] Turning to the later nineteenth century, Kenneth W. Warren argues that the crushing social and political burdens of Jim Crow made questions of utility inescapable for black writers. Warren suggests that African American literary expression cohered as a recognizable tradition through "instrumental" and "indexical" imperatives—that is, through understandings of texts written by black authors as "having been written to achieve a social end" on the one hand and as "an index of black integrity" on the other. The expectation that literary texts would be judged according to the identity of their author and with respect to the sociopolitical pressures they exerted on behalf of the race structured African American literature under Jim Crow, notwithstanding individual writers' actual intentions and despite widespread resistance to such programmatic claims on artistic expression.[56]

The thinkers in this study inherited a conception of literature as an expression of cultivation and refinement, as coterminous with an aesthetic sensibility that was a marker of education and privilege, even as their own participation in cross-class reform ventures challenged and even transformed this limited notion of culture. Lawrence Levine and Alan Trachtenberg have each articulated what we might call the "social control" thesis regarding the social function of art in the decades following the Civil War. In their analyses, elites threatened by the upheavals of urbanization and industrialization put their faith in high culture as a moralizing force and a means of arresting social chaos. Building on this thesis, David Shumway contends that by the end of the century literature had accrued new meanings and values that stemmed from its "historically persistent association with learning and its new, narrower identification with the class-specific quality of taste," as well as from "the utilitarian value of producing social cohesion around the dominant culture." Commentators ranging from Henry Ward Beecher to William James crafted a vision of culture that sought to insulate it from the marketplace and from the unruliness associated with working-class, urban life. Theirs was an essentially Victorian understanding of the social function of art, one shaped by the writing of John Ruskin and Matthew Arnold and immortalized in the middle-class Chautauqua adult education movement.[57]

These ideas clearly informed the way the reformers and writers I address approached literature as a social practice. Yet as influential as these nineteenth-century progenitors were, I argue that the sands of culture shifted at the dawn of the twentieth century, when new institutional forums emerged to validate and publicize the belief that literature was a privileged vehicle for the remediation of social problems. Among the broad cultural developments that supported this idea of literature's renewed social utility is the ascendant success culture of the United States, which saw etiquette guides and magazine columns, as well as reading manuals, becoming increasingly popular due in part to a suite of technological advances that made prescriptive texts newly affordable and accessible for a wide reading public.[58] But the culture of success also thrived because it drew strength from—indeed, it relied on—an ethos shared with reform institutions. As I have already suggested, turn-of-the-century reformers developed new curricular and pedagogical practices based on the premises that minoritized men and women could learn correct manners, behavior, and taste and that these changes activated broader social transformations. Furthermore, both etiquette manuals and reform institutions propagated a belief in reading as a mechanism of self-improvement. This confluence helped naturalize a utilitarian vision of literary value. Whole emergent genres of U.S. writing paid tribute to literature's utility: for instance, undercover texts often doubled as makeshift reading-advice manuals, embedding object lessons that illustrated the high stakes of reading, while the novel of manners—a paradigmatic genre of the period—absorbed and reflected this contemporary fixation on class, conduct, and social relations.[59]

But we cannot appreciate how the coalescence of etiquette and reform shaped U.S. literature without considering the extraordinary literary countertradition forged within and against reform culture. The marginalized populations targeted by settlements, clubs, and colleges pushed back against the literary and social politics of reform by appropriating its very terms, painting pedagogical endeavors as a frivolous exercise in manners. Emma Goldman described settlement house methods as "teaching the poor to eat with a fork." Her contemporary Jacob Gordin's antireform play, *The Benefactors of the East Side,* condemns settlements on the grounds that they teach Jewish immigrants to "study a cookbook and learn the rules for holding a napkin and using a knife and fork" and pass it off as cultural enlightenment.[60] Critics bemoaned the way African American vocational colleges displaced liberal culture in lieu of "practical knowledge" of hygiene, housekeeping, and etiquette, and student protests in the 1920s specifically attacked the tendency of such institutions to dilute literary and academic learning by placing excessive emphasis on conduct.

Even if their staff and clientele were somewhat self-selecting, then, reform institutions were able to influence the broader literary field through the rousing public debates they catalyzed. Stakeholders often hashed out what reading for reform actually meant and what its implications for art, activism, and citizenship might be. These debates played out in print, including in fiction: for example, turn-of-the-century racial-uplift novels invariably feature at least one scene in which characters debate the political stakes of uplift.[61] They played out, too, in the many essays and manifestos of the Harlem Renaissance movement, in which black authors reevaluated art, especially literature, as a practical tool in the campaign for civil rights, using the conceptual vocabulary pioneered in African American colleges twenty years earlier. These public conversations about literature's social contingency—its reported power, to name only three examples, to train white female factory workers in the temporal rhythms of industrial labor, to socialize new immigrants in the normative values of U.S. culture, and to make manual labor more palatable for African American students—constitute a central node in the history of racial, class, and gender formation during this tumultuous period. It was not simply by enabling or obstructing cultural access for upwardly mobile citizens that reform institutions made their mark on the literary sphere. Rather, by instigating a much larger public conversation regarding the stakes of this simultaneously paternalistic and democratic pedagogical gesture for benefactors and beneficiaries alike, the collaboration between literature and reform shaped how U.S. authors wrote about relations of inequality. The stakes of reform for reading, writing, and publishing turn out to be a signal preoccupation of U.S. literary culture.

It is no surprise to learn that beneficiaries were sensitive to the way they were represented in print. What is more curious, however, is the fact that reformers developed their social policies in careful dialogue with contemporary literature. They justified their institutional practices not just by pointing to the measurable social and economic needs of users, but also by referring to such factors as the "literary exploitation of the East Side" or to "the injustice done [to working women] by the writers of fiction."[62] Reformers endorsed modes of self-making that directly responded to the characterization of social types and plots of decline that marked even the most sympathetic fiction of the era. Literary and reform culture thus come together in the print public sphere, where social tracts and imaginative texts collaborated in making representation itself a mode of political activity. Each chapter in *Reading for Reform* charts instances of what Michael Warner calls "instrumental publicness" at the intersection of writing and reform, where publicity itself seemed poised to enact social change.[63]

Yet beneficiaries often blanched at the social politics of exposure. The upwardly mobile women who populated working girls' clubs protested reform writing's tendency to depict them as morally vulnerable even as they participated fully in Progressive reform culture. And the factory workers among whom class-passing writers temporarily labored dismissed undercover literature as dishonest and self-indulgent, utterly unconvinced by the genre's claims to veracity and reformist power. Many Jewish immigrant authors rejected the public efforts Jewish philanthropists made on their behalf as disingenuous at best. "As we of the dark, unhealthy, unclean 'Ghetto' read all that is said about us, we asked ourselves what sins have we committed, whether of omission or commission, that we are in the mouth of every man and woman whom fortune has kindly placed in a brownstone home nearer Central Park than our tenement houses happen to be," wrote one anonymous columnist.[64] Reform's belief in the power of representation to change public perception and subsequently social conditions translated into contests over who controlled the official narrative of marginalized groups. What made these debates so complex was the fact that reform institutions relied almost exclusively on philanthropy to keep themselves afloat. When reform's benefactors and beneficiaries battled over the politics of representation in these years, then, their conversations were shadowed—and sometimes overdetermined—by this dependency.[65]

One key way to assess the social work of literature within reform sites is to examine the reading formations these institutions nurtured. I draw on the tools of reception studies and book history to position readers as a crucial link connecting the work of literature and reform—both the historical readers who frequented classes, clubs, and libraries within uplift agencies and the implied and empirical readers of reform-minded literary texts. Following James L. Machor, I approach reception as "a product of the relationship among particular interpretive strategies, epistemic frames, ideological imperatives, and social orientations of readers as members of historically specific—and historiographically specified—interpretive communities."[66] The settlement house, working girls' club, and black college were all committed to literacy as an ideology and to a conception of reading as a socializing activity. Within each of these institutions, reformers were eager to regulate the reading habits of their beneficiaries. Settlement workers took an especially active role in organizing literary circles and dispensing reading advice, partnering with librarians to publish lists of recommended books for immigrant and first-generation readers. And texts born of Progressive reform efforts, like Washington's *Up from Slavery* and Dorothy Richardson's *The Long Day,* facilitate a mode of reception I call "reading for reform," taking care to comment on—and often to condemn—the reading practices of working-class, immigrant, or African American men and women. While I do not overlook the hegemonic cast of this reading formation, an attitude of strict critical reproach does not do justice to the complex social work that reform institutions attempted, since many organizations made reading the site and measure of opportunity at a time when disempowered groups had limited access to literary culture or to higher education. My approach, then, is to historicize reading for reform as impulse and act and to show how these reading practices were constitutive of racial, gender, and class formation in the modern United States.

Institutional periodicals were a primary vehicle for articulating the social value of literature. Organizations published these journals—*Alliance Review,* the *Christodora, Far and Near,* the *Fisk Herald,* and more—on a monthly basis over a number of years. They reached a national audience of socially engaged readers whose subscriptions kept the institutions afloat. Although these periodicals were inextricable from their pedagogical origins, their form and content were nonetheless often envisioned along literary lines. The editorial board of the *Alliance Review*, a settlement house periodical, described its mission as follows: "We beg to say that our chief lines of development lie not in making the *Review* a newspaper, consisting of the reports of the clubs and classes in the Alliance, but in making this little periodical a literary journal to embody discussions on current topics of importance to the East Side community and in this way to enable it to be of value to its readers."[67] In the pages of these periodicals we see benefactors and beneficiaries addressing one another directly, even if mediated by the supervision of powerful editors, and the essays, stories, and manifestos published within hash out the meaning of social reform in theory and practice. For example, in a lyrical essay published in the *Alliance Review* in 1901, a client proposes that stenography is analogous to language, music, and geometry in terms of the discipline it instills in practitioners, locating women's waged labor on a scale closely relative to artistic expression.[68] Many articles in *Far and Near* encourage an instrumentalist—and economic—relation to poetry, informing working-class readers that reciting poetry will help work hours tick by more quickly, infuse their lunch breaks with erudition, and raise their spirits. The house journals of African American colleges showcased writing by students, professors, and recent graduates and played a vital role in the intellectual life of black communities. It was writing published in institutional literary journals that galvanized the student protest movement in the 1920s and helped foment the Harlem Renaissance. And undercover narratives invariably appeared first in serial format, in periodicals ranging from both genteel and muckraking magazines to academic journals. Not only did Progressive reform culture flourish in tandem with the rise of popular magazines and professional journals, then, but the circulation of print materials—from the internal dissemination of a memo and the semipublic distribution of an annual report to the wide circulation of an institution's literary journal—also helped consolidate disparate, local reform projects into a national literary-reformist culture.[69]

Finally, *Reading for Reform* traces the intellectual genealogy of reform institutions within the field of U.S. literature. In the chapters that follow, I use reform institutions, and particularly their practices of contact and proximity, to periodize U.S. literature in a new way. I engage the traditional categories of late nineteenth- and early twentieth-century U.S. literary history primarily as an index of literature's changing social utility and reformist power across four pivotal decades, from the 1890s to the 1920s. Taking reform institutions seriously as sites where literary values were produced and mediated serves to remap this period of literary history around articulations of social complexity that span sentimentalism, realism, naturalism, and modernism but that upend the developmental narrative that typically attends the way critics engage with these concepts. For instance, while sentimental identification, realist empiricism, and modernist polyvocality are all at work in Richardson's *The Long Day*, I propose that the undercover genre is better defined by a distinctive aesthetic of sociability born of the fraught effort to watch, listen, and speak across boundaries of class and station. Attending to formal and generic innovation as a measure of social complexity makes writers as little known as Lillian Wald, Dorothy Richardson, and Bessie and Marie Van Vorst and as established as Booker T. Washington, Nella Larsen, and Edith Wharton collaborators in shaping U.S. literary history. This approach to periodization and form also drives the argument about modernism that I develop across four chapters. In the late nineteenth and early twentieth centuries, many early modernist and avant-garde authors were seeking not to make art more useful but, rather, to liberate it from concepts of social utility altogether, and the authors I explore here were as likely to bemoan the instrumental relations between literature and reform as they were to celebrate them. Viewed in the light *Reading for Reform* casts upon them, writers who challenged the idea of literature as handmaiden to Americanization, training in manual labor, and racial uplift were making a case for a kind of modernist autonomy. This parallel story of literary freedom brings Yezierska, Larsen, Du Bois, and Gordin into an expanded conversation about U.S. modernism.

The subject of every chapter emerges at the intersection of individualistic and environmental explanations for social problems, engaging literary texts that deconstruct and defamiliarize reform. Each chapter explores a specific organizational–literary partnership, forged around a common social problem that produced institutional procedures on the one hand and texts and formal strategies on the other. Chapter 1 examines the settlement house, the exemplary Progressive institution in which reformers combined cross-class friendship, interior design, and a literary–cultural curriculum in order to Americanize immigrants and their first-generation children through the objects and practices of high culture. Here I focus on the question of assimilation within Jewish settlement culture, turning to Yiddish dramatist Jacob Gordin's 1903 play *The Benefactors of the East Side*, the fiction of Anzia Yezierska, and the reform writing of Henry Street Settlement founder Lillian Wald. My second chapter engages Edith Wharton's *The House of Mirth* (1905) and the growth of the working girls' club, an institution devised by elite American women for their white, working-class peers in order to provide a "genteel" refuge from the saloons, dance halls, and streets that were common sites of working-class sociability at the turn of the century. I suggest that the club, and its logic of social comparison, provided a conceptual vocabulary for Wharton as she narrated her protagonist's relationship to an asymmetrical social world. My third chapter addresses philanthropic African American colleges and the early twentieth-century literary critique of racial uplift. I read the educational philosophy of Booker T. Washington and W. E. B. Du Bois, reformist accounts of black education and upward mobility, and the fiction of Nella Larsen as responding to the uplift politics of colleges like Hampton, Fisk, and Tuskegee. My final chapter traces the emergence of undercover literature in the context of turn-of-the-century social reform movements. I argue that so-called undercover writers made practices of reading and writing themselves forms of reform activity, in conjunction with the institutions I chronicle in the previous chapters. What might it mean for art to be practical, or to read for reform? Can positioning literature as a repository of social knowledge contribute to social and economic betterment in the real world, and if not, what *can* reading for reform do?

1

Sites of Contact

THE SETTLEMENT HOUSE

Partway through Rose Cohen's 1918 memoir *Out of the Shadow: A Russian Jewish Girlhood on the Lower East Side,* the young author-to-be attends a public lecture on Shakespeare at Lillian Wald's Henry Street Settlement. For Cohen, a Jewish immigrant who works in the garment industry, the event is fraught with mixed emotions. The other women assembled there are so educated and refined, so evidently "of the type that [she] looked upon as 'teachers,'" that her blood runs cold with mortification. She is ashamed of her poverty and inability to read English and immediately regrets her decision to attend. Yet when Cohen sits across from the lecturer and takes hold of a volume of Shakespeare, she finds that the book suddenly glows with symbolic power. "I felt the light full upon me," Cohen writes, merging her anxious sense of being scrutinized with the book's totemic power. "It was on my hands, it shone into my lap, it seemed to shine right into me, showing my ignorance." Although she can scarcely follow the thread of conversation that evening, Cohen walks home to her tenement apartment feeling proud of her encounter with elevated secular culture. Shakespeare is no longer alien to her, however daunting his language remains.

As the memoir proceeds, Cohen continues to recount her coming of age on the Lower East Side by referencing the books she received at nearby settlement houses. The volume of Shakespeare reflects Cohen's pursuit of erudition, Louisa May Alcott's *Little Women* signals her fledgling connection to genteel American girlhood, and the New Testament points to her growing religious and generational alienation. She charts her narrative of Americanization through these various intersections of settlement reform and literary culture, and her memoir of a Jewish immigrant girlhood has, in turn, come to hold a valuable position in the annals of early twentieth-century U.S. literature.[1]

Out of the Shadow models two distinct and crucially linked ways of approaching the literary history of the settlement house. As a historical document, Cohen's memoir describes the way literature functioned as a recreational activity, as a measure of social and cultural progress, and as a mechanism for communicating particular ideas and values to immigrant clients—in other words, as part of the institution's approach to social reform. The settlement movement put books, reading, and even the near-talismanic *idea* of literature to use in Americanizing immigrants like Cohen, placing as much emphasis on practices of reading, discussion, and performance as on literary objects themselves. But as a work of literary expression, *Out of the Shadow* joins a sizable corpus of novels, memoirs, short stories, poems, plays, periodical writing, and reform tracts about the settlement house, an archive so substantial that it constitutes a veritable subcanon of modern U.S. literature. Included in this subcanon are not only imaginative writings but also organizational records, meeting minutes, annual reports, and other bureaucratic forms that provide a kind of institutional architecture for the literary culture that flourished at settlement houses. The authors of what we might call settlement literature are as various as the texts they produce: they are reformers and volunteers, regular clients and occasional visitors, and writers commenting at a remove from the institution on its meaning and impact. The task of interpreting these texts and of understanding their place within U.S. literary history demands that we synthesize these two critical approaches, especially because their authors so often forged their working definitions of literature within the pedagogical context of the settlement house.

In this chapter, I suggest that the settlement house was a key site for defining the meaning and circumstances of literary value at the turn of the twentieth century. Yet this literary history is also necessarily a chronicle of dissent. For every immigrant memoirist who dutifully traces the origins of his or her book back to a settlement reading room, one finds another author whose writing is alive to the striking inequalities of reform. In fact, one of the main claims of this chapter is that settlement literature often structures itself in opposition to the aesthetic and social norms of the settlement, painting the institution's curriculum as artistically moribund, politically dubious, and generally dangerous in its zeal to divest literature of pleasure and autonomy. Some of the most important Jewish American writers of the early twentieth century honed their authorial voices in just this way. The Yiddish playwright Jacob Gordin proves a fitting counterpoint to Cohen in this respect. His one-act play *The Benefactors of the East Side* (1903) assembles a cast of characters strikingly akin to the philanthropists and working-class immigrants that people *Out of the Shadow*, and it is similarly written from the perspective of reform's beneficiaries. Unlike Cohen, however, Gordin challenges the entrenched social and aesthetic hierarchies that organize immigrant aid. In fact, *The Benefactors of the East Side* contends that settlement houses fostered an approach to literature that actually impaired immigrants' ability to engage with artistic and intellectual materials in a nontrivial way. The play's witless philanthropists propose to "save the population of the East Side" by banning "serious books" and offering in their place a suite of preposterous "educational tools," from cheap cookbooks to public baths administering "general enlightenment."[2] Gordin's satirical drama ultimately suggests that the fraught interpersonal dynamics of reform—the anxiety and shame Cohen cannot help but feel in the face of her educated benefactors—telescope larger, pressing questions of social power.

Far from being a contradiction, the disparity between Cohen's paean to settlement literary culture and Gordin's antisettlement invective indicates that the institution was a genuine site of sociopolitical and artistic contestation in the years before and after the turn of the twentieth century. As I develop this argument in the pages to follow, I range broadly across literary styles and movements, including sentimentalism, realism, and modernism, as well as genres. I engage this motley crew of concepts to show that the settlement house, with its curious methods of conjoining art to social practice, shaped and was in turn shaped by the larger literary sphere.

SETTLEMENT HOUSE GENEALOGIES

While Rose Cohen paints reformers as uniformly formidable and Jacob Gordin evokes their comical ignorance, settlement workers in fact brought diverse motivations and life experiences to their work. The roots of U.S. Progressive reform's signal institution lie in late-Victorian England, where a minister named Samuel Barnett and his reform-minded wife, Henrietta, established the first settlement house in London's East End in 1884. With the support of Oxford and Cambridge Universities, the Barnetts purchased a house in an impoverished neighborhood and invited their friends to move in and devote themselves to sharing "the best thoughts and aspirations of the age" with their neighbors (a privilege for which residents paid a small fee).[3] Toynbee Hall, as the new community was named, was heralded as a revolutionary new model for reform: several of the young social workers who would spearhead the movement's American wing visited in its early years and were inspired by its example.[4] The settlement house movement found a ready client base in the United States among the roughly twenty million new immigrants who passed through the gates of Castle Garden and Ellis Island between 1881 and 1924, the majority of whom hailed from southern and eastern Europe.[5] Settlement houses grew in number and influence around the turn of the century as immigration rates continued to climb; there were seventy-four settlements across the United States by 1897, two hundred by 1905, and over four hundred in 1910. A visitor to New York City's East Side could not walk the three blocks from Grand to Rivington without tripping over half a dozen "homes."[6]

The landscape of settlement work in the urban United States comprised women's institutions (college settlements), organizations allied with predominantly male universities and their departments of social science (university settlements), Christian and Jewish settlements, and settlements targeting an African American clientele, usually in cooperation with black churches, among other local permutations. Across this broad spectrum, settlement workers shared an overarching commitment to modalities of proximity and influence.[7] As careful students of history, they were convinced that earlier reform campaigns had floundered because privileged reformers kept themselves personally and geographically remote from the people they wished to help. They believed it would be impossible to resolve the social problems that fractured U.S. society as long as rich and poor, immigrants and native-born Americans were separated by so many intersecting social, cultural, and physical barriers, though white reformers were content, on the whole, to keep their institutions racially segregated.[8] Idealistic college graduates erected institutions in the heart of urban working-class neighborhoods, and they moved into settlement houses in order to work closely with the poor on what they hoped would be neutral ground. The buildings blended public and private space: lower floors were typically divided into libraries, classrooms, and meeting rooms, and upper floors were used as residents' bedrooms. The settlement movement was built on an infrastructure of cross-class exchange within the vastly unequal urban ecology of the modern United States, primarily New York City, Chicago, Philadelphia, and Boston. And while acculturating immigrants and their first-generation children remained the fundamental goal, the movement's most liberal participants believed that these interactions would also rejuvenate individual reformers and enrich U.S. society as a whole—embodying the optimism that was a hallmark of the Progressive Era.[9]

The first generation of reformers used their era's rhetoric of imperialism in describing their work, calling themselves "pioneers" or "settlers" on an "urban frontier." This colonial language was redolent of both the missionary enterprise and the rugged westward expansion, suggesting a technology of social control, even if not malign intent. Deeply flawed though it was, reformers used this rhetoric to bring attention to a "city wilderness" that desperately lacked effective infrastructure.[10] They joined other Progressives in lobbying the municipal government to address congested streets, dangerous tenements, and unregulated labor conditions. At their worst, reformers believed, the cramped spaces of the ghetto incubated the most pernicious social tendencies of their time: radicalism, vice and crime, religious orthodoxy, and ignorance of the norms, democratic conventions, language, and culture of American life. Though they sometimes celebrated the colorful family life of their neighbors, settlement workers were convinced that the ghetto hindered immigrants' upward mobility because it sequestered them from Americans who would model the language, behavior, and customs of their new land. They organized settlement house programs around what they considered to be essential compensatory experiences.

From the beginning, the settlement's primary goal was to Americanize immigrants and their first-generation offspring in order to ease their adjustment into U.S. society and facilitate their upward mobility.[11] But the meaning and objective of Americanization differed according to the ethnic composition of an institution's board of directors and its particular social mission. From the perspective of a nondenominational and thus implicitly Protestant settlement, the purpose of Americanization was to preserve the coherence of the state and spread the tenets of democracy. Jewish settlement workers had still other motivations: their interest in cultivating democratic allegiance joined a more self-preservationist impulse to protect the financial, cultural, and social capital accrued by a previous generation of Jewish immigrants, who had arrived from Germany. Acutely aware that social and political repression had historically accompanied European ghettoization, Jewish reformers urged their eastern European clients to Americanize in part to ensure that unofficial ethnic ghettos did not turn into permanent fixtures in the United States.[12]

Settlement house policies aimed primarily at cultural assimilation. Some institutions pushed a fairly restrictive model of Anglo-conformity; others, such as Hull-House, maintained a more capacious vision of immigrant cultural retention. Even the most liberal wing of the movement promoted a fundamentally hierarchical view of cultural value, presuming a teleology in which immigrants would shed aspects of their foreign cultures as they cultivated their American selves. Yet settlement workers did not envision beneficiaries becoming identical to an Anglo-Saxon model.[13] If contact across social boundaries promised to enliven the intellectual and personal lives of settlement workers as well as underprivileged clients, as reformers insisted, then cultural change was never completely one-sided.

PEDAGOGIES OF INFLUENCE: LITERARY, SPATIAL, AND PERSONAL CONTACT

Paul Boyer has explained how the theory of "positive environmentalism" shaped urban reform efforts at the turn of the century, documenting how the era's reevaluation of urban space as a potential wellspring of civic and moral well-being manifested in groundbreaking tenement reforms and the construction of parks, playgrounds, statues, and fountains. John Dewey was a proponent of positive environmentalism, writing in 1908 that effective social policy was based on "the intelligent selection and determination of the environments in which we act."[14] But within the settlement house's cultural milieu, environment had reformist value beyond the merely physical. It is more accurate to say that the movement developed a *pedagogy of influence*. This term names a version of positive environmentalism that encompasses not only architectural matters but also the relationships among people, and between people and particular cultural objects and practices, transacted within the ameliorative space of reform.

In what follows, I argue that the movement's pedagogy of influence worked in and across three interconnected domains: the settlement house's literary curriculum, its interior space, and its doctrine of personal relations. I further contend that the *concept* of influence underlying these three spheres provided the theoretical justification for the institution's discourse of literary value. The pedagogy of influence effectively blurred the boundaries between the literary and the social, the aesthetic and the political, so that reformers borrowed the language and ideals of high culture to describe concepts as seemingly remote as the layout of a club room or the cultivated tone of a settlement worker's speech. Most significantly, the pedagogy of influence created a problem of social and cultural power to which all settlement literature responded: exactly which individuals, cultural objects, and practices should have powers of transformation over whom?

Liberal culture became a primary vehicle for the settlement movement's Americanization program, particularly at Jewish institutions. The Educational Alliance, a Jewish settlement located in New York City's Lower East Side, was unparalleled in its dedication to cultural pursuits. The Alliance's official position read, "Our pleasures stand just as much in need of education as do our minds, and . . . it is vitally important to the civic, economic and moral welfare of a community that the pleasures of its citizens be of the highest character."[15] This meant, in effect, cultivating a taste for reading and offering cultural experiences apart from dance halls, vaudeville, and Yiddish theater. The Alliance and other settlements put their literary curriculum in place through libraries, reading rooms, and a system of clubs, classes, and circles, which were abundant and wildly popular. In 1899 the Alliance had twenty-seven literary clubs and societies (including the Tennyson Literary Society and the Eggleston Literary Society for men and boys, the Alcott Circle and Grace Aguilar Literary Society for women and girls), and forty-three that performed a combination of literary and other activities; these numbers remained fairly steady in the years before and after the turn of the century.[16] Smaller institutions hosted fewer literary clubs, but in a similarly high proportion. These typically met once a week and followed a preordained course of study and performance, and they were usually segregated by age and gender.

Settlement club members read and chose as their club namesakes canonical authors, such as Shakespeare, Sir Walter Scott, or Tennyson, or popular periodical authors favored by young people, such as Eugene Field, Edward Eggleston, and Margaret E. Sangster.[17] The all-female Christodora House's Loyalty Club maintained an ambitious literary agenda: for two months in 1908, they held weekly meetings on Robert Louis Stevenson in which members read excerpts from his biography, set his poetry to music, and wrote essays describing how Stevenson's courage and perseverance could be applied to their own lives. At the end of the Stevenson unit, each club member took home a sentimental token: a picture of the author with lines of his verse printed on the back. In the months to follow, Loyalty Club members would discuss the representation of children in the works of George Eliot and William Makepeace Thackeray, recite the poetry of Josephine Preston Peabody and Tennyson, learn about Helen Keller, and put on a play. Settlement literary clubs advocated what we might call *cultural generalism,* disseminating classic works of literature and middlebrow texts in equal measure. Even when a club's avowed goal was to study a particular author, the larger purpose was always to create the conditions in which immigrants might form a lasting cathexis to culture. Developing patrons' sense of cultural discernment and ability to choose "wisely" was important: in 1895, the Educational Alliance described its class in English literature as "more like a reading circle, where the object is to inspire and cultivate a taste for the best literature."[18] These clubs and classes were, in Thomas Augst's terms, a site of mass literacy in which "ordinary people learned to make the business of living an individual exercise in literary taste."[19]

This generalist tendency reflected the scholarly commitments of the many literary academics who worked at settlement houses and tended to favor one side of a growing rift between generalists and specialists within emergent departments of English.[20] The conviction that a general familiarity with literature would lend immigrants and their U.S.-born children an air of refinement and therefore support the Americanization process determined the kinds of texts settlement workers chose, as well as their methods of distribution. In fact, reformers believed it was possible— dangerously so—for patrons to become *too* adept at one particular artistic field over the rest, thereby unhinging their development along generalist lines. Becoming too proficient in one artistic skill threatened to counteract the modulated temperament and character that settlement pedagogy worked so hard to instill. An editorial entitled "An East Side Art Club" in the *American Hebrew,* an English-language Jewish magazine, describes the venerable intellectual and artistic capacities of immigrants who frequented reform institutions but warns of a danger in "the intensity of the love for a single phase of artistic expression. . . . The East Side is threatened by a passion for art, a passion which is hurtful to the living of the higher life, for it produces a deplorable one-sidedness." This writer urges teachers and reformers working in immigrant neighborhoods to offer a carefully modulated cultural literacy.[21]

As these examples suggest, the settlement movement aimed to instrumentalize culture, making literature amenable to an Americanizing agenda without completely erasing its pleasurable qualities. The movement popularized the view that reading had distinct social value in a tenement district. "Realizing that books have been the formative influences in the lives of most persons, the members of the Settlement give a strict supervision to the reading of each one taking books," one journalist observed after visiting the free library at the College Settlement, an institution on the Lower East Side run by female college graduates.[22] Helen Moore, librarian at the nearby University Settlement, made the related point that the settlement library owed "even more sympathetic attention" to the poor. "Its duty is to free them from the notion that the mere possession of books and unrelated facts constitute an education, and to help them [grasp] that books and facts are not an end in themselves, but only a means toward mental training and self-development."[23] In other words, immigrant and working-class readers needed to understand literature as a process, more a practice or ritual than simply a neutral body of texts. Moore cautions that tenement dwellers must be taught to read with particular sensitivity; after all, reading materials would be readily assimilated into their evolving American selves, furnishing a road map for future behavior.

Even within self-proclaimed literary clubs, reading and interpretation were only part of the settlements' literary regimen. Members spent just as much time writing and performing; enacting mock trials, recitations, and debates; and publishing journals. These activities were designed to serve as elocutionary exercises, opportunities to hone English speech and accent, and as a way of building confidence. Literary clubs also regularly staged minstrel shows under the auspices of "culture." The fact that white ethnic clients rehearsed this racist performance mode as part of their own elevation shows how entrenched was the institution's cultural regime in the conventions of Jim Crow America. Ultimately, settlements were committed to cultivating white citizens who would step without question into its social norms and racial categories.[24] Women's and girls' clubs typically combined cultural study with practical skills training and ideological instruction: women studied Ralph Waldo Emerson, Nathaniel Hawthorne, and Louisa May Alcott, but they also learned to sew and to cultivate charitable impulses. Even when female club members gathered for the purpose of discussing *The Merchant of Venice,* for example, the larger goal was "to cultivate a taste for those domestic virtues that tend to make home-life happier and brighter."[25] Jewish settlements even endorsed writers who took on explicitly Christian themes: a 1901 issue of the *Alliance Review* journal includes clergymen and theologians on its summer reading list. While this recommendation might seem out of place in an institution that honored the Jewish heritage of its funders, volunteers, and clients, it suggests that reformers valued literature above all for its ability to communicate "universal" (read, white Christian) moral lessons—that is, to influence beneficiaries' development in spheres apart from but adjacent to the literary. The presence of Christian writings in the literary curriculum of a Jewish institution attests to what Joan Shelley Rubin describes as "multiple canons, made up of texts deemed 'good' because they conserved the values governing the conditions of their use."[26] Because reformers were convinced of their capacity to socialize beneficiaries through the medium of culture, literature was both ubiquitous—every settlement had literary clubs and a reading room and professed to value cultural enrichment—and also handmaiden to extraliterary imperatives.

The pedagogy of influence is especially visible in the settlements' approach to theater. From clubs' trifling reenactments to full-scale theatricals, drama formed a major part of the institution's cultural curriculum. Whereas reading maintained residual associations with the schoolroom, drama was uniquely positioned to cultivate joyous enthusiasm. Acting permitted clients to embody the character of another, as though testing patterns of behavior that might one day come naturally to them. Shannon Jackson observes that theater's use value "in the reformist cultivation of aesthetic and moral sensibility lay in the embodied, environmental, and enacted nature of the medium itself, one that uniquely facilitated the transformation in sensibility and behavior."[27] Settlement workers believed that drama held special potential as a medium of personal growth. It was also useful for imparting lessons in manners and behavior, as a 1940 history of the Christodora House in New York City articulates:

> Children of the rich ... rarely want to live as the poor live; but the poor want life to be colorful—to be what they are not and to have their imaginations stirred by pasteboard scenery and the flummery of stage clothes—to have their gutter vocabularies changed into noble speech. Many a high purpose was formed at Christodora by playing make-believe—by witnessing and acting good plays; and a higher and more beautiful world opened itself through the medium of the stage to the children whose imaginations were cramped by poverty.[28]

This account is notable for the way it conflates assimilation with practices of dramatic performance. The idea that clients would internalize and naturalize their contact with the materials of U.S. culture was a key axiom of the pedagogy of influence. But here, the great promise of "playing make-believe" at the settlement house is that it leads to a more instinctive performance of American norms, a performance that does not feel like acting because "make-believe" has given way to "high purpose."[29]

This gloss of the settlement's literary and dramatic curriculum should make clear that settlement workers were strongly indebted to Matthew Arnold's program for working-class education. While Arnold's vision of literature as an ennobling social and moral force was well known to most settlement workers, many Jewish reformers would in addition have been familiar with Arnold's German Romantic models. Arnold based his theories on the Enlightenment educational reforms that had assimilated Jews as citizens into modern Germany and Austria through their involvement in the cultural arena, a paradigm Jonathan Freedman calls "assimilation-by-culture." Freedman argues that for Arnold, as for German educator Wilhelm von Humboldt, assimilation meant becoming "reoriented into a new form of subjectivity appropriate to life in a 'civilized' or cultured world: one in which feeling, sensibility, and responsiveness to the finer emotions and the finer cultural productions was a guarantee of belonging to the larger collective identity." This project of civilization, Freedman continues, "is a matter of affect, of sentiment—of being responsive in the proper way to the feelings encoded in art, literature, and music."[30] The settlement movement institutionalized an updated model of assimilation-by-culture, encouraging cultural and literary fluency as a guide to and measure of a transformed subjectivity. This is even more interestingly the case at Jewish settlement houses, where German–Jewish benefactors passed on a revised version of the same assimilation-by-culture paradigm to which they were themselves heir. The volunteers who led Longfellow circles and accompanied minstrel shows did not understand themselves to be passing on an Anglo-American cultural legacy alien to their own experience. Rather, they were confident that their own present acculturation—their own categorical, but still somehow provisional, American success story—was the best possible proof that assimilation-by-culture was effective.

Yet the benefits of literary and cultural attainment could not have their intended effect just anywhere—certainly not, reformers believed, in tenements whose crowding and dim lighting made it impossible to read or study. Settlement workers were convinced that this environmental obstacle would drive tenement dwellers to the streets and dance halls in search of leisure, and they therefore designed their institutions' interiors to be ideal settings for reading. Their goal was to offer working-class visitors a quiet place for cultural engagement. But reformers also sought to create a physical atmosphere that would perpetuate the social work of literature. The settlement house's spatial coordinates—interior layout, decoration, and genteel atmosphere—became an important domain of influence, serving as an adjunct to the institution's literary curriculum. From the first, the movement described itself in domestic terms, identifying as a "home among other homes."[31] Yet as Jackson notes, the urban working-class home and the settlement house had distinct, often oppositional spatial legacies. Many reformers had lived most of their lives in spacious homes with the parlors, drawing rooms, and privatizing subdivisions that were the markers of Victorian comfort, and they sought to reproduce key elements of bourgeois domesticity within their institutions. The mere experience of navigating different rooms and domestic objects inside the settlement forced users to experience the spatial and behavioral conventions of middle-class domesticity, reinforcing the social instruction they received in classrooms and clubs.[32]

Settlement workers drew on the Victorian conviction that decor helped create character, a notion that supported the institution's broader mandate of cultivation, assimilation, and reform. Settlements often scrambled to remain solvent, yet institutional records from the movement's early years emphasize the importance of fresh flowers, attractive divans, framed pictures of important personages, and a generally genial atmosphere.[33] Domestic rhetoric buttressed the work of female settlement workers in particular. The Christodora House, for example, aimed to have "the order of a well-appointed home—the order which grew into beauty. Flowers graced the office desk, tables, pianos."[34] A journalist's report on the nearby College Settlement invokes Matthew Arnold as it adds more detail to this description:

> Although the exterior of the building is dingy and unattractive, the interior is all "sweetness and light." The visitor upon entering the parlor is impressed with the air of refinement which pervades the apartment as his eye makes note of the really fine engravings on the delicately-tinted

walls, the well-bound books on the cabinet shelves, and the objects of *virtu* scattered about with the careless grace that suggests the presence of cultivated women.[35]

This account describes an emblematic Victorian parlor through the eyes of an imagined male visitor. Importantly, this female journalist advertises the then-nascent project of settlement reform by describing a room conspicuously *not* made for use. As Katherine C. Grier has argued, the parlor was the "'comfortable theater' for middle-class self-presentation" in Victorian America, a site for the display and cultivation of the public self that set the tone for the rest of the home. The objects strewn about the room do not belong to working-class clients; rather, they are "objects of *virtu*"—art objects or antiques—that bespeak "the presence of cultivated women." The settlement's physical structure emerges here as a metaphor for the ideal recipient of its philanthropy, a rough and uninviting exterior giving way to a pleasant interior suffused with "sweetness and light." Commentators continued to emphasize the pedagogical value of space even as Victorian domestic symbolism gave way to a more stripped-down, modern aesthetic. The expectation remained that clients would "paraphrase" aspects of the settlement's physical space by re-creating those ideals in their own smaller homes and that they would absorb the social lessons encoded in those spatial dynamics just as they would from a conversation, novel, or dramatic performance.[36]

Reformers regularly linked the settlement's domestic organization to the project of spreading English literacy and high culture. One writer boasts of the "double work" performed by the Girls' Home Culture Club at Chicago's Maxwell Street Settlement, which was frequented by Jewish "working girls" with a special interest in reading:

> About twenty working-girls from seventeen to twenty-two years old are being directed in their reading by an able teacher, who gives informal talks on the choice of books, and aids in the interpretation of the best English novels. . . . A taste for good literature once formed, there is little danger of relapsing into trifling enjoyments. The Home Culture Club does a double work. Meetings are held at the homes of the members, who take great delight in making their humble living-rooms bright for the occasion.

Home-making comes to be a part of the educative processes of the club, with its resultants of neatness, friendliness and hospitality.[37]

In this account, reading and homemaking operate along a single axis. Their aesthetic and pedagogical value is presumed to be the same, as book selection becomes home decoration and literary interpretation slides into cheerful hospitality. Reformers aligned cultural expression with domesticity through the normative logic of gender socialization, in which a penchant for literature was commensurate with "making . . . humble living-rooms bright." More importantly, though, this alignment exemplifies a larger practice of tying literary value to social progress. The settlement house measured cultural enrichment less by its intellectual benefits than by its ability to eradicate tenement domesticity, transforming slum apartments into "bright" homes modeled on the institution's own interior.

Descriptions of settlement house interiors are ubiquitous in settlement literature across genres, including the reform novel. Zoe Beckley's 1918 novel, *A Chance to Live,* evokes settlement space in terms that mirror journalistic and institutional accounts. Beckley's young heroine steps tentatively into a New York settlement and instantly takes note of her genteel environs:

> Her first impression was of unbelievable spaciousness and cleanness. . . . She got a quick picture of gray-blue walls and hangings, and golden lamplight glowing upon a long table, at which girls were reading. Without examining the furnishings in detail, she felt the quality of everything. She knew that the pictures hanging in discreet spaces were good pictures, well framed. That the tables and chairs and bookcases were of artistic rightness, though very plain. All was quiet, orderly, warm, and handsome. So much so that Annie felt vaguely uncomfortable and afraid of it.[38]

"Very plain" but also spacious, clean, and supported by all-encompassing "artistic rightness," the settlement house emerges here as an eminently respectable and cultured setting—indeed, as the site of reading.

In another reform novel, Isaac Kahn Friedman's 1901 *By Bread Alone,* the settlement's interior is organized around the imperatives of culture: "A portrait of Shakespeare, another of Tennyson, one of Dickens . . .

smiled literature down on the room; a revolving book-case was ready to turn under a Braun's copy of Burne-Jones' 'Golden Stairs,' which faced that artist's 'Venus' Mirror.'" There is a striking consistency between the methods reformers used and the accounts put forward by varied novelists and journalists. In these literary descriptions, we see how newfound associations between reformist space and literary value became a generic convention of the reform novel.[39]

Alongside its literary curriculum and interior design, the settlement's pedagogy of influence operated through personal contact. Settlements sought to put people from different class locations—and frequently, different religious and ethnic backgrounds—into close association. Indeed, faith in the power of personal contact managed to unite otherwise distinct factions of the movement: reformers believed that placing immigrants and the working classes in close proximity to the elite was essential to their uplift. One 1889 editorial explained that settlement workers "fully believe with Tolstoy that 'Enlightenment is not propagated by pictures,' not 'chiefly' by the spoken word, or the medium of print, but by the infectious example of the whole life of men."[40] When a college-educated woman met with a group of young adults for a weekly meeting of their literary circle, every dimension of that interpersonal contact—conversation, mutual affection, the leader's wardrobe, accent, and comportment—was understood to be reformist praxis.[41]

As the nucleus of settlement life, clubs proved an ideal context in which to cultivate relationships across social boundaries. Reformers considered clubs an important model of political organization and understood their formation as a step toward democratic citizenship, with each group's American leader as guide and mentor. No matter what a club's theme or primary activity, the club room was the space in which "right ideas" were inculcated into young people's minds, where reformers could "help [each person] to become a well-rounded human being" by fostering close personal relations between reformers and clients.[42] Similarly, the Educational Alliance's 1899 annual report made the point that clubs were "the most feasible way of bringing culture home to the [clients] and of entering into intimate relationship with them in a way that ought to benefit everybody concerned.... Of course, in work of this character, the emphasis is to be laid on the personal influence of the directors."⁴³ But given that literary clubs and circles were also a principal vehicle for the settlement's literary curriculum, it is somewhat jarring to recognize that the clubs' larger structural task was simply to bring working-class immigrants and affluent Americans into a room together.

Settlement orthodoxy held that cross-class proximity was essential to the growth and education of reformers as well, in part because it generated truths that could not be learned in books. One 1893 essay contends that intimacy with the poor would make reformers more effective civic campaigners, "[equipping them] with certain individual facts and general truths regarding the character and lives of the young friends of the [settlement] that are most useful guides in the work," and Addams described the settlement as "an attempt to relieve, at the same time, the over-accumulation at one end of society and the destitution at the other."⁴⁴ Yet social reform was never merely a selfless gesture: in the next section I argue that settlement literature coheres as a subgenre precisely in response to the vexed nature of this social relation. For all the educational advantages settlements offered to beneficiaries, they were equally conceived as an intellectual project for the benefit of privileged reformers in which the goal was to generate knowledge outside of but adjacent to the university. When settlement theorists portrayed their institutions as "universities in the slums," then, they were not referring to a low-cost college for the immigrant poor; rather, they were describing the settlement as a social laboratory generating pragmatic forms of knowledge.⁴⁵

The settlement movement answered to powerful emotional needs within the white middle and upper classes. In the late nineteenth century there began to grow a feeling that too much leisure and unmitigated privilege was plunging a whole generation into nervous depression, and by the 1870s a range of psychological, literary, and journalistic texts were reporting on the problem of "neurasthenia" among affluent Americans. Many people diagnosed as neurasthenics, Addams among them, saw reform work as a critical means of recovery. "Vital contact" with social inferiors promised to rejuvenate "inauthentic" reformers who had been "cultivated into unnourished, over-sensitive lives"; it would reintroduce them to a lost "reality."⁴⁶ The settlement house was thought to offer "a message of life and hope to that increasing body of men and women in these days who are stifled and crushed under the gifts of society become impediments through disuse."[47] Addams went so far as to claim that the "undirected" female settlement worker was nearly as desperate as her "destitute" beneficiaries.[48] Settlement work seemed a welcome point of contact with "real life" for female college graduates in particular, who were the ones most commonly diagnosed with neurasthenia at the turn of the century. Several years after trying out Dr. S. Weir Mitchell's rest cure for neurasthenia (and writing about it in her famous short story "The Yellow Wallpaper"), Charlotte Perkins Gilman lived for several months in 1895 at two Chicago settlements, Hull-House and Unity Settlement—though she didn't savor the experience.

Many reform novels echo the institutional conviction that cross-class contact worked, in its peculiarly reciprocal way, to reform beneficiaries and regenerate benefactors. Vida Scudder's 1903 *A Listener in Babel* follows a young woman on her quest for meaning by way of contact with the "other half." Protagonist Hilda Lathrop—an American raised in Europe and trained as an artist—has always "stifle[d] in class isolation," and she moves into an urban settlement because "she had hoped that among those with whom primal experiences were more evident, the common ground of humanity would be easier to find." Scudder makes clear that bourgeois Americans will find transcendence not in books or religion but, rather, in their relationships with real people. Only when Hilda enjoys a picnic lunch with three settlement clients does she come close enough to the human source to have a revelation:

> An impulse largely intellectual had sent her to live among the poor: now, she met at close range the problems of poverty, and bad as they had seemed when stated in the mass, they choked her as she felt their pressure on three individuals she loved ... her dry faith in democracy [was] renewed by the treasure of fellowship with the humble. The reality which she had sought in vain throughout her girlhood was hers at last.[49]

Elsewhere in *A Listener in Babel,* Scudder is more interested in her protagonist's emotional journey than in working-class character development or the structural problems buttressing poverty. In this moment, however,

Hilda finally comes to have a sense of reality—she comes to see *herself* as real—through her brief intimacy with the poor, who assume a pivotal redemptive quality here and in a number of other texts penned by settlement workers and their sympathizers.

Scudder was a prominent reformer and a founder of the College Settlement Association, and her novel draws on personal experiences to represent the settlement mission as a whole. She and her peers maintained that their cross-class ties were distinct from charitable or patronage relationships. As one journalist reporting on the College Settlement described it, workers such as Scudder "have no air of my Lady Bountiful, or of the patroness. Their protégés are their *friends,* and are always treated as such."[50] But other writers, especially those identified with working-class, minority, and radical left positions, looked far less fondly on the notion that philanthropy's recipients should be expected to revitalize their benefactors or greet their offer of friendship as anything other than deeply condescending. Critics charged the settlement house with perpetuating unequal power dynamics, a claim to which I will devote the remainder of this chapter. In fact, one way to ascribe some genre conventions to the body of writing I have called settlement literature is to track the wildly various literary reactions, on both sides of the reformist encounter, to the practice of "helpful contact."

As we have seen, institutional and reform writing endorses the aesthetic development of underprivileged clients while also bemoaning the way excessive cultivation had damaged the privileged reformers who sought to share their culture. Personal contact thus entailed an exchange of cultivation between donor and client that, while mutual, was always asymmetrical. One did not have to be a critic of the settlement house to recognize that philanthropy was an inherently unequal mode of relation. In 1922, a historian of the movement observed that while elite women could choose to use their "education and character" as merely "a set of rules for parlor behavior," to the denizens of a "tenement district" those same qualities constituted "not ornaments but limbs"—these qualities were, in other words, critical to their survival. Another writer suggested in 1900 that the benefactor-beneficiary relationship "not only teaches the poor how to beautify their own sordid lives, but shows the rich how to give purpose to their sometimes futile ones."[51] Reformers envisioned an ideal symbiosis by which the elite would share their culture and receive in return some of the energy and authenticity of their beneficiaries.[52]

Opposition to the settlement's pedagogy of influence turned on a critique of the assumptions and cost involved in this reciprocal exchange. Addams was sincere in her belief that "the man who looks back to the person who first put him in the way of good literature has no alloy in his gratitude," but settlement literature tells an alternative story, and this literary counternarrative is a crucial complement—and challenge—to the mostly uncontentious institutional history I have charted so far.[53] Late nineteenth- and early twentieth-century U.S. print culture is peppered with debates about the settlement house. More often than not, commentators who placed a premium on literary and cultural autonomy—or who at least prioritized these over a reformist mandate—lambasted the institution. Most famously, Anzia Yezierska virtually built her writing career on a critique of Progressive immigrant aid. Michael Gold's *Jews without Money* (1930) contains a seemingly throwaway reference to settlement workers that marks the distance between the authentic Jewish working-class culture to which his novel claims special knowledge and the sphere of reformist intruders: "In summer, if a slummer or settlement house lady walked on our street with flowers in her hand, we attacked her, begging for the flowers. We rioted and yelled, yanked at her skirt, and frightened her to the point of hysteria." In John Dos Passos's *The Big Money* (1936), the young social worker Mary Smith's residence at Hull-House is quickly trumped by a more meaningful stint as labor activist. Eugene O'Neill's "The Hairy Ape" (1922) pillories wealthy settlement-worker-as-slummer Mildred Douglas, whose own aunt exclaims that her beneficiaries "must have hated [her], the poor that [she] made so much poorer in their eyes." Friedman's now-forgotten 1901 labor novel *By Bread Alone* scorns settlement workers' efforts to resolve serious social problems through lessons in poetry and culture, despite Friedman's having been a resident at New York City's University Settlement for several years. Countless other writers made direct and often dismissive allusions to the settlement house's ubiquity on the U.S. cultural landscape, often picturing the institution as an ineffectual way station in which characters tarried en route to more meaningful forms of activism.[54]

Most critiques came from writers on the left who were disgusted at the settlement's ambivalent attitude toward labor. Thorstein Veblen's *The Theory of the Leisure Class* argues that settlement work ratified the gap between rich and poor and inflated the elite's sense of superiority. Emma Goldman dismisses settlement reform as "teaching the poor to eat with a fork." In Jack London's *People of the Abyss*, an undercover narrative based on London's experience living in the East End of London, the author charges that settlement workers from nearby Whitechapel "do everything for the poor except get off their backs. The very money they dribble out in their child's schemes has been wrung from the poor."[55] Many leftist commentators larded their criticism with gendered invective, scorning the settlement house as the frivolous domain of women. Others pointed their antisettlement rhetoric at Addams, averring that her privileged background, and especially her father's occupation—he was a mill owner and landlord whose property holdings Addams inherited in 1881—made her essentially the capitalist enemy. What is most striking for our purposes, however, is the number of commentators who criticized the institution for instrumentalizing literature and culture. These works often took a humorous approach to their subject, like the 1916 article in *New Republic* claiming that the settlement was "an attempt to paint the wound of poverty with a camel's hair brush dipped in a weak solution of Ruskin, Prince Kropotkin and Florence Nightingale." Others were much more serious in their assessment of the costs of literary–social contact at the settlement house.[56]

THE COSTS OF CONTACT: JEWISH SETTLEMENT CULTURE AND WRITING

The most sustained attack on settlement pedagogy came from early twentieth-century Yiddish performance culture. By the turn of the century, almost every major city in the Northeast was home to a lively Yiddish drama scene, with the most vibrant based in New York's East Side. Yiddish writers, actors, and theatrical audiences congregated in coffeehouses and theaters located just steps away from prominent settlements like the University Settlement, College Settlement, Henry Street Settlement, and Educational Alliance, among others; indeed, many of these institutions sponsored Yiddish dramatic clubs and rented out their auditoriums for performances. However, these institutional alliances were based more on mutual convenience and recognition of a common audience than on a shared cultural or political ethos, as the riotous, bombastic, and unapologetically ethnic Yiddish theater's definition of literary, social, and political value clashed with the settlement's more genteel (but also, in its way, didactic) approach.

In 1900, a group of Russian Jewish artists, activists, and intellectuals from New York's East Side founded a cultural organization they named the Educational League. Jacob Gordin, an educator and Yiddish playwright who was renowned in the Jewish immigrant community as the author of *Siberia, A Jewish King Lear*, and *God, Man, and Devil*, was the countersettlement's founder and figurehead. (He also guided Henry James through the Lower East Side in 1904, a tour James later described in *The American Scene* as evidencing the "Hebrew conquest of New York.")[57] Gordin's main motive in founding the Educational League was to combat the settlement movement's influence among immigrant working-class Jews, especially what he saw as its tainted cultural offerings. His rival organization offered East Siders an alternative institutional route to secular enlightenment: offering adult students "knowledge for its own sake" in Russian and Yiddish, the Educational League focused on mathematics, science, and literature. It also disseminated radical texts and encouraged social activism, both of which were discouraged or outright forbidden at most settlements. In a 1900 letter to the *American Hebrew*, a periodical read primarily by the uptown Jews whose volunteer efforts and financial sponsorship supported the settlement movement, an unnamed representative of the Educational League (probably Gordin himself) described it as "an organic outgrowth of a strong demand among the adult immigrants for the elements of education unbranded by the Stamp of charity, free from any religious sectarian or class tendencies, singly and solely for knowledge as a means to gain a better acquaintance with the mighty universe around us."[58] The League put a premium on intellectual seriousness and rejected all pretensions to gentility or mannered cultivation as being utterly foreign to immigrants' real cultural life, but the claim that the League offered "an honest unpartisan education" with no ulterior Americanizing motives was more than a little disingenuous.[59] In fact, Gordin's countersettlement was no less didactic than its reformist rivals: its practice of integrating secular knowledge into a broader education in class-consciousness was also intended to acculturate adult immigrants into the Left. Moreover, the League also employed literature in its effort to move Jewish immigrants from parochial particularism to universalism, although in this case the favored genre was Russian realist fiction.[60]

Gordin was a divisive figure within the cultural life of the Lower East Side—Abraham Cahan, an eminent tastemaker of Yiddish America, expressed at first ambivalence and eventually outright loathing toward Gordin—and he came into his career as a playwright only haphazardly. Gordin had been a teacher and journalist in his native Russia, but when he failed to find steady work at a Russian-language newspaper after emigrating to the United States in 1891, he overcame his preference for the language of Tolstoy over the "jargon" of Hester Street and began writing plays in Yiddish to support his large family. By the turn of the century, Gordin had established his reputation as an artistic reformer committed to raising the tone of the Yiddish theater, which was dominated by plays derided as *shund* (trash) for their mechanical, sensationalistic plotlines. Gordin's theatrical reform involved removing the Yiddish theater's conventional song-and-dance numbers, vaudevillian jokes and stunts, and melodramas and replacing them with a newfound moral seriousness and loyalty to the letter of the text. His "problem plays" were influenced by (and often freely borrowed from) the critical realism of Henrik Ibsen, Anton Chekhov, and Gerhart Hauptmann, and his characters—always recognizably the mothers, fathers, children, and lovers of the Jewish ghetto—spoke the common prose of the East Side. Gordin's particular definition of literary realism had social criticism at its core: he believed that using the tools of verisimilitude to expose political truths could not help but lead to social transformation, since the urgent need for radical change was manifestly "the real." Even the best of his plays do not read today as realist by any contemporary definition, but they were pivotal in moving the Yiddish stage toward an author-based, literary-centered theater. Importantly, Gordin's depiction of Jewish immigrant reality was inextricable from his educational activism, which was fundamentally a downtown counterargument to uptown philanthropy.[61]

Though Gordin's realism went hand in hand with his view of social reform, he was much less congenial toward the reformism of the settlement house, which competed (often ineffectively) with the Yiddish theater for the hearts and minds of the Jewish East Side. Gordin's campaign against the settlements reached its height with the performance of his play *The Benefactors of the East Side* in 1903. This one-act play was unusual Gordin fare in several ways. It was performed at a benefit for the Educational League in front of an audience of two thousand people in the Grand Central Palace in midtown Manhattan rather than in a downtown Yiddish theater; in order to drum up support among English-speaking potential donors in attendance, *Benefactors* was also the sole Gordin play to be written and performed in English.[62] *Benefactors* was what we might call occasional drama, written in direct response to a meeting between the Educational Alliance's board of trustees and a handful of East Side representatives at which the latter were not given sufficient opportunity to speak. The Yiddish- and English-language Jewish papers were flooded with commentary in the aftermath of this disastrous event, including an inflammatory article penned by Gordin himself for the January 1903 issue of *Di Zukunft* (The future). The February fund-raising ball for the Educational League sought to capitalize on the animosity this meeting provoked among East Siders and their potentially generous sympathizers: announcements for the ball read, "We do not need anyone's pity and benevolence." The characters and plot of *Benefactors* were an obvious send-up of the Educational Alliance: a wealthy philanthropist invites a group of concerned individuals to his mansion to discuss the problems of the Jewish ghetto, all except one of whom are blind to the ghetto's real problems and suggest a series of insufficient or outright ludicrous reforms. Notable characters include Mr. Morris Goldberg, a labor agitator who serves as Gordin's stand-in and the play's hero; Hutchins Fish Lobster, a wealthy non-Jewish reporter modeled on journalist Hutchins Hapgood; Reverend Dr. Knobel, whose name translates to "Dr. Garlic" and parodies

Reform Judaism's adoption of the Christian appellation "Reverend"; and the philanthropic host, Mr. Ashley Jefferson Joske, who was clearly modeled on Jacob Schiff, Alliance founder, principal financier of the Henry Street Settlement, and millionaire.

Reform appears, from the beginning, as a peculiarly Jewish obsession: in the opening monologue an Irish servant complains that her boss and his wife "are contaminated with the evil spirit of reform, [which is] a purely Jewish invention." A journalist arrives soon thereafter and promises to publish a glowing article summarizing the events of the meeting, though he doesn't plan to linger for longer than a minute. *Benefactors* immediately does away with the idea that uptown reform amounts to anything more than a parade of pointless meetings and an exchange of social niceties. It also expresses Gordin's deepest suspicions about the settlement movement's strategy of mixing culture with reform, its intellectual vacuity, and its fetishization of "cultivation." One guest and would-be reformer believes that classical music will save the needy; another suggests that developing a strong "physical culture"—a common period expression and a popular class at many settlements—could alleviate crime in the ghetto. Other characters are equally foolish: they mix up the Strauss of *Zarathustra* and the Strauss of "The Blue Danube," extol the Enlightenment potential of cookbooks and bathing, laud Reform Judaism, and worry that proximity to immigrants will cause physical contamination. These misbegotten cultural reforms suggest the benefactors' deep fear of immigrant intellect. "We must forbid them to engage in philosophy, we must forbid them to pursue higher education, we must beat their whole way of thinking and remembering out of them. Don't give them serious books in the libraries," one attendee argues, recommending that punching bags replace reading material in immigrant homes.[63]

Most damning of all is Gordin's portrayal of the philanthropic Mr. Joske, who accuses Russian Jews of being "freeloaders and beggars" and praises Jewish reformers as national heroes:

> Our great fellow-citizen, Lincoln, who was also a great American, one who raised the banner of liberty in the struggle for the liberation of the slaves to attain their freedom, in the footsteps of that Lincoln do we

follow. Most assuredly the population of the East Side is not colored, but it *is* Romanian; they are not Ethiopians, but they *are* Russians and as such they are not in a position to take advantage of the blessings of good citizenship. They are easy prey for the anarchists and demagogues. It is true that persecution has made them beggars, but it is our duty as human beings to solve the great social problem for the sake of truth and love, for the sake of humanity and progress, for the sake of civilization and the brotherhood of nations, for the sake of mankind and this great difficult and complicated solution of the social problems of society, the community of the city of New York.

This piece of dialogue telescopes many of the critiques of settlement pedagogy that can be found throughout turn-of-the-century print and periodical culture. It accuses reformers of racism, an overweening sense of self-congratulation, blind patriotism, and belief in their own godlike capacity to instill "truth, love, humanity, progress, civilization" in the new immigrants. This parallel drastically deflates the settlement movement's accomplishments by showing its distance from the real heroes and monuments of U.S. history. Furthermore, by suggesting that Joske/Schiff and his colleagues see themselves as white saviors and their foreign beneficiaries as African Americans—or at least "almost as lowly"—Gordin identifies the racism underlying immigrant aid.

The play's main goal may have been to undermine the public efforts of philanthropists like Schiff (and, as we shall see, of reformers like Lillian Wald) to balance loyal Americanism with a purely religious form of Judaism stripped of any ethnic, national, or racial valences. This settlement model of the American Jew was, after all, anathema to Gordin's self-identification as a Russian and an intellectual. But in fact, Gordin's rebuttal of reformers' attempts to dilute Jewish particularity is one of the play's most impressive feats. The play shows the absurdity of comparing Lincoln's Emancipation Proclamation to Progressive reformers' efforts on behalf of immigrants—efforts that the rest of the play paints as utterly self-serving. However, in revealing this parallel to be fraudulent, Gordin does not so much reject the conflation of eastern European Jews with African Americans as actually affirm the immigrants' affiliation with alternative minority histories and "rescued" subjectivities, to borrow Peggy

Pascoe's terminology.[64] This rhetorical alliance hints at a political affinity between differently racialized groups of beneficiaries, serving to critique philanthropic condescension and resist the forces of homogenization.

The fact of racial difference subtly underlies the work as a whole. The characters spend most of the play excitedly anticipating the arrival of Hutchins Fish Lobster, who as a member of the "smart set" and the only non-Jew invited, is the meeting's most valued guest. At the play's climax, the union leader, Mr. Goldberg, attacks the reformers' stupidity and arrogance and defends Jewish cultural integrity:

> Naïve people, the body of the East Sider is sick because he falls under the yoke of hard work, because he lives in dark holes, because he wanders around breathing polluted air! And you want to fix everything with a punching bag! . . . The lady who mixes up the composer of waltzes with the famous Richard Strauss thinks she can save the East Side with music. A moralist who does not know how to make blood-pudding proposes that they should study a cookbook and learn the rules for holding a napkin and using a knife and fork. It is very uplifting when people undertake to help the uneducated, to be the friends of the unfortunate, the leaders of the unknown. But to do this one needs understanding and awareness and not false love.

Goldberg's impassioned speech causes the other Jewish characters to despair that he has "disgraced the Jewish people in the eyes of the entire Christian world"—that is, in front of Fish Lobster. "Enough! Enough," the Jewish philanthropists shout. "This is a scandal! . . . In the name of God, leave this place! . . . A calamity! What will the gentlemen say about us?" Meanwhile, the esteemed Gentile smiles and mutters to himself and the audience, "*This* is an authentic Jew; this is what I like."

Many in Gordin's audience would have been familiar with Hapgood, a writer for the *Commercial Advertiser* whose book *The Spirit of the Ghetto* had been published one year earlier. Hapgood distinguished himself from his senior contemporary Jacob Riis by reporting "sympathetically on the character, lives and pursuits of certain East Side Jews with whom he [had] been in relations of considerable intimacy."[65] Hapgood's "sympathy" was the distinguishing factor. Unlike Riis, Hapgood found the Jewish district picturesque and its denizens utterly captivating, and he took a positive approach to the ghetto in his reform-minded writing; he even lived for a time at the University Settlement. He was a close associate of Abraham Cahan and a fan of the Yiddish theater, writing admiringly of Gordin in *The Spirit of the Ghetto*. But Gordin's suggestion here, embedded in Hutchins Fish Lobster's twinkle-eyed satisfaction at the noisy, fractious scene surrounding him, is that Hapgood too is an opportunist, poaching off the narrative potential of New York City's immigrant Jewish population. The ethnic melee of Jewish reform culture rejuvenates the fictional Hapgood and fortifies his imagination so that he might continue to rise in his career as a literary ghetto sympathist—as indeed Hapgood's next major publication, *Types from City Streets* (1910), would explicitly spell out: "The very lowest people, like the very highest on the social scale, come very close to the facts of life. They are, through poverty, through toughness, through crime, brought up against the 'limit.' . . . If you can get very close to experience, and not have your nervous system shocked by so doing, you have acquired culture and implicit literature."[66] As the play's already-compromised philanthropists and would-be reformers become desperately sycophantic in their efforts to secure Fish Lobster's approval, he is revealed to be the true power broker in the reform–philanthropic relation—as well as the watchful audience for this public performance of intercommunal dissent. It is curious that Gordin depicts the Jewish philanthropic class as obsequious fans of Hapgood, considering how many of them spoke out against the realist methodology of both Hapgood and his ghetto tour guide, Cahan. An editorial in the *American Hebrew* gave *The Spirit of the Ghetto* a withering review, claiming that Hapgood knew nothing of Jewish life and should be ignored; another assailed the contemporary school of "slum fiction" for advertising the Jewish ghetto's ills in embarrassing and exaggerated detail.[67] Jewish reformers actively managed the public image of Jews, identifying literature as an important carrier both for "positive" messages, as in the settlement's literary curriculum, and for negative impressions, as in "realist" fiction, urban reportage, and the Yiddish drama, which the patrician class also generally reviled.

The Benefactors of the East Side is a fascinating account of antireform sentiment among the immigrant working class and a suggestive portrait of uptowners. In the archive of Jewish settlement writing, Gordin is superseded in antireformist vehemence only by Anzia Yezierska, whose wide-ranging experience of reform culture included being a recipient of Jewish philanthropy and, later, serving as a teacher of domestic science at the Educational Alliance (working under her Americanized name, Hattie Mayer). The period in which Yezierska actually participated in settlement work made her Gordin's immediate contemporary, though her own writing did not appear in print until 1915. Her novels and short stories are set in a Jewish immigrant milieu dotted with better-housing bureaus, social betterment societies, charity organizations, night schools and colleges, homes for working girls, and settlement houses, a fictional world that divides along the fault line of the "clientelist" binary between benefactor and beneficiary.[68] She continually indicts the elite benefactors of the East Side for their willing blindness to Jewish immigrants' crippling poverty—the only problem requiring their direct intervention, in her view. Furthermore, her work joins Gordin's in identifying the intellectual and artistic context for the perennial conflict between reformer and client. Several stories in Yezierska's collection *Hungry Hearts* feature striving immigrant women turning to reform institutions for access to literature and the arts, suggesting that the success or failure of benefactors can be tracked through their literary investments.[69]

Yezierska protests the homogenizing Americanization efforts of the settlement house in her 1923 novel *Salome of the Tenements,* grafting a critique of reform and philanthropy onto a plot involving a love story between immigrant Sonya Vrunsky and John Manning, a wealthy WASP settlement worker. The novel posits a direct link between the settlement's methods of acculturation and Manning's cold, passionless character: "What did you get me for?" Sonya asks him. "To make me over? To make me part of your social experiment—part of your Christian reform?" Yezierska pillories the very notion of Progressivism and scientific rationality, depicting the settlement house as a superficial and misdirected endeavor. But whereas Manning is robotic in his reflexive Progressivism, Sonya's most pronounced characteristic is her disregard for reason as a quality antithetical to beauty—a trait Yezierska attributes here, as in many of her narratives, to her protagonist's immigrant Jewishness. And though

Sonya searches for aesthetic beauty everywhere she looks, Yezierska's metaphors for the benefactor–beneficiary relationship are drawn from the arts as well. The philanthropic class sees immigrants as part of a "melodramatic vaudeville," while Sonya indicts their own efforts as "fit for jokes in comic papers"; in contrast, the protagonist's own "shop of the beautiful" will offer democratized beauty to ghetto dwellers. Across Yezierska's body of work, reform organizations first appear to her fiercely independent but needy heroines as rare beacons of opportunity but quickly reveal themselves to be "a lie, like all settlements are lies." She continued to put the settlement house and allied reform institutions at the center of her narratives as she consolidated her oppositional authorial voice.[70]

Despite the sheer number of patrons, philanthropists, and reformers crowding Yezierska's texts, her collected works are actually less insightful than Gordin's satire when it comes to the effect of social reform on middle- and upper-class Jews. *The Benefactors of the East Side* ignores reformers' genuinely benevolent motivations. Instead, it presents desperation and self-consciousness as the root of their commitment to immigrant aid. In its depiction of fretting philanthropists who equate Goldberg's radical monologue with a reputation-eviscerating scandal, *Benefactors* protests the social censorship that would perceive all performances of overt Jewishness in public as a potential threat to community survival. And as the Gentile character's pivotal assertion that "*this* is an authentic Jew" indicates, it is specifically ethnic performances of immigrant Jewishness that bedevil the cast of benefactors, rather than the Jewish radicalism or poverty that are its analogues. This climax also permits Gordin to issue a veiled affront to contemporary critics of his dramatic form who alleged that he, like his hero Goldberg, "looked for all bad qualities in Jews—thievery, murder, swinishness—and put all that on the stage" under the guise of realist representation.[71] By implicitly allying Goldberg's radical insights with his own innovative literary technique, Gordin integrates his critique of settlement philanthropy with a defense of his *literary* model of reform. His goals are personal as well as propagandistic and institutional here: Gordin wrote *Benefactors* for performance in English in order to persuade an audience who possessed the implicit power as English speakers both to advertise his literary prowess to a broader constituency and to increase the influence of the Educational League. In short, Gordin's antireformist screed is also an advertisement for the very realism his farcical and hastily composed play scarcely embodied.

The Benefactors of the East Side's insights had ramifications beyond Gordin's activist and literary agenda, shedding light on the anxieties of Jews whose full acceptance within the U.S. mainstream was still far from secure at the dawn of the twentieth century. For uptowners, the decision to become involved in settlement work was experienced as a duty both to the newcomers and to themselves, and this group became the new immigrants' fiercest advocates and sternest critics. Self-interest, Susan M. Ryan reminds us, is a complement rather than an adversary to genuine benevolence. An editorial in the *American Hebrew* urged readers to approach reform in the spirit of both generosity and self-protection: "All of us should be sensible of what we owe not only to these . . . coreligionists, but to ourselves, who will be looked upon by our gentile neighbors as the natural sponsors for these, our brethren." Jewish reformers and philanthropists tended to mix public avowals of support with subtle statements of reprobation meant to distance themselves from their beneficiaries. They insisted that they shared none of the immigrants' offensive attributes, that "the boisterous, ill-mannered, pushing Jew is disliked much more heartily . . . by the highbred Jew than by any other man," and they simultaneously threw themselves into reform projects, founding settlement houses, boardinghouses, and schools and writing for Progressive periodicals.[72] Some, like Jacob Schiff, Felix Adler, Julia Richman, Belle Moskowitz, and Lillian Wald, were among the most public faces of Progressive reform and philanthropy. The generation of social reformers to spearhead the settlement movement was the first in which the Protestant tradition was not the primary moral compass and main source of financial and human capital.

Zeroing in on the problem of Jewish representation in board rooms and drawing rooms, in print and on stage, *The Benefactors of the East Side* compels us to ask, What real social concerns were dramatized when its reformist characters despaired at the possibility that Jewish settlement associates might be cast in a negative light? Commentators in the Anglo-Jewish press constantly measured the weight of obligation against the potential harm that affiliation with the immigrant poor might cause. One settlement worker described mixed motives, claiming, "[As] German Jews, proud of ancestry and desirous of self-preservation; as American Jews, anxious that the spirit of Judaism should continue to live in its highest manifestations; as American citizens, who see the need of continuing to assimilate and Americanize the immigrant, all of us are bound to help the social democracy of the settlement." Another spokesman reasoned, "[We] belong to the minority, and the minority is always judged by its lowest representative. Our duty therefore is to raise our race."[73] Comments attesting to the self-preservationist dimension of social reform work are easy to find in the English-language Jewish press, and they stand out in sharp contrast to the more generalized concern for "society" that mainstream periodical coverage of the settlement movement tends to express.

This perceived threat, I want to suggest, was another significant cost of settlement contact. Jewish patrons attended settlements in large numbers, owing to the high number of such institutions clustered in majority-Jewish neighborhoods like the Lower East Side. No other ethnic community was comparably active on both sides of the philanthropic relation. The heyday of the movement, from the 1890s to the early 1920s, marked the first time since the antislavery movement that a minority group had achieved such a high profile as leaders, beneficiaries, *and* chroniclers of a social reform institution. This troublesome proximity made many American Jews uneasy. The settlement movement brought to a head essentially political disputes between affluent and typically conservative German or "uptown" Jews and working-class, often radical eastern European or "downtown" Jews.[74] Although settlement work certainly boosted Jewish reformers' cultural capital through the coin of philanthropy, it also endangered their incipient status within the white mainstream by associating them in the national consciousness with Jewish immigrant beneficiaries, who were the object of enormous and mortifying public attention during this period in reform writing, slum fiction, exposure journalism, and urban travelogue. However "other" the Yiddish-speaking, working-class immigrants may have seemed to the Americanized Jewish settlement leaders, then, the latter were keenly aware that the broader culture considered them part of the same social unit. The traditional conception of Jewish communal identity only confirmed this view. Jewish reformers feared that this aggregation of *all* Jews under the banner of their "lowest representative" would serve nativist and anti-Semitic ends.

This sense of social peril among Jewish benefactors had rhetorical repercussions as well. I now want to suggest one further way in which the fear of being "disgraced ... in the eyes of the entire Christian world" is borne out in the archive of Jewish settlement literature by briefly turning to the writing of German–Jewish reformer Lillian Wald, founder of the Henry Street Settlement in New York, where Rose Cohen first encountered Shakespeare with a mixture of pride and shame. Wald's prose reflects anxieties about ethnic agglomeration not in the content it broaches but, rather, in the rhetorical techniques it deploys. In this final section, I argue that the fraught nature of assimilated Jews' social status in the face of the new immigration encouraged them to develop increasingly self-protective representational strategies in their writing, strategies that imposed some distance between writers, readers, and the philanthropic beneficiaries associated with their texts. This literary response to the settlement's pedagogy of influence was among the factors that changed the genre of reform writing at the turn of the century.[75]

The Henry Street Settlement was financed by Jacob Schiff, served an impoverished Jewish clientele, and maintained a strictly secular, universalist agenda from its founding in 1893. Wald's biographer Marjorie Feld has outlined Wald's efforts to distance herself from the Judaism of her settlement's immediate context, describing her difficulty in balancing a consent-based identity with her reliance on the personal, financial, and professional support of a network of German Jews, as well as the press's tendency to identify her, against her wishes, as a "Jewess."[76] As such, Wald's personal and professional life was marked by conflicts over Jewish identity that the settlement house catalyzed and that *Benefactors* brought to light. (Wald was a figure well known to Gordin and a close colleague of Schiff, whom Gordin satirized as Joske; it was perhaps only her singular record of achievement that spared her from inclusion in Gordin's satire.) Wald turned to literary form to resolve these challenges: she developed a prose style that managed to effectively describe immigrant need while avoiding the kind of human portraiture that might suggest that Jewish squalor was in any way endemic to the group. In doing so, she managed to institute some distance between herself and the problematic Jewishness of her own settlement work. In answering complex affective, social, and literary needs, Wald's writing allows us to glimpse an alternative genealogy for the newly objective, unsentimental cast of Progressive reform writing, and it suggests the central role of the settlement house in diffusing status anxiety across the Jewish American literary canon.

Consider the opening chapter of Wald's well-known *House on Henry Street*, a social scientific memoir published in 1915 based on a series of articles that had appeared in *Atlantic Monthly* earlier that year. *The House on Henry Street* focuses on sites of human habitation that are only abstractly peopled, describing tenements, streets, and cities in great detail. This is particularly the case in the book's first and most frequently cited chapter. Here Wald recounts the "baptism of fire" that cemented her commitment to public health–centered settlement work, a life-altering event that began when a student in her home-nursing class begged Wald to treat her ailing mother. Over the course of the chapter, Wald closely tracks her physical surroundings as she makes her way through the Lower East Side toward the patient's tenement apartment. She moves "over broken roadways—there was no asphalt . . . over dirty mattresses and heaps of refuse . . . between tall, reeking houses whose laden fire-escapes, useless for their appointed purpose, bulged with household goods of every description." She continues onward, through "Hester and Division streets . . . past odorous fish-stands, for the streets were a market-place, unregulated, unsupervised, unclean," all the way to "a tenement hallway [and] up into a rear tenement," and finally into the bedroom where a desperately ill woman lies. Wald condenses the whole mission of Progressive reform into this description of her travels through city streets: dilapidated roads, unregulated commercial activity, lack of public and domestic hygiene, and tenement housing, which together "[lend] themselves inevitably to many forms of indecency." This experience produces in Wald the need "to know and to tell," to gain knowledge through helpful involvement with her neighbors and to share that knowledge with the nation.

Although Wald goes on in later chapters to discuss her friends and neighbors by name, human figures are not rhetorically powerful tools in this account of her "baptism of fire." Detailed description of the blighted urban landscape serves as the book's evidential foundation. By locating social need in a journey rather than a person, stating that "[all] the maladjustments of our social and economic relations seemed epitomized in this brief journey and what was found at the end of it," Wald summarizes Progressive reform's fundamental innovation: its commitment to shifting the burden of causation from individuals to conditions and to offering environmental explanations for social problems. As a public genre that aims to produce concrete change in the world—a form of literature founded on the premise that it ought to *make something happen*—reform writing is the natural adjunct to Wald's Progressivism. But her literary Progressivism had specific motives that stemmed, at least in part, from her ongoing struggle to be seen as a representative of the "universal brotherhood of man" rather than as "an American Jewess."[77]

Wald gave what amounts to a lesson in literary interpretation in an address to the National Council of Jewish Women in 1896 on the problems of the immigrant East Side. Explicitly called upon to speak as a Jewish woman reformer to an audience of Jewish women, Wald instructs her listeners to "read" the physical environment as a surrogate for human beings, both on city streets and on the page.

> Read each figure a human being. Read that every wretched unlighted tenement described is a description of *homes* for people—men and women, old and young, with the strengths and weaknesses, the good and the bad, the appetites and wants that are common to all. Read in descriptions of sweatshops, factories and long-hour working days the difficulty, the impossibility of well-ordered living under them.... Say to yourself: "If there is a wrong in our midst, what can *I* do? Do *I* owe reparation?"

As her address proceeds, Wald acknowledges that it would be easy enough to name the specific social attributes of these human beings, such as their background and religion, but suggests that it would be better to obscure those details in the interest of circumventing the prejudices of a U.S. public eager to heap blame on immigrant Jews. She goes on: "It is unjust to say of our neighbors, the greater number of whom are Russian or Polish Jews, that they are the least clean, the most unlovely and ungrateful, [as an] equal depth of poverty will create the same conditions of filth and unattractiveness, whether found among Russians, Italians, or Irish." That Jewish immigrants live in special squalor, she continues, "is a generalization to be denied."[78] Wald's account of surface and depth, symbol and meaning within the modern city emerges as a description of her own emerging literary technique, still in development in 1896. The reading lesson she presents to the Jewish bourgeoisie extends her liberal universalist and self-protective ethic of care into a literary methodology.

Other Jewish reformers of Wald's social milieu betray similar motivations as they endorse her narrative technique. Emil Hirsch, a prominent Reform rabbi and philanthropist based in Chicago, also elevated a rhetoric of conditions and environment over portraiture. In a 1902 letter to the *New York Times,* Hirsch urges writers to avoid caricature by meditating on the conditions that produce urban inequality.

> [The] men and women who look upon the poor Jews as curiosities, and even the cheap novelists in quest in the Ghetto for material to work up in sketches [are] lacking always in the deeper understanding of the terrible injustice done to the poor Jews by making them to be freaks. Among these "slumming" visitors I include also the cheaper class of reportorial writers, who do not scruple to caricature the Ghetto Jew because they fail to remember that what they deem in him to be congenital characteristics and about which they love to jest are, after all, acquired traits easily removed with the change of conditions.[79]

Social workers like Wald and Hirsch were aware that their writing had a significant part in shaping the way Americans perceived immigrant and working-class communities, and they took seriously writing's ability to educate the public as well as to potentially devastate a cause.[80]

Scholars have charted the displacement of sentimental narrative strategies from the center to the margins of nineteenth-century reform writing as realism and naturalism came to dominate U.S. literature across genres and as social work became an increasingly professional venture. The language of reform writing became more objective and "scientific" when writers turned to facts and figures instead of to moralizing injunctions organized around human portraiture.[81] To grasp how the social concerns of Progressive reformers inflected their prose, it is helpful to recall what reform writing looked like during the antebellum period. This earlier "age of reform" was marked simultaneously by the urgency of abolitionism and by a distinctive sentimental narrative style characterized by direct address, highly stylized characterization, and thematic focus on human suffering and connectedness. Sentimentality, as Joanne Dobson puts it, is "designed to convey the primary vision of human connection in a dehumanized world," and antebellum reformers used sentimental rhetoric to remind privileged readers that they were emotionally, physically, and psychically tied to the suffering they read about.[82] Antebellum reform writing's direct appeals aim to "[put] listeners and readers in [the sufferer's] shoes, to heighten that listener or reader's sense of shared, common peril."[83] Reform texts from this period invariably place a human subject—the desperate slave, the drunkard, the fallen woman—at the center of their arguments. In one account by abolitionist Lydia Maria Child, for example, the "everlasting slave" haunts the writer's psyche and her representational strategies: "I *want* to do other things, but *always* there is kneeling before me that everlasting slave, with his hands clasped in supplication." Antebellum reform writing also accommodated an antisentimental strain, but these early instances of dispassionate discourse remained exceptional until the rise of Progressive reform.[84]

What we learn from comparing antebellum and Progressive Era examples is that risk and representation always travel hand in hand when it comes to the genre of reform literature. Midcentury reform writers risked comparatively little by describing the other-in-need in terms of sentimental pity because an identification with the slave, the drunkard, or the prostitute did not significantly threaten their own social standing. This is most obviously true for affluent white reformers who were at a great social remove from the groups they wished to help, but it also holds true for reform writers whose race, gender, or personal experience put them in closer proximity to the needy population in question. African American antislavery activists pose an important counterexample to Wald and her colleagues here. Like Jewish settlement workers, black abolitionists were at the forefront of their movement. Unlike the former, however, black abolitionists had little incentive not to emphasize the deeply personal suffering of enslaved people; oppressed and subjugated even in freedom and restricted from accruing wealth or broad influence in society at large, black reform writers faced an arguably lower threshold of social liability.[85] Furthermore, whereas Jewish reformers like Wald feared being conflated with a marginalized population, the racist logic of the nineteenth-century United States kept black abolitionists at an irretrievable distance from the white center of power no matter what financial, cultural, or social capital they might possess. For black abolitionists, sentimental tropes were an important means of gaining a hearing in a broader reform culture devoted to "acknowledging the corporeality of personhood" in their prose.[86] It was, instead, the *content* of their writing that potentially put them at risk: think, for instance, of the way sentimental form enables Harriet Jacobs to affirm her womanhood in *Incidents in the Life of a Slave Girl*, even though her story contains illicit sexual content that threatens to expunge that womanhood, and her very humanity, in the eyes of genteel white female readers.[87]

The human portraiture that defined sentimentalism had moved to the margins of reform writing by the twentieth century. Gilded Age reformer-writers such as Helen Campbell and Jacob Riis are intermediary figures in this genealogy, producing work in the 1880s and 1890s that melded sentimental and empirical aesthetics.[88] A heightened taste for facts and statistics interceded between the hybrid rhetoric of Gilded Age authors and the desentimentalized prose of Progressive reformers. But I am arguing that there was another critical intercession: the simultaneous influx of immigrants coded as others into the national body and of affluent Jews into the executive meetings, institutional parlors, and editorial boards of the social reform scene. As narrative description became a liability for this donor class eager to maintain its unprecedented material comfort and social acceptance, tropes that had been emblematic up to the late nineteenth century—emotionally resonant descriptions of a suffering child's face, a detailed portrait of a family in need—faced generic decline. There was never an "everlasting immigrant" to convince sympathetic middle-class Americans that the settlement project needed their support. The object of activist energies shifted both rhetorically and practically from individual victims to the health of the whole civic body.

The intrusion of Jews as major leaders, writers, *and* beneficiaries within a reform matrix was a triangulation never before achieved within the world of U.S. social work. From the start, Jewish Americans expressed anxiety over the way such a triangulation eroded the discrete self-other relationship between benefactor and beneficiary. This anxiety proved fertile ground for the socially conscious literary production that emerged from the settlement movement: it prompted Gordin's educational activism and composition of *Benefactors,* and it encouraged Wald to employ self-protective representational strategies in her prose to impose the necessary distance that money alone could not do. Wald's environmentalist writing thus registers the double bind of intracommunal settlement work. She knew that the social status of acculturated American Jews like herself was made increasingly vulnerable by the ongoing discussions of Jewish criminality and immigration restriction that her own reform work sought to temper. If reform writing could effect real change in the world, as Wald believed, might it not also cement one's social position within it?

Reformers did not conduct their work in a vacuum. They published their work in every manner of periodical, newspaper, and book and collaborated with social workers, politicians, and educators who did not always share their background or perspective. Within these print venues—journals like *McClure's* and the *Survey* and edited collections like *The Literature of Philanthropy*—authors shared literary tropes and devices that first emerged in distinct institutional contexts. Thus, while a unique set of social concerns galvanized Jewish settlement workers, their reform writing ultimately resembles that of their non-Jewish colleagues: all tended to diminish characterological representation and focus on environmental conditions once those tropes had begun to evolve and circulate in the broader culture of reform. Yet the fact that writers made moves toward the same style at the same historical moment does not mean that their motivations and causes were shared as well. We can understand the newly unsentimental cast of Progressive reform writing as a version of what Peter Demetz has called the "realist syndrome." This syndrome names the way in which literary conventions that "originated as so many separate innovations in the work of many separate authors . . . become gathered together, integrated in both idea and practice into a recognizable transpersonal *style*."⁸⁹ Approaching Progressive reform writing as a syndrome makes space for both critical truths about the genre posited in this chapter: first, the fact that by the early twentieth century representational distance was a generic convention of reform writing for authors of varying backgrounds, and second, the idea that Wald cultivated literary style as social practice.

I have argued that the settlement drew from a variety of sources and antecedents, developing an approach to literature that knitted together Victorian notions of moral uplift and the social power of art with Progressive ideas of objectivity, research, and environmentalism. I have also sought to show that the institution ultimately became its own vital if contentious source for twentieth-century literary and cultural production. The formal and generic heterogeneity of settlement literature—from reform novels, amateur poetry, and Progressive memoirs to politically charged Yiddish drama—reflects these diverse origins.

Yet historians have recorded the settlement movement's relation to literary culture in the twentieth century as a narrative of decline.⁹⁰ Beginning around 1910, reformers began phasing literature out of settlement pedagogy. Literary clubs were reconfigured as social or athletic clubs, while dances, parties, and summer camps displaced the older order of communal reading, writing, and performance. By the 1920s, few settlement clubs engaged in literary activities of any kind.⁹¹ The changing nomenclature of one Christodora House club is emblematic of this shift: the group that began in 1908 as the Webster Club soon changed its name to the Webster Literary Club, then to the Webster Literary and Athletic Club, and finally, by 1915, settled on the Webster Fraternity. The Christodora's Hawthorne Club underwent a similar transformation. In 1915, one member acknowledged that the club had broadened its topical range, writing, "From being solely literary, our club, though still emphasizing that department of work, now admits of any activity whatsoever, and there is nothing, be it music, drama, art or science, which does not find in our club a proper theater for its expression."⁹² Literary societies across the institutional spectrum underwent similar transformations. Where settlements scaled back literary offerings, drama, art, and music programs were often instituted in their place. By the second decade of the twentieth century, the Educational Alliance, always a leader in its literary pursuits, was more interested in advertising its Art School, which opened in 1914 as the nation's first community art center. What explains this move away from literature? After the turn of the century, the settlement movement shifted its priorities away from erudition and toward recreation and leisure as paths to Americanization. These new programs still aimed to bring culture to clients, but they divorced cultural enrichment from the liberal–humanistic tradition. At the same time, settlement workers decided to redirect energy toward the immediate needs of newcomers and scaled down their work among the Americanized and U.S.-born—the very demographic most receptive to an English-language literary curriculum. The Educational Alliance's 1916 annual report observed, "Methods of today are radically different from those deemed successful in the past. Ten or more years ago the ideal club had prefixed to its name, as a sort of justification, the term debating, literary, etc." In its place, the Alliance "incorporated manual work in [its] club plans so that each club performs some definite work, without detracting from its social functions." Vocational training would better prepare immigrants for the U.S. workforce than a literary circle, which is reduced here, in retrospect, to a mere "justification" for socialization.[93]

By the time the Americanization crusade cohered into an organized political movement at the onset of World War I, literature had ceased to be the settlement's privileged vehicle for cultivation—a word whose prestige was also in retreat. This socializing function migrated to the public school system. Settlement workers, always fearful that their institutions would become obsolete if they replicated services freely available elsewhere, dropped literature from their curriculum just as the public schools made it a primary vehicle of their Americanization program.[94] Meanwhile, by the late nineteenth century, literature had emerged in the universities as what Michael Warner calls a "knowledge subject." Newly formed departments of English professionalized the study of literature, casting an authoritative shadow on amateur practices like those found at settlement houses. Settlements were among the public literary institutions that were effectively displaced when literature became a professional vocation and English was installed as an academic discipline within the modern research university.[95]

In part, then, settlement literary culture fizzled out because of structural changes within the spheres of social reform and education—namely, the need to keep cultural offerings fresh, to serve the most disadvantaged constituency, and to distinguish the settlement house from adjacent institutions. But as I have sought to show in this chapter, the settlement movement also operated within a larger, complex literary field. The institution invented a set of uses and definitions for literature that changed in relation to forces exceeding its agenda for reform. I would argue that the diminished role literature eventually came to play within the settlement movement registered, in an oblique way, the profound reconfigurations of literary value then underway in the broader cultural sphere. For the moves toward specialization, expert credentialism, and professionalism that weakened the settlement's claim to literary authority are also practices central to the growth of modernism. By 1915, experimental, avant-garde aesthetics and criticism were introducing new ideas about what literature could do in the world. Writers and critics aligned with early modernism tended to promote an autonomous view of literature and often emphasized the primacy of formalism; the work of "new poets" such as Edna St. Vincent Millay, Amy Lowell, and Vachel Lindsay and the critical advocacy of Harriet Monroe reflected an insurgent belief that literature should not be expected to teach social or moral lessons. As countless critics have enumerated, this principle was also entangled with anxieties about the role of literature in the marketplace and about the commercialization of art in an era of mass culture.[96] At the risk of generalizing the complex work of diverse authors, then, it seems fair to conclude that modernist writers in the United States, as elsewhere, wished to circumscribe the instrumental functions commonly assigned to literature.

When viewed in light of the rise of modernism as a cultural formation, it becomes possible to read the settlement house in much broader terms as a modern institution of literature in which thinkers explored and anatomized the literary problem of autonomy, a problem whose aesthetic dimensions were inextricable from social questions of immigration, assimilation, class, and ethnic identity. In the end, how better to understand

Yezierska's and Gordin's critiques of the settlement house—their claims that homogeneity and quietism marred the institution's literary culture and social programs alike—than as a radical bid for autonomy, an appeal to escape from the curtailments of "influence"? As I have shown in this chapter, settlement houses were materially transformed by debates about the social utility of literary art waged within its quarters and without, and this transformation suggests that there are important parallels and intersections yet to be drawn between the settlement house and other literary institutions—salons, journals, publishing houses—that are more transparently bound up with the career of modernism as a transnational artistic formation.

As Pierre Bourdieu reminds us, literary practices accrue meaning through the interactions of different producers, critics, and cultural authorities and the positions they occupy on the broader field of power. Participants in reform culture made use of inherited literary forms and practices while also engendering alternative, often competing definitions of cultural value: at the settlement house, "literature" could mean personal and spatial cultivation or intellectual immersion; it delivered education in some moments and pleasure in others; it could serve as an introduction to conventional social mores or as a vehicle of self-expression; in literature, some ethnic writers found ways to creatively oppose Americanization, while others found in it rhetorical resources capable of protecting racial and class status. These expressions of aesthetic and political friction contributed to the self-consciously social tenor of late nineteenth- and early twentieth-century U.S. writing. The following chapters will continue to chart this process in new and occasionally overlapping institutional contexts, beginning with the working girls' club movement.

2

The Problem with Comparison

THE WORKING GIRLS' CLUB

> *No* novel worth anything can be anything but a novel "with a purpose," and if anyone who cared for the moral issue did not see in my work that *I* care for it, I should have no one to blame but myself.
>
> —Edith Wharton, letter to Reverend Morgan Dix, 1905

Edith Wharton is not often described as a novelist with a humanitarian social ethic. With some important exceptions, the majority of her fiction explores the world of the U.S. upper class and its culture of consumerism and commodification.[1] Yet even her damning portrayal of New York City's elite society, *The House of Mirth,* draws its vocabulary and model of social relation from an unlikely working-class source: the so-called working girl problem. Her thoughtful observations about inequality and cross-class affiliation become clear if we turn away from *The House of Mirth*'s Van Alstynes and Dorsets and attend to its treatment of the dynamics of social reform. Take, for example, Lily Bart's first encounter with the "underworld of toilers" at a working girls' club:

> Her visit to the Girls' Club had first brought her in contact with the dramatic contrasts of life. She had always accepted with philosophic calm the fact that such existences as hers were pedestalled on foundations of obscure humanity. . . . But it is one thing to live comfortably with the abstract conception of poverty, another to be brought in contact with its human embodiments. Lily had never conceived of these victims of fate otherwise than in the mass. That the mass was composed of individual lives . . . this discovery gave Lily one of those sudden shocks of pity that sometimes decentralize a life.

Lily does not join her friend Gerty Farish in fully committing herself to philanthropy. Only for a moment is she "drawn out of herself by the interest of her direct relation with a world so unlike her own" before focusing once again on her own abiding social progress. Nonetheless, Lily experiences her first pangs of "spasmodic benevolence" when she begins to visit the working girls' club, and her sense of aesthetic and social comparison—already well honed—encounters genuine inequality.[2]

What Lily learns from her visit to the working girls' club is enough to make her "shudder sympathetically," but she is not roused to outrage.[3] In fact, she doesn't entirely hate what she sees there. As she discovers the dramatic contrasts of life for the first time, Lily also comes to realize the key part she plays in producing that contrast by performing the role of "lady" in the personal encounter between benefactor and working girl. And Lily, the narrator regularly reminds us, has always flourished in situations that generate flattering distinctions between beautiful and ugly, proper and inappropriate, ideal and inadequate. Over the course of *The House of Mirth,* Wharton steadily elaborates on Lily's passion for comparison, her knack for finding circumstances, backdrops, garments, and companions that will showcase her positive attributes and renew her sense of self. By putting the social and aesthetic practices of comparison at the center of her novel, Wharton draws extensively on the institution that best displays Lily's value by force of contrast, and that also shows Lily the importance—and precariousness—of a "pedestalled" existence: the working girls' club.

Wharton's brief but compelling depiction of a working girls' club brings readers into the world of turn-of-the-century social reform, a sphere where middle- and upper-class women found a ready outlet for their professional aspirations, as chapter 1 demonstrated. It is worth pausing over the question of why Lily's visit to the club delivers such a charge. Do these "human embodiments" of poverty help put Lily's own financial problems into perspective? Or, alternately, does feeling like someone who gives rather than one who takes simply bring pleasure to a character who has grown tired of living as a "mere pensioner [on] the luxury of others"?[4] These questions have been hard to answer, for critics have generally overlooked the novel's dialogue with contemporary debates about urban working women as social force and social problem. Consider, for example, critic Lawrence Buell's important account of Lily Bart's drift into a working-class milieu, which argues that her downward mobility is a voluntary form of "virtuous self-privation" driven more by her refined nature than by any wish for a classless society. Buell contends that the novel does not take charity or altruism particularly seriously, noting that none of characters in *The House of Mirth* participates in important reform projects like the settlement house. Even Gerty Farish's earnest work at a girls' club—a "genteel charity," in his phrasing—is untouched by Social Gospel discourse, which, he suggests, disengages it from the dominant humanitarian politics of her day.[5] Certainly, Wharton's tone is often satirical when it comes to Farish's self-abnegating do-gooderness, just as the novel gently mocks the activities of would-be reformers like Lady Cressida Raith, who performs missionary work in London's East End, and Carry Fisher, who casts aside her faddish interests in socialism and Christian Science in favor of municipal reform, reduced to a "latest hobby" in her hands. But Gerty's occupation as leader of a working girls' club in New York City in fact plays a pivotal role in the novel, a role hardly diminished by Wharton's characteristically satirical narrative voice.[6]

In what follows, I offer a new perspective on the significance of the working girls' club within the spheres of turn-of-the-century American culture and Wharton's best-selling novel. By organizing Lily's brief beneficence and subsequent decline around a working girls' club rather than, for instance, a settlement house or a reformatory, Wharton is able to unfurl a complex argument about the troubling politics of comparison, to which Lily's exclamation over "the dramatic contrasts of life" points as a kind of narrative key. As I will argue, working girls' clubs were structured around the pedagogical value of contrast between wage earners and the leisure class, virtuous and immoral working women, the refined and the fallen, and they aimed to publicize the similarities and distinctions among women by linking cross-class sociability to print culture. Though riven with unresolved conflicts at the nexus of gender, race, and especially class—or perhaps *because* it was riven with such conflicts—the movement sought to create a new social taxonomy of white working women at a transitional moment in U.S. modernity. Wharton used the club movement's rich conceptual vocabulary and its damning model of social categorization to plot Lily Bart's fluctuating relation to an asymmetrical social world.

THE WORKING GIRLS' CLUB MOVEMENT IN THE UNITED STATES

The working girls' club movement was part of a thicket of voluntary associations devoted to educating and uplifting wage-earning women in the late nineteenth and early twentieth centuries. The movement emerged in response to a new social phenomenon: the exponential growth of the female labor force in the United States from 2.6 million in 1880 to 4 million in 1890 and finally to 10.8 million in 1930.[7] Thousands of women left their rural and small-town homes and household economies for the city in these years, in search of new opportunities for employment. Most were young and unmarried, and many moved into urban lodging houses or boarded with private families.[8] Employment outside the home was not a new concept to poor women, and especially not to African American women, who worked for wages in much greater numbers than white women did in the decades after the Civil War. However, as more white women joined a burgeoning workforce in fields other than domestic service, observers declared the new feminization of city streets, cafeterias, and workplaces to be a profound reconfiguration of social norms.[9]

Wage-earning women had been gathering for purposes of self-improvement and social diversion in official and unofficial ways for decades. But even with such precedents, working girls' clubs received a great deal of attention when the first official societies formed in the mid-1880s, modeled on the mainstream, middle-class women's club movement but focusing their efforts on this new workforce and meeting in the evenings after work had let out for the day.[10] The first self-proclaimed working girls' society grew out of the efforts of Grace Hoadley Dodge, who served as the public face of the movement despite her determined efforts to keep her photograph out of print. Dodge hailed from an enormously wealthy and influential evangelical family. Her grandfather founded Phelps, Dodge and Company, one of the nation's largest copper-mining operations, and was a founding member of the New York City YMCA. Other family members were noted abolitionists, Native American rights activists, and temperance reformers. Grace Dodge followed in her family's tradition of philanthropic work to become the first president of the Young Women's Christian Association (YWCA) and a member of numerous social purity alliances and charitable organizations. She also founded the New York College for the Training of Teachers, later incorporated by Columbia University, in 1887. In 1881, however, Dodge was engaged as a Sunday school teacher at Madison Square Chapel when she arranged with one of her pupils, a silk weaver, to lead a group of working women in weekly discussions on topics related to homemaking. By 1884, this fledgling discussion group had evolved into a more democratic enterprise—Dodge had been too firmly ensconced in the role of teacher in the early years—which they named the Thirty-Eighth Street Working Girls' Society. Dodge's early club and those that followed duplicated many of the YWCA's philosophies and services, with two notable differences: working girls' societies were (nominally) secular rather than evangelical—YWCA membership required that women be church members—and typically had no residential function. Within a year of the founding of the Thirty-Eighth Street Working Girls' Society, clubs and societies (terms used interchangeably) cropped up across the Northeast and began making institutional alliances across city and state lines.[11]

Although the clubs were theoretically open to all wage-earning women, from domestic workers to college instructors, in reality the movement almost exclusively served the industrial, clerical, and retail employees who had gone by the name of "working girls" since the 1870s. Reformers and writers of all stripes connected the emergent category of working girls— women who took on jobs made possible by the expanding, modernizing city—to the problems of the city itself. As Priscilla Murolo has chronicled, most wage-earning club participants hailed from the middle to upper echelons of the female labor force.[12] Factory operatives—the movement's largest membership—generally worked in segments of industry where the rate of pay matched or exceeded the federal average for women. The movement's second-largest demographic was composed of office and department store employees, fields that explicitly excluded women with foreign accents and demanded evidence of education, polished manners, and dress. Thus, despite the actual ethnic and racial diversity of the U.S. female workforce at the turn of the century—three-quarters of the women in the urban female labor pool in the United States were immigrant women and their first-generation daughters in 1890—club members were primarily native-born, old-stock white American Protestants or the daughters of immigrants from northwestern Europe, and the majority were between fourteen and twenty-five years of age.[13]

Wharton's account of Gerty Farish's organizing prowess and Lily Bart's financial generosity captures the role of the club sponsor (any given club had at least one sponsor). At their core, working girls' clubs were cross-class ventures in which working women mingled—sometimes companionably, sometimes with friction and bad feelings—with wealthy, usually older leaders. Participants generally used the language of "ladies" and "girls" in describing their mixed membership, even as they sought through club activities to extend a bridge between the two class worlds such language described. Sponsors provided seed money and functioned as movement leaders, organizing the nuts and bolts of institutional life during the daytime hours that their wage-earning colleagues spent at work.[14] In many cases a woman's decision to participate in a club rather than a settlement house may have been simply a matter of convenience or access (and many were active in both movements). But volunteering at a working girls' club did imply a significant investment in traditional, even conservative notions of gender and respectability, not least because it permitted unmarried sponsors to continue living in their family homes. Like the settlement house, the club movement's interventions were spatial. Organizers aimed to provide a pleasant environment for single women to congregate and socialize after work, one far from the saloons, dance halls, and city streets that they believed posed a threat to women's moral integrity. The movement was thus one of many civic projects that designed a protected public space for urban working women—a space offering a taste of the privacy and comfortable insularity that wealthy women had the privilege to enjoy.[15]

Although their numbers were always modest—approximately seven thousand women had joined around 80 clubs in 1900, and over fifteen thousand members belonged to 125 clubs by 1918—young working women took advantage of the club's opportunities for self-culture, and their involvement signified a real commitment to pursuing "vernacular gentility" and joining the ranks of the middle classes.[16] Organizational life encompassed a range of activities that Alice Kessler-Harris has described as "constructive leisure": members listened to didactic talks on topics such as hygiene, etiquette, and fashion; received domestic and industrial training; attended classes in sewing, literature, art, and music; and met regularly to discuss club issues and socialize in a casual environment. In these endeavors, leaders were less interested in dispensing breadth of knowledge than in "[letting] them know a little of everything and everything of something."[17] Members engaged in charity work, enjoyed chaperoned dances and parties, established libraries, and published journals. Just as Nettie Struther convalesces in the mountains thanks to Lily Bart's financial bequest in *The House of Mirth,* club members raised funds to outfit rural vacation homes where workers could spend their summer holidays away from "the haphazard picnic-park dissipation."[18] The movement also took a conservative position on labor issues, particularly in its early years. In theory, the goal of dignifying and normalizing women's work outside the home was a potentially radical project in the 1880s and 1890s. But in practice, organizers encouraged wage earners to cultivate self-discipline, obedience, and respect for employers, as though good behavior would naturally yield the kind of workplace reforms more radical activists went on strike to pursue. Clubs fairly brimmed with tension as they evaded serious discussion of labor conditions and trade unions.

At a moment when reformers were turning to environment rather than personal morality or behavior to explain social problems, especially within the adjacent settlement movement, working girls' clubs stand out for a deeply individualist approach that seemingly carried nineteenth-century modes of benevolence into the twentieth century. As Christopher Castiglia notes, it was in the antebellum period that reform rhetoric "moved out of the structural life of American society and into the interior lives of its citizens," and the club movement certainly inherited this sense that the beneficiaries of reform should be encouraged "to work at internal integrity rather than to struggle with social negotiation." Yet club leaders considered self-reform and structural change to be connected in a uniquely modern way.[19] They often described club life as initiating a circuit of individual transformations that, taken together, constituted a genuine mode of social reform. "The deeds we do, like pebbles cast upon the surface of a lake, may reach now to far-off cities," Boston Association leader Edith M. Howes declared in a public defense of individual self-improvement's social impact. "We have proposed no great and definite social changes. We have in our membership a large and sympathetic interest in these grave questions of the day, but we feel that our special mission is the training of the individual intelligence to personal responsibility and the spirit of unselfishness upon which all great social reforms and wise institutions must rest."[20] After the century's turn, participants would more explicitly link institutional concerns to broader reform causes, and their language accordingly came to reflect the scientific spirit of Progressivism. Yet the fundamental linkage between self-reform and social reform remained a hallmark of the movement.

Club members also cited collaboration as a central goal and method of their movement. "Co-operation, self-help, self-support, the working with, instead of the old prescribed methods of working for, is the true spirit in which to help the working girl to higher, nobler aims," one leader explained.[21] Although the club model was well established by the time Dodge's movement took off, working girls' societies did not take the principle of alliance for granted; members put great stock in the belief that women banding together for their mutual benefit across the boundaries of class and station constituted a meaningful social mission. Their hybrid vision of reform joined an individualist ethic of self-improvement with a collectivist notion of cooperation: through "combination"—here understood as a species of cross-class friendship—women could generate knowledge, support, and amusement within a self-selecting community that was more than the sum of its parts.

The movement's official stance held that cross-class friendship forged on the shared ground of womanhood was a powerful means of "helping to solve questions in social ethics."[22] Members explicitly connected this democratic sociability to the more obviously political work of, for instance, keeping the streets clean, and they judged its educational effects to be on a par with the effects of reading, lectures, and museums. But what this solution to "questions in social ethics" really accomplished was the creation of a novel class fiction, a reform discourse that assimilated social and economic disparity to gender sameness and made upward mobility out of the masses concomitant with individual personhood. The movement's institutional "syntax of class" rendered class distinctions through the cultural vocabulary of gender, representing the middle class to which wage-earning members aspired not as a bounded class formation but, rather, as "a blur of spiritual or religious ideals, domestic virtues, and standards of comportment more regularly ascribable and more regularly attributed to gender ideology than to class position."[23] In its many strategic displacements—of class onto gender, of social change onto individual self-improvement, of political action onto interpersonal relationships—the working girls' club capitalized on the relative absence of a stable language for describing social class in the United States, while also crafting a usable reformist vocabulary all its own.

The key to the movement's slippery and obfuscating class discourse was the notion of being "busy." Here too Dodge was an innovator. In 1887, Dodge published an advice book called *A Bundle of Letters to Busy Girls on Practical Matters,* drawing on her conversations with wage-earning members of the Thirty-Eighth Street Society. In its opening pages, she explains that the first organization was formed for the benefit of girls who were "busy all day in factory, shop or office," but she goes on to describe the club's overall membership in vaguer terms as composed of "busy" women, "all . . . with little spare time."[24] Five years later, Dodge released a sequel entitled *Thoughts of Busy Girls* (1892), this time publishing essays in a familiarly prescriptive mode allegedly penned by wage-earning club members themselves. Here and elsewhere, Dodge and her fellow club members from all along the class continuum deployed the language of "busy girls" to forge cross-class unity, a rhetorical sleight of hand that equated the unpaid, voluntary labor of wealthy organizers who had "received [their] wages in advance" with the waged labor of less privileged members, who were also kept "busy" with work transacted outside the home. "A woman's club has been called a 'college for married women,' and surely a working girls' club could be called a school for busy girls," Dodge explained.[25]

From a broad historical perspective, this language reminds us that privileged but "busy" women like Dodge were instrumental in advancing women's professional status within the emerging field of social work. Yet within the cross-class world of the club movement itself, this language performed more delicate and often damaging ideological work. Leaders articulated their membership's shared project as one of keeping "busy" so that participants would be able to see themselves as holding qualities in common, especially since it was much easier to notice vast differences in appearance, lifestyle, and opportunity. The rhetoric of "busy" effectively separated activity from labor, making rich women something more than idle and poorer women something other than—*more* than—laborers. This same artful logic organizes the moral hierarchy of women's labor in *The House of Mirth*, dictating which forms of affiliation are thought possible; as we will explore later in this chapter, it is the "busy" typist Nettie Struther who forges a transformative friendship with a female patron, and the abject domestic worker Mrs. Haffen who scrubs that patron's staircase on reddened knee.

In the movement's institutional literature, very real economic and social distinctions melt into vague affirmations of "womanly character." "Appearances! Class distinctions! How such words melt away to nothingness when we stand face to face with eternal verities! Rich or poor, refined or rough, wise or ignorant, these are changing standards and count for little," one sponsor exclaimed.[26] Visible here is the will to wish class antagonism away—not, importantly, to be rid of class distinctions as a mode of organizing social life, but to avoid accounting for the actual material and psychological effects of those distinctions. Club sponsors expressed no desire to dismantle the class structure that produced mentors on one hand and protégées on the other. Quite the contrary: they understood the social hierarchy that produced "different grades of friendship" to be both natural and instructive.[27] Obfuscating class as material reality, privileged club leaders transformed it into a style of womanhood and a measure of character. The movement's individualism "indexed interior moral qualities to outward signs of social mobility, to winning and losing at the pitiless games of market culture," as Thomas Augst has described in a different context.[28] Accordingly, institutional records equate fine speech and avoidance of gum chewing with superior morals, refined taste in the arts with elevated thoughts. Slang is nowhere to be found—a notable absence given that urban women's work culture was the site of significant innovation in vernacular expression in these years. Sharing space under the broad cloak of gentility enabled members to dodge hard discussions about class conflict and racial prejudice, an evasion that ensured these issues would haunt the margins of the movement's language and practice at every turn.[29]

The movement's inherent conservatism guaranteed that it would never be taken seriously by commentators on the left. Socialist feminist Rose Phelps Stokes rejected institutions of this ilk on the grounds that "friendship in this narrow sense does not seem [to] fulfill the requirements of justice. What the working girl wants (like the working man) is fair hours of labor and fair pay for its product." Stokes argued that cross-class relationships could never replace structural and political change and that "welfare work" performed under such undemocratic conditions was "but a pacifying measure to secure her good will despite injustice or wrong." Stokes and others believed that the inequality of reformist "friendship" enacted a kind of class violence; club leaders insisted instead that the stark contrast between leisure-class and wage-earning members helped catalyze reform.[30]

In fact, I argue in the next section that the club's larger reformist project was to create new categories of social differentiation. It did so by generating a complex vocabulary of proximity, combination, and distance that made the organization's mission legible to—and available for adaptation and critique by—observers like Edith Wharton. Encompassed in this comparatist vocabulary was the movement's distinctive way of talking and writing about the relations among "busy" women, as well as the set of theories and methodologies that oriented its reforming activities. In a broad sense, the movement's comparatist discourse aimed to recast the categories to which white working women were seen to belong in the court of public opinion, distinguishing wage earners who joined clubs from those who flocked to dance halls and who crowded city streets. As socially striving working girls combined with upper-class ladies to become more similar in manners, conduct, and presumed moral value, they simultaneously disavowed comparisons with "low" working women, whose experiences and character were, they insisted, so utterly foreign to their own that they constituted a different species of woman altogether. This drive to compare and contrast categories of white womanhood constituted a collective response to the perceived "working girl problem" at the turn of the twentieth century. In the end, it was these taxonomizing practices that held particular appeal for Wharton's social imagination, for in forming a system by which upwardly mobile wage earners might exercise selective discrimination and brutally exclude women they perceived as outsiders, the working girls' club echoed the social machinations of the elite tribe that is Wharton's greatest subject.

THE LADY AND THE GIRL: COMPARISON AND PUBLICITY

If we take the movement's institutional documents at their word, wealthy club members meant to function as a kind of living etiquette manual for wage-earning women who wished the public to recognize, with Lily Bart, that "the mass was composed of individual lives," each one an upwardly mobile striver who scarcely resembled the images of uncouth and sexually vulnerable working girls that circulated in turn-of-the-century publications, spawning entire subgenres from shopgirl fiction to white slave narratives. Club leaders believed that offering themselves as models of true womanhood promised to elevate the social and moral standing of white working women. In doing so, they displayed an investment in the logic of exemplification that borrowed from the still extant nineteenth-century practice of charitable friendly visiting.[31] One prominent club leader described the movement as "a little world" powered by a comparatist political system: "When a girl belongs to a club she is brought into contact with a large number of other women, who probably have had a different experience of life from her own, and who hold different views. She can learn how they look at life, can compare her views with theirs, which will widen her mental horizon and give her the chance of forming truer opinions."[32] Here, the material effects of class disparity are papered over with rosier kinds of differences—of "experience of life" and "views"—and those distinctions become the grounds for self-improvement. Comments like these make clear that the learned practice of discerning important contrasts within a group of people was as consequential as the actual friendships that may have developed between busy women.

Working girls' clubs made the social distinctions among members of their own voluntary community an object lesson not only in standards of behavior but also, more importantly, in the necessity of making comparison a habitual part of social experience and an engine of self-improvement. One sponsor wrote the following of this continual process of evaluation: "[The club] means opportunity to measure her actions by new and nobler standards; to gauge herself by women of fewer limitations, wider knowledge, and sweeter courtesies. It means opportunity to lift her womanhood to a clearer ideal, for nobility of character comes from nobility of aims."[33] Club leaders believed that proximity among rich and relatively poor would reveal undeniable contrasts in manners, behavior, and lifestyle to working women, generating, they hoped, neither envy nor crass imitation but a genuine will to elevate the self. This dubious process of "measuring actions," "gauging herself," and "lift[ing] womanhood" became the club's reform methodology. Accordingly, the movement made interpersonal comparison a new discipline of attention, a mode of relational thinking, and a gendered form of human cognition.[34]

Upper-class leaders knew that their primary occupation within the club was to serve as role models, and so they sometimes admonished one another to exercise vigilance lest their less privileged club mates measure themselves against a faulty ideal. "Let the more favored sisters ... always take the utmost pains to have their own speech and demeanor irreproachable," one sponsor advised, connecting elite women's obligation to serve as a worthy example to the aspirational consciousness of wage earners. "No girl likes to appear conspicuous, or unlike the companions whom she respects and loves, [so] she will insensibly modify her defects of speech and manner, and in time become as quiet and modest as they."[35] Another sponsor made the point that "those who have helped us the most [are] not always those who have given many gifts ... but rather those who have expected the most from us; who have made us ashamed when we were frivolous or false, who have made us aware in their presence of fair possibilities, whose kind eyes, even when absent, have reproached us with their constant vision of the thing we should be."[36] It is hard to imagine a clearer articulation of the regulatory ideal of absent power than this appeal to "kind eyes" that look accusatorily "even when absent," an appeal that instructs wage earners to internalize the eternal judgment of the elite along with their manners and style. Here it is worth putting a finer point on exactly how social contrast begets elevated character. If, in the logic of these formulations, being in the presence of individuals who represent life's "fair possibilities" would translate into constant awareness of "the thing we should be," then developing an aspirational consciousness was more essential to self-improvement than a shorter workday or higher wages, as these structural changes would better conditions without altering the individual who experienced them. In this way, the profoundly conservative ethics and aesthetics of comparison came to stand in for social activism.[37]

Crucially, however, club leaders describe cross-class comparison as a mechanism for shaping *all* female consciousness, including their own. They often made the point that comparison helped them guard against laxity in personal, aesthetic, and social affairs and offered a meaningful sense of their own value. In a widely republished editorial that first appeared in the *Century* magazine in 1891 and that Wharton's sister-in-law Mary "Minnie" Cadwalader Jones would later cite in her account of the movement, Florence Lockwood urged her fellow volunteers not to cover up their advantages for fear of offending working women. "It is shirking our responsibility as women of a leisure class when we attempt to pretend that our conditions of life are the same as theirs," Lockwood explains. She also implores wage earners not to resent the "difference of conditions" that made club work both necessary and possible. Lockwood suggests that for sponsors, the subjective impact of cross-class reform work was felt most acutely in the terrific pressure of being looked upon as a role model. "One cannot . . . lead a life outside the club willfully inconsistent with the light in which one appears to the girls," she contends, "for, never mind how little we desire to be looked upon as examples, we are looked upon as such even by the girls with whom we have least personal contact, and we are apt to find that their belief in us, and constant reference to us, is a pretty sharp reminder of our own shortcomings."[38]

Wharton recognized that cross-class comparison produced a powerful sense of self-worth in benefactors. This compensation is at the heart of Lily's psychology, for as much as she revels in the glow of her visit to Gerty's club, we see even more clearly how crucial that opportunity to measure herself against the working girls has been to her sense of self when she *loses* the capacity to play the lady, drifting downward into a desultory boardinghouse life. For Lily, leading the kind of life that no longer yields the esteem of her coworkers at the milliner's shop represents a tragic loss of self.[39] If one begins to identify the emotional texture of Lily Bart's story in the reformist record, however, the echo of Thorstein Veblen is perhaps stronger still. In his 1899 *The Theory of the Leisure Class,* Veblen outlines a hierarchy of influence ruled by the American leisure class, a group whose example holds prescriptive force for each class stratum lying beneath it. Lockwood's comments exemplify the idea of "invidious comparison," a social practice Veblen defines as "a comparison of persons with a view to rating and grading them in respect of relative worth or value—in an aesthetic or moral sense—and so awarding and defining the relative degrees of complacency with which they may legitimately be contemplated by themselves and by others."[40] Veblen illuminates the relations of power at work in the club movement here. Leaders found it pleasurable and deeply affirming to associate with wage earners, since any measurement that defined "relative worth or value" in terms of social, economic, or cultural capital would inevitably reinforce their privilege and authority. "No one who has not had the experience can realize the pleasure and stimulus of being looked up to and followed, however undeservedly, by a clubful of hard-working girls," Lockwood declares, uncannily predicting how, in the fictional world of *The House of Mirth,* "the admiration and interest [Lily Bart's] presence excited among the tired workers at the club ministered in a new form to her insatiable desire to please."[41]

Though Veblen never mentions the club movement by name, it is not hard to imagine that this organization and its reformist affiliates served as material for his searing argument.[42] But while these insights go far to situate the working girls' club within the larger social ecology of its time, there are aspects of the movement's particular formulation of comparison that Veblen cannot quite capture—most notably, the fact that the institution's methods of "pointing the contrast between themselves and the lower-lying humanity" supported a whole, albeit deeply flawed, theory of social reform. For instance, Veblen suggests that "the pervading principle and abiding test of good breeding is the requirement of a substantial and patent waste of time," but the idea that women gained social status by advertising their capacity for conspicuous inactivity cedes no space to the emergent gender and class politics of being "busy." Nor did invidious comparison exist solely to burnish the "superior status" of wealthy women. Club leaders tried to argue that comparison with social betters also benefited working-class women. By their reasoning, wage-earning members' obvious economic inferiority—an inferiority that was, of course, truly "invidious" only to the extent that it meant enduring long hours in tiring and often dangerous employments with dramatically insufficient rates of pay, cramped domestic conditions, and other structural inequities of working-class city life—would not incur a low self-image. Rather, it would inspire wage-earning women to cultivate the positive qualities sponsors evidently modeled—the platform that made social mobility possible.[43]

How must it have felt for working-class women to hear themselves, and the potential of their young lives, represented in this egregious way? And how can we evaluate the emotional and practical uptake of a theory that essentially links one woman's self-aggrandizement to the self-abnegation of another, a theory so premised on hierarchy in all its brutal forms? The archive offers few easy answers. Wage-earning club members' voices come through the historical record heavily mediated by the reformers, editors, and publishers who framed their words, and thus they can be only partially reconstructed. Moreover, the rank and file surely practiced self-censorship when they encountered more powerful individuals and institutions that had the weight of social and cultural authority behind them. But while rolling eyes and fuming anger leave no trace in the archival record, wage-earning women must have been inwardly resistant, and even outright defensive, in the closed company of their peers. The greatest opportunity to piece together their convictions lies in the movement's two official literary journals. *Far and Near*, published between 1890 and 1894, regularly featured editorials and letters penned by wage-earning members, in addition to publishing poems, stories, and articles by authors who were not directly involved with the movement but reflected its values. Its successor, the *Club Worker*, ran from 1899 to 1921 and mainly published the writing of sponsors and affiliated reformers, detailing club news and avoiding the kind of polite debate that had filled the earlier periodical. The titular "worker" referred not to women who worked for wages but to the organizing labor of the increasingly professionalized cohort of "busy" leaders, and the *Club Worker* dealt almost exclusively with their concerns.

One 1891 editorial in *Far and Near* acknowledges that cross-class relations may well breed hostility and resentment in wage earners, but the writer deems this frustration just another motivating force:

> Whatever inspires the working woman with the desire for a better material life is a force in the solution of the great social and economic problem. Just here lies great encouragement for working girls' clubs, in that they do create a desire for a higher standard of living as our objectors assert. Dissatisfaction with the present must precede the ambition that takes the next step higher. Whatever the club reveals of art, literature, science, society and ethics, and thereby inspires the club member with a longing for a better material life, not only develops her individually in nobler lines, but tends to make firmer and surer the foundations of the new industrial era.[44]

While conceding that becoming familiar with the advantages of the upper classes bred "dissatisfaction" and "longing," the writer insists that this frustration would make working girls into even more tenacious strivers. This profoundly inadequate explanation of the nature and possible rectification of working women's "dissatisfaction" represents the club movement's official policy on cross-class friendship's painful underbelly. And though resentment only rarely punctures the placid surface of official publications—both institutional journals refused to publish anonymous letters, which surely blunted criticism—wage-earning club members were clearly offended by some of the implications of invidious comparison, not least because it remained taboo to discuss the concrete effects of class disparity or the feelings of embarrassment and anger that cross-class proximity often occasioned. "I have yet to see a club where the class distinction did not stick out conspicuously, and I should like to know if our attitude toward it is quite consistent or disingenuous," one member wrote in a 1909 letter to *Club Worker*. "Of course, I know that we must always compromise between the ideal and the possible, but I should like the compromise to be a bit clearer." Her letter was roundly ignored.[45]

The stakes of these internal struggles felt so high because working-class women and their allies were already on the defensive. Beyond the club room walls, there was a growing consensus that cross-class comparison actually *corrupted* the virtue of wage earners. When club participants insisted that these modes of affiliation were uplifting, then, they spoke out, if only indirectly, against a chorus of voices enumerating the risks of class mingling in places like department stores, so-called palaces of consumption in which the wage earner's opportunity to observe the wealthy up close could not help but stoke her envy along with her consumerist desires.[46] This discourse typically centered on retail work, but the department store was merely the most visible setting in which social mixing served to accentuate the asymmetry between rich and poor. In popular magazines, highbrow journals, and reformist venues, writers worried that working women were becoming too familiar with standards of living, especially dress, they could never afford on their own. These debates were inextricably tied up with anxieties over women as consumers. Theodore Dreiser's *Sister Carrie* (1900) is the emblematic example of this kind of thinking in American fiction. Recall, for example, how Carrie's walk down Broadway in the company of a wealthier friend garners critical glances at her clothing, leading her to believe that "it must be evident to many that she was the less handsomely dressed of the two." Carrie immediately experiences a keen longing "to feel the delight of parading here as an equal."[47] Commentators worried that working women who compared themselves to wealthier women would inevitably seek out money, goods, and glamour in dance halls and saloons, among unscrupulous men willing to provide tickets in exchange for sexual favors, known at the time as "treating." Within a public discourse that left little room for marginalized populations to communicate their experiences on their own terms, the fact that so many new opportunities existed for wage earners to measure themselves against privileged women registered as a profound vulnerability to the forces of evil.[48]

Working women's struggles received sustained attention across the various organs of print culture in these years. Part of this attention boiled down to a fixation on the wage-earning modern woman as "a figure of fantasy . . . a marker for the future, for what has yet to take place," as Jennifer Fleissner has observed.[49] But it is also important to note that the turn-of-the-century "working girl problem" represented a new iteration of a long-standing tendency in the United States to project concerns about industrialization onto the bodies and minds—and imagined sexual practices—of women who worked for wages. For example, moral reformers and authors of "sentimental seamstress" narratives drew on the trope of the fallen woman in their writing of the 1830s, contending that female employment led ineluctably to sexual victimization. As Lori Merish explains, early nineteenth-century reformers inscribed a sympathetic but ultimately damning literary formula of exploitation and decline—a tragedy of economic determinism—that governed representations of white female wage earners for decades to follow. In these same years, women factory operatives working at the textile mills in Lowell, Massachusetts, were forced to weather "an extraordinary amount of observation and analysis." Mill owners invited prominent members of the public, from President Andrew Jackson to Charles Dickens, to tour the mills and scrutinize their female employees. Louisa May Alcott picks up on this cultural dynamic when, in her 1876 working woman novel *Work,* the protagonist tries out a number of different employments but balks at "the fatigue and publicity of a shop."[50] The inclination to scrutinize and objectify working women and to interpret their lives through the prism of tragedy was therefore not a new social development when members of working girls' clubs rallied against it. What *was* new at the turn of the century, however, was the way that emergent venues for cross-class and cross-gender mingling, from the dance hall and the department store to the working girls' society, energized public concern about breadwinners' welfare.

And yet club members were disturbed by this regard for working women's needs. From their perspective, widespread concern turned wage earners into victims of conditions they were powerless to change.

This was true even when that solicitude was conveyed sympathetically or supported by statistical analysis: their work was not dignifying but coarsening; their travels on city streets subjected them to unwanted attention; and their chastity was a matter of suspicion. "From her post behind the counter the shop-girl examines every detail of costume, every air and grace of these women whom she despises, even when longing most to be one of them," observed reform writer Helen Campbell in her 1889 *Prisoners of Poverty,* "and it is small wonder that when sudden temptation comes and the door opens into that land where luxury is at least nearer, she falls an easy victim," becoming part of "the army of women who have chosen degradation." Turn-of-the-century reformers made modest strides beyond the flat-out moralizing of earlier social discourse that had reflexively aligned women who moved independently through city streets with the figure of the prostitute, but even Progressives perceived only a very thin line dividing working woman from "easy victim."[51]

Lurking beneath the decorous surface of the club movement's bureaucratic writings and public declarations is this specter of working-class sexuality unloosed from the protection of family and community. Michael Trask has shown how social scientists, reformers, and common citizens alike twinned the apparent crisis of an urban female workforce with the problem of unruly sexuality as homologous forms of disobedience. "The problem of erotic threat," Trask contends, "always originated as a response to a phobia about social mobility." As Progressive Era reformers associated with settlement houses and antiprostitution campaigns worked not only to "protect" laboring women from the varied blights of city life but also to distinguish between regular and irregular forms of sexual expression, they helped produce a vision of working-class female sexuality in which activities like socializing in mixed-gender groups, or going on a date without a chaperone, might signify as an updated, modern form of prostitution.[52] Even Emma Goldman saw the laboring woman's proximity to wealth as a force directing her into sex work.[53] Across multiple print forms and with varying degrees of reformist intent, but traveling always under the cover of grave concern, depictions of struggling and fallen working girls unraveled the hard work club participants put into "[defending] the fair name of *woman* that the public in general will cease thinking that the factory girls are unladylike," as one member put it.⁵⁴ The activism of the working girls' club members, such as it was, evolved as a response to their sense of having been thrust onto the public stage without any power to control public opinion.

One of the movement's strongest motivations, then, was to combat the impression of female wage earners as a social problem. Indeed, many participants believed that cultivating public opinion was more consequential than engaging in conventional political activities such as pursuing the vote. The crux of the problem, as they saw it, was the fact that reformers, journalists, and fiction writers made generalizations about *all* working women, conflating them as uniformly rough, unvirtuous, or in need of rescue. The problem, in other words, was one of mistaken similitude: the public's inattention to social details that divided the category of working women onto separate planes and that distinguished, say, a dishonest domestic servant like Mrs. Haffen from a refined typist like Nettie Struther. This mistaken similitude unraveled the work of individuation to which the movement was committed and instead publicized an impression of working women as an undifferentiated mass. The theory and practice of comparison was thus designed to serve as a necessary social corrective: by emphasizing that their organizations were made up of busy "friends" rather than givers and receivers of charity and by explaining that rich and poor women were alike shaped by the rigors of comparative thinking, working girls' club members dodged the implication that they needed to be rescued. Yet this discourse was forwarded at the expense of the masses of wage earners who were admitted neither into the ranks of the club nor into the clubs' narrow definition of white womanhood.

The very first working girls' society resolved to organize into a club precisely because, in the words of its constitution, "there has grown up in the public mind a poor opinion of the characters, aims, and surroundings of working girls." Its members banded together in order to protest erroneous forms of ascription and "to bring about a change of public opinion."⁵⁵ As participants faced a print public sphere that was increasingly hungry for stories about working women's lives, the more lurid the better, they made it their mission to distance themselves from the category of wage earners that was the target of sympathy and reproach. In this sense, the working girls' club emerged as what Michael Warner would call a "counterpublic," since it was entirely "constituted through a conflictual relation to the dominant public."[56] By virtue of their willing participation in this counterpublic—not merely being women who earned wages but attending meetings and writing to unknown others in journals with national circulation—wage-earning club members remade their identities as "elevated" women. This counterpublic refused its members' classification as a problem population by forwarding an oppositional interpretation of working women's interests and character.[57]

In the pages of *Far and Near*, wage-earning members rallied indignantly in response to public misrepresentations of working women, misrepresentations whose leveling of all distinctions only confirmed the need for character-building organizations like their own. Before moving on to Wharton, let me offer one final example from the annals of this journal to illustrate the club movement's fraught negotiation with a public insistent on apprehending its members as a social problem. In the spring and summer of 1892, the journal's correspondence section hosted a lively debate about Edgar Fawcett's influential essay "The Woes of the New York Working Girl." Club members bemoaned the way working women were portrayed in fiction and reform writing. Fawcett's portrait of New York's white female working class was undistilled tragedy. "The road to ruin, as we call it, is so fatally easy to them; who shall dare to blame them if they take it? . . . It would be hard to think of any class of human beings more dismally handicapped from their births than are these same poor helpless victims of our massive social mistakes," he writes of their potential for uplift.[58] Although Fawcett's article was published in the reform journal *Arena* and indicted capitalism for creating the social ills of the late nineteenth century, his depiction of all wage-earning women as part of a singular class of innocent but degraded humanity, their fate sealed by an environmental determinism not even the strongest will could conquer, still rubbed club members the wrong way. In their view, even self-proclaimed reformers like Fawcett were complicit in spreading harmful misconceptions.

The problem, as they saw it, was both social and literary. "All of us smart under the injustice done us by the writers of fiction," wrote Laura

Cate of Boston's Shawmut Club, avowing that she expected more of nonfictional writing that advertised its claims as truth. "If [Fawcett] can not study from life he can at least read our journals and learn a few facts and figures in regard to the anatomy of the genus homo which he wishes to draw." Cate's response to Fawcett extends the club movement's reformist methodology into the literary domain. Fawcett, she argued, had observed a lower model of working womanhood and mistaken her for a representation of all wage earners. The result was a colossal misjudgment of categories that was unfair to "fair specimens" like herself: "It occurs to one to inquire why an author who wishes to represent the working woman does not seek a fair specimen from some of our clubs . . . whose ranks are filled with types worth reproducing, types neither weak, wicked, 'low nor lawless.'"[59]

Cate's account of the problems endemic to reform writing amounts to a nascent form of literary criticism. Alongside their attack on Fawcett's disingenuous prose, Cate's two letters also take aim at the slum fiction of late-Victorian author Walter Besant. Indeed, she uses Besant's writing as a platform for analyzing literary realism much as Henry James had eight years earlier in "The Art of Fiction," which responded to a lecture Besant had delivered by the same name. Her allusion to "types" that are and are not "worth reproducing" effectively chides Besant for selling an antiquated sentimentalism under the modern rubric of realistic representation. In Cate's view, it was clear from reading Besant's stories about the working girls of east London and the benevolent paternalists who loved them that "the business woman of his decade did not pose for his figure."[60] She goes on to claim that the stakes of fiction are particularly high—and Besant's depictions particularly stinging—because readers of the 1890s had come to expect a degree of verisimilitude in their reading material. "In these days of realism the public likes faithful representation rather than high-sounding unrealities, for it is often to the novel and novelist that the nineteenth century reader turns for a solution of problems whether of art, literature, theology, or sociology."[61] Cate's remarks take aim at unrealistic fiction that goads the public into forming faulty impressions of the various "types" of working people, to the detriment of club members. Reform-minded writers like Besant claimed to model their narratives on real-world examples, yet working girls still struggled to see themselves depicted faithfully in prose—they were effectively barred from the domain of realistic representation. As we have seen, the club movement circled repeatedly around the problem of "facts and figures." In asking what it would take for an "elevated" working woman to become a fact, the club movement generated a theory of representation that slid between life and fiction and between club room, street, and page.

These letters suggest that club members did more than simply protest the unflattering depictions of wage-earning women that appeared in print. In fact, they rejected the idea that literary representation should hold greater power to shape public perceptions of working girls than the evidence such girls themselves mobilized in their own bodies, speech, work ethic, and behavior. The club participant I have cited here gives voice to the convictions of what Laura Wexler calls the "unintended reader"—that is, any reader who apprehends literary material clearly written with a more privileged audience in mind (bourgeois, detached, unaffected) but uses the occasion of her own unforeseen act of reading to generate "stunningly vibrant political insights into the nature of class distinctions."[62]

It is crucial to note, however, that no manner of vibrancy could make the club movement's political vision equitable or just. Instead, participants simultaneously refused social determinism as a norm governing working women's lives *and* asserted hard, exclusive boundaries in the name of a certain politics of respectability. This dual gesture—visible in club members' writing and in all dimensions of their communal work—signified a serious effort to clear a place for working girls outside the circle of the social problem. Against the view of writers like Campbell, Besant, and Fawcett, then, club members maintained that women capitulated by *choice* to capitalist and sexual vice, and not as a natural outcome of their labor in the public sphere. "Our breadwinners are, I contend, as chaste as our middle and leisure classes, if for no other reason than that they are busier and necessarily more self-denying," wrote club affiliate and future Department of Labor investigator Clare de Graffenried in 1893. "The vast majority choose want rather than dishonor."[63] A speaker at a movement convention conveyed a similar sentiment, along with a familiar impulse both to mandate new forms of exclusion and to reject constructions of wage-earning women as a problem population: "It is said that members if not in our rooms would spend their evenings in improper places in the city [and] that the Society is intended to rescue girls from such places. Let me say emphatically this is not so."[64] Yet another speaker confirmed, "There are many different classes of working girls; some spend their leisure hours on the street, nights; some by doing just nothing at all; but many are willing to and do improve their evenings at the working girls' clubs."[65]

Alliance with privileged women enabled wage-earning club members to construct the most invidious comparison of all between "different classes of working girls," who existed, in their view, in distinct moral universes. They stringently distinguished "virtuous" from "immoral" wage earners, "projecting fears of working women's immorality onto a corrupted subgroup" of "rough," "bad," and "unvirtuous" girls.[66] The need to shore up distinctions within the growing category of working womanhood is the constant subtext of the movement's reformist practices and public declarations. We see this same commitment to disaggregation in the movement's abiding racism and anti-immigrant sentiment—African American members were seconded into a few segregated societies and were never granted any power within the larger association—and in its long-simmering debate about domestic workers. With few exceptions, black women, household workers, and (to an only slightly lesser extent) immigrant women were not invited to undergo the club's rites of individuation.

This synecdochic thinking about the individual's relation to the public, in which any working girl might at any moment "be used as a representative of the whole," grounded the club movement in an individualist mode of reform based on vigilant self-policing. But the movement also policed the borders of modern womanhood. This faith in cross-class friendship migrates to *The House of Mirth,* and so too does this troubled vision of an American social ecology organized around the classification and ranking of women.[67]

I have dwelled on the working girls' club at such length not to simply pave the way for a critical comparison of club and novel but, rather, to open up space for thinking about comparison itself as a conceptual trope that powerfully shaped structures of social relation and classification, both in the realm of reform within which the organization played so ambivalent a role and within the contemporary imaginative literature that so often took reform as a theme or a metaphor. Comparative thinking emerged as a political sensibility that effectively linked together projects of individual self-improvement, social reform, and literary representation. To adopt Caroline Levine's terms, comparison was a *form* that gave order to patterns of sociopolitical experience and to literary texts, traveling freely across social and aesthetic materials.[68] Built upon particular expectations of commensurability and incommensurability, all acts of comparison are inevitably enmeshed in relations of power. Bruce Robbins observes that "comparison presupposes common norms; common norms, which by definition impose sameness on difference, presuppose a view from outside or above; the view from outside or above presupposes that the viewer is a holder of power."[69]

The terrain of comparison appears inexorably unequal when it comes to clubs for working girls. The expectation is always that the affluent club leader forms a kind of model and provides the "common norm," with the wage earner standing to profit from her example. The white working girl's potential future success—her transit from nondominance to relative dominance—depends on the assumption that her benefactor is already worthy of emulation, and it depends equally on the masses positioned below and outside her orbit. The imperialist politics of this scenario approaches the kind of tender violence—the conjoining of domesticity and brutality—that Wexler identifies as a signal ideology of the turn-of-the-century United States, a time and place marked by the "afterglow of sentimentalism." Wexler argues that "any meaningful enlargement . . . of the percentage of the population who can come 'inside' this magic circle still leaves behind the vast numbers who cannot qualify for entry under moral standards determined by arbiters who remain in power." Whatever small advantages it may have afforded club members, one can only conclude that the movement's politics of comparison "encourages a large-scale depersonalization of those outside its complex specifications at the same time as it elaborately personalizes, magnifies, and flatters those who can accommodate to its image of an interior."[70] These dynamics prompt Wharton to ask, What happens to elite women like Lily once they are no longer able to offer "common norms" for others to follow?

For all Wharton's evident conservatism, it is also true that she understood the dangerous exclusions and depersonalizations this model of comparison implied.[71] Wharton used comparison as a guiding trope and keyword in *The House of Mirth* in order to pose serious questions about similitude and difference, gender, class, identity, and belonging. The novel traces two plots of mobility—upward and downward—that conjoin at the nexus of comparison. These plots are related by means of chiasmus: Lily and Nettie meet at the working girls' club, at which point their social fates begin to diverge. The novel reveals the profit and the injury of comparatist thinking by playing the declining Lily against the striving club girl Nettie. Furthermore, it shadows both the lady and the girl with an "unflinching" and unreformed charwoman who cannot even enter the economies of mobility and friendship set forward in the club. Wharton's literary strategies—her exact descriptions, her incisive analysis, her precise calibration of formal detail and social implication, her abundant and ironic use of simile—convert the social structures she observed within turn-of-the-century U.S. culture into the formal, thematic, and interpersonal comparatism of her novel. Yet in arguing that *The House of Mirth* borrows this keyword from the working girls' club movement, I do not wish to claim that the author's sympathies lie with nondominant populations. In Wharton's novel it is *comparison itself* that becomes the social problem.

WHARTON'S ORGANIZED BENEFICENCE

Once we identify comparison not only as a predominant theme of the novel but also as the basis of the novel's loosely chiastic structure, new and unexpected readings of *The House of Mirth* arise. The specter of Lily's descent and Nettie's rise—the chiastic relation at the center of the novel—embeds a dynamic argument about class and determinism that spans the novel's intricate social hierarchy. Indeed, we find Wharton thinking critically—thinking politically—about social reform.

Perhaps the most obvious evidence that Wharton made questions of labor and social reform central to her fiction lies in her 1907 novel, *The Fruit of the Tree*. This follow-up to the best-selling *House of Mirth* is a social problem novel from start to finish, weaving together a tapestry of issues that include industrial reform, workplace safety, workers' compensation, euthanasia, marriage, and drug addiction. Wharton drew many of the novel's details about dangerous and unhygienic conditions within the modern textile industry from observations she gathered while taking a guided tour of the pulp and paper mills near her home in Lenox, Massachusetts. Yet even Wharton's so-called reform novel *The Fruit of the Tree* flinches in the face of radical reform and never endorses significant structural or political change.[72] In fact, many of the novel's ideas about reforming modern industry seem ripped from the pages of *Far and Near*. In the novel, John Amherst, assistant manager of the Hanaford textile mills, is a sympathetic boss who is committed to a platform of scientific management. His plans for ameliorating factory conditions include the intensification of personal goodwill between employers and employees (without unions) and the provision of ample opportunities for workers to engage in enlightened leisure. The eventual construction of a "pleasure-palace" of recreation and a series of model lodging houses for mill hands forms a major plot arc. Amherst's second wife Justine Brent has trained as a nurse, but her intimate connection to the local community of mill workers more accurately mimics the behavior of a settlement worker. By nature "a redresser, a restorer," she is familiar with local customs and maintains personal relationships with members of the community, all of which feed into her Progressive politics.[73] Justine identifies so intensely with the suffering of the mill hands that she actually threatens to lose herself in them. "I'm not philanthropic," she insists, somewhat disingenuously; "it's only that I'm so fatally interested in people that before I know it I've slipped into their skins. . . . If I could only remember that the other people were not myself!"[74] Philanthropy is the language in which Justine and John communicate their love for one another, and their shared interest in bringing reform to the New England textile mills mediates their courtship from start to finish.[75]

 Wharton put much of her own intellect and conviction into the character of Justine.[76] Yet she herself would not participate actively in reform work until World War I, when she directed a complex network of humanitarian organizations under the auspices of Mrs. Wharton's War Charities.

In 1914 Wharton founded the American Hostels for Refugees, which offered services to civilians rendered homeless by the war in France, and in 1915 she collaborated with the Red Cross to establish the Children of Flanders Rescue Committee in support of Belgian orphans and refugees. She also established sanitariums for refugees suffering from tuberculosis and ran sewing workrooms and lace-making classes for unemployed seamstresses in Paris. This highly successful venture in the Paris workrooms (*ouvroirs*) supported all manner of unemployed women who had lost their means of subsistence during the war—not only seamstresses but also secretaries and other professionals, which linked the focus of her wartime philanthropy to the female working-class context depicted in *The House of Mirth*.[77] But even as Wharton devoted herself tirelessly to war relief, earning a medal from the French Legion of Honor in the process, she insisted that she was not cut out for the labor of philanthropy. Her 1934 autobiography *A Backward Glance* confirms that she never stopped feeling "luke-warmness in regard to organized beneficence" but was nonetheless compelled to act by the harsh "necessities of the hour."[78]

It therefore comes as no surprise to learn that Wharton never volunteered at a working girls' society during her years in New York City, though she was aware of the movement by the time she began writing *The House of Mirth* in 1903. Her sister-in-law and close friend, Minnie Cadwalader Jones, active for decades in New York City reform circles, was her conduit to the world of the clubs. Jones contributed a chapter titled "Women's Opportunities in Town and Country" to a self-consciously modern women's conduct book compiled and published in 1894 by *Scribner's*; in it she positioned working girls' societies as a meaningful professional outlet for middle- and upper-class women (she described them as "societies for befriending working-girls").[79] Jones's interest lay with the wealthy sponsor: her chapter excerpts several paragraphs of Florence Lockwood's *Century* editorial (discussed above) that describe club work as a resource for affluent women, and she follows the rhetorical convention of associating "the worker" not with wage-earning women but with "the giver," a practice the *Club Worker* would later reinforce.[80] Tellingly, Jones also invokes comparison as a motivation and justification for cross-class club work. She notes that while men have numerous opportunities to learn from other people in the course of their daily lives—and to discover their strengths and weaknesses in relation to others—women often missed out on this valuable experience, "and it is much better that a woman should be able to compare herself with other women, than that she should have no standard of comparison at all." Jones would later apply her experience in the working girls' club movement when she volunteered at Wharton's sewing room project in Paris, an enterprise the sisters-in-law were proud to describe as "self-supporting."[81]

Whether or not Wharton's sister-in-law piqued her interest in working girls' clubs—Jones also volunteered for a time within the New York Association of Working Girls' Societies—the press provided enough coverage to substantiate her portrait of the movement in *The House of Mirth*.[82] But unlike *The Fruit of the Tree*, *The House of Mirth* does not wear its reform politics on its sleeve. The novel might more accurately be described as an exploration of one woman's subjectivity, a cautious excavation of interiority and consciousness. Focusing on "the contest between a defining interior life and a socially constructed self," as Jill M. Kress has so nicely put it, Wharton weaves Lily's thoughts, feelings, and perceptions into a broad meditation on the dynamics of philanthropy.[83] Issues at the heart of club reform—dependence and independence, self-realization and massification, generosity and obligation, morality and publicity, virtue and coarseness—animate the novel as a whole, implicating various characters and story lines as the novel proceeds. Indeed, we might say that the narrative explores the way people's changing affiliations both mirror and subvert the relations of reform, as the power dynamics governing any given situation shuttle characters between the positions of giver and receiver of aid.[84]

The question of what quality or mode of relation distinguishes the radiant Lily from the female masses grips the novel from its earliest pages, when Lawrence Selden, observing Lily as she waits for a train at Grand Central Station, explicitly compares her to the "shallow-faced girls in preposterous hats, and flat-chested women with paper bundles and palm leaf fans." From this initial, favorable comparison with the "average section of womanhood," the novel proceeds to track the changing degrees of differentiation between the lady and the crowd.[85] The working girls' club plays a crucial role in that process when it appears at a pivotal moment in the narrative.

Midway through the autumn of her twenty-ninth year, Lily Bart is enjoying a brief spell of confidence and ease after a period of financial uncertainty. She has recently received the first payments from Gus Trenor that she believes to have been returns on her lucrative investments but that are actually gifts from a man who expects—and will try to demand—sexual favors in return. Provisionally flush with money and humming with good will, Lily makes a series of visits to her friend Gerty Farish's working girls' club, where she donates a liberal fraction of the money Trenor has given her. This money makes it possible for the club's young office workers to repair to a rest home in the mountains for a salutary break from urban life and labor—the kind of vacation home that consumes many pages of *Far and Near*. Just as importantly, the money gives the office workers a role model in the beautiful Lily Bart. Although Lily comes to realize that her dealings with Trenor have "put her in his power,"[86] and although she will ultimately sacrifice her social and financial security in order to repay him and regain her sense of moral probity, her gift saves the life of a tubercular typist named Nettie Crane (later Nettie Struther), a woman whose own character has been compromised by premarital sex with a scoundrel who abandons her. As Lily's social status declines, Nettie's rises. The latter recovers, marries a kindly fellow worker and gives birth to a child, and fills the last hours of Lily's life with a personal warmth and domestic comfort she has never known. It is worth unpacking the stunning symmetry at work here, for Lily's tragic descent not only complements but in fact *produces* Nettie's upward mobility.[87]

Of course, Lily is hardly a saint: her charitable contribution is a self-serving gesture inspired by her brief "mood of self-approval." The donation leaves her more interested "in herself as a person of charitable instincts" than in the social problems that surround her in New York City. While "the other-regarding sentiments had not been cultivated in Lily," so that she is typically "bored" by Gerty's philanthropic endeavors, Lily's "quick dramatizing fancy seized on the contrast between her own situation and that represented by some of Gerty's 'cases.'" Merely "[picturing] herself leading a life such as theirs" makes her "shudder sympathetically," and she feels that by handing over Trenor's money she has "justified all previous extravagances, and excused any in which she might subsequently indulge." The entire exchange leaves Lily with "a sense of self-esteem which she naturally mistook for the fruits of altruism."[88]

Wharton comprehends the psychological advantages that come from sponsoring a working girls' club, and she presents us here with an archetypal scene of invidious comparison. The novel's careful calibration of the comparative dynamic driving Lily's decision to fleetingly embrace club reform reveals this choice to be essentially aesthetic or narcissistic rather than ethical or political. Lily is not gripped by the genuine struggles wage earners face; instead, her "dramatizing fancy" seizes upon a "contrast," and once she "pictures" herself actually living a life so dreary, she spontaneously hands over a donation. The perceived distance between the working girls' condition and her own brings more pleasure than outrage, for Lily's generosity is motivated by the linked demands of her imagination—her need to "picture herself"—and the ongoing project of invidious self-construction—selfhood premised on hierarchy—that proves essential to her survival.

Beyond its small role in the plot, the working girls' club also offers a useful paradigm for Wharton as she unfolds a nuanced argument about the problem of comparison. In *The House of Mirth,* comparatism is an aesthetic and a mode of authorial observation. It is also, most damagingly, the lens through which Lily is trained to perceive the social world and recognize herself as any self at all. Wharton's comparisons—formal, thematic, and social—make relations of similitude or difference a medium for confronting the gendered social codes of her time. As though testing out the reformist hypotheses of the working girls' club, *The House of Mirth* shows that comparison works only unevenly as a mode of resolving social problems.

I argued in the first part of this chapter that comparison became an important keyword of U.S. culture around the turn of the century, traveling between domains of fiction and sociopolitical life. Comparison is fundamental to Wharton's composition and to Lily's reflexive encounters with the world, sharpening the way both author and protagonist plot the vagaries of social circumstance. Critics such as Amy Kaplan, Mark McGurl, Lori Merish, and Carol Singley have remarked on Lily's public-oriented subjectivity, and as Singley notes, the novel is constructed "as a series of set pieces in which Lily carefully presents constructed images of herself."[89] Wharton condenses some of the novel's greatest themes into a catalog of backgrounds and contrasts that affirm identity. Only a few examples should suffice to show the multiple uses to which contrast is put in *The House of Mirth*. Lily's comment to Lawrence Selden that "the clothes are the background, the frame, if you like; they don't make the success, but they are a part of it" abbreviates a broader argument about the commodification of women, while the "exhilaration of displaying her own beauty under a new aspect" at the *tableaux vivants* links Lily's dramatic and gender performances. The right background can sharpen the performative effect of Lily's emotions—she "could be keenly sensitive to a scene which was the fitting background of her own sensations"—and enrich the tones of beauty, as when "Selden noted the fine shades of manner by which [Lily] harmonized herself with her surroundings." The force of contrast intensifies nature's loveliness and deepens the comfort of her repose. Even memories gain shape in Lily's mind by means of their "ironic contrast to her present situation."[90]

Because Lily's great talent is to "[adapt] herself to others without suffering her own outline to be blurred," she negotiates personal relationships so that the general bearing of her acquaintances strategically contrasts with and flatters her own.[91] Lily's relationships are practical in the sense that they facilitate her social access and enable her to travel seasonally and in the sense that proximity to a variety of different people—especially women—illuminates her own carriage and character in ways that are useful to her. But imagining another person as a living backdrop can only serve her purposes if that comparison points to a discrepancy in value in which she retains the superior position. For instance, she "was fully aware of the extent to which Mrs. Fisher's volubility was enhancing her repose," and her "dingy" but loyal friend Gerty "seemed to throw her own exceptionalness into becoming relief, and give a soaring vastness to her scheme of life." Lily's friends have always made her look beautiful and elegant, as though she is ideally suited to the atmosphere in which she dwells.[92] Her need to stand out in comparison to her friends and associates will eventually bring her sorrow.

While Lily's peripatetic lifestyle exemplifies U.S. leisure-class norms of the time, it also serves the purposes of a selfhood premised on comparison: new backgrounds, both physical and human, make identity visible again and again by pointing to what Wharton calls her "outline." Her "faculty for renewing herself in new scenes, and casting off problems of conduct as easily as the surroundings in which they had arisen" does not prevent Lily from dreaming of a permanent home "in which every tint and line should combine to enhance her beauty and give distinction to her leisure."[93] When the narrative periodically gives way to Selden's perspective, his observations are attuned to the way comparison functions to affirm Lily's superior beauty. In Monte Carlo, he is struck by "the way in which she detached herself, by a hundred undefinable shades, from the persons who most abounded in her own style. It was in just such company, the fine flower and complete expression of the state she aspired to, that the differences came out with special poignancy, her grace cheapening the other women's smartness as her finely-discriminated silences made their chatter dull."[94] Lily works hard to achieve visual grace through distinction, and Wharton points out, through Selden, her success in this venture until the final year of her life.

Contrast, then, is an indispensable method of self-making for Lily, and the habit of comparing herself favorably to her companions and surroundings provides a constant check on her place in the social marketplace. Yet she ultimately falls in the social ranks, felled by conflict with cruel gatekeeper Bertha Dorset, her repeated failure on the marriage market, and her refusal to pay back, in sexual favors, the money from Gus Trenor that she had invested in the club for working girls. Lily's downward mobility forces her to live and work in a milieu governed by indiscriminate, "promiscuous" social relations, a milieu that scrubs away at an outline reliant on invidious comparison. Lily is most perturbed by the utter lack of recognizable rules and structure beyond the threshold of the upper-class world to which she is accustomed, an absence she can only interpret—and that Wharton consistently refers to—as a "void."

But how does one compare oneself to a void? If social survival is based on contingencies of comparison, then finding herself in a milieu that lacks any structure threatens to unseat Lily's sense of self altogether.

Lily begins to lose her outline the minute she turns to the "social outskirt" of the Sam Gormers, where she has "the odd sense of having been caught up into the crowd as carelessly as a passenger is gathered in by an express train."[95] This decisively modern language of masses, mass transit, and mobility reworks the terms of Selden's initial glimpse of Lily at the beginning of the novel, a moment when her status is still assured and she conspicuously "stood apart from the crowd" at Grand Central Station.[96] Mattie Gormer's friendship affords Lily the superficial patina of luxury, but Mattie also has an "undiscriminating good-nature" and can offer only "slap-dash sociability." Her social stratum does not allow Lily to "mark a sense of differences and distinctions, [which] was hard enough to the lingering pride in [her]."[97] Finding no structured settings for identity and encountering a social rule book that suddenly forbids her to mark any "differences and distinctions"—activities that are among Lily's greatest talents—she begins to fade into the "moral lassitude" of indifference. She eventually finds herself "[swinging] unsphered in a void of social non-existence."[98]

In Norma Hatch, on the other hand, Lily finds a woman whose habits are marked by "an Oriental indolence and disorder" and whose sphere fails even more dismally as accentuating background. Life at the Emporium Hotel is not so much a stage on which Lily may prop herself as the dim and obscure world "behind the social tapestry, on the side where the threads were knotted and the loose ends hung." There, neither individuals nor environment constitute usable backgrounds because time and space themselves recede into an abstract, undifferentiated haze and people "seemed to float together [in] a blur of confused and retarded engagements." Wharton describes this social milieu using the vocabulary of slippery inertia; its interiors are dim, languid, pallid, and vague, its occupants somehow insubstantial and impermanent. Norma has hired Lily to turn her own "faint symptoms of developing an outline" into a full-fledged social personality. But because the questionable conditions of Norma's life have become Lily's own, this engagement lacks the hierarchical structure and ego affirmation that make philanthropic work pleasurable. In the novel's shifting dynamics of philanthropy, Lily has come to embody the contrary pole of an appraisal that props up Norma;

she descends to the position of beneficiary. Being of service in this way turns Lily into a backdrop, a supporting character for whom it is impossible to "[show] herself to advantage."[99]

Wharton renders Lily's downward mobility as a narrative of massification—of becoming part of the mass, first slowly and then all at once—unfolding her deindividuation by degrees. Part of what makes the book's denouement so tragic is Lily's keen awareness that she has become one of "thousands and thousands of women" struggling to earn a living. In the final stage of Lily's devolution, we see most clearly that a woman who has been socialized as a member of the leisure class can have no outline among the masses. Once Lily has resorted to living in a boardinghouse and working as a milliner, and an inept one at that, she feels utterly ungrounded, like "something rootless and ephemeral, mere spin-drift of the whirling surface of existence, without anything to which the poor little tentacles of self could cling before the awful flood submerged them." The social leveling of Lily Bart melts away all the distinctions that would otherwise buttress a self—even the lingering scent of boardinghouse meals diffuses the crucial boundary between bedroom and kitchen. Her social world at this juncture is so unstructured, so bereft of form and distinction, that acts of comparison are simply impossible for her.[100]

The scale of Lily's decline is measured quite explicitly in symmetrical terms. At the factory, she sits as one of several laborers in a line, all working to create hats that will serve as "ever-varied settings for the face of fortunate womanhood."[101] Her own outline faded, she now takes up the labor of buffing the physical and social lineaments of former friends. It is fitting that club sponsor Gerty is the one to recommend this line of work as a potential solution to Lily's troubles. Trimming hats is resolutely manual yet residually genteel labor, work that avoids machine automation and pays its employees well enough to land them in the upper tier of the female working classes. Long gone is the once gratifying "contrast between her own situation and that represented by some of Gerty's 'cases'" by the time Gerty's philanthropic regard inspires her to take Lily on as a "case."

Yet still, the difference between visiting wage earners as a beneficent upper-class lady and actually *becoming* one of the masses of workers is more profoundly a matter of consciousness than one of material deprivation.

Lily's losses register most forcefully in psychological terms.[102] For not only does Wharton narrate her protagonist's downward mobility in a rigorously comparative vernacular, but the novel also encourages us to judge the scale and impact of this material decline in terms of its capacity to unseat an identity that is deeply rooted in positive contingencies of comparison. In other words, part of what Lily loses when she is forced to take on the "point of view" of the working classes is the opportunity to profit from acts of invidious distinction. Among coworkers who are "awed only by success" and perceive her as "a star fallen from that sky," lacking any means to distinguish herself from the "insignificant," she can no longer cling to any pretense of superiority nor, therefore, of any value. Even when Lily feebly insists that she wants her coworkers to treat her as an equal, the fugitive hope that she might "before long . . . show herself their superior" invades her consciousness. How else could she imagine herself building a life among the milliners?[103]

Throughout the latter part of the novel, Wharton emphasizes that Lily suffers most keenly of all from this irrevocable loss of "her old standpoint." The author's careful calibration of the different modes of relation Lily may maintain with the working classes underscores the disparity between altruistic regard and kinship premised on equilibrium: "In the days — how distant they now seemed! — when she had visited the Girls' Club with Gerty Farish, she had felt an enlightened interest in the working-classes; but that was because she looked down on them from above, from the happy altitude of her grace and her beneficence. Now that she was on a level with them, the point of view was less interesting."[104] Lily articulates her self-perception and class-consciousness in terms of spatial dynamics. In her world, individuation — selfhood itself — requires the structured hierarchy that her practices of social and aesthetic comparison have always confirmed.

Alongside this narrative of Lily's massification is a parallel story of working-class individuation in which the working girls' society again plays a pivotal role. When Lily pays her first visit to the club, she recognizes an essential humanity within the still-inchoate forms of the poor, whom she sees as "bundles of feeling . . . clothed in shapes not so unlike her own." Out of this mass of "bundles" and "shapes" that she can only discern by recourse to her own more determinate form—a mass that, as I have been arguing, serves to give her form its outline—Lily comes to know Nettie Struther. At first, their connection perfectly embodies the philanthropic ideal. Nettie holds her idol in the highest regard; she thinks of Lily as "being so high up, where everything was just grand," delights in reading about her exploits in the newspaper, and uses her as a guide for her own self-improvement. After recovering from the disease that sent her to a sanatorium and then starting a family, Nettie hopes that somehow Lily will have occasion to meet her once again and appreciate her formidable progress. It is not a stretch to say that both women understand their relationship through the lens provided by the working girls' club movement. They explicitly connect their friendship to the prospect of broader social amelioration, individually remarking that the high esteem in which they hold one another helps rectify the fact that "things were so queerly fixed in the world."[105]

Wharton uses this cross-class relationship to make Nettie's outline more distinct both as a minor character within the novel and as a turn-of-the-century social "type" her audience would recognize: the club girl type. When the novel describes Nettie's kitchen as "extraordinarily small and almost miraculously clean" and the young typist brags about having managed to carve a parlor out of her working-class apartment, it constructs her as a prototypical club girl—sprung, in all her gentility and striving, straight from the correspondence section of *Far and Near*.[106] As readers, we see Nettie break off from the amorphous mass of working girls just as her former benefactor watches the "vast gulf" that once separated her from that mass disappear.

Lily's and Nettie's fortunes have reversed by the time they meet again, when the working girl finds Lily sitting alone "on an empty bench in the glare of an electric street-lamp," vulnerable and in need of rescue.[107] Now it is Lily who is "in great trouble," and Nettie the one to offer emotional and material support to her weary mentor. And it is in Nettie's warm tenement kitchen that the novel's threads regarding individuation, massification, and the dynamics of reform finally come together, offering some resolution to a novel whose ending critics generally find disappointing. Confronting Nettie as a flourishing young wife exposes Lily to "the results of her spasmodic benevolence, and the surprised sense of human fellowship took the mortal chill from her heart." The language of "spasmodic benevolence" echoes Wharton's earlier account of Lily's impulsive philanthropy; it reminds us that Nettie's act of goodwill mirrors Lily's past generosity. This circularity helps correct the impression that Lily's beneficence had been exclusively a vanity project: though her support for wage earners was initially motivated by self-regard and effectively stripped her of her income, her benevolence has nevertheless had the positive result of renovating Nettie, enabling her to build a life that offers Lily the first "vision of the solidarity of life" she has ever seen.[108]

But where does this "solidarity" come from? What is it good for? And why can't it rescue Lily too? After swallowing too many drops of chloral, Lily spends the last moments of her life fantasizing that she cradles Nettie's daughter in her arms. The working-class baby is an apt symbol for the "solidarity of life" the protagonist longs for, a living culmination of the gift economy that commenced when she first donated money to Nettie's club.[109] Yet Wharton makes it clear that there are important consequences to having forged this solidarity within a site of cross-class reform, not all of which are salutary. Lily dies because she cannot survive outside of the very economy of social comparison that permits Nettie to flourish.

POOR LITTLE WORKING GIRL

Wharton's rendering of the tender friendship between Lily and Nettie parallels public understanding of the working girls' club movement in the years after *The House of Mirth* was published. We see, for example, the same extravagant indebtedness that Nettie feels for Lily in a 1910 editorial about Grace Dodge published in the *World Today*. In "What Grace Dodge Has Done for the Working Girl," Edwin Wildman triangulates benefactor, beneficiary, and selfhood as he quotes an anonymous breadwinner who attributes her own "solidarity of life" to her club leader's example. Compare Wildman's club girl to Wharton's:

> The woman looked around the pretty comfortable room in which we sat, then at her little daughter standing at her knee. Then she raised her eyes,

"She made me," she said simply. This is not an unusual answer for one of Miss Dodge's "girls." Asked to define the help that has been extended to them they grow puzzled. Finally they sum it up in that one sentence: "She made me; everything that I am is due to her."[110]

This article's nameless working girl—quite possibly a fictional construction of the author and resembling Nettie to an uncanny degree—becomes an individuated self through her relationship with a club sponsor ("she made me"). Here as in *The House of Mirth*, "solidarity of life" means achieving the kind of domestic comfort that manages to integrate background with self, a process set in motion at the working girls' club but culminating in dress, home, and family.

Wildman may very well have read *The House of Mirth*, which was still a best seller in 1910. But whether or not there is any causal link between the two texts, this editorial shows that the trope of comparison functions in a remarkably coherent way as it travels across discursive spheres of fiction, the periodical press, and sites of reform. The same comparatism that provided a reformist methodology for the club movement serves as shorthand for practices of self-making in contemporary literary representations. In these examples, the process by which a working girl raises herself up by emulating a Grace Dodge or a Lily Bart enables her to construct a self that can ultimately thrive independently of human or spatial settings for identity. The achievement of an improved, individuated self—what the anonymous club member calls "everything that I am" or the novel names Nettie's "solidarity of life"—mitigates the ongoing need for a benefactor.

Nettie is not the only wage-earning female character in the novel. Others include a fellow milliner at Mme. Regina's named Miss Kilroy, the forewoman Miss Haines, and unnamed parlor maids and boardinghouse attendants. But aside from Nettie, Wharton devotes sustained attention only to Mrs. Haffen, a charwoman who is kept at a conspicuously far remove from the cross-class social economy that unites Nettie and Lily. Wharton uses Mrs. Haffen's status as a domestic worker with privileged access to the wastebaskets of the upper classes as a convenient device for driving the story forward. Amy Kaplan argues that the love letters Mrs. Haffen sells to Lily, which she finds in Selden's room at the Benedick and wrongly believes Lily to have written, "become a central medium for exchange throughout the novel." Importantly, the letters hold out the promise of "an alternative narrative to the plot of decline which Lily follows," since she always has the option to sell them and live off their dividends or to use them to threaten Bertha in exchange for reinstating her place within elite society.[111] Yet I would argue that Mrs. Haffen is equally important in her structural capacity as a foil to the "poor little working girl" Nettie Struther. The charwoman embodies all the corruption and vulnerability that the club girl evades as she charts her upward course; she is positioned at the farthest reach outside of the "magic circle" of womanhood delineated by club reform.

Whereas Nettie is remarkably pliable and imitative, Mrs. Haffen is most notable for her obstinacy. When Lily first brushes by Mrs. Haffen while descending the stairs of Selden's apartment building, she is taken aback by the woman's unsolicitous manner. Potentially serious hazards lie in the way of a single girl spotted leaving a bachelor's apartment on her own, and those hazards are not significantly diminished by the fact that Lily classes her observer as only marginally higher than nobody at all. It is no surprise that the status-conscious Lily takes little heed of a domestic worker scrubbing the staircase of an apartment building, but it is worth noting that even Wharton's syntax draws our attention to Mrs. Haffen first as "no one" and after that as a "creature": "There was no one in sight, however, but a char-woman who was scrubbing the stairs.... What did the creature suppose?"[112] Wharton's language primes us to read the precarious woman as spatially and socially outside, below, and apart, even as she plants herself directly in Lily's way.

Wharton takes pains to describe the charwoman's appearance and behavior in order to contrast it unfavorably with Lily's, as per usual, but she also focuses on her because she violates so many of the rules of etiquette typically demanded of a woman in her station. Mrs. Haffen is red-fisted and crimson-elbowed from toil, her hair thinning and colorless, her complexion sallow and pockmarked; her clothing and bonnet are "battered." While this visual depiction is certainly meant to reflect Mrs. Haffen's lifetime of manual labor, it also constructs her as slovenly, careless, and utterly—even aggressively—ungendered: she is not the kind of woman to have modeled herself on a leisure-class lady. Most telling in these descriptions is Wharton's attention to the domestic servant's unsettling gaze. Instead of politely looking away to give Lily some semblance of privacy as she leaves Selden's flat, the charwoman "looked up curiously" and "continued to stare," her "persistent gaze" lingering in Lily's memory after their encounter has ended. Nor does Mrs. Haffen remove herself from the lady's path to ease her passage, forcing Lily to press against the wall as she slips uncomfortably down the stairs. When Lily chances on Mrs. Haffen at work in Mrs. Peniston's home weeks later, Wharton redoubles her emphasis on the woman's willfulness and invasive stare. Again poised on "crimson elbows," the charwoman looks at Lily with "the same unflinching curiosity, the same apparent reluctance to let her pass," and "without a word of excuse, she pushe[s] back her pail and drag[s] a wet floor-cloth across the landing, keeping her eyes fixed on Lily while the latter swept by." Blocking, pushing, and dragging, Mrs. Haffen wields the tools of her labor as weapons against propriety.[113]

It is not a stretch to say that Wharton has constructed the domestic worker as the genteel working girl's nightmarish double. More than this, the novel urges us to compare them—and then to question the grounds of our comparison. Whereas Nettie reads avidly and speaks in her best approximation of educated speech, Mrs. Haffen is the only character to communicate in a working-class dialect; whereas the novel's club girls tell Gerty that "it was as good as a day in the country just to look at [Lily]" and Nettie eagerly makes of her an idol, there is no respect or admiration behind Mrs. Haffen's steely gaze.[114] The charwoman's cross-class evaluations yield something more perverse—but ultimately more pragmatic—than the desire to improve herself. Comparing her own financial situation to Lily's—her husband is unemployed, and she cannot make ends meet by her labor alone—merely underscores the bleak necessity of selling wealthy people's secrets. Mrs. Haffen understands the social codes that govern her world and recognizes that there is more to gain in blackmailing Lily than there is in seeking to befriend her. Given that "the poor has got to live as well as the rich," as Mrs. Haffen calmly observes, existing circuits of rumor and gossip about Lily's assumed indiscretions must be transformed into capital. She negotiates the price of the stolen letters with "unabashed" confidence.

Mrs. Haffen's strenuous efforts to protect her own imperiled family actually hasten Lily's downfall. After all, Lily must spend a significant portion of her scarce income just to purchase and confiscate Selden's letters. Yet I also wish to point to a degree of moral ambiguity in Wharton's doubled portrayal of the charwoman. Consider the matter of sickness and recovery: both Nellie and Mrs. Haffen endure illnesses that threaten their financial standing. But while the novel romanticizes Nettie's survival instincts, nobody sent Mrs. Haffen to a sanatorium in the mountains free of charge. Instead, she had to pay out of pocket for "an operation that ate up all [they'd] put by," leaving her no choice but to resolve her financial quandary through blackmail.[115] The domestic servant's miserable behavior reflects the fact that no benefactor has ever looked upon her as a worthy beneficiary or potential friend.

The figure of Mrs. Haffen enables Wharton to touch upon a secondary reform sphere dedicated to regulating domestic service. The "servant question" was a period term for the challenges middle- and upper-class Americans professed to face in attracting and retaining household staff in an increasingly industrialized economy. It was also a catchall term for the social problems that imperious reformers claimed ran rampant in the service class. Progressive reformers interested in the so-called servant question championed day work, rather than live-in work, as a "modern" labor development that secured some measure of independence and the prospect of a family life for household workers. Yet despite sporadic inclusionary efforts from club leaders, who were less sensitive to finely grained class distinctions within the laboring classes than wage-earning members were, not even the most "modern" domestic workers were truly welcome at working girls' clubs. Women penned endless articles in *Far and Near* on the various problems associated with domestic service, generally making the point that they would prefer not to "combine" with servants at all. It was also hard for most club leaders to imagine new friendships blossoming across the hard boundary that divided mistress from servant. As there were few opportunities for upward mobility within the sphere of household labor, the occupation was ill matched with the larger goals of the working girls' club movement.[116]

Nosy, immoral, and dishonest, a thief, and bearing no interest in uplift and scant respect for her employers, Mrs. Haffen embodies all the negative traits that club members invoked to justify their exclusions: she is the problem servant of Progressive reform in every respect.[117] In constructing her as Nettie's antithesis, Wharton again borrows from the comparatist vocabulary of the working girls' club movement. Just as the women who were barred from the ranks of the club—the "rough" and "unvirtuous" ones, the ones who used slang or had accents, African Americans, domestic workers—ultimately defined the contours of that movement, Mrs. Haffen proves integral to the social taxonomy of *The House of Mirth* by illuminating the novel's profoundly uncommon ground.

Even if Wharton draws heavily on the language and ethos of the working girls' club, then, she also points to irrevocable flaws in the movement's comparatist worldview. For with Wharton's portrait of Mrs. Haffen in mind, Lily's epiphany about working girls being human beings—her realization that "some of these bundles of feeling were clothed in shapes not so unlike her own"—is suddenly more striking for its exclusivity than for its beneficence.[118] Both Lily and the club movement whose dictates she espouses are careful to articulate that only *some* members of the mass ever develop an outline. One of the things the novel asks us to think about, then, is the fate of those shapes that are in fact *unlike* Lily's own. Mrs. Haffen exemplifies the type of laborer Laura Cate and her cohort collectively disavowed: a woman who is debauched not because she performs wage work in the modern city—Nettie and Miss Kilroy do that too—but because she knowingly makes bad decisions.

The question of likeness and comparability also crops up as a key formal strategy within the narrative. As Wharton traces Lily's trajectory from a relation of dissimilarity to potential similitude with the lower classes, removing the invidious distinction that is so essential to her character's self-imagining, she explores that comparative thematic at the level of the sentence. *The House of Mirth* is rife with similes that compare two apparently unequal quantities but assert, as similes do, a fundamental relationship or likeness between those objects or conditions. Wharton's similes often describe seemingly humorous or superficial situations: "Mr. Gryce was like a merchant whose warehouses are crammed with an unmarketable commodity," Wharton writes of Lily's almost-suitor, while "[to] attempt to bring [Mrs. Peniston] into active relation with life was like tugging at a piece of furniture which has been screwed to the floor." These witty, epigrammatic phrases lend the novel a densely ironic narrative fabric.[119]

Wharton's fondness for this figure of speech—it occurs again and again in *The House of Mirth*—suggests a fundamental linkage between linguistic simile and the novel's meditation on similitude and disparity. At times, these similes compare two conditions that seem so incommensurable that one wonders whether there is any ground for the comparison at all. For example, on the subject of Lily's aunt, Mrs. Peniston: "The idea that any scandal could attach to a young girl's name, above all that it could be lightly coupled with that of a married man, was so new to her that she was as much aghast as if she had been accused of leaving her carpets down all summer, or of violating any of the other cardinal laws of housekeeping."[120] Just as Lily's residence in the Emporium Hotel or the boardinghouse produces comparisons that ought not be made—what kinds of settings are these for a figure like Lily Bart?—these similes push readers to question whether such disparate situations belong in the same sentence. Is Lily's potential ruin truly commensurate with a convention of housekeeping? If not, is there a greater inequality to which this asymmetrical comparison implicitly points? Throughout the novel, Wharton places Lily in many different settings in order to reveal the inadequacy of various backdrops to the ongoing needs of her selfhood and to point to a self-annihilating mismatch between character and conditions. This concern extends to a meditation on language and its ability to contain and express contradiction.

Wharton's similes frequently make much more serious comparisons, and in these cases the content of the evaluation combined with the broader questioning that the simile form always provokes—how and why are these things related?—inscribes the novel's investigation of comparison into the form of the narrative. Early on in the novel, the narrator claims that in her restless movement, "all [Lily] wanted was the taste of new experiences: she seemed like some cruel creature experimenting in a laboratory."

Wharton summarizes the position of Lily's upper-class milieu through simile as well: "The dreary limbo of dinginess lay all around and beneath that little illuminated circle in which life reached its finest efflorescence, as the mud and sleet of a winter night enclose a hot-house filled with tropical flowers." Moreover, of Lily's capacity to survive in a harsh social universe, Wharton writes that "inherited tendencies had combined with early training to make her the highly specialized product she was: an organism as helpless out of its narrow range as the sea-anemone torn from the rock"; of her ability to love and receive love in return, "the fact that [Selden's love] struck deeper, that it was inextricably wound up with inherited habits of thought and feeling, made it as impossible to restore to growth as a deep-rooted plant torn from its bed." Wharton's weightiest comparisons employ metaphors drawn from biology, natural science, and evolution—social privilege as a hothouse, a refined woman as an unmoored sea anemone—linking the problem of Lily's "torn" selfhood to naturalist imagery and argumentation.[121]

COMPARISON'S SOCIAL PROBLEMS

Critics typically categorize turn-of-the-century novels that employ this kind of scientific and deterministic language as works of naturalistic fiction. Late nineteenth- and early twentieth-century naturalist thinking in both its European and American forms revolved around the idea "that people were not free, that their destinies were controlled not by themselves but by their environment."[122] From Wharton's use of simile to her suggestion that Lily's dependence on invidious comparison ultimately leaves her ill equipped for existence outside the leisure class, *The House of Mirth* fits the paradigm of naturalism in many ways. (Wharton's other narratives of dwindling fortune, including the novella *Bunner Sisters* [written 1892, published 1916] and the short stories "A Cup of Cold Water" [1899], "The Pelican" [1899], and "The Rembrandt" [1900] use the naturalistic mode to varying degrees.)

Within the body of scholarship that examines *The House of Mirth*'s naturalism, it has become something of a commonplace to assert that Lily's inherited traits and early training made it impossible for her to survive in any environment other than the luxurious one to which she is accustomed. Naming Jean-Baptiste Lamarck, Charles Darwin, and Herbert Spencer as influences on Wharton's naturalism, critics have found in her novel abundant evidence that Lily falls victim to social, biological, and environmental conditioning.[123] Without retreading ground that has been covered elsewhere, I will simply note that Wharton sets the tone for viewing Lily in this light from the novel's earliest pages, when Selden scrutinizes the protagonist and decides that she "was so evidently the victim of the civilization which had produced her, that the links of her bracelet seemed like manacles chaining her to her fate."[124] The language of determinism—civilization and its victims, bracelets as shackles, inescapable fate—structures this early glimpse of Lily just as it rounds out the conclusion: as Richard A. Kaye has explained, Wharton revised certain sentences toward the end of the novel to emphasize that tragically stalled timing, rather than Selden's rotten character, was responsible for Lily's decline.[125]

I want to argue that the contemporary working girl problem serves as another key frame of reference for Wharton's literary naturalism here. Yet this reference can be hard to see, for the author extracts a narrative of social determinism typically imposed on working-class women and, in a curious transposition, applies it to her declining leisure-class heroine. In making the point that Lily ends up the way she does because of where she comes from, Wharton draws on contemporary debates about working women's morality and inevitable victimization—the essential unfreedom at the heart of their seeming liberty in life and work. Elizabeth Ammons remarks that "typical women in [Wharton's] view—no matter how privileged, nonconformist, or assertive (indeed, often in proportion to the degree in which they embodied those qualities)—were not free to control their own lives, and that conviction became the foundation of her argument with American optimism for more than twenty years."[126] What Wharton found in the reformist discourse of the working girl problem was a new source of knowledge, a new and supple language, for understanding the social parameters of women's freedom and constraint. As we have seen, the assumption that urban working-class spaces damaged their inhabitants made turn-of-the-century conversations about working women profoundly deterministic. This was the exact terrain into which club members inserted themselves when they argued that women were in fact free to determine their own fate, whether upward or downward. They insisted that comparative thinking was a force stronger than environment, a force capable of removing wage earners from the category of the social problem altogether.

Wharton shows that this is precisely how it works for Nettie Struther: she manages to flourish despite living a life that threatens to consign her to failure. "[Lily] had known Nettie Crane as one of the discouraged victims of over-work and anaemic parentage: one of the superfluous fragments of life destined to be swept prematurely into that social refuse-heap of which Lily had so lately expressed her dread," Wharton writes, using the language of the victimized working girl to frame her characters' unexpected reversal. "But Nettie Struther's frail envelope was now alive with hope and energy: whatever fate the future reserved for her, she would not be cast into the refuse-heap without a struggle."[127] Finding a husband certainly helped Nettie escape the "social refuse-heap," but it is also true that having forged a comparative habit of mind abets the typist's upward mobility in a manner that proves impossible for her mentor. Here, then, Wharton identifies both the success and the failure of comparison as a social practice. For all its commitment to working women's upward mobility, the working girls' club movement imagined only stasis for the wealthy. It always assumed—indeed required—that the class status of affluent leaders would remain stable, and comparative thinking offered no guidance for sponsors when that status did not hold. But it turns out that Lily lives in a world that is considerably more unstable, more painfully marked by social contingency at the upper as well as lower end of the economic spectrum, than the one she has been trained for.[128] The working girls' club movement prompts us to think about Lily's decline, then, as a form of entrapment caused not only by material or environmental forces—naturalism's usual story—but also by the aesthetic and psychic orientation through which she understands such forces to function. As Stephanie Foote notes, Lily simply "cannot imagine being a real person outside of the class culture that has rejected her."[129]

While Wharton borrows from the working girls' club movement in a number of important ways, then, she does not unthinkingly endorse its mode of social categorization. She also shows that there is horror in what is left behind. In triangulating the linked fates of Lily, Nettie, and Mrs. Haffen, Wharton shifts from modeling her novel on contemporary reform culture to exposing the cracks and fissures within that culture, particularly the mismatch between a comparatist worldview and the actual social world. Noting how comparison works in *The House of Mirth*, and where it fails, should help us see Wharton as political in a new way. Her critique of comparison is not as radical as we might wish it to be from a twenty-first-century perspective—but then again, neither was Progressive reform itself. The club movement's eagerness to prove that not all women who worked for wages occupied the same base rung of the social ladder was ultimately regressive, serving to divide and punish more than unite women across the race and class continuum. Literary and historical narratives of the Progressive Era often overlook the movement in part because its conservative goals fit uneasily with the politics of coalition that developed in these years. With these defects in tow, however, the movement's discourse of determinism and comparison provided an important language for writing about women, class, friendship, and social mobility across genres. More than in formal politics proper, the significance of the working girls' club movement resides in its creation of a keyword that operates politically as it moves between site, street, and text. In this way, both *The House of Mirth* and the club movement emerge as reformist entities, slightly out of step with the dominant reform politics of their day and yet nonetheless reaching out, in the oblique and repeated expression that seals Lily's letters, to something "Beyond!"[130] My next chapter takes questions of reform, uplift, and the stakes of social mobility further into the twentieth century, asking how the African American college emerged as a site for debate over racial and literary politics in the Progressive Era.

3

Correlation and Conformity

FROM THE AFRICAN AMERICAN COLLEGE TO THE HARLEM RENAISSANCE

Booker T. Washington had a cache of anecdotes that he was ready to deploy at any minute to illustrate his ideas about African American life in the rural South, and he told those stories again and again in his career as educator, writer, and race leader. One of his most famous anecdotes is the maritime allegory that animated his speech at the Atlanta Exposition in 1895. At the height of this so-called Atlanta Compromise address, Washington describes a vessel of thirsty men lost at sea who learn to cease looking far afield for a source of water and finally "cast down [their] buckets where [they] are"—that is, they decide to drink up opportunities for education and employment in the rural South without challenging the social and legal restrictions of Jim Crow.[1] Washington's anecdotes encouraging black southerners to entrench themselves in the local, to find sustenance within the impossible constraints of existing socioeconomic conditions, are well known; he devoted an entire book—the 1898 collection *Black Belt Diamonds*—to quotations from his public addresses and talks to students that sketched out a vision of black progress along these lines. Less well understood is the curious role that literature and books played in Washington's vision of the proximal good life, yet these too enlivened many of the stories he would tell most frequently over the course of his career.

Here is one iteration, from the 1904 sequel to Washington's successful 1901 autobiography *Up from Slavery,* entitled *Working with the Hands*:

> At least once a week, when I am in the South, I make it a practice to spend an hour or more among the people of Tuskegee and vicinity—among

the merchants and farmers, white and black. In these talks with the real people I can get at the actual needs and conditions of those for whom our institution is at work. When talking to a farmer, I feel that I am talking with a real man and not an artificial one—one who can keep me in close touch with the real things. From a simple, honest cultivator of the soil, I am sure of getting firsthand, original information. I have secured more useful illustrations for addresses in a half-hour's talk with some white or coloured farmer than from hours of reading books.[2]

This anecdote is typical of Washington's style in that it is framed in a series of dichotomies, here between the real and the artificial, the concrete and the imagined, the near and the far. These dichotomies map onto broader distinctions—between local and global, rural and urban—that structured Washington's political thought and that helped endear him to white philanthropists and businessmen between 1881, the year he founded Tuskegee Institute in rural Alabama, and his death in 1915. But what is most alien to his conception of gathering "useful" information here is the prospect of spending "hours . . . reading books." In his pragmatic appeal to real-life experience as a privileged source of knowledge, Washington depreciates reading as a degraded form of learning. He situates the book as a secondhand medium—an object utterly removed from the "actual needs" of the common people. Anecdotes that take on just this narrative shape and political tenor appear in nearly every one of Washington's more than a dozen published books, differing only in their minutest details.

At first glance, Washington's literary anecdotes appear to reinforce the infamous disagreement between the so-called Wizard of Tuskegee and W. E. B. Du Bois, serving as evidence that the former was an enemy of the liberal arts and the latter their champion. Indeed, negative appraisals of books and reading were central to what Carla Willard calls Washington's "story style."[3] But to say that literature was simply a convenient straw man for Washington is to miss the full range of his orientation to literary practice, for he was able to make books and reading core elements in Tuskegee's vocational model of education without contradicting his stated aversion to the reading of books for their own sake. The key distinction, which I will elaborate in the pages to come, concerns the question of literary *use*. Rather than dismissing books outright, Washington devised, implemented, and relentlessly publicized an original method for making books "useful," a method he named "*dovetailing*" or "*correlation*" (he used these terms interchangeably, as will I in what follows). The dovetailing method tethered books and reading to the essentially industrial and agricultural project of educating "real people [with] actual needs," instantiating an instrumental relation to literary practice that I will call vocational realism.[4] Evident as much in his own prose as in the curriculum at Tuskegee, Washington's vocational realism sought to do away with the troubling spatiotemporal distance between words and things, reading and reality, by foregrounding a pedagogy of simultaneity and overlap. Vocational realism grew from the tenet that "an ounce of application is worth a ton of abstraction."[5] This move to educate head and hands together fundamentally shaped the function of literature within black modernity—a formation marked by the inequalities and exclusions of "racial time."[6]

Washington was among the most noted public figures of the Progressive Era, and he is also a key figure linking the multiple reformist and literary sites I explore in this book's other chapters: settlement house literary clubs, working girls' club periodicals, and undercover narratives all paid considerable attention to Washington, lauding him as a paradigmatically self-made man and a fine representative of his race. In this chapter, I contend that looking at the theory and practice of literary value in the context of black industrial education changes what we think we know about African American literature and culture from the period Rayford Logan dubbed "the nadir" (a period in African American history that extends from the end of Reconstruction in 1877 to the end of World War I) to the Harlem Renaissance.[7] I begin by describing the social, educational, and philanthropic landscape in which Washington's model of vocational instruction came to dominate paradigms of social reform directed at African American citizens. Turning to turn-of-the-century curricula and institutional documents from Tuskegee Institute and Fisk University, to private letters and lesson plans and speeches and autobiographies, I show how Washington reconfigured literary practice as a practical instrument of manual labor rather than a waste of precious hours. Next, I make a detour to W. E. B. Du Bois and the New Negro college protests of the 1920s to illustrate the long arm of Washingtonian usefulness in African American literary and intellectual history. Du Bois and his contemporaries rarely derided the idea of industrial training in general; rather, they denounced the way Washington's vocational realism distorted literature and words by making them useful to the here and now of the Jim Crow South. As I will argue here, the New Negro collegiate reform movements—a crucial but understudied dimension of the broader New Negro Renaissance—grew out of widespread frustration with the way Washington's methods continued to shape the intellectual and social conventions of historically black colleges and universities for years after his death. A similar fury drives Nella Larsen's 1928 novel *Quicksand,* as Larsen's protagonist discovers how comprehensively black education and racial uplift support white supremacy. In this novel, published thirteen years after Washington's death, Larsen engages the dovetailing method from multiple literary perspectives—including figurative language, aesthetic philosophy, and narrative structure—to reveal an enduring contest between social reform efforts and individual autonomy.

To understand the contest over literature's fraught social utility during the era Hazel Carby has named "the Age of Washington and Du Bois" and beyond, we must begin by acknowledging that Washington did not precisely dispense with book learning; rather, he articulated a novel method for making books instrumental to the way African Americans learned about and practiced manual labor.[8] To make this point, I situate the African American college as an important site of social reform and as a literary institution. As did the settlement house, working girls' club, and genre of undercover literature, the college made concepts of distance and proximity a constitutive part of its theory of literary value.[9] Yet unlike for the institutions I explore in chapters 1, 2, and 4, the bounds of Jim Crow utterly shaped the black college's politics of proximity. A further goal of this chapter, then, is to illuminate the important role of black higher education within modern U.S. literary history by shifting the critical issue of literary autonomy into the arena of Afro-modernity—a context that sheds new light on Larsen's modernist interventions. I chart a reformist genealogy of black expressive culture from the college to the Harlem Renaissance, two important and intertwined institutions of modern African American culture.

RACIAL UPLIFT AND AFRICAN AMERICAN EDUCATION

In the late nineteenth and early twentieth centuries, debates over the place of literature within the domain of black higher education occurred as part of a larger conversation about the urgent project of "uplifting the race." The umbrella ideology of racial uplift defined the parameters of African American educational institutions from common and normal schools (public schools and teachers' colleges) to liberal arts and research universities (including Fisk, Howard, and Atlanta Universities).[10] Racial uplift emerged in the aftermath of Reconstruction as a powerful doctrine of social advancement for African Americans subject to the subordination and disenfranchisement of the Jim Crow system. Although paradigms of racial uplift were generally premised on an evolutionary conception of progress derived from the Christian model of a Great Chain of Being, uplifters nonetheless brought diverse goals and convictions to the task of individual and communal empowerment. For many, including Du Bois, uplift described a philosophy of black leadership that emboldened well-educated, middle-class representatives to serve as guides and exemplars for the masses. It was the responsibility of this so-called Talented Tenth to function as a kind of aristocracy of elite, educated professionals. Members of the Talented Tenth would offer their intellectual capacity as concrete proof of racial progress and would contribute to the social betterment of the wider community by disseminating their specialized knowledge from within the professions.[11] In reality, the proportion of highly educated black professionals was closer to 1 percent of the total African American population at the turn of the century.[12]

A competing philosophy of racial uplift associated with Washington and Tuskegee espoused a more conciliatory view, urging that self-help and economic initiative for the rural masses rather than for an elite, mostly urban subset would elevate the race gradually and from below. Washington gained enthusiastic white patronage in part because his uplift philosophy did not directly contest conditions of sociopolitical inequality—his political challenges to white supremacy happened behind the scenes—insisting instead that progress would result from hard work within the confines of the present system. After all, as Kimberley Johnson suggests, education was the arena in which "white supremacy and its obverse, white paternalism, could be most visibly displayed, and the rewards of race and class could be distributed accordingly."[13] Vocational realism's mode of orienting literary practice toward the real, the tangible, and the present time and place took shape within this understanding of uplift.

Somewhere between these two poles, African Americans interpreted uplift more generally as a call to service and education. This ethos of institution building inspired the construction of countless churches, schools, business leagues, self-help organizations, and women's clubs, a veritable explosion of African American communal institutions that occurred in concert with—and as a consequence of—the systematic eradication of the gains of Reconstruction.[14] Even while truncated and unequal, education constituted the main modality of citizenship available to African Americans living under Jim Crow, which made the black school a crucial domain of politics and a prime locus of social reform. As the number of establishments for educating black students proliferated in the South following the Civil War, each institution developed a unique reformist mission that corresponded to the attitudes and convictions of its figureheads.[15] Educators and preachers formed the literate core of the emerging black middle class and constituted natural community leaders. "Every educated negro must be a reformer," Howard professor Kelly Miller insisted; "Educate! Educate! Educate! Get all the knowledge within reach, then use it for the good of the race," echoed journalist J. Max Barber.[16] The understanding that intellectual and cultural development carried a certain disciplinary power over minority subjects linked the African American college to the settlement house and working girls' club. "For the same reason that the North gives its disciplinary education to the children of these swarming millions from other lands," noted Henry Morehouse of the American Baptist Home Mission Society, "the South should give a similar education to the increasing swarms of children of the Negro race already numbering nearly nine millions."[17] The school became a principal site for defining and disseminating racial uplift.

Of course, African American writers and intellectuals elected literary representation to the same task in these years. In his field-defining book, *What Was African American Literature?* Kenneth Warren proposes that African American literature became such a privileged vehicle of black political expression precisely because of the antidemocratic forces of slavery and disenfranchisement. In this context, "the black literary voice could count for so much because, in political terms, the voice of black people generally counted for so little."[18] Other scholars of late nineteenth- and early twentieth-century African American culture have explored how distinct models of racial uplift infused literary representation. Gene Andrew Jarrett positions uplift as a powerful organizing rubric for African American literature in this period, as for cultural and political representation in general, arguing that postbellum writers and thinkers recognized the potential of literature to represent and advocate for collective interests. While authors such as Pauline Hopkins, Paul Laurence Dunbar, Sutton Griggs, Frances E. W. Harper, and Charles W. Chesnutt and periodicals like *Colored American Magazine* and *Voice of the Negro* made uplift a constitutive feature of their literary projects, the intersections of uplift and literature proved equally important in an adjacent arena—the African American college. Scholars have not fully explored the fate of literary culture within this sphere, generally overlooking the impact of black higher education on modern American literature.[19] And yet black colleges and universities were the contested breeding ground for writers and artists, and the very nerve center of the so-called best of the race. At the same time that uplift discourse emerged as a dominant theme of the black literary tradition, debates raged within educational communities regarding the proper place of books in the African American college curriculum. How, educators and philanthropists asked, should books be put to use in the classroom toward the ends of social reform? As the contested value of what was then called a "literary education" divided black higher learning into divergent pedagogical models of liberal education (book-centric courses in mathematics, science, English, and the classics) and industrial education (hands-on training in farming, brickmaking, carpentry, sewing, and other trades), "method" emerged as a central problem within the domain of racial uplift. Debates over the methods of uplifting the race focalized on the troubling use value of books and reading and doubled as a rubric for social practice.[20]

Why have literary critics been slow to recognize how profoundly the contest over collegiate pedagogy has influenced African American literature? One explanation may be that this issue has long been embedded in the higher-profile debate over the relative efficacy of a liberal arts or a vocational education. This historical crisis in the humanities dominated the way people discussed the contingencies of black economic and cultural life in the postbellum period, and the roots of this crisis lie to a great extent in the philanthropic infrastructure that determined the parameters of black education. The earliest institutions of higher education for black students were established by missionary organizations in the 1860s and 1870s—the American Missionary Association, the Freedmen's Aid Society of the Methodist Episcopal Church, the American Baptist Home Mission Society, and independent boards of northern missionaries—and were designed on the model of Oberlin or Williams College. Yet most freed African Americans had received abysmal lower training, if any at all, and by necessity enrolled in the common and secondary school programs.[21] Even as self-styled colleges and universities proliferated by the turn of the century, relatively few students graduated from them with advanced degrees. In 1899–1900, for instance, only fifty-eight of the ninety-nine extant black colleges had any collegiate students at all.[22] The most rigorous institutions were committed to filling in the foundations of their students' academic knowledge so that they could progress into the collegiate program, where educators introduced curricula, textbooks, libraries, codes of discipline, and standards of qualification and advancement that approximated northern models as closely as possible.[23]

Importantly, the divide between liberal arts and vocational modes of higher education was not absolute: institutions such as Atlanta, Howard, and Fisk Universities wove some manual labor into their curricula as part of the boarding system and as a means of strengthening character by emphasizing the dignity of labor. However, the rise to prominence of Washington's model of vocational training in the years following his 1895 Atlanta Compromise address coincided with a shift in the structures of power supporting black education, a seismic change that did much to undermine the place of "arts and letters" within that system. With their own financial resources dwindling, the missionary organizations that had disseminated the liberal arts gradually ceded power and influence to new philanthropic foundations. The Peabody Education Fund, the John F. Slater Fund for the Education of Freedmen, the Julius Rosenwald Fund, the Phelps-Stokes Fund, the Anna T. Jeanes Foundation, and the General Education Board collectively assumed almost exclusive financial support of—and control over—black education in the South. The center of philanthropic influence shifted from nineteenth-century New England to twentieth-century New York City, and from missionary to corporate motives, as industrial education came to dominate the field of black education. The philanthropists who controlled black education imagined a future for African American citizens primarily as manual laborers in the rural South, often colluding with white supremacists in the view that "literary education—the knowledge of books—does not seem to produce any good substantial results with the Negro," as Mississippi governor James K. Vardaman put it in 1904.[24] An editor of the *New Orleans Times-Democrat* argued that same year that "the higher education of the Negro unfits him for the work that it is intended that he shall do, and cultivates ambitions that can never be realized."[25]

To an extent, setting vocational institutes such as Hampton and Tuskegee against liberal arts colleges such as Howard and Fisk is an unfair comparison. The former were normal schools devoted to training teachers for the newly emerging black common schools across the rural South and not, strictly speaking, colleges at all.[26] Students typically departed industrial institutes with the equivalent of a tenth-grade education. And yet these different institutions were inextricably linked as nodes within the system of black education. The dependence of *all* schools on philanthropy in the face of limited state support for black education made the choice between industrial or collegiate institutions a zero-sum game.[27] But whether one accepts Washington's educational philosophy as a virtue of dire necessity or as a base capitulation to racism, it is an indisputable fact that industrial schools pledged to prepare black men and women for the very southern labor force that fed the business interests of the philanthropists who funded them. In return, Hampton, Tuskegee, and the many "little Tuskegees" that followed received financial support that far outweighed the funds accorded to strictly academic institutions. "Except in the rarest of occasions, I am bitterly opposed to the so-called higher education of Negroes," wrote Tuskegee trustee, General Education Board chairman, and railroad magnate William H. Baldwin Jr. in 1899, just after he was named vice president of the Southern Railroad. Industrial philanthropies extended virtually no substantial financial aid to liberal arts colleges until 1920. In this context, black colleges had to fight to maintain a stringently academic focus.[28]

Educators in both the "practical" and "intellectual" camps mobilized metaphors of uplift to defend their distinct curricular philosophies. One article written by a white teacher at Virginia's Hampton Institute expressed its support for vocational pedagogy by engaging racial uplift's hierarchical and evolutionary meanings. In "Reflex Action of the Carolina Troubles," Alice M. Bacon, a regular contributor to Hampton's house periodical the *Southern Workman* and a member of its editorial staff, made the devastating 1898 race riot in Wilmington, North Carolina, a rhetorical device through which to remonstrate against a graver ill: a curriculum founded on books and reading. The white author's intention in referencing the Wilmington massacre is clear from the first line, which moves swiftly from the terrorism she euphemizes as "race feeling" to the "salvation" Hampton offers: "Deplorable as are the recent ebullitions of race feeling in the Carolinas, they are not without their uses in working out the ultimate salvation of the Negro and so of the white man at all." To Bacon, locating "salvation" in literary pedagogy produces graduates who "know" but cannot "do," a familiar (and typically anti-intellectual) charge against the work of Howard, Fisk, and Atlanta.[29]

Bacon's anchoring of intellectual uplift in the twin metaphors of "a rope ladder" and "a key" is worth quoting at length.

> We are apt to think that our books are the key to our civilization, and that by putting that into the hands of an alien he can enjoy with us all the elevating influences that civilizations affords. As a matter of fact, if we place that key in the hands of a man and give him no further aid he is no nearer to our position than he was before. Our civilization is built upon a lofty elevation, a cleft in the rock up to which we have painfully toiled

by a rope ladder let down by long vanished races to our aid. If instead of letting down a rope ladder we merely fling down a key and call to the Negro to come up and enjoy our privileges, we are but mocking him, for he can not so much as see the key hole. It is by this ladder of painfully acquired character, of slow growth in industrial and mechanical attainment, that the Negroes must come up to us, and while some of the Negro's friends at the North are saying he must have the key and nothing else, and some of his friends at the South would take away the key altogether, it is the real and undeniable fact that there can be no dispute among his friends as to whether the rope ladder is necessary, however loudly they may contradict each other as to the precise point in his upward journey at which he should be given the key.

Now Hampton and Tuskegee and other Southern schools are working along the rope ladder theory. Whatever tumult rages about their ears concerning just how much or how little literary education should be given the Negro, these schools stick to the faith in which they were conceived, and keep steadily at their work of fitting men and women to meet the *present* conditions, studying carefully the while whatever changes may occur, and altering from year to year their methods, though not their aim.[30]

In referring to an antagonized "literary education," Bacon refers broadly to a humanistic education that included the classics, language study, mathematics, science, and English. Whereas reading great literature may exercise "elevating influences" on white readers who already enjoy civilization's lofty perch, books emit no comparable power in the hands of a black reader. As Bacon sees it—and she articulates a widely shared perspective—universities furnish black students with literary riches *as though they were white people,* not noticing that this "key" opens a door to civilization that is too high up for any African American to reach while still entrenched, as he ought to be, in the "*present* conditions." Mixing spatial and evolutionary valences of the "uplift" metaphor, Bacon argues that a literary education unlocks no doors at all in the here and now of Jim Crow; this key cannot expedite a future "privilege" that has not yet arrived and for which black citizens are not prepared. In the alternative metaphor of the "rope ladder" that enables "slow growth," it remains unclear whether there *is* any key accompanying the ladder, nor is there any promise of equality atop the "cleft in the rock." Bacon's description emblematizes the common view that education should afford African Americans a manual foothold in the rural South—but no more. The implication, of course, is that black students were to be only gradually "civilized" and to have limited access to any books at all.

Advocates of a liberal arts education deployed similarly hierarchical, evolutionary metaphors to defend a sharply divergent conception of intellectual uplift. Kelly Miller, African American professor of mathematics and sociology at Howard University and future dean of its College of Arts and Sciences (1907–19), protested that advocates of industrial training had "lost the power of binocular vision." They ignored the crucial fact that "[the] two forms of education are not antagonistic, but supplemental." In "The Education of the Negro," a 1902 report conducted for the U.S. Bureau of Education, Miller insisted that poverty and low literacy rates did not fit the masses for exclusively manual vocations but, rather, *increased* their need for a "literary education": "Just as it is more needful for the crude rustic lad to study English syntax than it is for the son of a refined family who gains facility of speech by familiarity and use, so it becomes all the more necessary for the colored youth of crude antecedents and environments to gain culture and refinement through the medium of the school." As though referring directly to Bacon's "long vanished races," Miller insists that "no greater mistake can be made than to suppose that the colored race must pass through every variety of physical and mental vicissitude which the Caucasian race has undergone before it can attain like renown. This erroneous supposition lies at the basis of much of the opposition to the higher education of colored youth." Here, Miller combats the evolutionary racism of his time while defining uplift as a force generating individual and community coherence; he clings to a fundamentally vertical model of uplift while reversing Bacon's terms. "A race can not lift itself independently into civilization any more than a man can sustain himself by pulling against the straps of his own boots," he writes. But moral, social, and economic mobility depend on access to intellectual capital: "We can not reach the sky on a pedestal of brick and mortar. . . . The negro needs a wider and a larger range of visions, [and] such influences can be brought to him by means of the higher culture only." The school, he argues, must guide the black student beyond present conditions, and not simply fit him for conformity within them. Thus Miller arrives at a conclusion opposite to that of Bacon: when it comes to racial uplift, "the architect must plan before the artisan can execute. The idea comes from above and descends until it strikes the basis of popular needs, and then rebounds, bringing the concrete fulfillment up toward the level of the ideal from which it sprang."[31] The forcible power and alacrity inherent in this metaphor of a race's upward "rebound," as distinct from its "slow growth," testify to the superiority of an intellectual, book-based curriculum as a means of elevating the race.

I cite Bacon and Miller to begin to suggest how the conversation around black education and literature hinged on the question of method: which methods would succeed in bringing an institution's curricular philosophy together with its particular definition of racial uplift? Bacon's outright dismissal of "literary education" would seem to mount an absolute divide between the two institutional models, as though no form of literary engagement could be found within schools like Hampton and Tuskegee. Yet officials at these institutions did in fact integrate classically academic features into their industrial program as part of a new, self-consciously modern method of educating black pupils. Advocates of industrial training did not wage outright war on the arts and letters. Instead, that movement's figurehead and principal architect, Booker T. Washington, transformed books into instruments of a practical approach to learning and to manual labor. Thus as two distinct models of black education emerged at the beginning of the twentieth century, each in its own way made literature the agent of a distinct reformist mission.

To date, educational historians have examined the way African American vocational institutes removed books from the classroom in their capacity as participants in the industrial education system, a movement whose proponents included Jane Addams and John Dewey.[32] In contrast, I show that the debate over the methods of racial uplift focused on more than just whether or not African Americans were encouraged to read; rather, the debate was over how they were to use literacy and whether books could literally be categorized as tools, akin to hammers or shovels.[33] Looking past the content of the curriculum, I examine "dovetailing" (also called "correlation") as an emergent pedagogical method of applying the liberal arts to the field of manual training. The correlation method, I argue, generated a paradigmatic vocabulary that shaped African American literature and culture and that later provided the conceptual contours of the Harlem Renaissance. Washington's contemporaries and immediate successors were as concerned with the way his industrial pedagogy distorted literature and words under the weight of Jim Crow realism as they were with the near absence of printed words on the syllabi of vocational institutes.[34]

AGAINST ABSTRACTION

Although Washington used "correlation" and "dovetailing" as synonyms, the *Oxford English Dictionary* (*OED*) designates subtle and illuminating differences between the terms. Most broadly, "correlation" means "the mutual relation of two or more things (implying intimate or necessary connection)." And yet the relation need not be *inherently* "intimate or necessary." A subsequent entry defines correlation as "the *action* of correlating or bringing into mutual relation" (italics mine), implying that the actor has some agency in identifying and forging a connection between things. While used slightly less frequently in published material about Tuskegee's methods, "*dovetailing*" was nonetheless Washington's preferred term for describing his pedagogy, perhaps because the word's etymological rootedness in a manual trade helped identify—or, indeed, correlate—the term with the educational method it represented, thus nicely figuring his institutional brand. In carpentry, the term "dovetail" refers to "a fastening or joint composed of tenons cut in the shape of an expanded dove's tail, fitting into mortises of corresponding shape." The *OED* defines the transitive verb "to dovetail" as "to unite compactly as if by dovetails; to adjust exactly, so as to form a continuous whole." The intransitive verb "to dovetail" means "to fit into each other, so as to form a compact or harmonious whole or company." Each uniquely resonant term is suggestive of a broader politics—correlation involves the act of forming relations, with all the troublingly "necessary" implications of that connection, while dovetailing points up the goal of forming a unified and harmonious whole through that action—intimating that Washington's pedagogical concept was designed to find sites for application beyond the school.

At a basic level, a pedagogy of correlation aimed to "make [different] tracks of learning intersect" by integrating academic lessons in science, mathematics, geography, and English into students' daily acquisition of vocational skills.[35] For credit in both English and blacksmithing, for instance, students would write a composition about the process of forging machinery in the shop, altogether replacing compositions addressing, say, a poem or historical event or any other concept accessible on the page rather than through direct engagement with the material world surrounding Tuskegee, Alabama. Instead of sitting in a classroom poring over books and then heading out into the field or shop, students spent their time pursuing trade experiences that could be made, at least nominally, to correlate with linguistic and intellectual development—a temporality of overlap rather than sequence. (In practice, a vocational "class" entailed on-site occupational experience, with teachers present to guide students along.)

To industrial educators, the objects and practices of literary culture were absolutely central to the burgeoning manual competency of their students. For one thing, the arts and letters possessed inherently uplifting qualities that promised to elevate rote tasks by association. Wrote one Tuskegee educator, "Wood and iron evoke no enthusiasm for serving one's fellows and one's community; a material infinitely more subtle and delicate must be used. But, it is precisely this spirit of social service that Tuskegee must arouse . . . so the school is glad to use the incentives supplied by history and literature."[36] On one level, this vision of intellectual and high culture as incentives to perform manual labor and make it palatable positions literary engagement rather conventionally as a form of social control, reflecting a common view of high art as a mode of refinement and character building. As the earlier chapters of this book have already shown, this view of literature as a vehicle for refining underprivileged subjects—women and immigrants as well as people of color—was conventional at the turn of the century, though Washington's innovation was to make the pleasures of literature inextricable from manual labor. However, many advocates found instrumental value in literature for reasons far less sanguine than its arousing and incentivizing qualities. The white principal of Hampton Institute, Washington's alma mater, heralded dovetailing as a method uniquely suitable to the way African Americans already used

English. "The harnessing of words to things in the work of daily life has been of incalculable use to a race inclined to be 'somewhat venturesome' in the use of words," declared H. B. Frissell in 1908, deeming correlation "the great principle" of modern education.[37] Frissell's words make clear that while the correlation method may have been designed to enhance otherwise tiresome manual tasks, an equally important function was its capacity to discipline black literacy. It institutionalized a relation to language and literature that strictly adhered to the linguistic and imaginative ambit of Jim Crow employment and that therefore can only be described as impoverished.[38]

It is worth noting that the pedagogical and political significance of dovetailing has been recognized in art as well. A 1922 statue by sculptor Charles Keck that still stands at the center of what is now Tuskegee University features a seminaked man sitting atop a blacksmith's anvil with an oversized book in his lap, while Booker T. Washington holds a veil above his head. Keck's *Lifting the Veil of Ignorance* effectively immortalizes the mission of industrial colleges by representing dovetailing both as educational method (anvil and book together) and as a key operation of racial uplift ("civilization" is surely nigh for the semiclothed student). But the statue also suggests dovetailing's political ambiguity, since it can be understood to show both the lifting and the lowering of the veil, as the narrator of Ralph Ellison's *Invisible Man* famously reminds us.[39]

Washington spent a great deal of time advertising his pedagogical innovation. Correlation seemed to put in practice the broader idea of the "dignity of labor," the great theme of his career and a common watchword of Progressive Era discourse north and south. In doing so, he was able to articulate the material contributions his method made to the political and economic interests of the white South. "If a community has been educated exclusively on books and has not been trained in habits of applied industry, an unwholesome tendency to dodge honest productive labour is likely to develop," Washington wrote in *Working with the Hands*.[40] As late as 1911, years after his techniques had been accepted and widely imitated across the United States, he explained his methods to Tuskegee students in a Sunday Evening Talk.

Instead of picking up a book in arithmetic, printed in Boston, or Chicago or somewhere up there—suppose the teacher just gets courage enough and summons common sense enough to say that Johnny Jones' father, who lives a quarter of a mile from the school has a pig, and instead of working out the old, dead, abstract problem in arithmetic which some fellow in Chicago wrote, she suggests going over to John Jones' father's house and weighing his father's pig. . . . John Jones' father will scratch his head and say: "I did not know that this is what you mean by education, that my boy would come home and weigh my pig and tell how much my pig will bring. I always thought education meant what a pig in Chicago or New York would bring. I didn't think it would calculate the cost of my pig."[41]

In an anecdote nominally devoted to mathematics, Washington fixates on books—printing, writing, and reading them—demonstrating how vocational realism drew under its umbrella the liberal arts writ large. His concern lies as much in the distant form of the book as it does in the specific application of mathematical precepts to local agriculture. Washington equates the math textbook with a kind of experiential remoteness akin to the distance between rural Alabama and "Boston, or Chicago or somewhere up there," figuring the decision to cull intellectual cultivation from the agrarian South rather than the alien, urban North in heroic terms as a gesture of "courage" and "common sense." Equally heroic is the decision to eschew abstraction as hostile to the immediate concerns of a farmer with his pig.

Washington's words signify in complex ways here: while the decision to turn toward the homely object lesson just up the road holds pragmatic value as agricultural pedagogy, it also panders openly to sectional differences and suggests that reading and abstract thinking could have no possible relevance for black inhabitants of the South. The minute an instructor replaced the book with the pig, or culture with agriculture, the education of black students began to forge "a common bond between the two races and an opportunity for co-operation between the North and the South," as Washington put it in a 1912 article for the *Nautilus* magazine.[42] In his address about Johnny Jones's pig—this was another of his oft-repeated anecdotes—as elsewhere, Washington's thinking returns to this central idea of *relation*. As he saw it, the traditional literary methods practiced in liberal arts colleges bore no relevance to the lives of the black masses, whereas the correlation technique furnished a crucial relation between student and knowledge by couching the latter in the language of everyday life. Students were still encouraged to "read up," to borrow Amy L. Blair's notion of reading as a mechanism of upward social mobility, but this aspirational reading was to be absolutely pragmatic, with the scene of likely future employment kept entirely in mind.[43] Of course, educators' stated intentions do not necessarily determine the actual practices of historical readers. To observe that the library building at Tuskegee, constructed in 1900 after Andrew Carnegie donated $20,000 to the school, stocked more books on agriculture and industry than it did works of fiction and poetry does not mean that an industrious young student could not manage to lay hands on *Hard Times* through some other means—though public libraries were closed to African Americans in the state of Alabama until 1918.[44] Notwithstanding the idiosyncratic behavior of individual readers, this instrumentalist reading formation shaped a "practical" approach to literary practice into the twentieth century.

Washington's *Working with the Hands* explains what a dovetailed lesson actually looked like. A skilled teacher might correlate two divergent subjects—spelling and constructing a wood chest—by asking his students to spell the name of each tool and piece of construction material as it was exhibited to the class. The lesson plan walks through instructions for building a cedar chest, capitalizing and italicizing the relevant spelling words: "Then with these *Sprigs* we put on this *Moulding*, which should be cut in a *Miter*, or we may cut it by this *Bevel*, which can be changed to a *Square*. We now put on these *Butts*—not *Strap-Hinges*—with *Screws*."[45] This schema ensures that the student's expanding literacy dovetails with the tasks he will be expected to undertake as a carpenter. In one remaining example of a dovetailed composition written by a Tuskegee student, a pupil of brick masonry narrates "the most interesting incident" in his shop experience: "When I began to plumb one side of the pier the other side would bough out. I was really outdone because I couldn't build it like I wanted it, due to the fact that the bricks had absorbed a large quantity of water."[46] Other students describe learning to wipe a lead joint in plumbing class and to use magnets in the electrical training room. These essays were graded by industrial instructors for their technical competence and by English teachers for their linguistic correctness. They do indeed demonstrate grammatical competence and a strong command of the language and practice of the relevant trades, as student-writers documented their burgeoning vocational prowess.

These compositions studiously erase any distance between representation and experience, and they manifest these efforts in vernacular prose of such minute detail and mechanical precision that they too earn the title of vocational realism, that particular mode of expression rooted in the practical pedagogy of Tuskegee and similar institutions. To Washington, the chief advantage in this method of composition was that its author is "writing something in which other students have a practical interest [and] naturally feels responsibility for the statements that he makes—a responsibility that he would not feel if he were merely putting together facts that he had gathered from some encyclopedia or other second-hand source of information."[47] Reading and writing, Washington contends, acquire personal urgency within the Tuskegee classroom (or workroom). But precisely in their abiding vocational realism—their technical and formal economy, the locality of their experiential and imaginative scope—these compositions betray a linguistic and cultural landscape that is circumscribed by the sociopolitical conditions in which students were forced to live in the South. Tuskegee students, after all, were being primed to work on the lower rungs of the industrial workforce and in the same agricultural fields that had been the occupational site of slave labor, and corporate philanthropists saw little social or financial value in the broad exercise of black literacy. By regulating black literacy through correlation, vocational institutes sought to forge a relation to language so utterly attuned to the current sociopolitical conditions as to be constrained by them. In fact, one-time Tuskegee professor E. Franklin Frazier would write in his 1957 account of the black bourgeoisie that students and faculty were instructed not to be seen publicly carrying books around campus, lest visitors get the mistaken impression that the institution "was training the Negro's intellect rather than his heart and hand."[48]

Washington's campaign to dovetail the Tuskegee curriculum commenced immediately following his Atlanta Cotton States address. Beginning in November 1895, Washington peppered his daily memos to faculty with incitements to integrate the new method into their daily classroom routines. In March, he was still demanding that Tuskegee's teachers institute "uniformity to a larger extent in aims and methods" by "[putting] into operation the correlating of the literary and industrial work," and reprimanded them for deigning "to ridicule the use of the term 'dove tail' which [he] had used."[49] Faculty members blanched at these demands, particularly the "literary people" who had been educated at Oberlin, Harvard, Fisk, and Atlanta. Some were dismissed from their posts for refusing to correlate their academic lessons. While the stated aim was to make Tuskegee's curriculum more efficient, professors may have sensed the president's broader goal of "blotting out differences between the literary department and the industrial department," as Washington put it in a letter to his trustees—a blotting that dealt a serious blow to the school's academic bona fides.[50] Four years after introducing dovetailing into the curriculum, a group of Tuskegee's most influential trustees—a group that included John D. Rockefeller, Collis P. Huntington, and J. P. Morgan—promised to launch a new endowment for the school on the condition that Washington reform the curriculum to an even greater degree. By 1900, Washington had strengthened Tuskegee's manual offerings and abridged its academic profile even further. Money and books streamed in and out of black colleges in roughly inverse relation, as Washington's influential method itself correlated with the choking constraints of life in the segregated South.

Beyond appealing to industrial philanthropists, "dovetailing" did much to assuage the southern white population's fears regarding the prospect of higher education for black citizens. Washington was well aware of the relationship that obtained between the pedagogy he promulgated and the conditions of white supremacy. He was familiar too, of course, with the laws that had prohibited black literacy in his own lifetime. While there had been "open antagonism or indifference" to the idea of black education before he built up Tuskegee, the minute [it] appeared that as a result of industrial education the negro would not only, for example, study chemistry but apply that chemistry to the enrichment of the soil . . . [and that] the negro was not only learning geometry and physics but applying his knowledge to blacksmithing, brickmaking, housebuilding and what not; at that moment there began for the first time to be a common bond between the two races and an opportunity for co-operation between the North and the South in the matter of negro education.[51]

In addition to giving black pupils marketable skills, then, correlation also offered a way of working around racist antipathy toward the idea of black intellectual cultivation: Tuskegee students would "not only" learn chemistry, geometry, and physics but would also, more importantly, forge "a common bond" across racial lines and encourage sectional peace between North and South—surely a cause worthy of philanthropic investment. If "one of the saddest things [Washington] saw . . . was a young man, who had attended some high school, sitting down in a one-room cabin, with grease on his clothing, filth all around him, and weeds in the yard and garden, engaged in studying a French grammar," then an educational program that made academic subjects relevant to black life characterized by "filth" and "weeds" served as a species of social reform amenable to the racist structures of the Jim Crow South.[52] And indeed, one white professor at an Illinois normal school praised Washington's correlation technique in a letter to the director of the General Education Board, commending it for inculcating "the very minimum of the 'make believe' and superficial and the maximum of the real, the genuine, the education."[53] Washington credited his educational method with bringing about an "interdependence—a dovetailing of [black and white] business interests," framing the sociality of correlation as a kind of interracial friendship.[54]

Literary historians have described the rise of English studies in majority-white universities in these same years as a story in which emergent professional scholars gradually supplanted traditional humanistic critics and in which the study of modern literatures and languages displaced the classical curriculum.[55] But Washington's power to shape how books were used—or not used—in the classrooms of historically black colleges and universities constitutes an alternative historical trajectory. In this parallel narrative of the fate of English, proponents of modern literary studies were not opposed to classicists but, rather, necessarily allied with them in a shared quest to preserve space for intellectual activity that would remain autonomous from the language and practice of manual labor.

"FICTION I CARE LITTLE FOR"

Dovetailing was certainly politically strategic, offering a way of working around racist antipathy toward the idea of black intellectual cultivation. However, even as it instantiated a unique form of vocational realism, its method of tethering words to things also reflected clear antiliterary sentiments.[56] This antiliterary rhetoric functioned, at times, as shorthand for a sociopolitical orientation toward the "practical" that "the literary" was believed to contradict, as when Washington claimed in his Atlanta address that "no race can prosper till it learns that there is as much dignity in tilling a field as in writing a poem."[57] Here, the curtailment of poetry writing stands in synecdochic relation to social and political aspirations endlessly deferred. Across the archive of Washington's published writings, from autobiographies to essays and speeches, he consistently expresses animosity toward the idea of reading literature for its own sake.

In *Up from Slavery*, the book that cemented his celebrity and helped raise crucial funds for Tuskegee, Washington recounts how his own early education in the "school" of slavery prepared him to become a race leader suited to the twentieth century. Washington adopts the generic conventions of the slave narrative in the tradition of Frederick Douglass and Olaudah Equiano, depicting his rugged acquisition of literacy while at work in a salt furnace and subsequent construction of a makeshift library out of a dry-goods box as key features of his coming-of-age. And yet despite the foundational importance it grants to achieved literacy as a symbol of freedom and self-determination, *Up from Slavery* evinces a strong suspicion of reading books. "The older I grow, the more I am convinced that there is no education which one can get from books and costly apparatus that is equal to that which can be gotten from contact with great men and women," Washington writes. He vowed that "[instead] of studying books so constantly," Tuskegee students would "learn to study men and things."⁵⁸ Nearly all Washington's published writing expands on the idea that "too great a gap has been left between the Negro's real condition and the position for which we have tried to fit him through the medium of our text-books."⁵⁹

The dovetailing method thus institutionalized a view of the book as a secondhand medium. This pedagogy insisted on the distinction between "studying about things through the medium of books, and studying things themselves without the medium of books," so that rural African Americans would recognize that "there is just as much that is interesting, strange, mysterious, and wonderful; just as much to be learned that is edifying, broadening, and refining in a cabbage as there is in a page of Latin."⁶⁰ Of course, Washington's contemporaries in the field of fiction proposed oppositional viewpoints: novelist Charles W. Chesnutt, for instance, favored accumulating knowledge from books at second- or even thirdhand, arguing, "[We] form our conceptions of the lives and characters of others from what we read about them in books. This is true even of those who seldom read a book, they learn what little they know by association with those who have read and studied books."⁶¹ *My Larger Education* (1911) details how Washington, who in his earlier years had been ashamed to lack the classical training that was the mark of an educated man, came to realize that "authors, in their books, were after all merely making use of their own experiences or expressing ideas which they had worked out in actual life, and that to make use of their language and ideas was merely to get life second hand." He vowed to "learn something from every man [he] met; make him [his] textbook."⁶² In addition to presenting his program for black education as the rational course of action for a disenfranchised race eager to attain economic security, then, Washington framed his method as a revelation about the superiority of the "real" and concrete over the abstract and secondhand.

In this formulation, two distinct forms of knowledge emerge as cognates. On the one hand, there is the knowledge attained directly from one's own life experiences; on the other, the knowledge gained and subsequently described by an author in the course of his or her own life experience, which is not necessarily any more significant than readers'. The difference is a matter of degrees. To Washington, the book mediates between self and knowledge, materializing a sense of remote and obstructed knowledge that the black school nominally exists to banish. He suggests that the striving black self and the published author are basically equivalent in their potential to live productive, edifying lives and in their ability to furnish a "textbook" for others, either through merely living or through the process of writing and publishing a text. This conviction carries important principles of self-determination, self-help, and racial pride in the context of an institution with an entirely African American faculty and student body, even as it presents the choice between reading a book for its own sake and experiencing "the world around me" as a zero-sum game.[63]

Washington calibrates his antiliterary prejudice to the material forms and genres of literature. Books, unsurprisingly, are more problematically indirect and secondhand than newspapers—"I like to deal at firsthand with the raw material and this I find in the newspapers more than in books"—and biographies are the best, because most proximate, of all books.[64] Washington forcefully derides fiction, dismissing it as a trivial and dangerous genre. In this sense, Washington's theory of literature renews antifictional prejudice of long duration in the United States and elsewhere, as Cathy Davidson has documented in her classic text *Revolution and the Word*.[65] "Fiction I care little for," Washington writes. "Frequently I have to almost force myself to read a novel that is on everyone's lips.... I like to be sure that I am reading about a real man or a real thing."[66] Within the logic of dovetailing, a work of fiction is useless inasmuch as the black reader can form only an imaginative, and not a practical, relation to its narrative. That is, fiction might be literary realism, but it is not vocational realism; its use value is limited. Whatever instructive quality fiction possesses lends itself to changes of thought and feeling—abstractions—and not automatically to concrete actions with results that can be measured in economic terms. Thus, Washington's motivation in publishing his own prose was partly to publicize a relation to literacy that conformed to turn-of-the-century readers' desire for "facts rather than generalities or sermonizing."[67]

Washington's own writing style reflects this emphasis on literary utility. With not an adjective out of place, his unadorned prose—shaped, to be sure, by his amanuenses and sometime ghostwriters Edgar Webber, Max Bennett Thrasher, and Robert E. Park—confirms his status as a man of facts and realistic argumentation. He sought to engender a similar style in his students' prose as well, scolding an English teacher that "there are too many big words" in Tuskegee student compositions. "The sentences are too long and involved. . . . Let them use the same kind of language in writing that they do in talking."[68] The literary style of vocational realism helps reify a correlated literacy in which vectors of reading, writing, and speaking form a continuous whole. Through literary style, the dovetailing pedagogy, and a pragmatic relation to literary form and genre, vocational realism coheres as a distinctive theory of literary and intellectual practice.[69]

In arguing that Washington's pedagogical invention and antiliterary doctrine together index a theory of representation in which any representation of a thing is resolutely inferior to the thing itself, I intend to point to a set of dichotomies that structure Washington's writing and shape the whole pattern of his career as race leader: between words and things, abstract and concrete, secondhand and direct, principle and reality, thinking and doing. Given the great influence Washington's method held within educational and philanthropic circles, it is worth asking what effect vocational realism might have had on black literary production more broadly. After all, this understanding of literary value challenged the notion that reading, writing, and abstract thought as practices constitutive of a distinctly *literary* rather than industrial vocation would contribute in a meaningful way to the social progress of the race. If "the visible, the tangible . . . is ten times more potent than pages of discussion," as Washington alleged in *Up from Slavery,* then a literary and intellectual tradition would seem largely incompatible with a "realistic" vision of African American survival.[70] But even so, we see clear traces of dovetailed thinking in the work of Harlem Renaissance writers and theorists, for example, who drew on the language of correlation only to innovate on its central terms. What I am proposing, then, is that vocational realism helped institutionalize this dichotomous cultural vocabulary within the sites of black expressive culture, shaping the African American literary tradition in decades to follow.

DOVETAILING IN THE NEW NEGRO ERA

W. E. B. Du Bois was not opposed to vocational education in general and recognized that Hampton and Tuskegee filled an important role in preparing black men and women for work in agriculture and industry. However, he *was* eternally suspicious of any method that served to degrade the intellectual integrity of a collegiate education.[71] Across his rich body of work on the subject of education, Du Bois expressed concern that the theory and practice of vocational realism collapsed the boundaries that sustained the black university and safeguarded their autonomy of thought, expression, and action. In an editorial published in the *Crisis,* for example, he insisted, "It is not true that . . . you can at one and the same time educate the race in modern civilization and train it simply to be servants and laborers. Any one who suggests by sneering at books and 'literary courses' that the great heritage of human thought ought to be displaced simply for the reason of teaching the technique of modern industry is pitifully wrong."[72] Here and elsewhere, Du Bois critiqued the spatiotemporality of dovetailing, its method of offering training in literature and in labor "at one and the same time." Yet while he praised schools like Fisk and Atlanta for bringing black students "into contact with the standards of modern culture," making them "missionaries of culture" who stood to uplift the race precisely through their intellectual training, not its evasion—Du Bois was a faculty member at Atlanta from 1897 to 1910—he found that even the best centers of liberal learning had capitulated to the principles of correlation.[73]

Let me turn now to two moments of public address in which Du Bois explicitly attacked the correlationist discourse that linked knowledge to immediacy and undermined the relevance of an intellectual and literary tradition to black learners. In the first, on June 17, 1908, Du Bois stood in front of an audience of faculty and graduating students at Fisk University to deliver a commencement address. He was a Fisk alumnus, having attended the university between 1885 and 1888 and having graduated with a bachelor's degree. But now instead of praising the accomplishments of a later generation, Du Bois damned the university for allowing industrial training to encroach on its academic curriculum. Conceding that "[there] can be no doubt that the college curriculum of the past generation shamefully neglected the World of Things—the tangible visible universe and its laws and ways," he continued,

> It is certain that in the university of tomorrow, the field of knowledge will include a knowledge of what the present world has done and is doing with its physical resources as well as a knowledge of its Thoughts and feelings. For this momentous change in curriculum, all true educators are looking and preparing; but this does not mean a stampede to industry as a substitute for life—to mechanics as an antidote for thought, or to technique in place of Reason. Simply because in the world of education, we are fighting for change and larger fulfillment of true prophesy, does not mean that any industrializing of a college curriculum, or any substitution of hands for brains, is the true heralded change. For it may easily happen (and this is the gist of my message) that a mere specious and popular promise of longer and easier life, may prompt the Galilean spirit of 1908, as it did in 1608, to seek to establish the mechanical success of the future building by tearing down the spiritual foundations of the past.[74]

Du Bois's speech took aim at recently implemented changes to the Fisk curriculum, which had historically held fast against the Tuskegee model of education. But now, Du Bois warned, Fisk was prioritizing financial security over intellectual integrity. In 1906–7, his alma mater had introduced a new department of Applied Science and used funds supplied by the General Education Board and its subsidiary, the Slater Fund, to hire new professors of agriculture, mechanical arts, and domestic science. It also instated certain key features of the dovetailing method by, in Du Bois's words, "denominating a series of lessons in the training of servants [as] a course in mechanical engineering" and by deeming "the milking of cows [a course of] cultural study."[75] These changes to the curriculum were clearly attempts to ensure the school's economic survival: Fisk was located in the bustling center of urban Nashville with no farmland in sight, and it had long offered the same liberal arts education provided at majority-white institutions. Mobilizing familiar dichotomies drawn from the vocabulary of dovetailing—industry/life, mechanics/thought, technique/reason, future success / historical foundations—to condemn

Fisk's "tearing down" of its intellectual tradition, Du Bois criticized the liberal arts institution he most cherished as a means of inciting reform.

Du Bois's 1908 Fisk address refers more generally to the destructive relationship between the vagaries of philanthropic funding and the fate of black intellectual culture in the early years of the twentieth-century—to evidence, that is, that the dovetailing method had seeped into the most rarefied of educational institutions. College administrators found that the easiest route to an enhanced endowment lay in becoming more "vocational," whether by simply adding the word to their name and hoping for the best or by genuinely integrating industrial classes into the curriculum, as the philanthropists had pressured Washington to do in 1900. No subject was under greater threat within this arrangement than the classics, which still represented the most elite form of cultural capital. Studying dead languages and literatures was anathema to a practical orientation, and white bureaucrats, philanthropists, and erstwhile educators found it dangerously liable to produce citizens who would challenge the white supremacist order. The classics loomed as large in black universities as they did at comparable white institutions, where studying Greek and Latin was a fundamental part of the curriculum into the early twentieth century. Students at liberal arts–focused institutions could expect to learn Latin and Greek in addition to studying modern languages, and to read Caesar, Virgil, Xenophon, Homer, Plato, Horace, and Cicero.[76] Yet the ire of white educational reformers toward the classics was wholly disproportionate to the miniscule number of black students actually pursuing classical studies in the South. Knowledge of the classics was threatening in that it represented intellectual equality and civic participation. Historian Adam Fairclough has demonstrated that once philanthropists assumed greater control over schools, including Fisk, these institutions—once "colleges" and "universities" but now, in many cases, renamed "institutes"—invariably eliminated Latin and Greek and replaced interracial boards with exclusively white trustees.[77] The president of Georgia State Industrial School was forced to resign in 1921 when he refused to follow orders to "cut this Latin out and teach these boys to farm."[78] Administrators of the Jeanes Foundation, founded in 1907 to train teachers for work in rural schools, encouraged even elementary schools to industrialize, offering bonus funds as a reward to teachers who augmented manual training, dropped Latin, and found ways to "[correlate] the industry with language."[79]

It became clear just how entwined were the social and the academic in the theory and practice of dovetailing when agents of the General Education Board offered starved liberal arts institutions philanthropic support with the caveat that "their methods [become] adjusted to the civilization in which they exist," or when they criticized colleges for producing students who refused to "co-ordinate their lives with the social and industrial requirements of their civilization [because colleges] impeded the substitution of 'training' for book learning," as two white administrators phrased it.[80] And in Du Bois's view, it affected the African American community as a whole—not simply those privileged enough to be enrolled at Fisk in 1908—when vocational realism infiltrated the liberal arts college. "We are the University," he insisted. "For us the trustees hold this property; as our representatives these teachers teach. If this republic of letters suffers harm, the guilt lies on us and on our children's children."[81] This threat to "book learning" persisted well into the twentieth century.

Du Bois redoubled the reformist intent of his 1908 address in the next speech he delivered at Fisk, in June 1924. The educational tide had not significantly turned for black colleges in the sixteen intervening years.[82] This second address, "Diuturni Silenti," would inspire waves of student protest and infuse contemporary literature—including, as I will argue, Nella Larsen's *Quicksand*—with a New Negro politics grounded in the conditions of black higher education. A brief account of Fisk's sudden transformation in 1924 will help explain Du Bois's and Larsen's engagement with the institution. Earlier in the year, president Fayette McKenzie had succeeded in raising a million-dollar endowment for his school, gathering contributions from the General Education Board, the Carnegie Corporation, and the Slater Fund, as well as from prominent northern individuals. Unusually, McKenzie also raised $50,000 from white citizens of Nashville in what was a rare gesture of support for black higher education. Though the foundations had previously donated millions in financial aid to Hampton, Tuskegee, and the Little Tuskegees, none had offered such a grand sum to a liberal arts institution, nor had white citizens ever participated so actively in fund-raising. Thus this endowment came freighted with a demand for "compromise"—really appeasement—in the form of proof that Fisk students were social moderates despite the elite "literary training" they received in university. McKenzie responded to this demand by promptly disbanding the student government, the athletic association, and the *Fisk Herald,* one of the oldest and most respected campus literary publications in the nation. He forbade Greek letter societies, denied a request to start a university chapter of the NAACP, prohibited radical literature from the university library, and instituted a severe code of discipline and a strict dress code that disproportionately affected female students. While black and white colleges across the nation generally maintained strict rules of conduct in the early twentieth century, none regulated student behavior so stringently and at such cost to self-expression.

Du Bois's two Fisk orations do more than merely expatiate on views of higher education expressed more famously in *The Souls of Black Folk,* and indeed they form an important supplement to his classic work. Whereas Du Bois's 1908 address attacked the intellectual and curricular ramifications of correlation, his 1924 speech condemned the social pedagogy of conformity and conservatism that had overtaken this citadel of liberal education. Fisk now prohibited freedom of thought, expression, and behavior; students, he argued, should boycott the school until it had loosened its draconian social codes and made room for alumni on the board of trustees. In the months to follow, Du Bois commissioned a ferocious publicity campaign against Fisk and its "tainted philanthropy," as he termed it in a *Crisis* editorial, "Gifts and Education," resurrecting the *Fisk Herald* among a group of dissident alumni.[83] Students took even stronger measures. They papered campus with a list of grievances, petitioned trustees to consider their claims to academic freedom, and funneled letters of dissent through Du Bois to newspapers across the country, inaugurating the first significant rebellion on an African American university campus. After an evening uprising in a male residence hall in which Nashville's notoriously racist police brigade was called in to enforce order, a majority of Fisk students boycotted classes for ten weeks, causing McKenzie to resign from the presidency in April 1925.

The Fisk uprising was a signal moment in African American modernity for several reasons. Self-possession, independence, and bold claims to cultural capital and political power—all constitutive features of modernity—were clearly in evidence.[84] Significantly, the (white) president who was appointed in McKenzie's wake added courses in African American history and literature, developed a social science department under *Opportunity* editor and New Negro Renaissance figurehead Charles S. Johnson, and brought specialists on African and African American culture to Fisk campus for national conferences; in his first address to the Fisk community, students credited President Jones for rejecting "mid-Victorian ideals."[85] Du Bois hoped that Fisk students' success in bringing about collegiate reform would lead to further social protest: "They have the power, they have the wealth, but glory to God we still own our own souls and led by young men like these at Fisk, let us neither flinch nor falter but fight and fight and fight again."[86] And indeed, following the Fisk demonstrations, collegians across the nation rose up against curricular and disciplinary constraints, with significant uprisings overtaking Howard, Hampton, Tuskegee, Lincoln University, and Wilberforce University between 1925 and 1929. Students who participated in the 1927 rebellion at Hampton argued that they could no longer possess "a Du Bois ambition" alongside "a Booker T. Washington education" and demanded higher intellectual standards. In the spring of 1925 Alain Locke was briefly fired from Howard for his participation in the 1925 campus protest, and in 1926 Mordecai Johnson became Howard's first African American president. Though the individual cause of each rebellion varied, all combined social protest with intellectual engagement and galvanized national attention through the extensive coverage they received in the black press. Collectively, the protests indexed important changes in the tenor of black educational politics.[87]

The students' protest rhetoric brought together the institution of the college with the doctrines of self-expression and self-determination as dual foundations of an uplifted, modern black self. Davarian L. Baldwin has argued that New Negro selfhood was founded on an understanding of modernity as a break with the controlling structures of white supremacy, patriarchy, and philanthropy, and student protesters called attention to the particular virulence with which these structures came together at black colleges, to the detriment of their social, intellectual, and artistic freedom.[88] We might understand the modernity of the college protests in another way still, by noting that student activists rejected the "racial time" of vocational realism. Against a backdrop of chronic underfunding and scant political support for black higher education, the New Negro college uprisings instantiated a signal form of time appropriation, a process Michael Hanchard defines as a distinctly "Afro-Modern" revolt against the "unequal temporal dimensions of racial dynamics" that forced African American students to wait interminably for goods, services, and information that had grown obsolete by the time of their arrival.[89] Crucially, the student activists forwarded their mandate on the basis of an accelerated temporality, demanding immediate and unqualified access to the intellectual goods of modern American life. In doing so, they rejected the spatiotemporality of vocational realism as it persisted in the 1920s: recall that Washington offered his pedagogy of simultaneity—"head and hands together"[90]—as a solution to the perceived "gap" or lag inherent in intellectual activity undertaken without practical application. New Negro student activists succeeded in rerouting the direction of black higher education by reimagining an Afro-modern education as being grounded in acts of reading, writing, and speaking freely—free, that is, of the many constraints of vocational realism.

My purpose in sketching out these New Negro uprisings is to point to the discourse of correlation that lay at their core. If, as Gene Andrew Jarrett and Henry Louis Gates Jr. have argued, the period between Reconstruction and World War II was "the era of the myth of a New Negro, a New Negro in search of a cultural renaissance capable of accommodating it," then the 1920s college uprisings did much to catalyze that renaissance.[91] The major public events that institutionalized the Harlem Renaissance as a cultural movement overlapped with the duration of the Fisk rebellion, including the 1924 Civic Club "coming out party" celebrating the publication of Jessie Redmon Fauset's novel *There Is Confusion,* and *Survey Graphic*'s "Harlem" issue of March 1925. Moreover, the college protests make clear how deeply entrenched the Harlem Renaissance was in the social, historical, and intellectual currents of the South, not only by means of the southern migrants making their way northward in these years but also, crucially, in the contested program for industrial learning that took root in places like Nashville, Tennessee, and Hampton, Virginia. One Fisk trustee grumbled that rebellious students were turning "the noble Fisk into a place of jazz," equating demands for collegiate reform with that definitively modern black musical form.[92]

Du Bois objected most stringently to the way Fisk had dovetailed its social apparatus with the demands of white benefactors who sanctioned apartheid capitalism. His dispute with white philanthropy was "more than opposition to a program of education. It was opposition to a system and that system was part of the economic development of the United States at that time," as he put it in an autobiography published in 1968.[93] The philanthropic foundations that supported the liberal arts so unevenly also made unequal access to education a core part of Jim Crow policy. One system of inequality fit seamlessly into the other. The General Education Board's aim, for instance, was to create an "orderly and comprehensive *system*" of segregated learning that was "territorially comprehensive, harmoniously related [and] individually complete," one that would "discourage unnecessary duplication and waste and encourage economy and efficiency."[94] As it happens, Nella Larsen forwarded a similar critique of an "orderly and comprehensive system" in her 1928 novel *Quicksand,* creating a peripatetic heroine who discovers that school, pedagogical method, educational system, and ideas of racial uplift all dovetail uncomfortably with the broader constraints of white supremacy. I want to suggest that *Quicksand* offers a meditation on correlation as social form.

THE NEW NEGRO IN THE SYSTEM: NELLA LARSEN'S *QUICKSAND*

Quicksand opens onto the scene of a young teacher in distress. A litany of small insults and larger political assaults have marred Helga Crane's tenure as English instructor at Naxos, a southern educational institution that constitutes, in her view, nothing more than "a show place in the black belt." Most recently, Helga and the rest of the campus community had been forced to sit through the patronizing and racist homily of a visiting white preacher, whose proclamations about the obedience of "the Naxos products" filled her with "hot anger and seething resentment." It was bad enough that the preacher exhorted members of the community to behave submissively and keep their political aspirations in check; but the fact that the all-black audience at Naxos greeted his speech with enthusiastic applause brought Helga's rage to a boil. "The South. Naxos. Negro education. Suddenly she hated them all."[95] She decides to resign from her teaching post midway through the semester, with no next step in mind beyond her immediate escape north to Chicago.

When the principal presses Helga about her decision to leave Naxos, she at first offers an explanation that doesn't quite match her fury. "I—well—I don't seem to fit here," she stutters, seeming to drastically understate the case. But in fact Larsen's language is precise and even strategic when it points to Helga's lack of "fit" and describes Naxos as a "machine . . . a big knife with cruelly sharp edges ruthlessly cutting all to a pattern." Helga, Larsen writes, simply cannot achieve "the unmistakable Naxos mold"; she is incapable of being as "conformable," "naturalized," and, again, "fitted [for her] niche" as her peers. She finds herself unable, or perhaps unwilling, to conduct herself "in the manner of the Naxos products" and looks upon her students as unwitting "automatons" subject to the constraints of a "cruel educational machine." But the students, teachers, and administrators at Naxos cannot be held responsible for Helga's seeming failure to assimilate to the culture of the institution, for she recognizes that it is not so much the fault of the school as it is "the fault of the method, the general idea behind the system."[96]

Helga's escape from Naxos establishes a pattern of enthusiasm and acclimatization followed by hostility and migration that she will repeat many times over the course of *Quicksand*. But why is she stuck in this perpetual cycle of political and affective ambivalence? At Naxos, in Harlem, in Copenhagen, and finally in rural Alabama, Helga begins to assimilate to the conventions of her social environment and even grows to love it. Her disenchantment begins when she recognizes that the environment's governing ideas and methods do not fit with the autonomous life she wants to lead. In describing her protagonist's inability to adapt to

Naxos as a lack of *fit*, Larsen suggests that concepts that appear to join together quite naturally—a woman and her environment, a teacher and her school, a "race woman" and the surrounding ideology of uplift— somehow resist correlation when it comes to Helga. There is "a lack somewhere."[97] Larsen's industrial metaphors—a knife and its patterns, the processes of fitting a niche, achieving a mold, becoming a product— serve as commentary on the prevailing methods of black education and the philosophy of uplift that subtends it. And this critique is not limited to the early chapters of the novel, those that actually take place at Naxos. From *Quicksand*'s mechanical metaphorics to its discourse of aesthetics and overall narrative structure, Larsen's larger concern in the novel is with the very *idea* of correlation as a normative method of forging a whole out of disparate parts, a strategy that in its effort to fit things together disregards individual differences.

Larsen establishes her protagonist as a frustrated literary pedagogue from the first. Sitting in her tastefully decorated sitting room, Helga flings her teaching supplies—books and papers—across the room, "seeing in the mess a simile of her own earnest endeavor to inculcate knowledge into her indifferent classes." The narrator goes on:

> Yes, it was like that; a few of the ideas which she tried to put into the minds behind those baffling ebony, bronze, and gold faces reached their destination. The others were left scattered about. And, like the gay, indifferent wastebasket, it wasn't their fault. No, it wasn't the fault of those minds back of the diverse colored faces. It was, rather, the fault of the method, the general idea behind the system. Like her own hurried shot at the basket, the aim was bad, the material drab and badly prepared for its purpose.[98]

Here Larsen addresses both the local and the broader contexts of "method" at once. Part of what angers Helga is simply her impossible position as an English teacher in a school that places a higher priority on transmitting conservative social lessons than on scholarship—or, put another way, her condition as an English instructor teaching the vocabulary of manual labor. Each school day begins with "five hours of work and so-called education" in which "the material [is] drab and badly prepared for its purpose," but

Helga's fellow teachers still manage to be rigorous in imploring students to "*please* at least try to act like ladies and not like savages from the backwoods."[99] Training in bourgeois social codes exceeds and finally inhibits intellectual development at this particular black school. But seen in the broader context of the novel as a whole, Larsen's meditation on method transcends the specific institution of the school to encompass a critique of all institutions that seek to incrementally reform Jim Crow and that therefore persist in existing within it.

Helga discovers that she is not alone in her disgust for Naxos when her friends in Chicago and Harlem heap scorn on the southern institution. Even Dr. Robert Anderson leaves his position as principal to become a welfare worker in New York, a city whose "continuously gorgeous panorama" Helga genuinely loves at first, before she hates it. But she soon discovers that the ethic of racial uplift that reigns in Harlem merely reproduces the dynamics of suppression and imitation that soured her experience at Naxos, making the urban North as suffocating as the South. Her friend Anne Gray is "obsessed by the race problem" but still expresses contempt toward the black masses, silently cultivates the manners and cultural proclivities of white people, and polices the boundaries of Helga's prospective interracial relationships. Lecturing race woman Mrs. Hayes-Rore is committed to educating and uplifting African Americans but is a devastatingly unoriginal thinker and writer herself: her lectures are "merely patchworks of others' speeches and opinions," pasting together quotations from Frederick Douglass, W. E. B. Du Bois, and Booker T. Washington with "a few vinegary statements of her own." Furthermore, she intimates that Helga will fit more seamlessly into the Harlem bourgeoisie if she agrees to hide her scandalous white origins. Meanwhile, Helga's former fiancé, James Vayle, rises through the ranks to become assistant principal of Naxos despite holding plainly eugenicist views about the need for "Negroes of the better class" to keep pace with the fecundity of the African American masses, the very demographic his institution professes to serve. The black working classes stymie Vayle's desire for racial progress, as their intransigent poverty and seeming lack of civilization form a counterweight to the upward mobility of the race.[100]

In their efforts to elevate the black community, the novel's reformers, educators, and race women cannot accommodate—and in fact are actively hostile to—real differences in race, class, and national origins. The problem, of course, is that these differences govern Helga's identity as an orphan of mixed Danish and African American heritage. And so in each of these varying geographical and institutional settings, Helga experiences an epiphanic moment that reveals the hypocrisy lurking near the heart of racial uplift, provoking her "hot anger and seething resentment" and stirring her to "[recoil] in aversion."[101] There are a number of differences among the black college, bourgeois Harlem, modernist Europe, and the southern black church, but all these sites ultimately demand some degree of conformity and assimilation from Helga. Each partakes of the same "method, the general idea behind the system" that we might call *assimilation*—not just the pressure to assimilate to one or the other side of the color line, which George Hutchinson has astutely noted, but assimilation as Helga's lived experience of correlation as social form.[102] These vignettes establish the violence of conformity as *Quicksand*'s central problematic.

Quicksand is in many ways a profoundly antisocial novel. It is suspicious of all modes of relation, from those within organizations like the church and the school to those between individual relatives and romantic partners. Critics have offered a wide range of interpretations of the novel in the decades since Larsen was "rediscovered" and restored to the canon by black feminist scholars in the 1980s.[103] In her classic *Reconstructing Womanhood,* Hazel Carby identifies Helga's biracial status as "a narrative device of mediation" that renders her both insider and outsider to the racial discourse she encounters, and most subsequent criticism has situated Helga's alienation, cultural dualism, and perpetual movement within the thematic frames of sexuality and the color line.[104] And while issues of race, gender, and sexuality are, of course, absolutely central to Larsen's work, it is also the case that her disappointed narrative of antiassimilationism and retrenchment is built on the social, political, and rhetorical scaffolding of the African American school—itself a crucial site for defining modern conceptions of race, class, and belonging. Larsen's critique of the methods of race uplift joins a conversation about the theory and practice of black higher education that was many decades long by 1928. While public discourse on black intellectual culture was no longer as exclusively focused on institutions of higher learning by the time *Quicksand* was published, the novel reveals the particular salience of these pedagogical debates to the New Negro moment.

Larsen was intimately familiar with the two schools I have chronicled in this chapter. At age sixteen, she attended Fisk University for the 1907–8 academic year, and from 1915 to 1916 she worked as head nurse at Tuskegee's John A. Memorial Hospital and Nurse Training School before resigning in disgust at the work conditions she found there. Although Larsen finished her term of study at Fisk at the end of the 1907–8 school year, she did not witness Du Bois's incendiary speech at her commencement ceremony that June. A mere four days before Du Bois delivered his "Galileo Galilei" address, a young Nella Larsen (then known as Nellie) was suspended from Fisk along with ten other students, seven of whom were women. She was expelled for "[dressing] in a manner contrary to the wishes of several of the faculty," as one Fisk employee put it in a letter to the college president that was later taken up in a faculty meeting.[105] Larsen's decision to break dress code amounted to a small-scale rebellion against the university's restrictions on women's freedom and self-expression, a refusal to comply with the social regulations that structured the college's vision of racial uplift. She had permanently departed Nashville once Du Bois arrived. However, the reformist spirit of her small revolt lives on in the older author's furious commencement message of a few days later, even if the timing of the two events was nothing more than coincidence. (Or perhaps it is no coincidence at all; could it have fed Du Bois's righteous anger to know that ten Fisk students had just been expelled for reasons that were essentially superficial and that clearly demonstrated the conservative values held by the university administration?) There is evidence that Larsen's aesthetic presentation rankled authorities at Tuskegee too: the biographical narrative she composed to accompany Knopf's release of *Quicksand* characterized her time as head nurse there as follows: "Her dislike of conditions [at Tuskegee], and the school authorities' dislike of her appearance and manner were both so intense that after a year they parted with mutual disgust and relief."[106] Booker T. Washington regularly emphasized that women's dress, appearance, and "physical culture" were matters of great importance, noting in *Working with the Hands* that "special rules governing the conduct of the girls are made known to each girl upon her arrival" at Tuskegee.[107] No doubt Larsen's passion for color and fashion violated many of those rules.

Critics have discerned many autobiographical notes in *Quicksand*, and the issue of "[dressing] in a manner contrary to the wishes" of others is no exception.[108] Helga Crane shares the young Larsen's love of bright colors, sartorial finery, and aesthetics, possessing an intense "urge for beauty" and a lifelong desire for "nice things."[109] Helga's artistic sensibility assumes momentous importance from the first page. When the novel begins, we find her sitting in a bedroom whose décor and general aesthetic orientation convey important details of her character: there is a "single reading lamp, dimmed by a great black and red shade," a "blue Chinese carpet," and a stool covered in "oriental silk." The room manifests a "rare and intensely personal taste." Helga may continually fail to fit into any organized social institutions or communities, but an "observer would have thought her *well fitted* to that framing of light and shade" (italics added).[110] She fits, that is, within her own aesthetic universe, if nowhere else; color, clothing, and aesthetic judgment provide the kind of wholeness for Helga that Naxos, Chicago, Harlem, Copenhagen, and Alabama never do.

Helga's self-expression, evident in the clothing she chooses to wear and the way she decorates her personal space, signals an autonomous streak that cannot be assimilated to the various racial schemes through which she moves. Her acquaintances' and institutional affiliations' efforts to regulate her appearance fuel the cycle of attachment, dejection, and refusal that she repeats over the course of the novel. In a clear nod to Larsen's own expulsion from Fisk and to the similarly prohibitive culture she found at Tuskegee, Helga's colleagues at Naxos elect black, gray, brown, and navy blue as "the most becoming colors for colored people," discouraging yellow, green, and red, to the detriment of aesthetic felicity as well as race pride. Faculty members nominally committed to race consciousness are unable to perceive "the inherent racial need for gorgeousness" that draws Helga away from colors that "destroyed the luminous tones lurking in their dusky skins" and toward "dark purples, royal blues, rich greens, deep reds, in soft, luxurious woolens, or heavy, clinging silks." In contrast, her Danish aunt and uncle strive to exaggerate her "exotic" beauty by dressing her in "flaunting flashy things," intending to advance their social standing by capitalizing on her racial otherness. Helga's innate appreciation of color and dress and her discerning taste are powerless in comparison to her relatives' desire to exhibit her as a "strange species of pet dog" and make of her a winning spectacle. Aesthetics thus figure alternately as a vehicle of creative expression and even resistance, as when Helga seeks to counter the "suppression of individuality and beauty" at Naxos, and as an external threat to individual autonomy, as when her European relatives dress her in "an exotic, almost savage way" and encourage her to sit for a portrait that objectifies her in the manner of "some disgusting sensual creature." Observing the way her reform-minded friend Anne ostracizes the "beautiful, calm, cool" Audrey Denney, who dresses vibrantly and socializes with white people, breeds in Helga a deep disgust with Harlem, precipitating her departure. Critics generally agree that Helga's aesthetic and sartorial orientation symbolizes a capacity for artistic self-expression that she can exercise in no other context.[111]

Yet Larsen also represents aesthetics more capaciously as a site for the expression or containment of individual difference. In this way, she integrates aesthetic concerns into *Quicksand*'s larger critique of the institutional forces of conformity. Du Bois's 1924 Fisk address is instructive here. In it, he contends that a strict dress code is more than simply a rote disciplinary matter, because clothing is a uniquely expressive medium for those living inside the relentless ugliness of Jim Crow. "There was once a colored leader who sneered at the pianos in the homes of poor colored people," Du Bois begins, "but it was pointed out [that] it was a fine thing for the poor to spend on music even that which they might have spent on bread. Did it not show the innate beauty of their souls?" A university makes the same mistake when it "sneers and raves and passes all sorts of rules against the overdressing of its students, particularly of its women." As long as Jim Crow cars are "dirty, ugly, unpleasant" and black neighborhoods are "as muddy and nasty and unkempt and unprotected as possible," black citizens will "fill their starved souls with overuse of silk and color" and choose to "flame in their clothing."[112] Since ugliness is an effect of systemic racism, artistic expressions of beauty, from music to fashion, constitute a genuine political intervention. Larsen builds on Du Bois's insight that any institution that colludes with the forces of ugliness reaffirms its place in a correlated social system.

In many ways, then, *Quicksand*'s discourse of color and resistance reflects Larsen's own youthful protest and registers the impact of the 1920s collegiate reform movements. While not precisely allegorizing the Fisk uprisings—Helga's progress from the regulations of Naxos to her commodification in Copenhagen does not quite match the teleology of protest—Larsen weaves the major themes of New Negro collegiate reform into her novel. In so doing, she thickens the novel's social protest by showing how correlation continued to shape discourses of racial uplift in the midst of the Harlem Renaissance, a period that was generally understood to be characterized by "an unusual outburst of creative expression"[113] and "deliberate flight . . . from medieval America to modern."[114]

But if the novel is premised on Helga's flight from Naxos, what explains her decision to return to the South at the end of the novel? Following two years in Copenhagen and another several months back in New York, she marries "the grandiloquent Reverend Mr. Pleasant Green, that rattish yellow man" in a frenzy of religious and sexual excitement. Helga and the reverend marry just one day after they meet at a storefront church service in Harlem and he presides over her sudden religious conversion. In other words, Helga makes these momentous decisions hastily—and with no more forethought than she exercised in resolving to leave Naxos. She quite literally falls into the church in the midst of a rainstorm, "drenched and disheveled" and suffering from "frayed nerves," and similarly falls into marriage "in the confusion of seductive repentance." She and her husband take up residence at his parish in rural Alabama, where Helga assumes the role of hybrid teacher–settlement worker among neighbors whom Larsen depicts quite flatly as the uneducated black folk masses—a "scattered and primitive flock." In the first flush of her new life, experiencing an initial exhilaration with which readers are now familiar and of which they are thoroughly suspicious, her "young joy and zest for the uplifting of her fellow men came back to her." Helga is fired up with reformist energy: she vows "to subdue the cleanly scrubbed ugliness of her own surroundings to soft inoffensive beauty, and to help the other women to do likewise," and she tries "to interest the women in what she considered more appropriate clothing and in inexpensive ways of improving their homes according to her ideas of beauty." She devotes her attention to matters of wardrobe and etiquette and promises to help the women understand why "gay" and "frilly" items of clothing are "not quite the proper things for Sunday wear." She has lofty plans of starting a sewing circle that will instruct "wild" children "in ways of gentler deportment."[115]

Helga seems oblivious to the many layers of irony built into her new position, in which her task is to leverage her own aesthetic sensibility in the service of uplift, while ambivalent parishioners politely ignore her efforts to reform them just as she shrugged off the clothing police at Naxos. After all her struggles, Helga has now become the arbiter of racial convention. Her erstwhile romantic rival in Alabama, Clementine Richards, even considers *her* "a poor thing without style." In her efforts to become a "helpmate" to the uplift of her new community, Helga enacts the same conformist gestures that had alienated her from Naxos, Harlem, and Copenhagen, trying on for size a role that ultimately doesn't fit. Once again, she encounters that familiar feeling of "dissatisfaction" and "asphyxiation," and she longs for independence more completely than ever before. Yet this time she has children whom she refuses to leave behind. By the end of the novel, Helga has fallen irretrievably into the quicksand of unhappy motherhood, thinking only of "freedom and cities, [and] clothes and books" as she prepares to give birth to her fifth child.[116]

In depicting Helga this way, Larsen surely capitalizes on ironies her protagonist never detects. For whatever idealism may have inspired Helga before the story opens, the character we encounter in *Quicksand* is not at all fond of reform; in fact, she seems to possess precisely the inverse of a "joy and zest for the uplifting of her fellow men." She belittles herself for having once been one of "those immature people who have dreamed dreams of doing good to their fellow men." Later she oozes sarcasm toward uplift activities at the Chicago YWCA and at welfare institutions in Harlem. Larsen is characteristically sharp on this point: "'Uplift,' sniffed

Helga contemptuously" in response to her friend Anne's account of "the needs and ills of the race." Helga's struggle all along has been to preserve individual difference within institutional structures of belonging, to remain a unique and autonomous self while also fitting in as a member of a collective. That she jumps at the opportunity to serve as a "helpmate" to the masses in the South suggests that she never quite escapes from the clutches of this desire in all its perversely circuitous and regressive force. Yet Helga turns to teaching and reform work in Alabama under the rubric of her newfound religious belief, only to find that the "fatuous belief in the white man's God" is a system of belief akin to those she encountered at Naxos and in Harlem, and one that suffers from the same overarching weaknesses and hypocrisies: clannishness, elitism, conformism, and allegiance to racist systems of oppression. Helga eventually marvels at how "the white man's God must laugh at the great joke he had played on them." Thus both times that Helga is lured south for the purpose of uplift, the racist underpinnings of organized religion extinguish her fleeting passion for reform when she discovers that even the balm of spiritual belief finds its place within the Jim Crow system. Furthermore, in both moments of recognition and despair, Helga turns instinctively to a book—first to Marmaduke Pickthall's *Said the Fisherman* and later to Anatole France's "The Procurator of Judea"—only to quickly abandon it. She is a frustrated English teacher and literary aesthete to the very end.[117]

Scholars have long puzzled over a conclusion that seems to present Helga in an uncharacteristic light.[118] But the narrative symmetries linking the beginning and ending of *Quicksand* suggest that Helga's final social configuration in the Deep South is hardly unanticipated. These continuities obtain not in Helga's progressive character development or in a satisfying plot resolution but, rather, in Larsen's ongoing critique of method. As I have argued, Helga's antiassimilationist quest for a better "fit" consistently registers as ambivalence, manifesting in swift and often surprising changes of heart and conviction. We might say of the protagonist's relentless seeking after autonomy-within-community that she faces the same philosophical difficulty that critic Leela Gandhi articulates in relation to the problems of anti-imperialist friendship: "Can I oppose radical individualism with community while opposing communitarianism in such a way that I don't return to a position of radical individualism/autonomy?"[119] Or to put it, presumptuously, in Helga's terms, Can I find a community that will serve as my home but also let me be who I am, an environment that will neither assimilate nor exile me for all of the ways I don't fit? Rather than resolving that problem—Larsen's conclusions never do that—*Quicksand* ends on a note of irresolution that renders Gandhi's individualism–communitarian dyad an open question. Helga's final institutional identity as a minister's wife is finally not at all surprising in light of the novel's abiding dialogue with sites of social and educational pedagogy: school and church, education and religion prove to be basically equivalent means of "adjust[ing] exactly, so as to form a continuous whole," ways of binding individual to community that ultimately falter under the constraints of Jim Crow. In this way, *Quicksand* stages one of the central conceptual problems of the Harlem Renaissance: by what method should black artists and intellectuals forge a collective identity?

"DESPITE THE WAILING OF THE PURISTS"

> A people may become great through many means, but there is only one measure by which its greatness is recognized and acknowledged. The final measure of the greatness of all peoples is the amount and standard of the literature and art they have produced. The world does not know that a people is great until that people produces great literature and art. No people that has produced great literature and art has ever been looked upon by the world as distinctly inferior. The status of the Negro in the United States is more a question of national mental attitude toward the race than of actual conditions. And nothing will do more to change that mental attitude and raise his status than a demonstration of intellectual parity by the Negro through the production of literature and art.[120]

Elsewhere in the literary archive of the Harlem Renaissance, debates over correlation continued to structure discussions of literature as a vehicle of social change. It was owing to a series of transformations in concepts of literary method that a self-conscious "civil rights arts movement" was able to emerge in the 1920s with Nella Larsen as a central, if predictably ambivalent, contributor. Larsen participated in the Harlem Renaissance both as the writer of two feted novels and as a librarian at the 135th Street Branch of the New York Public Library, where she arranged influential lectures and exhibits under the leadership of Ernestine Rose.[121] By the time the Harlem Renaissance reached its high point in the second half of the 1920s, industrial training had ceased to be the default mode of black education and dovetailing was beginning to recede from regular practice. Campus rebellions across the nation, new and expanded sources of financial support for black education, and a general wave of modernization that introduced the elective system to black and white universities alike were beginning to change African American higher education.[122] In the 1920s, Tuskegee added a separate College Department, and by 1930, twenty-one thousand black students were enrolled in colleges or universities across the nation, an increase of more than ten times the 1919 figure.[123] By 1933, Du Bois himself could assert that "the industrial school has almost surrendered its program."[124] Although institutions of black higher learning continued to train the intellectual elite, there was also a sense by mid-decade that the cultural center of gravity had shifted with the Great Migration from a university system that had historically struggled to keep books in the classroom to a cultural movement founded on the reformist power of literature in its diverse material formats. The ongoing conversation regarding the social utility of the literary arts for black citizens came to orbit around the myriad institutions of the Harlem Renaissance rather than the institution of the college. Kelly Miller noted in a 1926 editorial, "The cultural life of the race is not now focusing at Fisk nor Atlanta, or Howard or Wilberforce, but in New York," and he urged black colleges to incorporate into their curricula the "new cultural motive in the direction of the Negro Renaissance."[125] Echoing Miller's sentiments, the president who replaced Booker T. Washington at Tuskegee leaped to connect the turn-of-the-century college's success in fostering interracial partnerships, professional development, and racial leadership to the new cultural movement centered in the North. "What was then the faith of the few has become the conviction of many," Robert R. Moton claimed in an essay that appeared in the anthology *The New Negro*. "The confidence sown then is bringing forth a harvest of good-will now, and the field is being enlarged continually."[126]

Of course, many of the black artists, writers, and intellectuals who produced work associated with the Harlem Renaissance had attended the colleges we have surveyed in this chapter, and they carried those formative experiences into their work. Claude McKay left his home in Jamaica to enroll at Tuskegee in 1912 but swiftly grew to dislike "the semi-military machine existence" he found there and transferred to Kansas State College before moving to New York City in 1914, and James Weldon Johnson formed impressions during his years at Atlanta University that no doubt shaped his portrait of the institution in *The Autobiography of an Ex-Coloured Man*, to name only two examples. Institutions of black higher education were a powerful force in the literary culture of the Harlem Renaissance in ways quickly discerned through biography alone.[127]

Many scholars have ably described the institutional contours of the Harlem Renaissance, and I won't rehash their efforts here. But it is worth noting that these two reformist contexts—the college and the arts movement—were, in many ways, institutionally and intellectually continuous.[128] Whatever the individual goals of novelists and poets who are now included in standard historiographies of the Harlem Renaissance, the public figures (many of them university professors) who choreographed the events and assembled the publications that advertised the Renaissance to the world—W. E. B. Du Bois, Alain Locke, Charles S. Johnson, Kelly Miller, Jessie Redmon Fauset—imagined the movement as fundamentally an expansive educational exercise. The movement provided an institutional structure through which to expose the broader public to African American writers and themes and was a means of bringing white readers "into contact with the general world of letters to which they have been for the most part timid and inarticulate strangers," as Charles S. Johnson put it in an editorial announcing the 1925 *Opportunity* literary prize.[129] Harlem Renaissance writers and culture brokers tied the New Negro's "racial awakening" to cultural expression both as a key to interpreting art (a critical method) and as a justification for art's value (a social purpose).

The university and the Harlem Renaissance were also connected through shared structures of patronage and philanthropy. William H. Baldwin Jr., white railroad heir and Urban League board member, helped finance and advertise the movement, inviting relevant white dignitaries and philanthropists to Renaissance cultural events just as his father had done for Tuskegee. Millionaire philanthropists J. G. Phelps Stokes, Julius Rosenwald, and William E. Harmon expanded their attention from education to the arts in the 1920s, establishing foundations to promote black literary and cultural expression. As the movement's literary institutions—periodicals, anthologies, literary competitions, books—came to embody the uplift of a "new" race, Renaissance culture brokers rescripted the arts and letters as a practical vehicle of social reform.

We have seen how proponents of vocational education found manual training a more practical avenue to collective uplift than book learning. In similar fashion, leaders of the Harlem Renaissance were strategic in electing literature an instrument of reform. The turn-of-the-century college and the Harlem Renaissance are most strongly linked in this conceptual way: through the question of literary method. In the years following World War I and the Red Summer of 1919, it was by no means obvious that novels and poetry would catalyze the social changes necessary in the United States. And yet after a decade of quietly publishing black poetry and prose in the *Crisis*, W. E. B. Du Bois suddenly announced in the magazine's April 1920 issue that "a renaissance of American Negro literature is due."[130] Du Bois had long believed in the productive links between publication and activism, but he began in the 1920s to articulate and advocate for the precise connections between aesthetics and social justice.[131] He insisted in his provocative 1926 essay "Criteria of Negro Art" that literature "is part of the great fight we are carrying on and [that] it represents a forward and an upward look—a pushing onward," and, for a few years at least, he shifted the focus of the *Crisis* from documentary and sociological prose to more creative and belletristic writing.[132] Du Bois acknowledged that his detractors might question the value of "[turning] aside to talk about Art" for a civil rights organization like the NAACP, but he concluded that literature represented an untried method of "pushing onward," a newly useful vehicle in the "great fight" for collective uplift. Du Bois's view that "all art is propaganda and ever must be" incited a string of responses from Langston Hughes, George Schuyler, and others.

These documents would become foundational position pieces of the cultural movement.[133]

Du Bois's colleague at the NAACP, James Weldon Johnson, similarly conceived of the Harlem Renaissance along methodological lines. In a 1928 article published in *Harper's*, Johnson nominated "intellectual and artistic achievement by Negroes," or the "art approach," as the current "method of approaching a solution of the race question."[134] Johnson acknowledged that the literary approach was not precisely new—the "Negro has been using this method for a very long time; for a longer time than he has used any other method"—but argued that its novelty lay in the robust infrastructure the New Negro Renaissance offered for supporting and institutionalizing black literary production. The literary method was "new" inasmuch as the Harlem Renaissance connected black writers with a broader reading public.

Indeed, Harlem Renaissance critics of every stripe announced their interventions in the literary field by referring to the trope of social utility. In his introduction to the *New Negro* anthology, Alain Locke identified cultural production as one of the "constructive channels opening out into which the balked social feelings of the American Negro can flow freely." Conceding that increased political participation and representation promised the "greatest rehabilitation" for the race, he claimed that "for the present, more immediate hope rests in the revaluation by white and black alike of the Negro in terms of his artistic endowments and cultural contributions, past and prospective." In this foundational document, Locke's rhetoric of adjusting aims to conditions and of using available means "for the present" evokes the same discourse of immediacy and local context that Washington, Bacon, and others used to defend industrial education. And though literary representation figured a merely transitional phase in advance of greater social transformations to come, it enabled the New Negro cultural producer to become "a collaborator and participant in American civilization" rather than "a beneficiary and ward," progressing from "the arid fields of controversy and debate to the productive fields of creative expression." In Locke's view, literature is socially meaningful—politically strategic—because the public recognition it attracts will "prove the key to that revaluation of the Negro which must precede or accompany any considerable further betterment of race relationships." Literary "self-expression and spiritual development" will complement the "old and unfinished task of making material headway and progress," thus at once enriching a black cultural tradition and aiding in collective social advancement. Locke and Du Bois may have been divided on the question of propaganda and art—Locke claimed this was a monotonous conjunction—but both understood literature to be a forcible instrument of social expression.[135]

Harlem Renaissance leaders even reinterpreted Washington's antirepresentational preference for "the visible, the tangible" as being constitutive of literature's social power. Charles S. Johnson, one of the chief figureheads of the Renaissance, wrote an article entitled "The Social Philosophy of Booker T. Washington" that detected traces of the Tuskegeean's philosophy in the current arts movement. Written in 1928, Johnson's article interprets Washington's deferral of politics and embrace of economic progress as a canny means of trumping white racism: "Since men hold passionately to opinions which are founded upon intangible emotions, the wiser strategy would shift proof from a subjective to and [*sic*] objective plane, from immaterial belief to visual reality." Instead of challenging a white southern citizenry that oppressed its black neighbors, Johnson argues, Washington's method "would constantly divert attention from abstract and undefinable theories while it laid an unmoveable foundation at the base of this scorn." Johnson construes Washington's aversion to "the abstract" as an activist circumvention of white people's "abstract and undefinable" racial prejudices rather than as an intellectual position that shaped the course of African American intellectual practice for decades. Johnson begins by affirming the correlationist social philosophy on its original terms, but he takes his argument a step further by arguing that the foundation "of abiding culture and civilization" that Washington laid at Tuskegee is visible in the institutions of the Harlem Renaissance. Where Washington relied on the "objective plane" of economically "visual reality" to facilitate racial uplift, the contemporary school of black writers and artists, "in their new representations of Negro life are doing the very thing for which he found a phrase." That is, New Negro literary art—or "representation"—constitutes the very same "tangible proof" that Washington once located in *opposition* to intellectual and literary engagement. In this stunning feat of reinterpretation, Johnson asserts that the Washingtonian method had migrated wholesale to the Harlem Renaissance, where "art" now substituted for the earlier instrumentality of "work." Art, he concludes, "is but an elaboration of Washington's principles of stressing work rather than the rewards of work."[136] New Negro art becomes the concrete sign of progress that manual labor's tangible outcomes—the brick or the cabbage—had earlier figured for Washington.

Efforts to instrumentalize literature would again fall out of favor as Renaissance writers moved further afield in their propagandistic aims. Yet here too, critiques of older Renaissance statesmen would borrow from correlation's conceptual vocabulary. In 1926, a group of younger writers headed by Wallace Thurman founded a short-lived avant-garde literary publication called *Fire!!*, based on a theory of artistic value that diverged from those of the established Renaissance literati. *Fire!!* did not intend to use literature to undermine racism but, rather, sought to undermine the artistically moribund, conservative notion that art and uplift were necessarily linked. The problem, as Thurman saw it, was that "Negroes in America [felt] they must always exhibit specimens from the college rather than from the kindergarten, specimens from the parlor rather than from the pantry," thereby sanitizing literary subject matter and stifling formal experimentation.[137] Literary expression needed to be freed from the clutches of social utility and from "application" of every kind. As we have seen in the collegiate reform movement and in *Quicksand*, "freedom of expression" was a key concern of New Negro cultural politics, but many of the younger writers associated with the arts movement came increasingly to interpret this freedom within modernist and avant-garde paradigms as opposed to an older, social protest tradition. George Hutchinson's masterful biography of Nella Larsen has shown that the novelist was affiliated with both the avant-gardist and propaganda–Talented Tenth wings of the Harlem Renaissance without allying herself entirely with either group.[138] More importantly, Larsen's publicly noncommittal stance on matters of art, uplift, and literary method enabled her two brief novels to speak for themselves and enabled *Quicksand* in particular to weave the methodological foundation underlying these divisions into the fabric of its narrative.

Even if turn-of-the-century debates over educational methods helped establish the critical and artistic fault lines of the Harlem Renaissance, the terms of that debate were revised and in many cases overturned. Perhaps the greatest reversal of all is the way in which Harlem Renaissance artists and affiliates redefined "the modern." Late nineteenth- and early twentieth-century industrial training embodied the modern idea in American educational theory. Progressive educators, Addams and Dewey among them, saw in Washington's dovetailing method a logical extension of Pestalozzi's doctrine that education should be relevant to the real life of a particular community (think of the Tuskegeean's insistence that his methods responded to "actual needs"). Addams and Dewey understood correlation as an African American inflection of similar pedagogies found at Hull-House and Montessori schools and within immigrant-geared vocational institutes.[139] Such a discourse framed traditional book learning as pedagogically archaic by comparison; Washington named it "the old-time method of teaching" to shore up its irrelevance to the lives of black citizens, and even Kelly Miller begrudgingly agreed that humanistic study represented "the old ideal" in comparison to "the modern bias."[140]

Yet as I have sought to show in this chapter, the dovetailing method constituted a particular variety of modern education that was endemic to African American life under Jim Crow. The modernity of correlation cannot be easily generalized to the experiences of other groups. In *Democracy and Social Ethics,* Addams described a mode of educating immigrant and working-class students, who "use their hands and eyes all the time," that would "take actual conditions and [make] them the basis for a large and generous method of education."[141] Dewey, for his part, rejected any strict opposition between industrial and literary training and maintained that all modern education must be necessarily vocational.[142] However, these capital-*P* Pragmatic theories of education did not speak to the political reality of black students. Contemporary scholars repeat this critical miscomprehension to their peril: when Mark McGurl contends in an otherwise illuminating analysis of *Quicksand* that Larsen's novel "represents a transitional moment *within* the discourse of progressive education, when the movement's initial thrust toward the efficient assimilation and vocational training of the immigrant (here African-American) working class began to turn . . . toward the fostering of the child's 'originality' and capacities for self-expression," he conceives of the institution of the school as a generalizable case.[143] Such a position forgets that unlike the white immigrant, who might move freely among vocational institute, public high school, and state college, black students could rarely find either alternative or supplement to an educational system largely dictated by the vicissitudes of white philanthropy. That Progressive Era black education was designed "to form a compact or harmonious whole or company" and to fit so neatly within the "actual conditions" of the Jim Crow system is precisely why the stakes of the struggle were so high.

The practical lesson plans, conservative social codes, and abridged curricula of real colleges like Tuskegee and Fisk and fictional ones like Naxos were not the sorry prehistory of Progressive reform's enlightened plan for black students. These qualities were precisely constitutive of "the modern idea" in Progressive education in the late nineteenth and early twentieth centuries. The circumscription for which I have taken correlation and vocational realism as figures represented the very heart of the modern as it shaped African American intellectual opportunity well into the twentieth century, right up until collegiate reformers in the 1920s demanded systemic change under the banner of a new, and newly modern, racial consciousness. It remained for those organizers and writers to redefine modernity and social reform as joint features of African American intellectual and literary engagement and for later generations to continue the struggle.

In chapter 4 I explore one final conjunction of literature and reform by turning to a cohort of white American writers who immersed themselves in very different sites of modern industry and habitation. To undercover authors writing in the early years of professional social science and literary modernism, firsthand experience trumped the authority of books every time. Yet they also situated *writing itself* as an institutional setting of reform.

4

Forms of Mediation

UNDERCOVER LITERATURE

In 1892, Jane Addams stood in front of an audience at the School of Applied Ethics in Plymouth, Massachusetts, and issued an appeal for cross-class understanding. The lecture she delivered roused the packed audience of middle-class summer school attendees, and it soon reached an even larger public through various publication routes: first as an article in *Forum,* next in an 1893 collection of essays entitled *Philanthropy and Social Progress,* and years later as a core chapter in her 1910 memoir *Twenty Years at Hull-House,* where it was retitled "The Subjective Necessity for Social Settlements." Part of what made Addams's address so memorable for these different listeners and readers was the faith it evinced in cross-class intimacy as a powerful social force, a force capable of generating authentic social knowledge and a revivified democracy.[1] Her argument, in fact, makes social distance the defining problem of urban American modernity and white middle-class longing its most potent expression:

> You may remember the forlorn feeling which occasionally seizes you when you arrive early in the morning a stranger in a great city: the stream of laboring people goes past you as you gaze through the plate-glass window of your hotel; you see hard working men lifting great burdens; you hear the driving and jostling of huge carts and your heart sinks with a sudden sense of futility. The door opens behind you and you turn to the man who brings you in your breakfast with a quick sense of human fellowship. You find yourself praying that you may never lose your hold on it all. A more poetic prayer would be that the great mother breasts of our common humanity, with its labor and suffering and its homely comforts,

may never be withheld from you. You turn helplessly to the waiter and feel that it would be almost grotesque to claim from him the sympathy you crave because civilization has placed you apart, but you resent your position with a sudden sense of snobbery. Literature is full of portrayals of these glimpses.[2]

Addams's tone is strikingly melancholic here. She palpably yearns for direct, reciprocal contact between rich and poor, for a bridge more meaningful than fleeting observation, as she gropes toward Chicago's working classes in pursuit of "our common humanity." Yet even as she longs for this intimacy, Addams inserts some distance between herself and her feelings by speaking in the second person, commanding listeners to identify with an inner life described as essentially inauthentic.

If the unmet desire for "human fellowship" across class lines is the problem, then the settlement house—a site that exists to mediate and institutionalize cross-class fellowship—is Addams's solution. As earlier chapters of this book have shown, contemporary reformers and educators proposed a range of alternative sites of recuperation. Beyond the settlement house, the working girls' club, and the black college, a generation of modern writers and intellectuals also sought to infuse their work with "the barbarities of immediate experience," avidly pursuing what T. J. Jackson Lears has memorably called "the cult of experience."[3] Pragmatist philosophers John Dewey and William James provided an important conceptual framework for this endeavor when they theorized the epistemological importance of personal experience and the experimental quest for truth in their writing. This book has been principally concerned with these very themes: recall that Booker T. Washington's vocational realism represented a significant effort to eliminate any conflict between book knowledge and real, firsthand experience within Jim Crow, while the working girls' club movement endeavored to bridge the near and the far through friendships founded on comparison.

But what of the *literary* charisma that the "laboring people" held for Addams and her peers? Her appeal crystallizes a widespread tendency among turn-of-the-century authors working across genres to conceive of disadvantaged citizens not only as the means for a potential cure for the neurasthenia that besieged many privileged Americans at this time but also as a vital firsthand resource for their writing—a kind of pliant raw material for prose grown similarly moribund or unresponsive. When read at a different angle, then, it is possible to see Addams calling for more than just a more integrated urban civic culture. She also demands a new literary method capable of bridging the social and representational gaps that defined her age. After all, the problem of social distance also shapes the boundaries of literary expression. Addams notes that "literature is full of portrayals of these glimpses" of cross-class union; yet in using the word "*glimpses,*" she implies that such literary representations of this amity as do exist are strictly ephemeral, certainly more fleeting than the comparatively stable, durational work of "settling." She concludes, in fact, that no author has yet been able to represent the socio-affective moment of cross-class proximity and yearning in any meaningful way. "These longings are the physical complement of the 'Intimations of Immortality,' on which no ode has yet been written," Addams muses. "To portray these would be the work of a poet, and it is hazardous for any but a poet to attempt it."[4] And so—only slightly aslant of her lecture's central purpose—the Hull-House founder issues a tantalizing literary challenge: if social reform sites remove the "plate-glass window" that separates the middle-class spectator from the laboring mass, enabling the waiter to return his patron's sympathetic glance as though "civilization" no longer divides them, then what literary forms might effectively serve as adjunct to these class-bridging institutions? What might a *literary* practice of bridging gulfs and of protracting glimpses look like?

In this chapter I seek to answer these questions by turning to an archive of American literature that takes the cultural sensibility of cross-class proximity to its absolute limit. In the years immediately surrounding the turn of the twentieth century, dozens of privileged white Americans temporarily renounced their worldly comforts to live and work in disguise among the poor. Their overarching goal in journeying downward into the world of waitress, shop clerk, and factory worker was to gather raw material for articles and books. Some had trained as sociologists, and others worked as activists or reporters, which means that this genre can also profitably be read as a story about the birth of investigative journalism and social science. But the authors I address here set their sights squarely on literary accomplishment. The genre I will call *undercover literature* embodies in its very existence the commitment to modalities of contact, proximity, and comparison that animates Addams's address in "The Subjective Necessity for Social Settlements" and that further drives the social reform ventures that are the subject of this book.[5]

By the time the undercover genre took off at the turn of the century, reform writers and social investigators had already done much to document the wretched conditions of urban-industrial life, a pursuit that worked in concert—and occasionally in conflict—with a national infrastructure of reform institutions dedicated to ameliorating those conditions. But the authors of undercover narratives hoped to learn from the *subjective* experience of living and laboring shorn of their class advantages. They believed that the opportunity to interact as seeming equals in working-class work spaces and boardinghouses—terrain that felt, to middle- and leisure-class authors, like a rare plane of social equilibrium—would have potentially revolutionary opportunities for literary form and practice. I will argue that undercover literature rose to a position of relative prominence within early twentieth-century U.S. literary culture in part because its methodological embrace of firsthand experience tapped into a rich vein of Progressive Era social politics, but also because its methodology yielded novel forms of literary expression.[6]

The case of Cornelia Stratton Parker exemplifies several key features of undercover authorship. A former student of Thorstein Veblen at the New School for Social Research, Parker taught social economics at the University of California, Berkeley, and was widely known as a lecturer on "the labor problem." However, by 1920 she had come to believe that the problems of industrial labor required not an expositor who was purely academic and not one born and bred within the working classes but, rather, a writer willing to "see the world through their eyes." No longer simply a reader, this expositor would assume a "role": "In California I had studied the theoretical side of labor problems, guided university classes through factories and factories, and read, pondered, and theorized," she explained, but "I yearned to get a firsthand grip on what it was all about.... I wanted to work in factories so far as it was possible in the role of a *bona-fide* factory girl myself—no college graduate snooping or sob-sistering." Parker offered herself as mediator: she donned a faded dress "from the rag bag" and a pair of "very darned" stockings, unwrapped her first-ever piece of chewing gum, and became Connie Park, working girl.[7] She spent the winter of 1920–21 toiling in chocolate, brass, and dress factories, a bleachery mill, a laundry, and a hotel in New York City and its environs, and she wrote a book about her experiences titled *Working with the Working Woman*. Though Parker offers her revelations as though they are brand new, she was hardly treading new ground. By the time Harper and Brothers published her book in 1922, scores of affluent white Americans had written undercover texts, including such well-known authors as Stephen Crane and Jack London, and the genre was already winding its way out of fashion.[8] But the fact that Parker envisioned herself as something of an innovator at the border of literary and labor studies does not stop her from using remarkably common terms to describe her undercover methods—terms that had, in fact, become constitutive of the form after three decades of undercover writing. These terms appear in her book's final words, when Parker concludes that "what industry needs more than anything else—more, indeed, than all the reformers—are translators—translators of human beings to one another. 'Reforms' will follow of themselves."[9]

Much like Addams, Parker comprehends the dynamics of reform in terms of the distance between human beings. The conceit of built institutions like the settlement house and the working girls' club was that they contracted social distance by bringing people of diverse social, ethnic, and economic backgrounds into contact with one another, though, as we have seen, racial divides remained stubbornly and willfully unbridged. But undercover authors had technically belonged to both capital and labor; they had managed to actually traverse that social distance, or so they claimed, and they made that traversal the driving thematic and formal element of their prose. And so, in book after book, Parker and her peers position themselves as mediators and translators uniquely poised to interpret the language and convictions of each side. Self-proclaimed "gentlewoman as factory girl" Marie Van Vorst "hoped to be a mirror that should reflect the woman who toils," describing herself as "a mouthpiece for her to those who know little of the realities of everlasting labor." In the same volume—*The Woman Who Toils, Being the Experiences of Two Gentlewomen as Factory Girls* (1903)—her sister-in-law and coauthor Bessie (Mrs. John) Van Vorst similarly calls herself "a mouthpiece for the woman labourer" and states that she wished to "place [her] intellect and sympathy in contact as a medium between the working girl who wants help and the more fortunately situated who wish to help her."[10] Parker perhaps purposely overstates her claim that translators like herself will write books so keenly insightful that "reforms" would follow "of themselves." Yet this very overstatement indicates that undercover writers credited their prose with a special reformist power that built on, and potentially even superseded, the work of contemporary reform institutions, a literary and social proposition that it will be my task to unpack in what follows.

This chapter is organized into two parts. I begin by giving an overview of the undercover archive as a whole, looking at a variety of articles, stories, and books published between 1902 and 1922. I draw most of my examples from three particularly rich undercover texts: Parker's *Working with the Working Woman* (1922), the Van Vorsts' *The Woman Who Toils,* and Dorothy Richardson's undercover novel *The Long Day: The Story of a New York Working Girl* (1905). I argue that undercover writers principally drew on two varieties of firsthand evidence in their pursuit of immediate experience: the poor and working-class people with whom they lived, toiled, and, most importantly, conversed; and the transformations in their own perception and behavior that came as a result of this rare cross-cultural intimacy. Although these texts differ from one another in important ways, the problem of social distance—as well as the politics of cross-class proximity—frames how each represents the language and literacy of marginalized populations. What this suggests is that the social and political concerns of contemporary reform institutions had been transformed into core elements of literary form and genre by the early twentieth century.

In part because the genre was so materially, economically, and ideologically embedded in Progressive reform culture, undercover literature both reflected and precipitated period debates about the value of reading and writing as tools of social amelioration. Undercover writers made firsthand experience the basis of a new mode of U.S. writing, yet they simultaneously commenced journeys "down and out" because they believed that literature had lost its usefulness as a source of social knowledge. They argued that Americans could no longer count on articles and books to explain how the other half lived; to produce writing with genuine sociological and literary value, authors had to be willing to experience hardship in a direct, unmediated way. Down-and-outer Walter Wyckoff, for instance, declares that the "slender book-learned lore" he acquired in college had shown him nothing of the "vital knowledge of men and the principles by which they live and work," and Parker's literary origin story emerges from her frustration with experiencing industrial turmoil only "second or third hand through books." She acknowledges that "reading about it is better than nothing" but finds that "being an active part of it all is better still. It is one thing to lounge on an overstuffed davenport and read about the injurious effect on women of long hours of standing. It is another to be doing the standing."[11]

If Edith Wharton's comparatism and Booker T. Washington's dovetailing pedagogy seem to inflect Parker's language in this instance—think here of Lily Bart discovering through her visit to Gerty's girls' club that "it is one thing to live comfortably with the abstract conception of poverty, another to be brought in contact with its human embodiments," or of Washington pointing out "the real difference between studying about things through the medium of books, and studying things themselves without the medium of books"—that is because the problem of acquiring unmediated social knowledge under conditions of bare inequality preoccupies all three.[12] However differently these authors define the most pressing social problem of their day—whether it be the training and enfranchisement of black citizens, the freedom and mobility of women, or the hazards of modern industrial labor—each one uses relations of proximity to frame both the problem and its potential resolution. As though adhering to an unwritten rulebook, undercover writers assert the priority of experiential immediacy ("doing the standing") over the printed word ("[reading] almost nothing"). In conflating stereotypical beliefs about working-class vitality with the pedagogical priority of personal experience on the one hand and the fog of class privilege with book learning as varieties of impediment on the other, undercover writers helped make firsthand knowledge a collective sensibility of late nineteenth- and early twentieth-century U.S. literature writ large.

However, there are two competing claims about literary mediation being made here, for undercover authors identified a contemporary crisis in literary authority—the waning power of books and reading in the face of modern social disorder—only to frame that crisis as the source of their own innovation as writers. In other words, they ultimately produced *texts* that had as their express purpose to "[translate] human beings to one another" through prose—to mediate the burgeoning social knowledge of their readers. It then remained the responsibility of those readers to implement reforms along the lines suggested by authors who had experienced both darkness and daylight. But I argue that rather than overlooking the paradoxes that attended the undercover genre, authors actively managed those contradictions by commenting self-reflexively on the promise and purpose of reading for different class constituencies—a literary-social formation I have been calling *reading for reform*. By focusing attention on reading as a social and political activity, undercover writing forged new relations between the practices and institutions of reform on the one hand and literary production and reception on the other.

One way to understand undercover literature, then, is as an ur-genre for the alliance between social reform institutions and modern U.S. literature that we have been examining in this book. Undercover literature achieves this special status, I will argue, because it is fundamentally concerned with bridging gaps—in social, spatial, and epistemological terms and in terms of literary form, movement, and practice. Yet as we shall see, the acts of border crossing that authors undertook ultimately reinforced the social distinctions that motivated their journeys in the first place. As virtually all critics of the genre have noted, undercover writers established a "pernicious dynamic that reified class and race hierarchies under the guise of challenging them."[13] Their work reflects a "common enough schizophrenia among social reformers of the turn of the century" that plays out in calls "for both social justice and social control," as Keith Gandal puts it; it is fed equally by humanitarian impulse and utter condescension and strikes a precarious balance between sympathy and censure.[14] But even if we grant the arguable claim that sympathy for the poor held some measure of value as motive or outcome, undercover writers inarguably enacted their sympathy through a literary method founded on theft. They bridged social gaps in order to capture for themselves knowledge and authority that rightly belonged to their unwitting interlocutors in "the underbrush."[15]

Undercover writing was limited in its capacity to achieve the social advances to which it aspired. Yet these texts warrant careful consideration precisely because they are so uniquely possessed by their own use value, so certain of an absolute fit between the social practice and literary form of going "down and out." The genre therefore stages questions that have been at the heart of *Reading for Reform:* What are reading and writing good for? Who has the authority to speak for—and in this case, as—marginalized populations? What might it mean to read or write for reform?[16] To answer these questions, let us examine the distinct literary features and historical antecedents of the genre.

DOWN AND OUT IN NEW YORK AND CHICAGO AND PITTSBURGH

Undercover literature muddies the waters between fiction and nonfiction, yet certain constraints and commonalities bind this seemingly unwieldy archive into a recognizable literary genre.[17] Class-passing texts are fundamentally stories of experience. They follow a trajectory that moves from decision, transformation, and immersion to discovery, revelation, and retreat. Furthermore, they express a strong air of factuality and referentiality, making claim to "a privileged representational intimacy with hard 'reality' or irreducible materiality."[18] Undercover narratives are always recognizably based in the historical present, and they maintain that the world of the story corresponds to the real world. In practice, this means that they often invite readers to conflate author, protagonist, and narrator as one intrepid class-crossing figure—so that, for instance, "Cornelia Stratton Parker," "Connie Park," and the first-person narrator are one.

Most frequently, writers frame their undercover narratives as the unvarnished transcription of actual experience, but some stories and novels feature middle-class characters who pass into and then resurface from the sphere of manual labor within the fictional world of the plot; some such are W. H. Little's *Sealskin and Shoddy* (1888), Margaret Sherwood's *Henry Worthington, Idealist* (1899), Jack London's "South of the Slot" (1909), and Upton Sinclair's *King Coal* (1917), among many others.[19] Authors often combined the imaginary and the factual both in their accounts of the undercover research they claimed to have committed and in their narratives' generic complexity. Examples in this hybrid mode include Stephen Crane's "An Experiment in Misery" (1894), the two articles and two books published by Boston settlement worker Alvan Francis Sanborn, Dorothy Richardson's 1905 *The Long Day* (to which I shall return later in this chapter), and *Four Years in the Underbrush,* published anonymously by Scribner's in 1921 as the alleged work of a well-known southern novelist. Whether fictional or nonfictional, undercover narratives demonstrate a wide tonal and political range and display varying degrees of literary embellishment.

Several features of the early twentieth-century literary marketplace proved significant to the consolidation of the genre. Foremost is the issue of money. Undercover writers received financial support not from the philanthropic sources that funded adjacent reform ventures but, rather, from mainstream publishing entities whose prime motivations were prestige and profit.[20] Furthermore, their work sold well because it circulated in a highly synergistic print culture that blurred the boundaries between the book and magazine industries. Most undercover texts appeared first as serial articles in general monthly magazines and were later published in lengthier form by book publishers who owned or maintained editorial oversight over those periodicals. For example, Marie and Bessie Van Vorst's writing was serialized in the muckraking *Everybody's Magazine* in 1902 and 1903 before it was published months later by Doubleday, Page and Company, a firm that managed the editorial content in *Everybody's* from 1900 to 1903. Similarly, Cornelia Stratton Parker's undercover writing was published by both the periodical and the book wing of Harper and Brothers. By 1909, the genre was ubiquitous enough that Charlotte Perkins Gilman and O. Henry could casually reference—and parody— "literary imposters" in their fiction, and literary critics could characterize class-crossing authors as a "little body of adventurers who have been in forbidden lands and have brought back something strange at the cost of their lives." Some undercover books even became best sellers.[21]

But undercover literature also took off because it catered to the particular literary taste of American readers in the early years of the twentieth century. Indeed, even this brief overview will no doubt indicate that undercover writing possesses diverse literary and social scientific antecedents. Within the U.S. literary tradition, the genre draws on conversion and captivity narratives; the mid-nineteenth-century urban gothic and city mysteries genres; travel writing; tenement, seamstress, slumming, and Social Gospel literature; and the early twentieth-century sociological novel. The language, characters, and plotlines of undercover writing also borrow from nineteenth-century labor fiction focused on the industrial work environment. The latter was overwhelmingly written by white authors who had never experienced the constraints of manual labor firsthand. Its iconography of wage-earning "types" makes its way into early twentieth-century undercover writing—alternately virtuous, vulgar, or frivolous wage-earning women chief among them—and so too does the tendency to craft characterizations that "reveal less who is being looked at than who is looking."[22]

Undercover writing also shared key narrative techniques and motives with Jacob Riis's pioneering urban exposé of 1890, *How the Other Half Lives*. Riis's hybrid text combined documentary photography, statistics, and literary anecdote in unprecedented ways, and its commercial success proved that the "other half" made compelling subject matter for an economically comfortable readership interested in crossing borders and closing social chasms from the safety of their homes. Undercover writers capitalized on this public fascination with physical and narrative excursions into the so-called underworld, and most also shared Riis's reformist agenda. But while Riis's shocking, intimate images of urban domestic squalor established the existence of a profound social crisis that required immediate intervention, he often took the photographs without permission in the course of nighttime "raiding parties," which means that they also represent a serious assault on the privacy of lower-class people. Indeed, *How the Other Half Lives* naturalized the idea that needy populations did not have any privacy worth protecting. This invasive sensibility surely authorized the even greater deceptions enacted by authors like Richardson and Parker.[23] To this middle-class literary tradition of observing and chronicling the "other half" at close view, undercover writers added a prolonged period of immersion, a more personal and subjective orientation, and the element of class disguise.

For female scholars, the undercover mode became an important means of gaining a hearing within academic disciplines that systematically excluded them. As Mark Pittenger has explained, the undercover genre is rooted in the methods of participant observation, social investigation, and investigative journalism and in the disciplines of sociology, economics, and anthropology.[24] Sociologists Annie Marion MacLean and Amy Tanner, who published articles about their time working undercover in department stores and sweatshops, pioneered participant observation techniques several years before the Chicago school of sociology would lay claim to that method. When women gradually outpaced men as undercover authors in the early twentieth century, their dominance within an increasingly recognizable literary tradition registered a gendered pursuit of authority within social scientific, reformist, and literary spheres alike.

Undercover authors are close kin as well with Progressive Era social investigators, who observed urban vice zones closely—sometimes in disguise—under the aegis of antivice organizations and industrial commissioners such as New York City's Committee of Fourteen and Chicago's Juvenile Protective Association. Social investigators issued factual reports on the conditions of urban-industrial capitalism that served as powerful ammunition in ongoing legislative campaigns.[25] Many undercover writers participated in reform initiatives—the settlement house, Consumers' League, and Waitresses' Union among them—that were adjacent to the work of social investigators. The Van Vorst sisters-in-law organized against Tammany Hall as members of the Women's Municipal League in New York (working alongside Grace Dodge and Lillian Wald, among others), and Bessie Van Vorst explicitly compared the insights she earned during "three weeks as a factory girl" to those she had previously gained "as an outsider in a factory girls' club," indicating that prior experience within social reform sites remained a touchstone for authors as they narrated their time down and out. Yet, crucially, they undertook their cross-class journeys as individual actors, possessing neither the institutional powers and protections nor the sponsorship of private reform groups that social investigators claimed for themselves.[26]

Finally, undercover writers also picked up the mantle of late nineteenth-century investigative journalists known as "girl stunt reporters." Their sensational mode of muckraking journalism enjoyed a brief spell of popularity in the 1880s and 1890s, just before the undercover literary mode took off in earnest. Following in the footsteps of groundbreaking Victorian masquerader James Greenwood, so-called sob-sister reporters would disguise themselves to gather material for their dramatic, high-profile newspaper exposés.[27] Their investigations went beyond urban-industrial contexts: the most famous writer in this tradition, Nellie Bly, masqueraded as an inmate in a mental asylum, a flower maker, and a recipient of medical charity who "Narrowly Escapes Having Her Tonsils Amputated," to name but three. Bly's great success in writing such stories as "Ten Days in a Mad-House," "The Girls Who Make Boxes: Nellie Bly Tells How It Feels to Be a White Slave," and "Nellie Bly as a Mesmerist," all published in Joseph Pulitzer's *New York World*, inspired a legion of daredevil imitators, including Nell Nelson, Elizabeth Banks, and Eva Valesh.[28] These stunt reporters baldly emphasized the performative dimensions of their work, and their primary allegiance was always to the story. They aimed to boost newspaper circulation and to entertain readers with their derring-do, but they were not necessarily concerned with cultivating sympathy or reformist indignation in response to the hardships they exposed. Nor did female stunt reporters ever lead readers to believe that they genuinely became another kind of woman—a disadvantaged one, for instance—rather than briefly and theatrically impersonating one. What distinguished undercover authors from the generation of stunt journalists that preceded them, then, was the sense that their writing existed to connect the scenes in which they had been immersed with a particular program of social amelioration, however deficient those proposed reforms turned out to be.[29]

This disciplinary kinship with the social sciences, investigative journalism, and social investigation secured a reliable market for undercover literature in its time. But new critical insights emerge when we wrest the genre from these primary associations in order to position it, instead, at the crossroads of Progressive reform culture and U.S. literature that is the subject of this book. Take, as an example, the gender dimensions of undercover writing. Men and women wrote these narratives in roughly equal measure, with women publishing slightly more after the century's turn. Yet I address women's writing almost exclusively in this chapter because white female down-and-outers were much more embedded in the traditions and institutions of Progressive reform than were their male counterparts—both in terms of the reformist agendas they proposed in their texts and in terms of their own backgrounds as teachers, reformers, and philanthropists, which shaped their literary expression in powerful ways.

What we find, in fact, is that affluent women passed into the very communities of factory and mill workers, department store attendants, and clerical workers that were targeted by white-dominated turn-of-the-century uplift institutions. Their male counterparts, by contrast, were far more likely to write about the indigent populations—hoboes, tramps, and transients—that such reform institutions consciously overlooked. Most famously, Walter Wyckoff traversed the United States on foot from Connecticut to California, publishing a two-volume account of his experiences as a homeless migratory laborer in 1897 and 1898. Male-authored undercover texts, bearing titles like *Tramping with the Tramps* and "Six Weeks in Beggardom," tapped into the ascendant masculine ideal of reinvigorated manhood and pastoral adventure that Theodore Roosevelt famously dubbed "the strenuous life" and thus can be read as part of a literary genealogy of male road narratives that includes Mark Twain's *Adventures of Huckleberry Finn* (1884), Jack London's *The Road* (1907), Jack Kerouac's *On the Road* (1957), and Jon Krakauer's *Into the Wild* (1996). But sleeping on the streets and taking to the open road was not a safe or viable option for women. Moreover, female undercover writers aimed to "reform, not merely pass through, the lives of 'the unknown class.'"[30] If we take social reform and U.S. literary practice as dual vantage points for comprehending undercover literature, then it suddenly appears a very female genre indeed.

"THE WAY THE GIRLS TALKED ... SET THE STAMP OF DIFFERENCE ON IT ALL"

At the center of every undercover narrative is a pivotal scene of transformation in which the protagonist assumes a working-class disguise and prepares to make her public debut as a quasi laborer. Bessie Van Vorst describes the working-class costume as a bridge between distant social worlds:

> Before leaving New York I assumed my disguise. In the Parisian clothes I am accustomed to wear I present the familiar outline of any woman of the world. With the aid of coarse woolen garments, a shabby felt sailor hat, a cheap piece of fur, a knitted shawl and gloves I am transformed into a working girl of the ordinary type. I was born and bred and brought up in the world of the fortunate—I am going over now into the world of the unfortunate.[31]

Having crossed over, she finds that her new wardrobe possesses near-talismanic power: "My disguise is so successful I have deceived not only others but myself. I have become with desperate reality a factory girl, alone, inexperienced, friendless." Other writers echo Van Vorst's sense that "coarse" and "shabby" clothing precipitates a profound subjective transformation. Her sister-in-law Marie charts a one-to-one correspondence between wardrobe and being, describing the way her previous leisure-class personality "slipped from [her] as absolutely as did the garments [she] had discarded." Facing the public in her "simple decorous work-clothes," the narrator announces her conversion: "I was Bell Ballard."[32]

Working-class clothing—so simple in substance but represented as an absolutely transformative mode of class disguise—becomes an important means of navigating a social status in transition. But embodying working-class experience is more than just a matter of wearing tattered apparel. In the next phase of the undercover figure's ritualized downward mobility, the protagonist learns to perform a host of new bodily cues, gestures, and behaviors that she associates with working-class conduct. Parker disguises herself in "earrings and the bar pin, the green tam and the lip stick," but chewing a stick of gum is what completes her "metamorphosis." "Some people have to go to a masquerade ball to feel themselves someone else for a change," Parker remarks. "Others, if they have been brought up by school-teachers, can get the same effect with five cents' worth of chewing gum."[33] In articles and books across the genre, undercover protagonists learn to occupy their bodies in self-consciously humble ways; one writes of cultivating "a hang-dog position of the head."[34] Privileged authors mine their own unsettled feelings about wearing ragged clothing and acquiring novel forms of embodiment as important forms of primary evidence in their own right.

Not only did authors draw on their own newfound proletarianization as raw material for their prose, but the people encountered in the social depths made up another kind of firsthand evidence. Indeed, undercover writing has an immensely sociable atmosphere. We learn countless names and employment histories, hear of boyfriends and families and wardrobes and gossip so idle its very mundanity becomes part of the stories authors want to tell. There are entire chapters devoted to chatty, character-driven interludes. Thick with description and long sections of dialogue, undercover narratives read at times as character studies of an other half whose supposed otherness is constantly put under pressure. In this sense, down-and-outers' pursuit of vital experience was keyed to the theoretical and aesthetic principles of literary realism. Realism, Michael A. Elliott notes, was a movement that "came to value the firsthand observation of group-based difference and to develop conventions by which that difference would be textualized." In general terms, realist authors "saw the mimetic possibilities of literary description as a necessary counterpart to democratic recognition," and they charged writing with the task of accurately reflecting—and thereby changing—the social world. Early twentieth-century undercover authors inherited the realist principle that representing everyday regions and figures in all their particularity, authenticity, and locality held political and aesthetic value.[35]

The undercover genre's allegiance to realism is revealed most powerfully in its fixation on lower-class character. Occasionally down-and-outers craft round characters imbued with nuance and intentionality, but more frequently their characters are flat and conventional, exhibiting the predictable behavior of generalized social types. "Maurice was the type, with the qualities absent.... Maurice was Labour—its Symbol—its Epitome," Marie Van Vorst effuses, and yet "he is one of the absolutely real creatures I have ever seen. Of his likeness types of crime are drawn." Later, in a different workplace across the Mason–Dixon Line, she notes that "the Southern mill-hand's face is unique—a fearful type, whose perusal is not pleasant or cheerful to the character-reader."[36] While this kind of stereotypical, typological characterization was common enough in early twentieth-century fiction, undercover writers also harnessed a formulaic approach to literary character to reinforce the reformist message of their work: that men, women, and children were transparently shaped by their domestic surroundings and by the degrading conditions under which they performed their labor. This too was in keeping with the tenets of literary realism, for "if sentimentalism depended on characters who could transcend their environment, then realism would by definition highlight the obstacles to transcendence," Kenneth W. Warren notes.[37] Yet means and ends are dramatically incommensurate here. Writers deploy exoticizing and primitivist tropes to describe working-class characters on the one hand while also praising their courage, wisdom, and solidarity on the other.[38]

The methodological embrace of proximity finds its corollary in rigorously empirical prose that is attentive to the appearance, morality, and—especially—speech of the working poor. For the class-passing writer's discovery of the other half is also, crucially, the discovery of an unknown language. Across the undercover archive, class-crossing figures call attention to the common slang, informality, and so-called vulgarity of working-class speech. Most of the time, this encounter takes the form of shocked revelation. "The way the girls talked was one of the phases of the life which set the stamp of difference on it all," Parker confesses, remarking that for the genteel writer in disguise, "if there is one thing you are more conscious of than all else, it is such proper English as you possess."[39] Frances Donovan is scandalized by Chicago waitresses' casual profanity, adducing that their regular interactions with male customers had lent to their speech "the incredible candor of men."[40] Annie Marion MacLean offers a more measured assessment of the "surroundings" that shaped working-class language, noting that it only stood to reason that "refinement of thought and speech would soon disappear in such an environment."[41]

For every account of hazardous work conditions, class-passing writers reflect on the worrying vernacular of restaurant and factory. These accounts range from fond but unflinching to moralizing and admonitory. Parker is the least censorious, but even she concludes her chapter on the New York City chocolate factory by quoting the unremitting slang her coworkers spoke. In doing so, she leaves the precise attribution for each instance of quoted speech obscure: "Lena's giggles and Ida's 'Lee-na, stop your talk and go to work! . . . Louie, stop your whistlin'! . . . My Gawd! Girls, don' you know no better n' to put two kinds in the same box?' . . . Hey, Lena, this yere Eyetalian wants somethin'; come here and find out what's ailin' her." In between sections of transcribed dialogue, Parker interlaces asides about the ubiquity of slang in the factory, and the absence of quotation marks implies that this slang has succeeded in blurring individual workers into an anonymous mass. "And 'round here, there, and every place, 'My Gawd! My feet are like ice!' 'Say, len' me some of yo'r cardboards—hey?'"[42] Parker takes care to explain that she does not hold her coworkers' nonstandard English against them. But the genre's overwhelming tendency is to make corrupted language a symbol of the damage manual toil inflicts over a period of years, a position that only affirms the prevailing belief that cultural degeneration and linguistic decay operate as tandem forces in modern American life.[43] As they calibrate their moralistic linguistic commentary in relation to the speaker's precise occupation—laundry workers' faulty speech is "indicative of loose living and inherent vulgarity," but the elegant speech of the women making artificial flowers bespeaks "clean minds and an intelligent point of view," in Richardson's *The Long Day*—language becomes a way for outsiders to categorize working-class communities by means of the internal hierarchies they ascribe to them.

The constant judgments leveled at the "box-factory vernacular" are meant to shore up undercover writers' difference from—and superiority to—their newfound peers.[44] These transcriptions of an unfamiliar language also engage the vogue for dialect that gripped American authors in the early twentieth century. When they record the vocabulary and diction of mill workers and waitresses, undercover writers participate in what Gavin Jones calls the "cult of the vernacular," a convention of postbellum local color realism pioneered by "upper-class writers who had what they thought was intimate contact with the dialect speakers of their locality." Like their late nineteenth-century predecessors, undercover writers fixate on "the phonetics of unfamiliar speech" and convey "a strong thematic interest in the cultural and political issues surrounding questions of linguistic variety."[45] In this spirit, Marie Van Vorst quotes her landlord in a South Carolina mill town—"I wa'n't sick when I come hyar, but them mills! They's suttinly tew hyard on a woman"—before switching into a more analytical mode, observing immediately afterward, "With every word she speaks this aged creature draws her own picture. To these types no pen save Tolstoi's could do justice. Mine can do no more than display them by faithfully transcribing their simple dialect-speech."[46] Van Vorst leverages her own artistic merit to claim that nonstandard speech tells its own story: she contends that it is possible to relay an accurate picture of working-class life simply by transcribing this speech without further elaboration. For authors reckoning with their dual investments in accumulating firsthand knowledge of the poor and translating the poor to a broader audience, juxtaposing standard and nonstandard speech becomes a metaphor for stark material difference and a measure of the great distance separating genteel Americans from denizens of the lower order.

Whereas turn-of-the-century critics saw literary representations of nonstandard English as "part of a sincere, democratic interest in recording the speechways of subaltern cultural groups," recent scholars are more likely to see them as "a means by which a social elite found cultural reassurance," or at least to perceive such bids for linguistic hegemony as "fraught with complex anxieties."[47] As I have been suggesting, both critical perspectives hold true to some extent in the case of undercover writing. But class-crossing authors bring additional political and genre-related motives to their documentation of working-class English. Their quasi-ethnographic rendering of the language spoken by marginalized people allows writers to meditate self-consciously on the core problem that underpins the genre—namely, the broader difficulty of communicating across social borders at all. In a crucial sense, then, it is merely a matter of aesthetic convenience that undercover writers choose to represent those boundaries as linguistic ones. Cross-class understanding is already difficult in social, political, and spatial terms, but the "damaged" and "mutilated talk" of the urban poor makes such understanding practically difficult too. Richardson goes so far as to endow her working-class characters with physical traits—cleft palates, inscrutably guttural voices—that make their speech even more incomprehensible. "Her English was so sadly perverted and her voice so guttural that I could make out her meaning only with the greatest exercise of the imagination," Richardson writes of a brief conversation between her genteel protagonist and a fellow boardinghouse resident.[48] The genre's characteristic blend of good intentions and blinding prejudice is clearly in evidence here, as Richardson's recourse to "sadly perverted" and "guttural" speech hints at a Lamarckian view of the cultural devolution of the poor. But she also worries that distance trumps intimacy when language is so hard to comprehend, obstructing the social change that only cross-class communication makes possible.[49]

And yet as a third modality of disguise, undercover writers cautiously integrate slang into their own speech so that they might blend in more easily with their new surroundings. "I speak bad English, but do not attempt to change my voice and inflection nor to adopt the twang," Bessie Van Vorst clarifies; her sister-in-law Marie struggles so much at first to cover up her leisure-class accent that she speaks in French to her French-Canadian landlord in Lynn, Massachusetts, passing herself off as an immigrant from Paris.[50] In order to mediate the social gap, undercover figures must not only translate the language of the poor to their readers. They are also compelled, like so many Eliza Doolittles in reverse, to learn to speak a new kind of English. One senses from their writing that this linguistic appropriation was among the greatest challenges authors faced during their time down and out. Parker even allows an especially highbrow coworker at the dress factory to coach *her* out of saying "ain't" as a way of cementing their friendship and to show readers how fully the power dynamic has shifted in the course of her undercover journey, even to the point of reversal. Actively performing dialect, in addition to transcribing it, indexes the close connection between the social practice of going undercover and the genre's achieved literary form.

Undercover writers' extensive focus on spoken language as a reflection of character grounds their prose in late nineteenth-century realism. But in their own code switching between class-inflected varieties of English, we can also detect a dawning sensitivity to the emergent conventions of transatlantic modernism, in which white modernists used "linguistic imitation" and "racial masquerade" as experimental forms of self-fashioning.[51] Michael North frames white modernists' attachment to the black voice as a rapturous form of rebellion and self-liberation. Appropriation of dialect was foundational to U.S. literary modernism, North argues, whether it arrived in white authors' racial ventriloquism or in black modernists' rejection of a racist dialect tradition. None of the authors I examine here can be rightly described as modernists, and it is important to note that their linguistic imitations do not cross racial lines. Yet their motivations—and their literary methods—were nonetheless resolutely modern. Speech, after all, served as a crucial mode of social discrimination in the early twentieth century in part because the forces we have come to call "modern"—rapid intranational and global migration and urbanization, the standardization and commercialization of dress—made it increasingly difficult to make such discriminations through traditional means.[52] In undercover writing, modern identity becomes *envoiced*—a matter of voice as much as embodiment, of aurality and orality as much as observation and visuality. Here we might also recall the fundamentally verbal and auditory terminology undercover writers used—the "translator," the "mouthpiece"—to define their intentions.[53]

Indeed, not only does undercover writers' linguistic borrowing across social borders position them as transitional figures suspended between the language politics of realism and modernism, but the sonic infrastructure of their prose also shows the genre departing from the primarily visual strategies of Jacob Riis to embrace aural methods that are additionally associated with women's charitable and social work. Riis famously dilates on the visual appearance of the poor and their domiciles in *How the Other Half Lives*. He hardly neglects their language—he worries about the cacophony of foreign tongues crowding out English in the slums of New York City—but we rarely hear those voices in action, nor is the particular content or manner of their conversation central to Riis's project. In contrast, Ellen Ross suggests that turn-of-the-century British women's writings about the slum are "striking . . . for their emphasis on the *aural.*" Ross argues that this literary aurality reflects the strategic position women often assumed as listeners and care workers within the feminized institutional orbit of philanthropy and social work.[54] While Ross's insights are pitched to a British context, they bring into focus the particular formal and generic qualities that undercover literature took on across the Atlantic. The undercover genre's sociable aesthetic—its chattiness, its orientation to listening as much as to looking—was forged at the nexus of gender and reform.

The genre's sonic infrastructure rests on two methods of communication: conversation and eavesdropping. Down-and-outers talk to their coworkers and housemates as much as they possibly can. Their assumption is that it is only possible to achieve such an easy back-and-forth when individuals normally separated by class and other social distinctions are provisionally situated on a level playing field, sitting side by side at the loom or in the cafeteria. Undercover writers suggest that seamless conversation—talk not stretched by the effort to find a common denominator or traverse any social gulf, as was explicitly the case inside reform sites—requires a degree of social parity. And they were not incorrect on this score. There were well-known codes, both spoken and unspoken, that sought to direct the way marginalized people spoke to those possessing greater social and institutional power, from hegemonic etiquette codes that presumed the lower classes owed verbal deference to the rich to professional codes that encouraged clients to remain guarded in their interactions with charity officers, teachers, and members of clergy lest their words be used against them. Genteel undercover writers craved an open channel of conversation that would allow them to bypass these codes, though it does not seem to have occurred to them that their considerable class privilege and condescension may have shone through even the most convincing disguise.

Conversation is also prized for its capacity to facilitate the cross-class friendships that prove crucial to navigating an unfamiliar social world. Luckily, undercover figures find their coworkers to be fairly chatty. Conversation is "the only resource among the poor," Bessie Van Vorst notes, and Parker concludes that factory girls' one universal quality is their willingness "to tell you everything they know on short acquaintance."[55] Failure to chat is therefore a major liability; Marie Van Vorst's struggle to induce one particular workmate to banter with her forms a central plot arc in the chapter focused on a Lynn, Massachusetts, shoe factory. Van Vorst ignores the other plausible explanations for Bobby's reticence—concentration, distraction, personal dislike—to conclude that she "was not talkative or communicative simply because she had nothing to say," having been overworked to the point of silent stupefaction.[56] Parker is similarly frustrated with her quiet coworkers, referring to them as "dead ones—the sort who would not talk had they been given a bonus and share in the profits for it." She becomes desperate to sit near more talkative factory girls even though she finds, when she succeeds in doing so, that they eat unpalatable "Yiddish" foods. "But at least there was conversation."[57]

The broad emphasis on cross-class talk produces an aesthetic of sociability that spans the whole undercover archive. But it is a profoundly fraught and unequal sociability, one that reflects the undercover figure's constant battle to control the flow of knowledge. Undercover authors give very little of themselves in return for the stories they collect, since the salient details of their own autobiographies must be concealed to protect the ruse of a worker identity. In some cases, workplace dialogue threatens to become *too* reciprocal, and talkative coworkers *too* invested in something like real friendship, stripping them of their power to control conversational encounters. Friendly coworkers "ask me questions, and I lie until I hate myself," writes Parker.[58]

These conversations are fundamentally one-sided affairs, but eavesdropping is even more so, becoming a key method of collecting evidence on the sly when the working classes do not perform according to script. The prevalence of eavesdropping in undercover writing grounds the genre in overheard moments and stolen knowledge. Bessie Van Vorst's section of *The Woman Who Toils* is marked by an insatiable hunger for closer friendships and better access to the truth of working-class experience. She strategically positions herself so that she will overhear her coworkers' gossip: "I hear fragmentary conversations about fancy dress balls, valentine's parties, church sociables, flirtations and clothes," she reports from the pickle factory, using conversations that strike her as trite as grounds for condemning the shallow pleasures of certain classes of working girls.[59] The practice of eavesdropping is nonconsensual and deceptive, but it also depends, in these texts, on some measure of intimacy and authenticity, since the person under surveillance is presumably unaware that she is being scrutinized and therefore feels free to be herself.[60] Undercover writers rarely express any doubt that working-class women's stories, as overheard and reconstructed later, offer unvarnished truths that trump the authority of books and more established academic ways of knowing. "I didn't take those jobs to see what working conditions were like—I had visited factories on end in my day," Parker clarifies. "My interest was solely in the human element concerned. What did the girls think about their jobs, work in general, life in particular and in general?"[61] But whatever confidence authors project about their literary method, the fact that undercover texts so readily embrace a mode of communication predicated on class surveillance renders suspect their claims to real intimacy with the poor.

Important questions arise here, questions that link the troubling politics of eavesdropping to the larger generic problems that undercover literature poses. How can we explain writers' shameless pursuit of working-class secrets when eavesdropping so clearly violated all existing rules of etiquette? One overly generous explanation is that they forgave their transgressions of right conduct because this private deception was thought to serve the public good. Ann Gaylin notes that in nineteenth-century literature, eavesdropping was deemed socially and morally sanctionable when the eavesdropper went on to use her stolen knowledge to prevent a crime or otherwise spread good.[62] Undercover writers no doubt believed that their appeals to broader sympathy and advocacy of concrete social reforms were outcomes "good" enough to authorize some duplicity along the way. Another explanation is that they failed to recognize that eavesdropping and then printing conversations that were recorded without consent constituted transgressions at all.

While these explanations may contain a grain of truth, they go too far in crediting the authors' innocence. What the undercover archive shows more plainly is that down-and-outers were utterly blinded by their own class bias. They were unable to see that poor people might have a desire for privacy, that they possessed inner lives and voices deserving of protection. Indeed, considering the class surveillance that structured late nineteenth-century reform ventures, from the charitable practice of friendly visiting to the nighttime raids of Jacob Riis, the undercover genre merely confirms that the working classes were rarely granted the right to privacy well into the twentieth century.

Distilled in the literary and social politics of eavesdropping are still larger truths about the undercover genre. Eavesdropping is often understood as a way of accessing truth in an unmediated way, since the people who are talking do not know that there is a hidden audience for their speech. We have seen too that readers of undercover literature were encouraged to accept the genre's revelations about social experience as unvarnished truths—every bit as unmediated as at the moment they were secretly overheard. The crucial point I wish to make concerns the role of readers in bridging the genre's multiple methodological and aesthetic interventions. Making eavesdropping a key feature of undercover writing places readers in a position structurally analogous to that of the author, and it therefore forces readers into a kind of class collusion. "What did they talk about? Everything, except domestic cares," Bessie Van Vorst writes. Her syntax suggests that she is answering an obvious if unasked question, as though readers too are listening in on her drama of experience, sharing her every concern.[63] When her undercover methods violate working-class privacy or breach appropriate conduct, then, her transgressions are in the service of readers' implied demand for the intimate knowledge the genre has convinced them is their due.

Undercover authors made bold assumptions about who would actually read their work, and felt that these assumptions gave them creative and ethical license to shape stolen knowledge into literary form. Parker is again instructive here. Months after returning home from the mill in upstate New York, Parker's secret was out: her former coworkers had discovered excerpts of *Working with the Working Woman* published in *Harper's Magazine,* and she found herself the subject of an angry article in the mill's house periodical, *Bleachery Life.* Parker had considered the author—she calls him Uncle Mat—a good friend during her time at the bleachery, but now he attacked her sneaky methods, branding her "A

Lady with Tiger's Claws." In his article, Uncle Mat singles out Parker's stereotypical representation of the mill workers' vernacular speech as particularly offensive. But what he objects to most is the flippancy with which she exposed her coworkers' private information, her ease in revealing intimacies her onetime friends had shared with her in confidence. That she did so with reformist goals in mind is of no consequence to him. Tellingly, however, Parker responded by claiming that she had never expected mill workers to read her work at all. "I could see his point, but *Harper's* to me had not been public print in their sense," Parker writes in a 1934 memoir that comments upon her earlier undercover narrative. "I had foolishly never visioned an operative reading *Harper's*, any more than the girls at the laundry or the dress factory, and, besides, in my own heart I'd cared so much for the girls I wrote about, it had never occurred to me that I was describing them in a way to cause resentment."[64] As I will suggest in the next section of this chapter, undercover writers shared with Progressive reformers and educators a very particular and highly tendentious understanding of what the working classes did and should read. Their own writing was also shaped by convictions about who would be reading their published work. And so Parker used actual first names, quoted vernacular speech phonetically, and told secrets freely—all because she never dreamed a mill worker could have any interest in the genteel *Harper's*.

I have been arguing that undercover authors imagined their writing to be an instrument of social reform because of its presumed capacity to traverse social and literary distances. The undercover figure's discoveries while living within the abyss—of language, of new social norms, of the impact of labor conditions on her own subjectivity—are intended to parallel and metaphorize the reader's own discoveries while traveling through the undercover text. In other words, Parker could not imagine a working-class readership for her narrative because the middle-class readerly double was a constitutive feature of its form. In her study of Victorian social fiction, Carolyn Betensky identifies a "fundamental analogy . . . between the hero or heroine of comfortable means who comes to know and care about the suffering of the poor through personal contact with them and the reader who is poised to know and care about the suffering of the poor through her reading of the novel." By means of this analogy, the social problem novel constantly shuttles traits back and forth between protagonist and reader. "While the reader's knowledge develops on the model of the self-styled social investigator within the novel," Betensky writes, "the character's burgeoning awareness and subsequent quest for more knowledge is itself modeled on the act of reading."[65]

Betensky's account has special purchase for U.S. undercover literature, for the genre's reputed power to serve as an instrument of social change lies at the intersection of representation and reception that I call *reading for reform*. These narratives translate the experience of working-class life and labor to a readership transparently imagined as white middle and upper class, and in doing so they seek to mediate the reader's own unfolding humanitarian consciousness. In presenting their narratives as conduits for reform in this way, undercover authors generated a distinct understanding of literature's use value for different class constituencies.

If the author's primary function is to serve as a reader surrogate, then it makes sense to think of undercover literature as, finally, a genre about the practice of reading. This self-reflexive quality becomes even more striking when one notices how frequently authors embed scenarios of good and bad reading in their writing. These scenes help authors bridge the gap between the immediate, firsthand knowledge they prize and the second-hand representations that their own published books proffer. Surprisingly widespread and always conceptually meaningful, these literary representations of reading practices serve as metadiscourse on the instrumentality of the printed word, and they also shed light on the social utility of the undercover text—its status as "artificial machinery" for resolving social problems.[66] What I argue is that representations of books and reading allow writers to meditate on the problematic gap between proximity and distance, on social action and textual representation, and ultimately on the relationship of literature to reform, the core issues at the heart of this book. To make this point, I will turn now to an undercover narrative that addresses these concerns in considerable depth: Richardson's *The Long Day: The Story of a New York Working Girl*. Richardson's protagonist is a genteel eighteen-year-old girl who has suddenly descended into poverty and must now repeatedly read the bodies, homes, and workplaces of the urban working classes to make her way through an unknown social world. As a novel with multiple levels of impersonation built into its production, plot, and reception, *The Long Day* relies heavily on reading as a metaphor—and articulates a new political purpose for reading in the twentieth century.

READING READING IN *THE LONG DAY*

To begin, let me outline the publication history that has led to some generic trickiness around *The Long Day*, such that the novel is not always included in critical studies of the undercover mode. The novel was first published anonymously in 1905 and is framed as the true story of a rural Pennsylvania schoolteacher's descent into industrial and factory work in New York City and her eventual return to prosperity. The first-person narrator alludes to a recent death in the family that triggered her fall in fortune from comfortable rural teacher to "[a] waif and a stray in the mighty city of New York."[67] The book's genteel "before" and "after" segments—downward and upward mobility tales, respectively—are limited to a few opening sentences and a highly schematic outline of the heroine's rise in the epilogue. The vast majority of the narrative is set in the trenches of working-class New York. Yet even though economic precarity has genuinely pushed the refined protagonist into the ranks of the working classes, she stumbles through her life in the city as an utter stranger to the experience of poverty and manual labor.

The real provenance of *The Long Day* is quite different from this cover story. Dorothy Richardson—not to be confused with the British modernist author of *Pointed Roofs*—began working as a journalist in the late-1890s, first with the *Milwaukee Sentinel* and then for the *New York Herald*. While reporting for the *Herald,* Richardson constructed a persona that she used when conducting investigative research: she became Dorothy Adams, an impoverished factory girl who had recently left the countryside for New York City. Hot on the heels of Nellie Bly's success, Richardson/Adams's stealth investigations fueled a series of popular newspaper articles about working women published in 1900 and 1901. She expanded these articles into longer magazine pieces for *Frank Leslie's Popular Monthly* in 1903 and

1904 and eventually folded them into *The Long Day,* published in 1905 by the elite Century Company.[68] Importantly, Richardson's articles are explicit about their basis in undercover exploration: the subtitle to one piece called "The Girl Who Lives on $5 a Week" professes that the author "Tries the Experiment and Tells How It Is Done."[69] After Richardson's work had been revised and substantially expanded into a book, however, her publishers decided to drop the "Dorothy Adams" moniker in favor of publishing the novel anonymously, reasoning that obscuring authorship would bolster the novel's credentials as *The Story of a New York Working Girl.* Whole paragraphs of Richardson's earlier articles reappear in her novel, but the Nellie Bly-like performativity and sensationalism disappear altogether.[70] The novel is thus a work of fiction and an undercover narrative at once, and it sold extremely well, appearing in three different editions between 1905 and 1906.

And yet even though *The Long Day* was published strictly under the banner of autobiography, the novel's premise of a genteel rural teacher transplanted to the city inflects every narrative detail with a class-passing plot. The protagonist is initially nameless, in line with the book's anonymous authorship, until a coworker bequeaths her the false name of Rose Fortune. This new name masks the protagonist's true middle-class identity just as "Connie Park" disguised Cornelia Stratton Parker's. Rose is legitimately poor—daily she counts a diminishing pile of pennies and worries about which boardinghouse or working girls' home will serve as her home that evening—but her history, values, and educated speech distinguish her at every turn from the people around her. And because Rose's middle-class rural background has left her ill prepared for the sights, sounds, and challenges of New York City, her process of acclimating to her new life within the lower working ranks subjects her to the very same set of shocking discoveries that confronts every undercover figure within the genre writ large.

Conventions of the undercover mode appear throughout *The Long Day* in only slightly displaced form. There is Rose's educated speech and genteel behavior, for one thing. A fellow factory worker and part-time prostitute named Henrietta comments on Rose's "kind of high-toned" way of talking, walking, and even standing, warning her, "You ain't going to have no lady-friends in the factory if you're going to be queer like that." Richardson sets standard and nonstandard speech in explicit juxtaposition, as when a group of paper-box makers mock Rose's genteel diction ("Eyether! It must have slipped from my tongue unconsciously," the narrator frets) before letting loose a steady stream of "ain'ts" moments later. Even an elderly homeless woman remarks on Rose's educated speech, commenting, "Ye don't speak as if ye be one of we uns, be you?" Like the middle-class investigator in disguise, Rose must adjust her middle-class speech and demeanor to match those of her new associates if she is to make her way in this new world.[71]

Richardson also solders the trope of working-class costume onto the narrative of Rose's worsening poverty. After working long hours and sleeping at a working girls' home without the luxury of a bath, Rose becomes alienated from her increasingly shabby appearance. She catches a glimpse of herself in a mirror and no longer recognizes the woman staring back at her. "I stopped and surveyed myself. Truly I was a sorry-looking object," she muses; "two successive mornings without soap and the services of a stout comb are likely to work all sorts of demoralizing transformations in the appearance of even a lady of leisure, to say nothing of a girl who had worked hard all day in a dirty factory." Rose realizes that she has appeared in public without gloves, handkerchief, or collar and begins "to feel for the first time what was for [her] at least the very quintessence of poverty. . . . Never before had [she] experienced this new, this infinitely greater terror—lack of self-respect."[72] Importantly, Rose wears her shabby appearance like an ill-fitting costume. For even as circumstances relegate a gloveless Rose to boardinghouse and sweatshop, the fact that she comes "from the country" serves as code for her ongoing social and psychological distance from the urban poor. Proximity and distance vie for narrative dominance. Even if the plot does not follow a middle-class character's journey down-and-out through conventional means, the embedded passing narrative makes pedagogies of cross-class contact and discovery paramount, even for readers unaware of the novel's curious publication history or its participation in the undercover genre.

The novel's passing theme becomes most explicit in the epilogue. The narrator steps out of the plot to issue metacommentary on its production, explaining how she managed to rise from manual laborer to published author of *The Long Day*. After hundreds of pages of misery, Rose's fate takes a turn for the better. Richardson recounts this shift quickly and programmatically. "Have I actually been through all that I have described? Yes, and more," the narrator insists. But she adds that in preparing to write her book, she had "reinforced memory by thorough investigation" by voluntarily laboring at the same trades she had worked in years earlier, "all the time living consistently the life of the people with whom I was thus temporarily associated."[73]

Let us review this stunning conceit. "Rose" lived the life of a manual laborer adrift in New York, worked her way out of that life, and then immersed herself in its depths once more to remember exactly how it felt, to capture its smells and cadences with greater accuracy. Though a curious explanation added late in the novel, the undercover claim turns out to be the only checkable aspect of the narrative, for Richardson never performed factory work out of true necessity. The undercover claim here also provides useful cover for Richardson—whose name was revealed shortly after the release of the book—lest astute readers should happen to notice that several identical paragraphs had appeared in 1902 newspaper articles by an investigative journalist named Dorothy Adams. Should readers identify Richardson and Adams as one and the same author, this would only support the former's claim in the epilogue to have risen from factory worker to stenographer and finally journalist and writer, while conveniently accounting for any details that might have changed between article and book. Furthermore, the undercover investigation story trades on the authority of journalistic and sociological empiricism to bolster the literary authority of this working-girl-cum-first-time-author-from-the-country.

Finally, this explicit class-passing trope protects the truth claim that was the novel's core appeal to readers. One review in the *New York World* praised the fact that the novel was "not written by a masquerader, or a sociological adventurer. The author has been a working girl from simple necessity." However, not all reviewers were equally credulous. Another cast doubt on the novel's truth claims: "Who the author is we do not know, but are able to declare her endowed with extraordinary powers of observation. Joined to an effective capacity for description, this anonymous writer owns a deep sympathy with the class she knows so well. One so gifted evidently never was a working girl—the publisher's specious announcement on the title page notwithstanding—except for the purpose acknowledged by herself [at the end]."[74] Richardson didn't want to be identified as another Van Vorst; she sought the heightened authenticity—and the literary novelty—that came from being a real "New York working girl."

But even as Richardson tells only partial truths about her methods, *The Long Day* can't quite get over its status as a passing narrative, in part because class disguise buttresses the novel's central claims about the politics of reading. Deceptions of various kinds traverse the story. Working-class characters regularly obscure or manufacture their social origins, as when a homeless woman describes her dubiously wholesome nuclear family, or when the corrupted factory girl Henrietta pretends to come from an aristocratic family. On Rose's first and only night as a boarder in Henrietta's flat, her roommate shows her a picture of her alleged family home, a "cheap chromolithograph" that Rose immediately recognizes as "a reproduction of a familiar scene showing a castle on the Rhine." She had seen that same iconic image many times in print and knows Henrietta's story to be false. But Henrietta curiously seems to have fallen for her own fiction, having "come to believe every word of what she had told [Rose]."[75] It is to the heroine's credit that she sees straight through these lies—sees them, that is, for the stories they are. To a certain extent, Rose earns her piercing insight because of her genteel origins and respectable small-town education. But more than this, Rose can discern truth from fiction because she is a model reader.

Rose's ability to read better than everyone she meets proves a significant advantage, and her capacities as a reader justify the novel's earnest faith in the power of storytelling. In each of Rose's many urban workplaces, women pass the time telling one another stories—tales from childhood, anecdotes about dating, summaries of cheap serial fiction. Here Richardson picks up on a common thread in autobiographical accounts by activists and sometime garment workers Pauline Newman, Clara Lemlich, Fannia Cohn, and Rose Schneiderman, all of whom testify to the importance of participatory reading in women's work culture of the early twentieth century. What makes narrative so powerful in *The Long*

Day is its capacity to foment friendships among strangers and cultivate sympathetic relations across class lines, as when Rose spends the length of one boardinghouse dinner telling her life story to a new friend, or when she and her favored coworkers give each other new, pretty names drawn from their favorite books. These sympathies are violently curtailed in the face of racial difference, for Rose refuses to recognize her black male coworkers as humans, let alone as friends. Toward the end of the novel, she works at a laundry alongside a crew of white women and "fifteen big, black, burly negroes who operated the tubs and the wringers" and express themselves with "demoniacal" gestures and shouts. The black male laundry workers do not even warrant the protagonist's consideration as men ("Don't any men work in this place except the foreman?" Rose demands of her female coworker, with the implication that readers should be outraged to find her laboring in such an environment).[76]

But if the link between narrative and friendship grants storytelling a central place in the novel's account of white working-class culture, Richardson also establishes the ethical import of literary taste and genre. *The Long Day* draws a strong connection between what women choose to read and how authors represent women in print. This connection is meant to guide our own reading of *The Long Day*. Richardson's perspective, while hardly uncommon for her time and context, is still harsh and unforgiving: she insists that literary and political narratives of working womanhood that are too sympathetic or idealizing make it impossible to actually effect any social change. The working girl "has become, and is becoming more and more, the object of such an amount of sentimentality on the part of philanthropists, sociological investigators, labor agitators, and yellow journals . . . that the real work-girl has quite been lost sight of," she writes, setting up a conventional opposition between representation and reality. "But fine words butter no parsnips; nor do our fine idealizations serve to reduce the quota which the working-girl ranks contribute to disreputable houses and vicious resorts."[77] Representations of working women are idealized, distorted, abstract: these are precisely the same qualities that undercover authors attribute to writing that is the product of a distanced relation to its object.[78] *The Long Day* seeks to minimize sentimentalism's gentle violence by proposing an alternative way to use stories. What is further suggested here is that there is an important connection between the kinds of books working-class people read and the sociopolitical function of the undercover text.

Richardson's concern that "fine words" and "fine idealization" are likely to worsen women's moral and social condition is at the core of her book's theory of reading. When people write about working women "in a light as false and ridiculous as that in which Don Quixote was wont to view the charms of his swineherd lady, Dulcinea," these representations hinder middle-class readers' willingness or capacity to help them. Furthermore, Richardson connects the reformist stakes of literary representation to the way in which her one-time coworkers actually read, for if sentimentalism actually threatens laboring women—a perspective shared by working girls' club members, for instance—their own reading practices harm them just as gravely. Only Rose possesses the insight of a seasoned reader; her box-factory coworkers consume the "false and ridiculous" narratives of "trashy fiction" at an alarming rate. At lunchtime they gulp down their meals in anticipation of "[stealing] away to a sequestered bower among the boxes, there to lose themselves in paper-boxed romance." In contrast to reading material that contributes to the reader's store of knowledge, working girls lose themselves in fevered consumption and are left "entranced," depleted instead of educated. The narrator blames cheap fiction for the box makers' tendency to fantasize rather than approach their real lives in a practical way: their escapist reading practices lead them to think more about the "bankers and millionaires who in fiction have wooed and won and honorably wedded just such poor toilers as they themselves" than about the "flesh-and-blood man of every-day life" whom they will one day marry. Here Richardson applies an older rhetoric of the dangers of fiction for female readers to the case of modern industrial labor. What kind of self-reform is possible, she asks, when women's mental and emotional energies are consumed by unrealistic fantasy?[79]

When the novel's factory women debate the value and content of fiction, share "wild laughter," and devise "doggerel rhyme" to pass tedious hours of routinized labor, we can understand them to be exercising aesthetic, imaginative, and intellectual faculties.[80] But to read them in this way would be to resist the novel's clearly articulated alternative philosophy of reading, which insists that literary engagement is only "positive" when it incites inward growth and outward action in readers; it is "negative" when its pleasurable qualities promote a scattering of attention beyond the real world. Good reading provokes independent thought; bad reading is passive and undisciplined. The pragmatic and wholly conventional view of reading as an instrument of social reform that Richardson offers bears a close similarity to Washington's vocational realism, discussed in chapter 3.

The Long Day falters as a work of literary fiction, and its conservative politics are likewise beyond repair. Yet these flaws make a different kind of sense when the novel is viewed within the paradigm of prescriptive literature—texts that instruct readers on matters of conduct, etiquette, and domestic activity. Indeed, *The Long Day* is perhaps best understood as a makeshift reading advice manual, one that makes its recommendations through object lessons that bring to light literature's alternately damaging and enriching social work. As Amy L. Blair has argued, books dispensing reading advice had existed since at least the sixteenth century in the form of guides for young gentlemen and college hopefuls and treatises on moral education directed at young women. A particular craze for reading manuals took hold between the 1880s and the 1910s, when vast numbers of such books were published in the United States targeting members of the emergent professional-managerial class who had achieved some measure of educational and economic capital yet still required guidance in matters of literary taste and consumption.[81] As my previous chapters have shown, the activities and publications of reform institutions—settlements, clubs, colleges, and vocational schools—brokered much of the literary and cultural advice aimed at racialized people and the working classes during this period. *The Long Day* brings together the twinned goals of contemporary reading manuals and of reform institutions in its capacity as a guidebook for working-class literacy that few industrial wage earners were ever likely to actually read.

In this context, Louisa May Alcott and Laura Jean Libbey emerge as dueling emblems of good and bad reading in the novel. Rose discovers with astonishment that her paper-box factory coworkers have never heard of her favorite book, Alcott's *Little Women*. They are "undisguisedly bored" when she attempts to summarize the simple plot, dismissing it as no story at all. "That's no story—that's just everyday happenings," one coworker charges. "They just sound like real, live people; and when you was telling about them I could just see them as plain as plain can be."[82] In drawing attention to the apparent flaws in such a literary analysis, Richardson constructs a dichotomy that brings together readers of *The Long Day* and the undercover protagonist on the one hand and the novel's laboring women on the other. She assumes that her own readers, like Rose, prize Alcott's classic novel and value her ability to represent "real, live people" with "plain" realism—undoubtedly the very impression Richardson hoped to make with her book.

The novel insists, moreover, that working women's preference for Libbey's sensational dime novels over Alcott's cozier mimetic fiction reflects a deeper crisis in individual character, a crisis with profound social reverberations. Richardson's undercover contemporaries used similar terms to lament the power that "bad" fiction exerted over working-class female readers. Libbey was one of the most popular American writers of the late nineteenth century and wrote over sixty fictional works that transposed a Cinderella formula onto the narrative of a young woman alone in the city, her fate at the mercy of men who either abuse or rescue her. Libbey's heroines are wealthy urbanites, well-bred ladies from the country, or working girls who receive a surprise inheritance over the course of the book; marriage offers their only path to upward mobility. Richardson is eager to convey the shallow appeal of this fiction. She devotes six full pages to transcribing the plot of Libbey's *Little Rosebud's Lovers, or A Cruel Revenge* as one factory worker recounts it. As the retelling rolls on, canny readers will not fail to note how banal is the storyline, nor the speaker's use of working-class dialect in describing it.

Critics have argued that the Libbey formula, a rare female version of the Horatio Alger success myth, produced images of natural-born ladies "marrying up" that strongly appealed to working-class readers like those that populate *The Long Day*.[83] The formula's easy appeal—the ease with which the fortunes of the dime novels' characters rise and fall, prompted by circumstances outside their control—is exactly why the narrator condemns it so strongly. "Girls fed on such mental trash," Richardson's narrator avows, "are bound to have distorted and false views of everything."[84] (It is significant that Rose spies a large collection of dime novels in Henrietta's flat.) From this perspective, the interdependence of "good" and "bad" reading in Richardson's theory of reading for reform becomes clear. For *The Long Day* is also a female success story, one in which the protagonist achieves social mobility through a route sharply at odds with that of a Libbey heroine. Rose rises through hard work and tireless study, virtuous behavior, and alliance with a female friend of comparable moral character, and not through luck or marriage to someone above her station. The process of achieving upward mobility is as meaningful as the outcome.

Richardson's quarrel with working women's reading practices doubles, then, as an argument about uplift. The fundamental problem, in her view, is that working-class readers identify so strongly with dime-novel heroines that they come to think of self-improvement as an instantaneous and unwilled event. By extension, fiction that propagates this kind of thinking obscures the fact that true journeys of upward mobility require rigorous self-discipline. Richardson employs an important plot arc around a character named Eunice to illustrate the danger of sensational narratives. Eunice and Bessie are Rose's two "lady-friends," intimate companions who bring some comfort to Rose before dying prematurely in manners both tragic and pedagogical. Eunice, a fellow inmate at a working girls' home, is tortured by repercussions from a sexual lapse in the recent past that resulted in a premarital pregnancy. We know from the start that she is doomed, and so, it seems, does she: Eunice presciently informs Rose that she isn't as strong as other girls who "get hurt—and hurt bad" but who manage to overcome their lapses by marrying men who love and forgive them, girls, one notes, much like Nettie Struther in *The House of Mirth*. But Eunice cannot manage to fight her way out of depression and rebuild her life because she sees no inherent dignity in labor. She diagnoses her fatal flaw quite efficiently. "If I liked work for its own sake, like you do," she tells Rose, "there'd be some hope for me living things down." When Eunice eventually bids Rose farewell and disappears, we can only guess from clues scattered throughout the episode that she has drowned herself in the East River. The narrator won't tell us for sure: "I never expect to know the fate of Eunice. It is only in stories that such things are made clear, usually, and this was only an incident in real life."[85]

Here Richardson fashions a narrative rife with the drama of a Libbey tale, and yet she declines to wrap up her story because she deems such unlikely feats of redemption—or even closure—the province of sensationalistic fiction. She leaves this "incident in real life" inconclusive to shore up distinctions between literary representation and firsthand knowledge and between melodramatic narratives that dupe readers into misunderstanding social conditions (as Libbey does to the box-factory employees) and those that lay bare the problems underlying those conditions (as *The Long Day* purportedly does for its own readers). Crucially, the Eunice anecdote registers as a lesson about the relationship of reading to social action only in the context of the box-factory workers' extensive retelling of the Libbey tale. Richardson asks that we recognize the moral distinction between the melodramatic but easily resolved travails of Little Rosebud and the senseless real-life tragedy of Eunice, which she claims to have viewed firsthand. The irony of this juxtaposition, of course, is that readers of *The Long Day* who have been schooled in the conventions of sensational fiction will have known from Eunice's characterization, from her shrieking in the night and her fitful, intermittent glances at the East River, that she was bound for tragedy. Advance knowledge that a plot will turn against its unknowing heroine is one of the dime novel's prime reading formations. Thus, an anecdote that Richardson frames as a lesson in the gravity of real-life happenings over dime-novel story lines draws heavily on the tropes and reading strategies of cheap fiction.

The Long Day's meditations on reading and social utility ultimately build toward a broader claim about intellectual method. Despite obfuscating the real balance of imagination to undercover reportage that fueled her own process, Richardson still suggests that writing informed by a particular experience of proximity—knowing both affluence *and* wage labor firsthand, talking and listening across the borders of class—infuses literature with social and ethical consciousness. This methodological argument first appears in a pivotal episode early in the novel. On the first night of her life as a factory worker, Rose lies in her dingy lodging house quarters, gazing at her new surroundings.

How different it all was in reality from what I had imagined it would be! In the story-books it is always so alluring—this coming to a great city to seek one's fortune. A year ago I had been teaching in a little school-house among my Pennsylvania hills, and I recalled now, very vividly, how I used to love, on just such cold winter nights as this, when the wind whistled at every keyhole of the farm-house where I boarded during the school year, to pull my rocking-chair into the chimney-corner and read magazine stories about girls who lived in hall bedrooms on little or nothing a week; and of what a good time they had, or seemed to have, with never being quite certain where the next meal was to come from, or whether it was to come at all.[86]

This paragraph offers a tidy précis of the undercover project. In the span of a year, but really over the course of one momentous day, Rose has transformed from a middle-class reader fascinated by the picturesque depictions of laboring women to an industrial laborer. A year ago, in other words, she occupied roughly the same social position as most early twentieth-century readers of realist–sociological fiction. After experiencing the travails of poverty firsthand, Rose can appreciate the distance between aestheticized representations of poverty and the reality of being a girl "who lived in hall bedrooms on little or nothing a week." The ability to appreciate that such a distinction exists makes her a more incisive writer—after all, we are reading Rose's "autobiography"—and interpreter of social circumstances. In this vignette, the narrator reflects on the distinction between firsthand and secondhand forms of knowledge and on the tension between proximity and distance that the undercover text exists to mediate. And embedded in her praise for the undercover method is an implicit warning that literature—whether "story-books" and "magazine stories" or class-passing novels—powerfully shapes readers' attitudes about the world.

But it is the epilogue that presents the novel's most explicit reading advice. The narrator breaks the narrative frame to explain how Rose managed to rise from factory laborer to published author in a matter of three years. Her social advancement, it turns out, has been highly systematic: after setting up a proper home with another genteel wage earner, Rose signs up for an evening stenography course and conducts a self-taught course of reading in her spare time. This autodidactic literary education has a two-part structure, moving from practical to theoretical analysis. Rose begins by reading every book at the library that she thinks might help her "solve the problem of earning a good livelihood." Her second phase entails a more rigorous and systematic course of reading, approaching the problem of women's labor from a scientific and economic perspective. Soon, Rose explains, she enrolls in stenography school, continuing all the while to exercise reading habits that are "of a most desultory, though always mercenary sort." Busy at work and in class from morning until night seven days of the week, at this point in her story "the Long Day began in earnest."[87]

Richardson's double entendre works on a number of levels. She alludes, of course, to the "long day" of a woman who works all day and attends school every evening. And she puns on the title of her own book to suggest that the hard work Rose performed in factories across New York City was actually nothing as compared to the demanding synthesis of wage labor and education that heralds true self-improvement. This metafictional wink captures the social work of undercover literature by confirming that social practice and literary form are one: *The Long Day* achieves its final form because of the author's own long, laborious days as recounted in the prescriptive epilogue—a feat of endurance that reportedly trumps the months of long working days described over the course of the novel.

In contrasting the productive reading that supported her protagonist's upward mobility with the flawed literary practices of the poor, Richardson constructs correct reading as a form of labor dependent on a scrupulous work ethic. Such a construction is fundamentally at odds with traditional understandings of reading as a leisure activity, yet it accords with the idea, commonly voiced in etiquette and reading advice manuals of the time, that "*how* to read is, for society, more important than *what* we read" and with the notion that "good" reading could support the development of discipline, memory, and perception.[88] *The Long Day* is a veritable treasure trove of ascetic Protestantism, preaching, as Kathi Weeks puts it, "the moral import of constant and methodical productive effort on the part of self-disciplined individual subjects."[89] Indeed, the narrator ultimately argues that the core problem with wage earners is their inefficiency and lack of skill as laborers, their willingness to be "*simply 'worked'*" like machines rather than "to work" intelligently.[90] Thus it makes sense that of all the books Rose reads, Booker T. Washington's *Up from Slavery* is the one to occasion an important turning point in her life. *Up from Slavery* "brought home to me as nothing else could have done what was the real trouble with myself and all the rest of the struggling, ill-paid, wretched working women with whom I had come in contact"—namely, that the "working woman is a new product . . . as new to the idea of what it really means to work as is the Afro-American citizen."[91] It is the narrator's conscientious reading that allows her to identify her experience as a white working woman with the (alleged) condition of African American laborers. Reading Washington's memoir furnishes a bridge between the two minoritized social groups—the "best" of whom, Richardson suggests, are striving ever upward. This nexus of reading and identification roughly parallels the one Richardson envisioned for her own book. As I have been arguing, the very purpose of undercover literature is to draw privileged white readers closer to the experiences of working people, to construct a bridge via reading where none existed before.

But the resemblances between Washington and Richardson go further still, for both *Up from Slavery* and *The Long Day* present their authors as exemplars of imitable social pedagogy: the latter offers its class-traversing heroine—Richardson's "self"—as an object lesson for educators and reformers concerned with the white female working classes. And both authors detail a profoundly disciplined approach to reading and to labor, efforts that lead directly to a happy ending. To Richardson, the material fact of the book itself exemplifies her success, and her book's potential utility for other readers justifies the considerable suffering she endured in producing it. "I can now look back upon the recent, still vivid past without a shiver; for there is comfort in the thought that what I have undergone is to be held up to others as a possible lesson and warning," the narrator declares.[92] Generically, then, *The Long Day* joins *Up from Slavery* as an instrumental text made for use.

Moreover, both Richardson and Washington encourage the structure of reception I have called *reading for reform*. This sensibility links their prose to the mission of Progressive reform institutions. The status of their own books as vehicles of reform for the upwardly mobile reader merely reifies the more generally "mercenary" reading formation they hope will take hold among working women and African Americans, respectively. Both authors advocate a version of what Blair calls "reading up," an orientation toward reading books not because they are intrinsically good but because they promise to elevate the reader in the cultural and social hierarchy.[93] She who "reads up" approaches books in a self-interested and utilitarian way as valuable cultural capital.

But there is a crucial distinction to be made here, for just as Richardson, like Washington before her, promotes an instrumental approach to reading for social advancement, she is aware that her book will reach mainly affluent readers—not, in fact, the laborers to whom she appears to dole out advice throughout the narrative. Unsurprisingly, working-class readers showed little interest in undercover narratives. These books were unaffordable and inaccessible, and workers' own long days left scant time or energy in which to consume them. Moreover, if the example of Parker's unexpected reader at the bleachery is any indication, then undercover writing's condescension and conservatism made them anathema to working-class readers. "I am sorry, but I'm too tired when I get home at night to read things like that article on Industrial Education. I'm sure I ought to know about it and think about it, but I'm too tired," one woman wrote to the editors of *Life and Labor*, the official journal of the Women's Trade Union League (WTUL).[94]

But while it's likely that few working-class and poor Americans checked out *The Long Day* from their local library, undercover writers' insights managed to reach this audience through a circuitous institutional route that brings social reform organizations back to the center of my argument. Undercover writers' actual and implied readers were people a lot like themselves: college-educated, philanthropically inclined, middle- and upper-class citizens—readers uniquely positioned to put undercover writers' recommendations into practice within existing sites of social reform. Undercover writers explicitly engage this readership by proposing concrete solutions to the social problems they document and by endorsing the work of specific reform institutions. Annie Marion MacLean champions the Consumers' League, Amy Tanner pushes for an eight-hour workday, and Frances Donovan praises the Waitresses' Alliance that offered her job opportunities and a support network. Maud Younger couches her advocacy of unions in criticism of the conservative politics of certain settlement workers, quoting a conversation between two coworkers: "'But Miss Morgan says that labor unions are never satisfied. They always want more.' 'Who's Miss Morgan?' asked 12. 'She's the directress of our club, and her father's president of a railroad.'"[95] Bessie Van Vorst draws on the resources of Hull-House while working undercover in Chicago (though she elsewhere equates reform institutions with the "fictitious duties" of "old maids"), and Marie Van Vorst advocates for child labor legislation and the expansion of kindergartens. When it comes time to offer institutional remedies, though, both Van Vorsts somewhat bafflingly neglect the truly impoverished female workers whose struggles they have illustrated most fully. Instead, they urge reformers to develop Tuskegee-like industrial training facilities for the upper echelons of woman wageworkers. Training "non-self-supporting girls" to do skilled labor such as lace making and bookbinding—work that can be done from home, far away from machines—would create a "new, higher, superior class of industrial art laborers."[96]

All undercover authors, in other words, situate their writing within a larger institutional web. Like earlier nineteenth-century reform fiction, which exhorts readers to "feel right" and sees the activation of a sympathetic emotional response as a legitimate reformist objective, undercover writers seek to stir feelings of outrage, sorrow, and compassion in their readers. But in this early twentieth-century genre, feeling right through reading is just one phase in a longer process of concrete institutional outcomes. The tendency to connect individual pursuit of social justice to larger organizations possessing institutional power and expertise was, after all, a hallmark of Progressive reform, and here it becomes a central feature of undercover writing.

For her part, Richardson acknowledges that the social problems her novel documents are structural and systemic. She notes in her epilogue that "the responsibility for these conditions of moral as well as physical wretchedness is fundamentally attributable to our present socio-economic system," but, curiously, she declines to discuss the socioeconomic system in theoretical terms or endorse the unions she heartily supports until the "idea of organized labor" has grown more popular among working women themselves. (As the introduction to *The Long Day* notes, only 1.5 percent of female industrial laborers were organized into trade unions in 1903.)[97] Instead, Richardson melds the discursive and behavioral mandate of the Protestant work ethic with the Pragmatist rhetoric of hands-on labor, placing all hope for social reconstruction in the individual woman, who must learn to value work in general and "making something with the hands" in particular.[98] Her conclusion turns, finally, to social reform institutions, elucidating the need for improved lodging houses and respectable parlors and for expanded opportunities for working people to attend kindergartens, settlement houses, Social Gospel churches, and vocational schools. It does not mention higher pay, shorter hours, or safer working conditions.

After the success of *The Long Day*, Richardson became a popular speaker at churches, universities, settlements, and working girls' clubs, delivering lectures that connected her novel to the institutional goals of the organizations that hosted her. Reviews of *The Long Day* indicate that professional readers also interpreted the novel as an adjunct to reform activity. The book's principal reviewers were people like Maud Nathan, the leading organizer in the Consumers' League, the Women's Municipal League of New York, and the General Federation of Women's Clubs; Frances Maule, a prominent suffragist whose assessment of Richardson's novel detailed the need for better lodging houses and vocational training; and Jack London, who used the book as a platform for explicating his own views of economic inequality. In her positive review of *The Long Day*, socialist feminist Rose Pastor Stokes (who also went by the name Rose Phelps Stokes) wrote that she expected the book to educate reformers about facts to which they remained willfully blind and to enlarge their reserves of empathy. And despite the novel's overtly literary mien, none of these reviewers positioned the book within the artistic contexts of realism or naturalism or in genres of fiction or autobiography. Similarly, Richardson's negative reviewers focused on her interpretation of social problems they claimed she did not adequately comprehend.[99]

The book's reception history indicates that *The Long Day* was viewed not only as a compelling story or as pressing social commentary, as one might expect, but also as a call to arms for educators and reformers to reexamine their methods. There is evidence that Richardson's novel did actually spark a certain amount of institutional change. The National League of Women Workers (the revised name of the Association of Working Girls' Societies) used *The Long Day* as a guidebook for correcting flaws within the movement, including some of the very shortcomings discussed in chapter 2 above. The 1908 document *A Brief History of the First Decade of the National League of Women Workers, 1898–1908* tells the story of that movement's bureaucratic history, with the location and attendance of annual league meetings, advertising sales for the *Club Worker,* and the appointment of new vice presidents serving as plot points. Amid this dry narrative, *A Brief History* admits that the 1905 publication of *The Long Day* threw a wrench into the movement's placid self-satisfaction. It states, "The picture drawn in *The Long Day* had kindled much anxiety for the working girl of very small wages, who must board alone in a large city." How could it be, the document asks, that conditions for working women in New York remained so grim almost twenty years after the working girls' club movement was founded in that same city? Richardson's novel made movement leaders so anxious about their own dubious accomplishments, in fact, that they decided to investigate the living and working conditions of their own members and to reach out to "girls who most need club opportunities"— girls like Richardson's onetime coworkers and housemates. The result of this investigation revealed that the club movement actually knew very little about the "outside life" of its wage-earning members. The undercover novel ultimately exposed the essential hollowness of the movement's much-touted cross-class intimacy, suggesting that friendship between rich and poor women did not stray beyond the spatial or epistemological parameters of the club room.[100]

But this incident left scarcely a dent in the larger infrastructure of Progressive reform, and it hardly seems to count as the kind of significant practical impact that undercover writers envisioned for their work. Tellingly, *The Long Day*'s most vocal detractor arrived at the same conclusion as the league, if from a more cutting vantage point. Union organizer Leonora O'Reilly wrote a scathing assessment of Richardson's novel in a 1905 review that was intended for the *New York Journal* but was never published. O'Reilly argued that elite reformers and undercover writers shared a fundamental misunderstanding of women's experience of wagework:

> The book sells like hot cakes at a fair—Ministers preach sermons on it. Critics vie with each other to review it. It becomes the topic of afternoon teas. . . . It appeals to those who could not be paid to listen to the patient, plodding every day life of the working woman until she is made picturesquely immoral, interestingly vulgar, and maudlinly sentimental. No, good Mr. Editor, Mr. Publisher, Mr. Sensational Minister and Lady Bountiful of afternoon teas, you may have paid your money for a *real* working girl sensation, but you did not get the *real* thing.

O'Reilly finds Richardson's portrayal of working-class language, behavior, and morals so tendentious as to undermine the whole premise of her book. "No working woman ever wrote like that about her class," she declares, and she insists that she had earned the right to forward her own corrective views on working-class experience "positively without fear of contradiction after an experience of over twenty years daily intercourse with them *as one of them.*"[101] O'Reilly's negative review of *The Long Day* forms part of a larger attack on the dominance of wealthy women within the purportedly cross-class alliance of the Women's Trade Union League, an organization O'Reilly helped found in 1903 alongside alumnae of the settlement house and working girls' club movements. She and other wage earners found themselves crowded out of the movement by the hegemony of well-meaning allies, class-privileged reformers whose ability to finance the burgeoning cause of women's unionization unfairly tilted the balance of power in their favor. O'Reilly attempted to resign from the WTUL in 1905, in part because she was outraged to see her colleagues supporting and publicizing *The Long Day*. The league had promoted the book—principal funder Margaret Dreier Robins wrote a mixed review for *Charities and the Commons*—and published excerpted chapters in its institutional materials.[102] *The Long Day* simply confirmed for O'Reilly, and doubtless for many other working-class readers, that the fundamental imbalance of power that characterized reform culture shaped adjacent literary experiments as well.

It is little surprise that O'Reilly's counternarrative ranges so freely between literary and labor critique here, considering how many material and conceptual vectors linked the work of reform organizations to the genre of undercover writing. What undercover literature establishes, above all, is that literature and reform were far more than merely analogous. Instead, they worked together in producing representations of working-class reality—representations that had the power to shape the social and political contours of that reality by directing the flow of sentiment, capital, and organizing power. In both scenarios, reformer-writers "paid [their] money for a *real* working girl sensation," constructing the working-class woman as a commodity to be bought and sold by the comfortable classes alone. By positioning her as a firsthand resource to further their own education and authorship, their own subjectivity, undercover writers evaded the task of reckoning with real conditions of urban-industrial capitalism. Moreover, they spoke as—and in the place of—the poor, the other potential expositors of city life, who, of course, possessed far greater intimacy with working-class reality but were rarely granted a public platform to elaborate on it. In this deeper sense, then, the undercover archive instantiates a mode of stolen authorship.

Such is the abortive legacy of the undercover literary project. For all their good intentions, class-crossing authors finally succeeded only in consolidating their own place within a now more coherently articulated class of socially conscious readers and writers, people of means whose knowledge of social facts authorized them to advocate for the poor. They sought little input from marginalized subjects in this endeavor; as I have argued, the voices of the "other half" emerge strictly in the highly mediated form of vernacular quotation. Class-passing writers transformed methodologies of conversation and eavesdropping into constitutive features of a new literary genre that selectively drew on features of realism and modernism: extended quotation and transcription, attention to the sound of nonstandard speakers' voices and to the shock of hearing slang and profanity, and a relentless search for fresh interlocutors and useful gossip. But these working-class interlocutors were "compelled to play not the leading roles but the human scenery before which the melodrama of middle-class redemption could be enacted, for the enlightenment of an audience in which they were not even included," as Laura Wexler aptly puts it. The most powerful class relationship the readers and writers of undercover literature forged is the one that strengthened their bond as members of a reform-minded middle class.[103]

In this chapter, I have suggested that the methodology of undercover literature linked writing to reform in two ways. First, undercover literature attempted to close the epistemological gap between firsthand experience and secondhand representation in books by channeling the former into the latter. Second, undercover writers used their experience of cross-class proximity to propose solutions to socioeconomic crises they believed to be rooted in similar conditions of social distance. These solutions replicated the platform of contemporary reform institutions and therefore magnified the significance of those sites within the field of American literature. Yet the genre's ultimate hollowness as a political or ethical force finally lies in another kind of distance, one to which undercover writers were seemingly oblivious: the tremendous, yawning gap between the structural problems Richardson and her colleagues represent and the fundamentally deficient individualist recommendations they so often propose. This chasm casts doubt on the genre's whole enterprise. Undercover writers held political perspectives that ranged from conservative to progressive, but they clung to the view that the working-class subject needed to commit to self-reform on an individual level. This, finally, is what "good reading" stood to effect.

Thus, Richardson's final recommendation that reform institutions disseminate "better literature" merely confirms undercover literature's vital place within the larger ecology of early twentieth-century reform and also confirms, by extension, the centrality of reform to U.S. literary culture. Her narrator puts it bluntly in the epilogue:

> There is a broad field awaiting some original-minded philanthropist who will try to counteract the maudlin yellow-back by putting in its place something wholesome and sweet. Only, please, Mr. or Mrs. Philanthropist, don't let it be Shakespeare, or Ruskin, or Walter Pater. Philanthropists have tried before to reform degraded literary tastes with heroic treatment, and they have failed every time. That is sometimes the trouble with the

college-settlement folk. They forget that Shakspere [*sic*], and Ruskin, and all the rest of the really true and great literary crew, are infinite bores to every-day people. . . . The taste for better literature could be helped along immeasurably if still another original-minded philanthropist were to make it his business that no tenement baby should be without its "Mother Goose" and, a little later, its "Little Women," "Uncle Tom's Cabin," "Robinson Crusoe," and all the other precious childhood favorites. As it is, the majority know nothing about them.[104]

Conflating intimacy with authority, the undercover author uses her firsthand knowledge of working-class taste to articulate a literary–pedagogical program that cannily avoids authors she believes will derail the work of uplift and endorses those that promise to "prepare the leaven for the loaf" of kindergarten, settlement house, and school.[105] Reading for reform reaches its apex here, at the point where literary practice and reform policy become interchangeable modalities of experience. By becoming a guide to the social mobility of others, Richardson translates her proximate encounter with poverty into the institutional protocols of social reform.

The onus finally rests on the undercover figure's real-life proxies, the historical readers of these narratives, to initiate the social changes a text can only prescribe. It remains as obscure in the archive of undercover writing as it does in other representations of humanitarian crisis whether the reader's textual encounter with the pain of others effectively mobilizes social action in the public sphere, or whether the act of reading itself stands as a valuable and sufficient gesture of social engagement. The question of what reading for reform can actually *do*—what new worlds it can bring into being—remains open.

Coda

TWENTY-FIRST CENTURY AFTERLIVES

This book has presented a constellation of microhistories at the intersection of social reform and U.S. literature. It might be tempting to glean from the contemporary invisibility of many of these once-prominent institutional and literary sites that they have had minimal lasting impact, their significance dulled beyond the temporal parameters of this study. After all, the working girls' club movement is now mostly forgotten; undercover literature languishes on unvisited library shelves and on the Internet Archive's Wayback Machine, many years out of print. But this is far from the case. If anything, recent events point to the enduring cultural afterlife of uplift institutions and reform literature. By way of conclusion, let me enumerate a few recent examples of this contemporary legacy.

On January 27, 2012, Hull-House closed after providing 122 years of ongoing social services to low-income Chicago residents. The Hull-House Association's board of directors cited bankruptcy, while laid-off employees claimed financial malfeasance on the part of the board. The direct, helping services Hull-House offered (child care, counseling, job training) were transferred to other community organizations. But the legacy of this association has not been erased entirely. Since 1963, the historical institution "Hull-House" has been living a double life as social service agency on the one hand and as a museum sponsored by the University of Illinois's College of Architecture and the Arts on the other. The Jane Addams Hull-House Museum was unaffected by the Hull-House Association's closure; it remains open in the original location on South Halsted Street, where it pays tribute to Jane Addams by maintaining a curatorial focus on arts education and social justice issues. The settlement house thus first evolved from its original status as a joint educational and reformist association to two discrete institutions of social work and cultural education and has now been reduced to the latter alone.

The elimination of a civic Hull-House and the retention of a cultural Hull-House tells us much about the uneven distribution of funding for institutions geared toward distinct, and differently empowered, communities: those who experience social need directly and those who visit cultural institutions to learn more about social need. But it also suggests the important place turn-of-the-century social reform continues to hold in the contemporary imagination. Although the densely populated neighborhoods of working-class Jewish, Irish, Italian, and Slavic immigrants that dotted turn-of-the-century American cities have long since disappeared, interest in the history of the urban ghetto has not abated. Today, built environments like New York City's Tenement Museum, founded in 1988, permit visitors to walk through an "authentic" urban tenement at 97 Orchard Street on the Lower East Side; its apartments are preserved and decorated in period style. In one apartment, narrow beds are pushed against the stove; in another, a small bedroom is given over to a makeshift tailor shop. The Tenement Museum invites visitors to imagine immigrant life in the late nineteenth or early twentieth century, and literary representations of the turn-of-the-century tenement, ethnic ghetto, and surrounding community organizations are central to this process of imagining: the museum's bookstore sells a large selection of immigrant literature in reissued editions, much of which addresses the importance of the settlement house to the Lower East Side and to an immigrant generation that has disappeared forever. The bookstore shelves display the autobiographies of Rose Cohen and Lillian Wald alongside Irving Howe's encyclopedic rendering of Jewish American history; indeed, most of the museum's recommended books deal to some degree with the settlement movement.[1]

In spite of the obvious deprivations the tenement's original inhabitants suffered and the vigorous efforts of reformers to abolish those social conditions, the institutions of the turn-of-the-century ghetto are the subject of intense nostalgia at both the Tenement Museum and the Hull-House

Museum. The settlement house and adjacent ghetto institutions emerge as deeply valued sites of cultural memory in the absence of any ongoing material place, functioning as a crucial node in the museums' narrative of social mobility and acculturation. Interestingly, the museums' fond retrospection on overcrowded tenements, bustling multilingual streets, and unmelted ethnics precisely reverses the tenets of Progressive reform, which aimed to change those very aspects of the immigrants' urban experience that the contemporary museums most treasure. Just as affiliation with working-class and immigrant communities once served as a balm for reformers in search of a "common life," here too direct contact with physical space and real historical figures constitutes the museums' pedagogical method; both institutions name and describe former residents of Orchard Street and South Halsted Street. Contemporary visitors reach out to the same historical milieu to rediscover the nation's roots, and perhaps also their own, in working-class urban space. Although nostalgia and social reform look very differently at the same cultural site, the modes of memorialization at the Tenement Museum and Hull-House Museum make clear that Progressive reform continues to galvanize new narratives into the twenty-first century, even as its legacy of providing direct service to underserved urban communities has been eroded.

The social and literary legacy of social reform persists in other nonprofit organizations as well. In New York City, 826NYC and Girls Write Now recruit well-educated volunteers to offer personal mentorship and literary training to talented young members of underprivileged groups. The participants in these programs publish journals and anthologies, read their work at high-profile public events, and, importantly, get into college at astronomical rates. (The Girls Write Now website declares that "100% of GWN seniors graduate high school and go on to college.")[2] Meanwhile, the Occupy Wall Street movement of 2011–12 and the more recent Black Lives Matter movement have made literature a cornerstone of their social and political projects. Beginning in the early days of Occupy Wall Street in the fall of 2011, the People's Library set up shop in Zuccotti Park as the literary-institutional analog to a leaderless movement. The library was entirely donated, collective, public, and open to all; its collection was made up of fiction and nonfiction, meeting minutes, mission statements, and press. After the New York Police Department destroyed the original collection of books, magazines, and pamphlets in their November 15 raid on the Occupy Wall Street encampment, activists resurrected the library as a mobile book-sharing system of shopping carts and crates that accompanied Occupy organizers at every public event. The library's slogan delineated its unique contribution to the protest movement: "Literacy, Legitimacy, and Moral Authority."[3] Occupy has spawned many other literary endeavors as well: communal reading events, a small press, the I-am-the-99% documentary project, a poetry anthology, and, of course, countless blogs and Twitter accounts. Since its formation in 2013 in the aftermath of the state-sanctioned murder of unarmed black teenager Trayvon Martin, Black Lives Matter has become a vital black-liberation movement, attacking racism and police violence through social media, mass protest, and public policy. The movement also maintains a significant literary profile, having inspired countless reading groups, syllabi, and reading lists. It has already shaped the black literary canon as well.[4] These pursuits ramify beyond the wish to garner support and visibility for the Occupy and Black Lives Matter movements. They are literary endeavors that weave reading and writing into the very fabric of twenty-first-century social reform. Turn-of-the-century efforts to embed literary engagement in the pursuit of social justice live on in these contemporary movements, promising to redefine the social utility of literature for a new, digital generation of activists, readers, and writers.

The cultural life of Progressive reform also lives on in the domain of performance art.[5] In 2011, artist Tania Bruguera founded a social service–driven arts project she named Immigrant Movement International (IM International) and began a three-year residency in an urban storefront in Corona, Queens. Bruguera is a well-known visual and performance artist from Havana, but IM International was grounded in a series of concrete actions responding to the experience of immigrant life in the United States—none of them overtly artistic. With funding from the Queens Museum of Art and the arts nonprofit organization Creative Time, Bruguera set up a rented storefront as a community space where she and a host of volunteers led workshops and classes offering English lessons, legal advice, and other practical services. During the first year of the movement's existence, she also pursued a fully immersive experience of immigrant life in New York City. Bruguera lived alongside several undocumented workers in a small apartment, struggled to subsist on an amount equal to their low wages, and forwent health insurance. While her period of cross-class proximity came to an end when her artist's residency concluded, the movement's social work nonetheless goes on: as of October 2018, IM International's website continually updates a Google Calendar in English and Spanish with details about upcoming events—ballet and guitar classes, *risoterapia* (laughter therapy), meetings of the youth and mother's groups. The website also lists the names of leaders, volunteers, and residents.

Bruguera's mission statement describes the IM International in spatial terms, as a "community space," "think tank," "lab," and "educational platform." Seemingly without intending to do so, Bruguera built a twenty-first-century reform site that replicates the goals and methods of the Progressive Era settlement house in nearly every respect and approximates the immersive techniques of undercover authors. Nowhere in the movement's parainstitutional literature does she reference the settlement house as an inspiration or harken back to other historical models. Yet elsewhere Bruguera describes her project as a case study in what she calls Arte Útil (Useful Art)—art that "[develops] new methods and social formations to deal with issues that were once the domain of the state."[6] Bruguera's ahistorical project is thus profoundly historical in its implications, as it draws an invisible line from Progressive reform institutions—which reformers initially founded to contend with the absence of state support for social welfare and then abandoned when such support was established—to the contemporary moment, marked as it is by the profound erosion of twentieth-century state-supported social initiatives.[7] Bruguera has not attracted the kind of positive attention she might have wished for her project: one *New York Times* article published shortly after she took up residency in Queens emphasizes her neighbors' ambivalence, painting her as a latter-day Van Vorst sister. Yet IM International nonetheless succeeded in establishing a more public and indeed institutional place for Bruguera's social service art. In July 2015, the city of New York appointed Bruguera the first artist in residence affiliated with the Mayor's Office for Immigrant Affairs. During her one-year residency, Bruguera used her creative platform to educate undocumented New York City residents about the city's new, free identification card.[8]

My final example concerns the flourishing genre of undercover literature. This literary and now televisual mode continues apace, spawning high-profile books and programs that follow—perhaps unwittingly—in the footsteps of the Van Vorsts, Parker, and Richardson. In early 2012, investigative reporter Tracie McMillan released a book entitled *The American Way of Eating: Undercover at Walmart, Applebee's, Farm Fields, and the Dinner Table,* which chronicles her months spent undercover performing low-wage, unskilled labor and subsisting on its meager wages. Her goal was to expose the corporate food hierarchy's pernicious effect on the livelihoods of its employees and on public health at large. Although McMillan's working-class upbringing distinguishes her from her genteel forebears of a hundred years ago, the fact that she uses undercover methods to begin with means that education, class, and lifestyle mark an important distinction between herself and her coworkers. "Like any stranger in a foreign land, I'm overwhelmed by the landscape around me," McMillan writes with Van Vorstian flair of her time stocking shelves at a Walmart in Michigan.[9] McMillan's reformist mission to extend public health campaigns into the realm of literary nonfiction draws extensively on the methods of her closest contemporary, Barbara Ehrenreich, whose 2001 book *Nickel and Dimed: On (Not) Getting By in America* has been enormously successful. *The American Way of Eating* also perpetuates the work of especially progressive undercover writers of the early twentieth century, for whom waitressing or factory labor was a prelude to union advocacy or endorsement of the eight-hour day.

In contrast, the popular CBS reality television show *Undercover Boss* (2010–) draws on the most conservative, individualist tropes from the undercover archive as it depicts business executives going into disguise as one of their own employees. Each episode shares an overarching goal—to become a kinder, more humane boss by heeding the voices of labor—and follows a set formula: a corporate CEO realizes that he knows very little about his own low-paid employees; he dons a fake moustache, jumpsuit, or weathered plaid shirt as necessary to impersonate one of those employees and becomes an entry-level employee at his own workplace to discover the "reality" of the labor conditions he legislates and profits from. We watch him struggle to perform necessary tasks and converse with two or three coworkers, for whom he develops a personalized concern. At the conclusion of every episode, the executive reveals his true identity to his new "friends" ("Surprise! I am the CEO of global 7-Eleven, not the slushy repairman!"), promises to institute local changes to his organization, and offers his "friends" sums of money to solve whatever issue plagues their private lives: they have, naturally, brought up their sick mothers, too-expensive weddings, mortgages in arrears, and aborted college educations over the course of his week undercover. The executive weeps as he reflects on his new knowledge, and his employees weep in turn as they receive a gift that will, he swears, solve all their problems. As in early twentieth-century narratives, the undercover boss's goal has always been to pursue cross-class contact as a valuable source of social knowledge. But because this contemporary undercover agent also possesses the power to sign a check or tighten safety codes, to raise his employees' hourly wages or indeed to fire them, he may use these relationships to craft a gentler workplace while leaving the structuring mechanisms of capitalism unmentioned and untouched. Gone is the author's conventional appeal for social action on the part of his readers: the undercover boss *is* the change he wants to see in the world.

Part of the pleasure of *Undercover Boss* for a recession-era audience has been the opportunity to watch a corporate millionaire fumble the seemingly mundane tasks of an entry-level worker and, of course, to see him cry. The show has earned its coveted Friday night time slot because the CEO debases himself by struggling to mop a floor, not because he has a heart of gold. But viewers also want to believe that corporate structures can change—and that populist cultural texts possess the power to change them. The model of "social reform" operating here is amorphous at best. In an editorial for the *Huffington Post*, newspaper mogul Arianna Huffington analogizes the "quiet desperation of the working classes" in *Undercover Boss* to Benjamin Disraeli's 1845 industrial novel *Sybil*, a tale of "two nations between whom there is no sympathy."[10] The problem of class disparity is also a matter of class distance, Huffington insists, which is why *Undercover Boss* is so helpful: it introduces executives to blue-collar laborers, and it introduces a diverse viewership to working-class TV characters. Huffington may be correct in electing reality television the social problem novel of the twenty-first century, but her belief in the good faith, cross-class reformism of *Undercover Boss* is at best ahistorical and at worst a privileged delusion. Or maybe her historical amnesia is a necessary symptom of *any* reformist narrative. The texts of culture—as American as Applebee's or 7-Eleven—are new again, each and every time, when they become vehicles of social change.

Acknowledgments

It is a pleasure to be able to acknowledge in print the many individuals and institutions whose support made this book possible. At McGill University, studying with Jackie Buxton and Erin Hurley started me off on this venture. At New York University (NYU), Thomas Augst was an exceptional mentor and dissertation supervisor, asker of the most stimulating questions. He, Patricia Crain, and Phillip Brian Harper were an ideal committee of engaged and challenging readers, and I remain grateful for their ongoing guidance and profound generosity. Thank you also to Elizabeth McHenry, Bryan Waterman, and Lisa Gitelman for offering valuable insights and acts of friendship. My years at NYU were shared with a graduate cohort of funny and caring geniuses. I am especially grateful that graduate school brought me the deep friendship of Jennifer Spitzer and Shirley Wong, my own personal axis of kindness. Jen and Shirley have given feedback on practically every word I have ever written, tone-checked countless emails, and been soul friends of the highest order.

I am fortunate to have found a wonderful academic home at Ryerson University. Two sequential chairs of English, Nima Naghibi and Andrew O'Malley, offered unfailing support and understanding as I completed this book. I am grateful to my colleagues in the Department of English for their warm collegiality, and especially to Jason Boyd, Colleen Derkatch, Lorraine Janzen Kooistra, Dale Smith, and Monique Tschofen for always being on hand with advice and encouragement. I thank the dedicated librarians and staff of the Ryerson University Library and Archives for tracking down sometimes obscure materials on my behalf. Generous travel support provided by the Faculty of Arts at Ryerson University enabled me to share earlier versions of this project at conferences. The preparation of my index was supported with a grant provided by the Office of the Dean of Arts at Ryerson. I am grateful to the American Jewish Historical Society in New York and Boston for use of materials in the Educational Alliance Collection, I–359; to the Rare Book and Manuscript Library of Columbia University for use of the Christodora House Records; and to the New York Public Library for granting me access to its archival collection.

The intellectual companionship of colleagues at other universities has enriched this book in many ways. For reading drafts, fielding questions, and thinking with me, I thank Toby Beauchamp, Mary Chapman, Julia Fawcett, Travis Foster, Josh Gang, David Hollingshead, Sheila Liming, Cannon Schmidt, Dana Seitler, Kate Stanley, and Autumn Womack. Stephanie Foote has been a rock star. Naomi Levine and Greg Ellermann have been world-championship friends since our collective coming-of-age in Montreal. For asking about the book sometimes, but mostly for filling my life with other things to care about, I thank my friends in New York City, Toronto, and further afield: you know who you are.

At the University of Minnesota Press, I thank Danielle Kasprzak for her encouragement and support in bringing this book into being. Anne Carter and Laura Westlund offered invaluable editorial assistance, Kathy Delfosse provided scrupulous copyediting, and Puck Fletcher prepared the index with precision and speed. The insights of two anonymous readers for the University of Minnesota Press improved this book exponentially. Rebecca Thursten lent her characteristic rigor and wit to my baggy endnotes when I really needed her.

My greatest thanks are reserved for my family. I am very lucky to have joined the extended Qadeer clan; thank you to Mohammad, Susan, Nadra, Keith, Razia, Ruby, Ahmer, Millie, Zuzu, and Ibi. The love and friendship of my brother, Benjamin Fisher, has sustained me from afar. I wish to express my profound love and gratitude to my parents, Valerie and Alfred Fisher, whose immeasurable support and faith in me have made everything possible; I cannot begin to enumerate the emotional and intellectual gifts they have given me. I wish my father could be here to see this book, which he cared about so much, come into the world at the same time as his first grandchild, Rose. Thank you to my beautiful Rosie for nudging me along to the finish line from in utero. And to Ali Shamas Qadeer: you were by my side the first time I cracked open *The House of Mirth* and for my first walk down Henry Street. The ideas that went into this book would simply be unthinkable without you. Every moment of my life has been the brighter for your irrepressible wit and curiosity, your fierce loyalty, and your boundless love.

Notes

INTRODUCTION

1. "Far and Near," *Far and Near,* no. 1 (November 1890): 1.
2. The elliptical reference to class difference here is characteristic of reform organizations that viewed social change through the lens of uplift rather than radicalism.
3. Maria Bowen Chapin was the editor of *Far and Near* and an active participant in the working girls' club movement. She would go on to found the Chapin School in 1901, which became one of the most elite all-girl prep schools in New York City.
4. Henry James, *Hawthorne* (London: Macmillan, 1879), 42.
5. On the genesis and significance of modernist autonomy in the late nineteenth and early twentieth centuries, see Andrew Goldstone's *Fictions of Autonomy* (New York: Oxford University Press, 2013). Goldstone argues that understandings of modernism's relative autonomy became the basis of "a new social formation for literature: a world of specialized and professionalized writers, publishers, and readers with their own particular rules of description and evaluation, their own claims to independence" (2).
6. See Susan M. Ryan, "Reform," in *Keywords in American Cultural Studies,* ed. Bruce Burgett and Glenn Hendler (New York: New York University Press, 2007), 198.
7. See Allen Davis, *Spearheads for Reform* (New York: Oxford University Press, 1968), and Judith Trolander, *Professionalism and Social Change* (New York: Columbia University Press, 1987).
8. Alexis de Tocqueville, *Democracy in America,* ed. J. P. Mayer, trans. George Lawrence (New York: Anchor, 1969), 513.
9. See Lisa A. Long, "The Postbellum Reform Writings of Rebecca Harding Davis and Elizabeth Stuart Phelps," in *The Cambridge Companion to Nineteenth-Century American Women's Writing,* ed. Dale M. Bauer and Philip Gould (Cambridge: Cambridge University Press, 2001), 262–83, here 273.

See also Lori Ginzberg, *Women and the Work of Benevolence* (New Haven: Yale University Press, 1990). Many nineteenth-century reform organizations were fed by the religious enthusiasm of the Second Great Awakening and maintained strong financial and ideological ties to Christian denominations. On the rise of the Social Gospel movement in the late nineteenth century, see Wendy J. Deichmann Edwards and Carolyn De Swarte Gifford, eds., *Gender and the Social Gospel* (Urbana and Chicago: University of Illinois Press, 2003).

10. Ryan, "Reform," 197.

11. See Alan Trachtenberg, *The Incorporation of America: Culture and Society in the Gilded Age* (New York: Hill and Wang, 1982). For an account of the late nineteenth-century United States as what Sven Beckert calls an "associational universe," see his "Bourgeois Institution Builders: New York in the Nineteenth Century," in *The American Bourgeoisie: Distinction and Identity in the Nineteenth Century*, ed. Sven Beckert and Julia B. Rosenbaum (New York: Palgrave Macmillan, 2010), 104.

12. Amanda Claybaugh, *The Novel of Purpose: Literature and Social Reform in the Anglo-American World* (Ithaca, N.Y.: Cornell University Press, 2007), 21. On philanthropy as a requirement of the upper classes, see the essays collected in Lawrence J. Friedman and Mark D. McGarvie, eds., *Charity, Philanthropy, and Civility in American History* (New York: Cambridge University Press, 2004). The classic expression of the so-called gospel of wealth appears in Andrew Carnegie's essay of the same name. Kathleen D. McCarthy makes the important point that postbellum American women were more likely than men to donate time rather than money; see her essay "Women and Political Culture," in Friedman and McGarvie, *Charity, Philanthropy, and Civility in American History*, 179–98.

13. See Francesca Sawaya, *The Difficult Art of Giving: Patronage, Philanthropy, and the American Literary Market* (Philadelphia: University of Pennsylvania Press, 2014). As Sawaya notes, corporatized philanthropy contradicted many of the values of U.S. Progressives. However, those values must nonetheless be understood as part of the larger culture of Progressivism (28). On the consolidation of the U.S. cultural elite, see Beckert and Rosenbaum, *The American Bourgeoisie*.

14. Jane Gorjevsky, "Documenting Russian and Eastern European Immigrant Culture in American Manuscript Repositories: Private Philanthropy Archives," in *Tracking a Diaspora*, ed. Anatol Shmelev (London: Routledge, 2012), 9–28, here 13. Before the formation of the Carnegie Corporation in 1911, the Carnegie Home Trust Company managed and administered Andrew Carnegie's philanthropic activities.

15. "Carnegie to Educators," *New York Times*, December 14, 1903.

16. Carnegie claimed that he was not "opposed to the higher education of the Negro" per se, yet he did not finance African American universities that actually delivered a liberal arts education, such as Atlanta University and Fisk University. Carnegie donated $620,000 to Tuskegee and $441,045 to Hampton. See David Nasaw, *Andrew Carnegie* (New York: Penguin, 2006), 714.

17. For influential accounts of the "literary institution," see Mark McGurl, *The Program Era: Postwar Fiction and the Rise of Creative Writing* (Cambridge, Mass.: Harvard University Press, 2009), esp. 151; Jeffrey Williams, *The Institution of Literature* (Albany: SUNY Press, 2002), esp. 2; Lisi Schoenbach, *Pragmatic Modernism* (New York: Oxford University Press, 2012); Lawrence Rainey, *Institutions of Modernism: Literary Elites and Public Culture* (New Haven: Yale University Press, 1998); Caroline Levine, *Forms: Whole, Rhythm, Hierarchy, Network* (Princeton: Princeton University Press, 2015); and James F. English, "Everywhere and Nowhere: The Sociology of Literature after 'the Sociology of Literature,'" introduction to a special issue on the sociology of literature, *New Literary History* 41, no. 2 (Spring 2010): v–xxiii. My theoretical understanding of institutions is informed as well by Pierre Bourdieu's now-canonical definition in *The Field of Cultural Production*, trans. Randal Johnson (New York: Columbia University Press, 1993); Michel Foucault's articulations in *The Archaeology of Knowledge and the Discourse on Language*, trans. A. M. Sheridan Smith (New York: Pantheon Books, 1972) and *Discipline and Punish: The Birth of the Prison*, trans. Alan Sheridan (New York: Vintage, 1995); and John Guillory's *Cultural Capital* (Chicago: University of Chicago Press, 1993).

18. See Bourdieu, *The Field of Cultural Production*, 136. It is also important to note that the very concept of an "institution" remained unsettled within turn-of-the-century social reform culture. Some reformers disavowed participation in anything so cold and anonymizing as an institution; others, aware that social service endeavors were feminized and had therefore been devalued throughout the nineteenth century, enthusiastically embraced the notion of an institutionalized reform sphere. Newfound institutional affiliations with academia and municipal politics lent authority and professional status to women's reform work in particular.

19. Michel Foucault, *Power/Knowledge: Selected Interviews and Other Writings, 1972–1977*, ed. Colin Gordon, trans. Colin Gordon, Leo Marshall, John Mepham, and Kate Soper (New York: Pantheon Books, 1980), 197, 96.

20. Barbara Cruikshank, *The Will to Empower: Democratic Citizens and Other Subjects* (Ithaca, N.Y.: Cornell University Press, 1999), 4, 48, 70.

21. Merve Emre has defined the "paraliterary institution" as "an institution

that uses literature to organize practices of self and sociality, but has little to do with the conventional sites and spaces of literary production"—for example, the American Express Company, whose expressive techniques and documents (advertising, traveler's checks) made it possible for American authors to travel abroad and reimagine themselves as artists in exile and, more broadly, helped construct Americans as international subjects. See Emre's "Ironic Institutions: Counterculture Fictions and the American Express Company," *American Literature* 87, no. 1 (March 2015): 107–35, here 113.

22. See Lisa Gitelman, *Paper Knowledge: Toward a Media History of Documents* (Durham, N.C.: Duke University Press, 2014), 5.

23. Charles Taylor, *A Secular Age* (Cambridge, Mass.: Harvard University Press, 2007), 5.

24. See Vida D. Scudder, "College Settlements," *Far and Near*, no. 38 (December 1893): 24. *Far and Near* was the official periodical of the working girls' club movement.

25. Cornelia Stratton Parker, *Working with the Working Woman* (New York: Harper, 1922), 242.

26. Levine, *Forms*, 64.

27. On "distant reading," see Franco Moretti, *Distant Reading* (New York: Verso, 2013). On "surface reading," see Stephen Best and Sharon Marcus, "Surface Reading: An Introduction," *Representations* 108, no. 1 (Fall 2009): 1–21, and Heather Love, "Close but Not Deep: Literary Ethics and the Descriptive Turn," *New Literary History* 41, no. 2 (Spring 2010): 371–91.

28. Thanks to Stephanie Foote for bringing this idea to my attention.

29. Pierre Bourdieu, *Distinction: A Social Critique of the Judgment of Taste*, trans. Richard Nice (Cambridge, Mass.: Harvard University Press, 1987), 100. On Bourdieu's own split or divided habitus as a result of upward mobility, see Deborah Reed-Danahay, *Locating Bourdieu* (Bloomington: Indiana University Press, 2005), 156.

30. See Pierre Bourdieu, *Outline of a Theory of Practice*, trans. Richard Nice (Cambridge: Cambridge University Press, 1977), 214, and Bourdieu, *In Other Words: Essays Towards a Reflexive Sociology*, trans. Matthew Adamson (Cambridge, Mass.: Polity Press, 1990), 63.

31. Drawing on turn-of-the-century social scientist J. Hobson's conception of the "art of social conduct," Cruikshank positions these modes of self-governance as "technologies of citizenship." See Cruikshank, *The Will to Empower*.

32. Bruce Robbins, *Upward Mobility and the Common Good: Toward a Literary History of the Welfare State* (Princeton: Princeton University Press, 2007), xv, 9.

33. See James Livingston, *Pragmatism, Feminism, and Democracy: Rethinking the Politics of American History* (New York: Routledge, 2001), 75.

34. James Livingston, *Pragmatism and the Political Economy of Cultural Revolution, 1850–1940* (Chapel Hill: University of North Carolina Press, 1997), 66, 77.

35. Jane Addams, *Democracy and Social Ethics* (Urbana and Chicago: University of Illinois Press, 2002), 92.

36. Addams, *Democracy and Social Ethics*, 88.

37. Booker T. Washington, *Up from Slavery* (New York: Oxford University Press, 1995), 114, 116.

38. Phillips, quoted in Adam Fairclough, *A Class of Their Own: Black Teachers in the Segregated South* (Cambridge, Mass.: Harvard University Press, 2007), 148; Baldwin Jr., quoted in James D. Anderson, *The Education of Blacks in the South, 1860–1935* (Chapel Hill: University of North Carolina Press, 1988), 91.

39. Nella Larsen, *"Quicksand" and "Passing"* (New Brunswick, N.J.: Rutgers University Press, 1993), 17. On the "Tuskegee Machine," see Marlon Bryan Ross, *Manning the Race: Reforming Black Men in the Jim Crow Era* (New York: New York University Press, 2004) 206. See also Tyrone Tillery, *Claude McKay: A Black Poet's Struggle for Identity* (Amherst: University of Massachusetts Press, 1992), 21.

40. Robbins, *Upward Mobility and the Common Good*, xii.

41. Jane Addams, "The Subtle Problems of Charity," *Atlantic Monthly*, February 1899, 66, 63, 74.

42. On the class-specific ways in which friendship was lived and defined in the nineteenth century, see Marc Brodie and Barbara Caine, "Class, Sex, and Friendship: The Long Nineteenth Century," in *Friendship: A History*, ed. Barbara Caine (London: Equinox, 2009): 223–78.

43. Hull-House was also a hub of queer sociality. On the queerness of Hull-House, see Shannon Jackson, *Lines of Activity: Performance, Historiography, Hull-House Domesticity* (Ann Arbor: Michigan University Press, 2000), and chapter 1 of Scott Herring's *Queering the Underworld: Slumming, Literature, and the Undoing of Lesbian and Gay History* (Chicago: University of Chicago Press, 2007). For a helpful synthesis of the criticism directed at Addams in her own time and after, see Jean Bethke Elshtain, *Jane Addams and the Dream of American Democracy* (New York: Basic Books, 2002), esp. 188.

44. See Maurice Hamington, *The Social Philosophy of Jane Addams* (Urbana and Chicago: University of Illinois Press, 2009), 5.

45. See Herring, *Queering the Underworld*, 35.

46. Earlier white reformers had deemed themselves "friend of the Negro"

or of the "Indian," but they were not oriented to proximity and friendship as praxis. Though the Charity Organization Society's signal practice of "friendly visiting" ultimately evolved into the casework method of social work, it also institutionalized ideas about the so-called unworthy poor, the culture and morality of poverty, and the dangers of "dependency" on welfare that have proven profoundly harmful. See David Huyssen, *Progressive Inequality: Rich and Poor in New York, 1890–1920* (Cambridge, Mass.: Harvard University Press, 2014).

47. See Sharon Marcus, *Between Women* (Princeton: Princeton University Press, 2007), 69.

48. Henry James, *The Princess Casamassima* (New York: Penguin, 1987), 248.

49. Sawaya, *The Difficult Art of Giving*, 67.

50. William Dean Howells, *A Hazard of New Fortunes* (New York: Boni and Liveright, 1889), 347, 234, 325, 332.

51. On "class fictions," see Pamela Fox, *Class Fictions: Shame and Resistance in the British Working-Class Novel, 1890–1945* (Durham, N.C.: Duke University Press, 1994).

52. See Stephanie Foote, *The Parvenu's Plot: Gender, Culture, and Class in the Age of Realism* (Lebanon: University of New Hampshire Press, 2014), 9.

53. Nancy Bentley notes that "a sincere belief in national uplift through art coexisted with a vision of social breakdown" in these years. See her *Frantic Panoramas: American Literature and Mass Culture, 1870–1920* (Philadelphia: Pennsylvania University Press, 2009), 73. Russ Castronovo observes that this period was also characterized by the kind of violence at home and abroad that made it hard to accept at face value any discourse that linked artistic value to national stability and civic order; see his *Beautiful Democracy: Aesthetics and Anarchy in a Global Era* (Chicago: University of Chicago Press, 2007), 5.

54. After Stowe, the classic nineteenth-century reformist literary texts are Rebecca Harding Davis's *Life in the Iron Mills* (1861), Elizabeth Stuart Phelps's *The Silent Partner* (1871), and Helen Hunt Jackson's *Ramona* (1884). As Sylvia Jenkins Cook, Amy Schrager Lang, Phillip Brian Harper, and Dale Bauer have pointed out, post-Stowe reform novels strive to bridge the gulf between rich and poor by constructing a sympathetic narrative voice. Louisa May Alcott's *Work* (1873) is also a paradigmatic novel in this tradition; see Glenn Hendler, *Public Sentiments: Structures of Feeling in Nineteenth-Century American Literature* (Chapel Hill: University of North Carolina Press, 2001).

55. Hendler, *Public Sentiments*, 49.

56. See Kenneth W. Warren, *What Was African American Literature?* (Cambridge, Mass.: Harvard University Press, 2011), 11–12.

57. See Warren, *What Was African American Literature?*, 10, 13. See also David Shumway, *Creating American Civilization* (Minneapolis: University of Minnesota Press, 1994), 14, and Lawrence Levine, *Highbrow/Lowbrow: The Emergence of Cultural Hierarchy in America* (Cambridge, Mass.: Harvard University Press, 1990), 177. Echoing Levine, Alan Trachtenberg argues that "[the] conjunction of culture with wealth and property on one hand, with surrender, self-denial, and subordination to something larger on the other, gave it a cardinal place among instruments of social control and reform"; see his *The Incorporation of America*, 147.

58. Etiquette manuals had circulated in the United States since at least the eighteenth century. Esther B. Aresty notes that sixty new etiquette manuals were published in the 1870s and 1880s, and that seventy-one etiquette books and at least 150 magazine articles on the subject were published between 1900 and 1910; Aresty, cited in Foote, *The Parvenu's Plot*, 40. Emily Post's *Etiquette* sold approximately one million copies in 1923. See Susan Goodman, *Civil Wars: American Novelists and Manners, 1880–1940* (Baltimore: Johns Hopkins University Press, 2003), 2–3; and Amy L. Blair, *Reading Up: Middle-Class Readers and the Culture of Success in the Early Twentieth-Century United States* (Philadelphia: Temple University Press, 2011).

59. Susan Goodman argues that etiquette manuals and the novel of manners "obliquely legitimized" one another and belonged to a shared interdisciplinary network. See her *Civil Wars*, 3, 5.

60. Emma Goldman, *Living My Life*, vol. 1 (New York: Cosimo Classics, 2011), 160; Jacob Gordin, *The Benefactors of the East Side*, unpublished translation by Stanley Bergman, 2009, in possession of the author, 11. The Yiddish original is published as *Di volteter fun der ist sayd*, in Yakov Gordin, *Eyn-akters* (New York: Tog, 1917).

61. Gene Andrew Jarrett, *Representing the Race: A New Political History of African American Literature* (New York: New York University Press, 2011), 209.

62. Morris R. Cohen, "The East Side," *Alliance Review*, March 1902, 354; Laura Cate, "Correspondence Column," *Far and Near*, no. 20 (June 1892): 164.

63. See Michael Warner's "Publics and Counterpublics," *Public Culture* 14, no. 1 (2002): 49–90.

64. See "A Voice from the Ghetto," *American Hebrew*, October 31, 1902, 674–75. The letter was signed "One of the Submerged."

65. Here, too, the airing of "class-related feelings" became even more vexed in the light of public exposure because most settlement house attendees, working girls' club members, and African American college students in fact held significant advantages over their contemporaries. These clients were

generally drawn from the upper echelons of the working classes or from the lower middle class. It cost a nominal sum to participate in organizational activities, but even the most modest amount surpassed what many working-class and poor people could afford. The average working-class family living in New York City between 1903 and 1909 earned approximately fifteen dollars per week, according to Kathy Peiss; membership in working girls' clubs typically cost twenty-five cents per month. Beneficiaries often drew attention to their status in invidious distinction to the individuals who passed through the doors of reformatories, antivice organizations, and the poorhouse, all contemporary agencies that served a more desperate population and that were imbricated in the workings of the criminal justice system. See Kathy Peiss, *Cheap Amusements: Working Women and Leisure in Turn-of-the-Century New York* (Philadelphia: Temple University Press, 1986), 12, 168.

66. See James Machor's "Introduction: Readers/Texts/Contexts," in *Readers in History: Nineteenth-Century American Literature and the Contexts of Response*, ed. James L. Machor (Baltimore: The Johns Hopkins University Press, 1993), vii–xxix, here xi.

67. "Editorial," *Alliance Review*, June 1901, 81.

68. Celia Cohen, "Stenography as a Mental Discipline," *Alliance Review*, May 1901, 54.

69. On the vibrant periodical culture of this period, see Nancy Glazener, *Reading for Realism: The History of a U.S. Literary Institution, 1850–1910* (Durham, N.C.: Duke University Press, 1997); Richard Ohmann, *Selling Culture: Magazines, Markets, and Class at the Turn of the Century* (New York: Verso, 1996); James P. Danky and Wayne A. Wiegand, eds., *Print Culture in a Diverse America* (Urbana and Chicago: University of Illinois Press, 1998); Carol J. Batker, *Reforming Fictions: Native, African, and Jewish American Women's Literature and Journalism in the Progressive Era* (New York: Columbia University Press, 2000); and Mark J. Noonan, *Reading the Century Illustrated Monthly Magazine: American Literature and Culture* (Kent, Ohio: Kent State University Press, 2010).

1. SITES OF CONTACT

1. Rose Cohen, *Out of the Shadow: A Russian Jewish Girlhood on the Lower East Side* (Ithaca, N.Y.: Cornell University Press, 1995), 251, 252.

2. Gordin, *The Benefactors of the East Side*, 9, 8.

3. From the first annual report of the Toynbee Hall Association, quoted in Arthur C. Holden, *The Settlement Idea* (New York: Macmillan, 1922), 13–14.

4. Stanton Coit studied at Toynbee Hall for six months before founding

the first American settlement, the Neighborhood Guild (later renamed the University Settlement), on New York City's Lower East Side in 1886. Jane Addams and Ellen Gates Starr made several visits to Toynbee Hall before starting Hull-House in Chicago in 1889, and prominent settlement leaders, including Robert Woods of Andover House, Vida Scudder of the College Settlement and Denison House, and George Hodges of Kingsley House, made the customary pilgrimage to Toynbee Hall before building their own U.S. institutions. See Daniel T. Rodgers, *Atlantic Crossings: Social Politics in a Progressive Age* (Cambridge, Mass.: Harvard University Press, 1998), 64.

5. See U.S. Bureau of the Census, *Historical Statistics of the United States, Colonial Times to 1970* (Washington, D.C., 1975).

6. See Davis, *Spearheads for Reform*, 12.

7. The historical legacy of the movement has been determined by the high-profile organizations I will call mainstream settlements, to reflect their disaffiliation from any particular ethnic, racial, or religious group. Institutions founded by and for Jews typically removed the residential function. There is some disagreement as to whether such institutions should be considered settlement houses at all, as opposed to the more general "neighborhood house" or "community center," but they were so much a part of the Progressive movement that scholars have overwhelmingly embraced this designation. The Educational Alliance changed its name from the Hebrew Institute in 1893 in part to fit into the secular settlement mold, and its website describes its early history as that of a settlement house. See http://www.edalliance.org/. For more on this debate across the twentieth century, see Morris Isaiah Berger, *The Settlement, the Immigrant, and the Public School* (New York: Arno Press, 1980); Boris D. Bogen, *Jewish Philanthropy* (New York: Macmillan, 1917); Andre Manners, *Poor Cousins* (New York: Coward, McCann and Geoghegan, 1972); and Isaac Spectorsky, "The Advantages of Jewish Settlements," *American Hebrew*, September 4, 1903, 512. The gender dynamics of settlement work also distinguish Jewish institutions from the mainstream model. Historians have painted a picture of the settlement house as an arena in which middle- and upper-class women gained professional authority in relation to a clientele composed largely of women and children. And indeed, with most settlements run and patronized by women, it does constitute an importantly female institution. Precise statistics on the gender composition of the U.S. settlement movement vary, but one 1911 investigation claimed that 53 percent of all U.S. settlements housed women only. Fewer than 2 percent of settlements were male only. See Dawn Keetley, *Public Women, Public Words: A Documentary History of American Feminism*, vol 2, *1900-1960* (Lanham, Md.: Rowman and Littlefield, 2005), 97. However, to cast the whole movement as

merely a site of feminized "civic housekeeping" ignores Jewish institutions, where the gender balance was more evenly balanced.

8. African Americans and Asian Americans were mostly ignored by the mainstream settlement movement, and majority-white settlement houses were overwhelmingly segregated spaces. Very few white-run settlements were built to serve communities of color in the early twentieth century, and those that did exist often functioned as segregated satellite campuses to the dominant white institution (leaders of Wald's Henry Street Settlement founded the Lincoln Street Settlement to support black New Yorkers, for example). Iris Carlton-LaNey discusses segregation in relation to black settlement houses in "The Career of Birdye Henrietta Haynes, A Pioneer Settlement House Worker," *Social Service Review* 68, no. 2 (June 1994): 254–73. A number of African American reformers organized important settlements on a self-help model, like the White Rose Mission established by Victoria Earle Matthews on New York City's Upper West Side in 1897. These institutions operated at some remove from white settlements and were often connected to specific churches. The relative dearth of institutions serving people of color illustrates the movement's investment in preserving and endorsing a vision of white identity. See Elizabeth Lasch-Quinn, *Black Neighbors: Race and the Limits of Reform in the American Settlement Movement, 1890–1945* (Chapel Hill: University of North Carolina Press, 1993).

9. See Paul Boyer, *Urban Masses and Moral Order in America, 1820–1920* (Cambridge, Mass.: Harvard University Press, 1992), 156.

10. Quoted in Lawrence J. Vale, *From the Puritans to the Projects: Public Housing and Public Neighbors* (Cambridge, Mass.: Harvard University Press, 2007), 76. For a sampling of the settlement movement's imperial vocabulary, see Robert Woods, *The City Wilderness: A Settlement Study* (Boston and New York: Houghton, Mifflin, 1899).

11. See Jane Addams, *Twenty Years at Hull-House* (New York: Penguin, 1998), 369. On Addams's relationship to Americanization, see James B. Salazar, *Bodies of Reform: The Rhetoric of Character in Gilded Age America* (New York: New York University Press, 2010).

12. Sarah Wilson charts the multiple, competing definitions of "assimilation" and "Americanization" in the early twentieth century, focusing on the cosmopolitan, Deweyan definition of the term. While several prominent settlement workers (most notably Addams and Wald) can be counted as "melting-pot thinkers" who embraced the cultural gifts of immigrant communities, the movement as a whole was more concerned with passing on American mores and behaviors to ethnic clients than with opening U.S.

culture to foreign influences. See Wilson, *Melting-Pot Modernism* (Ithaca, N.Y.: Cornell University Press, 2010).

13. For contrary views, see Ruth Crocker, *Social Work and Social Order: The Settlement Movement in Two Industrial Cities, 1889–1930* (Urbana and Chicago: University of Illinois Press, 1992), and Rivka Shpak Lissak, *Pluralism and Progressives: Hull-House and the New Immigrants, 1889–1919* (Chicago: University of Chicago Press, 1989).

14. Dewey, quoted in Boyer, *Urban Masses and Moral Order in America*, 180, 225.

15. Club Department of the Educational Alliance, "Editorial," *Alliance Review*, January 1902, 306.

16. Annual Report, 1899, box 1, folder 4, Educational Alliance Collection 1-359, American Jewish Historical Society, New York.

17. On Shakespeare's eminence with U.S. public literary culture of the long nineteenth century, see Nancy Glazener, "Studying Literature," in *Literature in the Making: A History of U.S. Literary Culture in the Long Nineteenth Century* (Oxford: Oxford University Press, 2016): 71–118.

18. Annual Report, 1895, box 1, folder 3, Educational Alliance Collection 1-359, American Jewish Historical Society, New York.

19. See Thomas Augst, *A Clerk's Tale: Young Men and Moral Life in Nineteenth-Century America* (Chicago: University of Chicago Press, 2003), 12.

20. Generalists aimed "to adapt the old college ideal of liberal culture to the challenges of modern times." By contrast, specialists sought to redefine the study of English by casting the discipline as a science requiring a high degree of expertise. See Gerald Graff, *Professing Literature: An Institutional History* (Chicago: University of Chicago Press, 1989), 85, 82; and Elizabeth Renker, *The Origins of American Literary Studies: An Institutional History* (New York: Cambridge University Press, 2007). Vida Scudder of Wellesley College was a noted generalist who worked in settlement houses.

21. "An East Side Art Club," editorial, *American Hebrew*, March 14, 1902, 512–13.

22. Hester Dorsey Richardson, "The College Settlement," *Lippincott's Monthly Magazine* 47 (1891): 785–90, here 788.

23. Moore, quoted in State of New York, "Social Settlements," *Eighteenth Report of Bureau of Labor Statistics of the State of New York, 1900* (Albany, N.Y.: James B. Lyon, 1901), 283–84.

24. The literature on Jews and blackface is vast. For two competing views, see Eric Lott, *Love and Theft: Blackface Minstrelsy and the American Working Class* (New York: Oxford University Press, 2013), and Michael

Rogin, *Blackface, White Noise: Jewish Immigrants in the Hollywood Melting Pot* (Berkeley: University of California Press, 1999).

25. Annual Report, 1903, box 1, folder 6, Educational Alliance Collection 1–359, American Jewish Historical Society, New York.

26. Joan Shelley Rubin, *Songs of Ourselves: The Uses of Poetry in America* (Chapel Hill: University of North Carolina Press, 2007), 246.

27. Jackson, *Lines of Activity*, 238.

28. Edward Steiner, "Christodora, 1897–1940," unpublished manuscript, n.d., box 3, folder 3, Christodora House Records, Columbia University Rare Books and Manuscript Library, New York. Edward Steiner was a frequent guest and lecturer at the Christodora House.

29. The idea of a serious theater for children was born at the Educational Alliance in 1903, when Alice Minnie Herts founded the Children's Educational Theater. Mark Twain actively participated in the Alliance's 1908 staging of his novel *The Prince and the Pauper*, and Frances Hodgson Burnett attended the 1904 staging of *A Little Princess*. Alice and Irene Lewisohn's theater troupe at the Henry Street Settlement was incorporated in 1915 as the Neighborhood Playhouse, one of the nation's first off-Broadway theaters, which earned renown for its experimental productions.

30. Jonathan Freedman, *The Temple of Culture: Assimilation and Anti-Semitism in Literary Anglo-America* (New York: Oxford University Press, 2002), 33–34.

31. This self-identification as fundamentally a home above all else would lessen after 1910, as the settlement movement was increasingly linked to larger municipal reform projects. See Mina Carson, *Settlement Folk: Social Thought and the American Settlement Movement, 1885–1930* (Chicago: University of Chicago Press, 1990), 59.

32. See Jackson, *Lines of Activity*, 153.

33. Reformers were also aware that settlement domesticity alienated young clients from their more traditional immigrant parents. For more on social reform, immigrant families, and the problem of the generation gap, see Sarah Chinn, *Inventing Modern Adolescence* (New Brunswick, N.J.: Rutgers University Press, 2008).

34. Steiner, "Christodora."

35. Richardson, "The College Settlement," 785–86.

36. See Katherine C. Grier, *Culture and Comfort: Parlor Making and Middle-Class Identity, 1850–1930* (Washington, D.C.: Smithsonian Institution Press, 1997), 3, 64. See also Robin Faith Bachin, *Building the South Side: Urban Space and Civic Culture in Chicago, 1890–1919* (Chicago: University of Chicago Press, 2004), 5.

37. Josephine Hunt Raymond, "The Social Settlement Movement in Chicago" (master's thesis, University of Wisconsin, 1897), 68–69.

38. Zoe Beckley, *A Chance to Live* (New York: Macmillan, 1918), 80. Note Anzia Yezierska's description of the settlement interior in *Salome of the Tenements:* "The service I feel myself called upon to render the East Side is to teach the gospel of the Simple Life. . . . I try to make my settlement house an exhibit of what I mean. I have studied out the furnishings with the most competent artists. Only the inexpensive materials are used. Cheap woods, muslins and cheesecloth, cotton and scrim, but combined in a way to bring about beauty." Yezierska, *Salome of the Tenements* (Urbana and Chicago: University of Illinois Press, 1995), 75.

39. See Isaac K. Friedman, *By Bread Alone* (New York: McClure, 1901), 278.

40. Mary H. Porter, "A Home on Halsted Street," editorial, *Advance,* July 11, 1889, unpaginated.

41. Although "helpful personal contact" remained a key feature of settlement praxis for decades, the implications of patronage and condescension lessened after 1900, as the rise of Progressivism brought with it a new spirit of liberalism and an appreciation for democratic relations between reformers and beneficiaries. Christine Stansell makes this point in her section on settlement workers in chapter 2 of *American Moderns: Bohemian New York and the Creation of a New Century* (New York: Holt, 2001). But beyond this important intervention, Stansell's account of the settlement movement makes too strong a claim for the reformers' democratic attitude toward immigrants. Stansell suggests, for instance, that the settlement movement as a whole was not closely affiliated with "the Americanizing movements of uplift" (63).

42. Annual Report, 1910, box 6, folder 4, Christodora House Records, Columbia University Rare Books and Manuscript Library, New York.

43. Annual Report, 1899, box 1, folder 4, Educational Alliance Collection 1–359, American Jewish Historical Society, New York.

44. Jean Fine Spahr and Fannie W. McLean, "The Tenement Neighbor Idea," in *The Literature of Philanthropy,* ed. Frances A. Goodale (New York, Harper and Bros., 1893), 32; Jane Addams, "The Subjective Necessity for Social Settlements," in *Philanthropy and Social Progress,* ed. Jane Addams and Robert Woods (New York: Thomas Y. Crowell, 1893), 1–26, here 22.

45. See Jane Addams, "A Function of the Social Settlement," *Annals of the American Academy of Political and Social Science* 13 (May 1899): 323–45.

46. Jane Addams, "The Subjective Necessity for Social Settlements," 6. On "vital contact," see Patrick Chura, *Vital Contact: Downclassing Journeys*

in American Literature from Herman Melville to Richard Wright (New York: Routledge, 2005).

47. Robert Woods, "The University Settlement Idea," in Addams and Woods, *Philanthropy and Social Progress,* 93. The classic account of the sources and expression of American "unreality" around the turn of the century is T. Jackson Lears, *No Place of Grace: Antimodernism and the Transformation of American Culture, 1880–1920* (Chicago: University of Chicago Press, 1994). On Theodore Roosevelt's notion of reinvigorated and restorative manhood, which critics have dubbed his "cult of the strenuous life," see also David E. Shi, *Facing Facts* (New York: Oxford University Press, 1995).

48. Addams, "The Subjective Necessity for Social Settlements," 16. See also Jill Conway, "Women Reformers and American Culture," *Journal of Social History* 5 (Winter 1971–72): 164–77, here 170–71.

49. Vida Scudder, *A Listener in Babel* (New York: Macmillan, 1903), 60, 85, 238.

50. Richardson, "The College Settlement," 789.

51. See Holden, *The Settlement Idea,* 87, and Helen Churchill Candee, *How Women May Earn a Living* (New York: Macmillan, 1900), 316.

52. The idea that one's own culture is the best gift one can give the poor also underlies cultural philanthropy. Andrew Carnegie famously makes this point in *The Gospel of Wealth*. On the role of "cultivation" in Addams's writing and activism at Hull-House, see Francesca Sawaya, *Women, Modern Work: Domesticity, Professionalism, and American Writing, 1890–1950* (Philadelphia: University of Pennsylvania Press, 2004), 19–35.

53. Addams, "The Subjective Necessity for Social Settlements," 25.

54. Michael Gold, *Jews without Money* (New York: PublicAffairs, 2004), 41; John Dos Passos, *U.S.A.* (New York: Library of America, 1996); Eugene O'Neill, *The Hairy Ape: A Comedy of Ancient and Modern Life* (Hazleton: Pennsylvania State University Electronic Classics Series, 2010), 131; Friedman, *By Bread Alone*.

55. See Thorstein Veblen, *The Theory of the Leisure Class* (New York: Oxford University Press, 2007), 341; Goldman, *Living My Life*, 1: 160; Jack London, *Novels and Social Writings: "The People of the Abyss" / "The Road" / "The Iron Heel" / "Martin Eden" / "John Barleycorn,"* ed. Donald Pizer (New York: Library of America, 1982), 176.

56. A fictionalized critique of Jane Addams' class background appears in Beckley's *A Chance to Live,* where a young factory worker sneers at the hypocrisy of wealthy settlement workers: "You think it's fine of her to go spending her father's cash to help the working girls! How did her rich father make his cash already! Ask her that! . . . My father was killed in a mill her

father owned. . . . There's dozens of men hurt in his mill every month and nobody ever hears a word about it. Her settlement house! Pah—I'd like to see it crumble in pieces!" (89). *New Republic* piece quoted in Davis, *Spearheads for Reform*, 17.

57. Henry James, *The American Scene* (New York: Penguin, 1994), 101.

58. Educational League Committee, letter in *American Hebrew*, July 13, 1900, 232.

59. *Arbeter tsaytung*, March 3, 1901, 2, quoted in Cecile Kuznitz, "'Who Is to Guide the Destiny of the East Side Russian Masses?': The Educational Alliance, the Educational League, and the Struggle to Become 'Good Americans,'" unpublished paper in possession of author, 30. I would like to express my sincere thanks to Cecile Kuznitz for sending me a copy of her paper.

60. See Hadassah Kosak, *Cultures of Opposition: Jewish Immigrant Workers, New York City, 1881–1905* (Albany: SUNY Press, 2000), and Tony Michels, *A Fire in Their Hearts: Yiddish Socialists in New York* (Cambridge, Mass.: Harvard University Press, 2005).

61. For more on Gordin's innovations as a realist, see Bettina Warnke, "Reforming the New York Yiddish Theater: The Cultural Politics of Immigrant Intellectuals and the Yiddish Press, 1887–1910" (PhD diss., Columbia University, 2001), chap. 4. For a discussion of Russian Jewish intellectuals' definition of realism, see Steven Cassedy, *To the Other Shore: The Russian Jewish Intellectuals Who Came to America* (Princeton: Princeton University Press, 1997).

62. *Benefactors* has a complex genealogy. It was hastily written—but never published—in English with some Russian inclusions, subsequently translated into Yiddish, and published in *Eyn-akters*, Gordin's 1917 collection of one-act plays, which revised and fleshed out the English original. To retrieve a fair approximation of the English text of the play, I have used a reverse translation from Yiddish back into English, cross-referenced with the original, and taken with the theatrical grain of salt that the performers in 1903 probably deviated from the script.

63. All quotations from the play are from Gordin, *The Benefactors of the East Side*. The reference to cookbooks is probably a send-up of a real *Settlement Cookbook* published by the Milwaukee Settlement House in 1903 and, amazingly, still in print today.

64. See Peggy Pascoe, *Relations of Rescue: The Search for Female Moral Authority in the American West, 1874–1939* (New York: Oxford University Press, 1993).

65. Hutchins Hapgood, *The Spirit of the Ghetto* (Cambridge, Mass.: Harvard University Press, 1967), 5.

66. Hutchins Hapgood, *Types from City Streets* (New York: Funk and Wagnalls, 1910), 15, 17.

67. See "For the Down-Town World," *American Hebrew*, November 7, 1902, 705. The letter was signed "One of the Submerged."

68. Hadassa Kosak describes as "clientelist" the early twentieth-century welfare practices that were based on an unequal donor-client relationship administered by a foreign Jewish elite. See Kosak, *Cultures of Opposition*, 39.

69. In Yezierska's "How I Found America," for instance, a factory operative reads Mary Shelley in the workplace, is disgusted to find essayists Joseph Addison and Richard Steele on her night school syllabus, and knows she has found the key to America when a congenial high school teacher reads to her from Waldo Frank's *Our America*. See Anzia Yezierska, *Hungry Hearts* (New York: Signet Classics, 1996).

70. Yezierska, *Salome of the Tenements*, 149, 134, 147, 178, 147. See also Meredith Goldsmith, "'Democracy of Beauty': Fashioning Ethnicity and Gender in the Fiction of Anzia Yezierska," *Modern Jewish Studies* 11 (1999): 166–87, esp. 172.

71. On critiques of Gordin's dramatic style, see Nahma Sandrow, *Vagabond Stars: A World History of Yiddish Theater* (Syracuse, N.Y.: Syracuse University Press, 1996), 151.

72. See Susan M. Ryan, *The Grammar of Good Intentions: Race and the Antebellum Culture of Benevolence* (Ithaca, N.Y.: Cornell University Press, 2003); *American Hebrew* editorial quoted in Gerald Sorin, *A Time for Building: The Third Migration, 1880–1920* (Baltimore: Johns Hopkins University Press, 1995), 10; "the boisterous . . ." from James Rosenberg, "The Gentile's Attitude toward the Jew as a Jew Sees It," *Menorah Journal* 11, no. 3 (December 1916): 271–76, here 274.

73. "German Jews . . ." quoted in Alfred Bettman, "A Few Limited Observations," in *Second Conference of Jewish Charities in the United States. Detroit, Michigan, May 26–28 1902* (Cincinnati: C. J. Krehbiel, 1902), 290; "belong to the minority . . ." quoted in Henry L. Feingold, *Zion in America* (New York: Dover, 2002), 147.

74. The literature on the uptown-downtown conflict is vast. For one representative text, see Lucy S. Dawidowicz and Louis Marshall, "Louis Marshall's Yiddish Newspaper, *The Jewish World*: A Study in Contrasts," *Jewish Social Studies* 2, no. 2 (April 1963): 102–32.

75. By "reform writing" I mean all nonfictional forms of narrative that described and endorsed solutions to the social issues addressed by reform movements. See Maria Carla Sánchez, *Reforming the World: Social Activism*

and the Problem of Fiction in Nineteenth-Century America (Iowa City: Iowa University Press, 2009), 11.

76. Marjorie N. Feld, *Lillian Wald: A Biography* (Chapel Hill: University of North Carolina Press, 2008), 75.

77. Lillian Wald, *The House on Henry Street* (New York: Holt, 1915), 7, 5, 8, 6. On Wald's resistance to being included in *Jewish Women in America*, see Feld, *Lillian Wald*, 6.

78. Lillian Wald, "Crowded Districts of Large Cities," in *Proceedings of the First Convention of the National Council of Jewish Women, New York City, Nov. 15–19 1896* (New York: Jewish Publication Society of America, 1897), 259, 260.

79. Emil Hirsch, "Dr. Hirsch's Recent Address," *New York Times*, December 7, 1902.

80. Elizabeth Ewen makes a related point in her *Immigrant Women in the Land of Dollars: Life and Culture on the Lower East Side, 1890–1925* (New York: Monthly Review Press, 1985), 77.

81. On the evolution of "objective" reform writing, see Boyer, *Urban Masses and Moral Order in America*; Batker, *Reforming Fictions*; Janice Koistinen-Harris, *Social Reform, Taste, and the Construction of Virtue in American Literature, 1870–1910* (Lewiston, N.Y.: Edwin Mellen Press, 2002); William M. Morgan, *Questionable Charity: Gender, Humanitarianism, and Complicity in U.S. Literary Realism* (Lebanon: University of New Hampshire Press, 2004); and Shi, *Facing Facts*.

82. See Joanne Dobson's "Reclaiming Sentimental Literature," *American Literature* 69, no. 2 (June 1997): 263–88, here 268.

83. Sánchez, *Reforming the World*, 182.

84. Child, quoted in Ryan, *The Grammar of Good Intentions*, 21.

85. Darryl Pinckney makes this point in "The Invisibility of Black Abolitionists," in *The Abolitionist Imagination*, ed. Andrew Delblanco (Cambridge, Mass.: Harvard University Press, 2012), 109–34, here 114.

86. Karen Sánchez-Eppler, *Touching Liberty: Abolition, Feminism, and the Politics of the Body* (Berkeley: University of California Press, 1993), 49.

87. On Jacobs's use of sentimentalism, see Franny Nudelman, "Harriet Jacobs and the Sentimental Politics of Female Suffering," *ELH* 59, no. 4 (Winter 1992): 939–64; see also Hazel B. Carby, *Reconstructing Womanhood: The Emergence of the Afro-American Woman Novelist* (New York: Oxford University Press, 1987).

88. Even if Riis's social agenda was essentially environmentalist—he pushed for new laws governing sanitation and housing and for the construction of parks and playgrounds—his pioneering use of photojournalism to capture life in urban tenements meant that his formal strategies still bent toward the

depiction of human subjects. His willingness to name chapters of *How the Other Half Lives* (1890) after ethnic groups and districts, from "Jewtown" to "Chinatown," indicates how little distance he posed between environment and identity in his prose. Riis and his contemporaries melded sentimental pieties with social science, creating a hybrid form of "moral realism" that is still residually present in the earliest writings of the settlement movement. See Robert Dowling, *Slumming in New York: From the Waterfront to Mythic Harlem* (Urbana and Chicago: University of Illinois Press, 2007), 21.

89. Demetz, quoted in Richard H. Brodhead, *The School of Hawthorne* (New York: Oxford University Press, 1986), 141. See also Claybaugh, *The Novel of Purpose*, 44.

90. See Jackson, *Lines of Activity*, 17.

91. The Christodora House's Poets' Guild and "Unbound Anthology," which began operating in 1919 and 1920 respectively, are notable exceptions to this general rule. See Joan Shelley Rubin, *The Making of Middlebrow Culture* (Chapel Hill: University of North Carolina Press, 1992), and Barbara Sicherman, *Well-Read Lives: How Books Inspired a Generation of American Women* (Chapel Hill: University of North Carolina Press, 2010).

92. "The Christodora Year Book," 1915, box 1, folder 12, Christodora House Records, Columbia University Rare Books and Manuscript Library, New York.

93. Annual Report, 1916, box 1, folder 8, Educational Alliance Collection 1-359, American Jewish Historical Society, New York.

94. Joan Shelley Rubin observes that educators made room for poetry in their curricula in the 1910s and 1920s to indicate respect for the humanistic capacities of immigrant students. But the idea of using literature for social ends was not the public school's innovation but, rather, its inheritance. See part 2 of Rubin's *Songs of Ourselves*.

95. Michael Warner, "Professionalization and the Rewards of Literature: 1875–1900," *Criticism* 27 (Winter 1985): 9; and Renker, *The Origins of American Literary Studies*, 2. On the fate of literature as a public value in the twentieth century, see Glazener, *Literature in the Making*, and David Shumway, *Creating American Civilization* (Minneapolis: University of Minnesota Press, 1994).

96. For key texts in this critical tradition, see Andreas Huyssen, *After the Great Divide: Modernism, Mass Culture, Postmodernism* (Bloomington: Indiana University Press, 1986); Raymond Williams, *The Politics of Modernism: Against the New Conformists* (London: Verso, 1989); Rainey, *Institutions of Modernism;* and Goldstone, *Fictions of Autonomy*.

2. THE PROBLEM WITH COMPARISON

1. In their focus on rural, mostly working-class New Englanders, *Ethan Frome* (1911) and *Summer* (1917) are the notable exceptions here.
2. Edith Wharton, *The House of Mirth* (New York: Bedford, 1994), 152, 153, 294; hereafter referred to as *Mirth*.
3. Wharton, *Mirth*, 119.
4. Wharton, *Mirth*, 95.
5. See Lawrence Buell, "Downwardly Mobile for Conscience's Sake: Voluntary Simplicity from Thoreau to Lily Bart," *American Literary History* 17, no. 4 (Winter 2005): 653–65, here 66. Elizabeth Ammons is an exception to the general rule that critics have overlooked the significance of the working girls' club in *Mirth*. She notes that the club is an important, ironic symbol in the novel. Ammons, *Edith Wharton's Argument with America* (Athens: University of Georgia Press, 1980), 40. There is also a brief but useful discussion of working girls' clubs as a context for Wharton's novel in Janet Beer, Pamela Knights, and Elizabeth Nolan, *Edith Wharton's "The House of Mirth"* (New York: Routledge, 2007), 31–32.
6. Recent Wharton critics remain divided in their assessment of her politics. Jennie Kassanoff sees her as a conservative chiefly concerned with the decline of the U.S. patrician class. See Kassanoff, "Extinction, Taxidermy, Tableaux Vivants: Staging Race and Class in *The House of Mirth*," *PMLA* 115, no. 1 (2000): 9–19. By contrast, Dale M. Bauer argues that Wharton did not sharpen her political perspective until later in her career. See Bauer, *Edith Wharton's Brave New Politics* (Madison: University of Wisconsin Press, 1995), xii. For an account that tracks the trajectory of Wharton scholarship, in which critical perspectives progress from seeing her as "simply too much a child of privilege to generate meaningful social commentary through her fiction" to more fulsome analyses enabled by feminist criticism, see Jennifer Fleissner, *Women, Compulsion, Modernity: The Moment of American Naturalism* (Chicago: University of Chicago Press, 2004), 456.
7. Joanne Meyerowitz, *Women Adrift: Independent Wage Earners in Chicago, 1880–1930* (Chicago: University of Chicago Press, 1991), xvii.
8. As Kathy Peiss has shown, "four-fifths of the 343,000 wage-earning women in New York were single, and almost one-third were aged sixteen to twenty" in 1900. See Peiss's *Cheap Amusements*, 5, 34.
9. In 1870, more than half of all women wage earners were domestic servants; by 1920, only one-sixth were. See Jean V. Matthews, *The Rise of the New Woman: The Women's Movement in America, 1875–1930* (Chicago:

Ivan R. Dee, 2003), 48. See also Alice Kessler-Harris, *Out to Work: A History of Wage-Earning Women in the United States* (New York: Oxford University Press, 2003), 123.

10. On the mainstream white women's club movement, see Anne Ruggles Gere, *Intimate Practices: Literacy and Cultural Work in U.S. Women's Clubs, 1880–1920* (Urbana and Chicago: University of Illinois Press, 1997); Karen J. Blair, *The Torchbearers: Women and Their Amateur Arts Associations in America, 1890–1930* (Bloomington: Indiana University Press, 1994); and Anne Firor Scott, *Natural Allies: Women's Associations in American History* (Urbana and Chicago: University of Illinois Press, 1992). On nineteenth-century progenitors to the working girls' club movement, see Ginzberg, *Women and the Work of Benevolence*.

11. Most working girls' clubs had a Protestant membership and maintained a religious tone, since cultivating "piety" was one of the movement's early commitments. On the formation and ideology of the YWCA, see Scott, *Natural Allies*. The Association of Working Girls' Societies was founded in 1885 and guided the movement under revised nomenclature until the 1920s, holding much-publicized regional and national conventions on a regular basis. Despite the existence of this central governing body, working girls' clubs were relatively decentralized organizations, often appearing as subsidiaries of other voluntary and uplift institutions such as settlement houses, YWCAs, and churches.

12. See Priscilla Murolo, *The Common Ground of Womanhood: Class, Gender, and Working Girls' Clubs, 1884–1928* (Urbana and Chicago: University of Illinois Press, 1997), 18. Murolo's book remains the most thorough historical account of the working girls' club movement. The fact that domestic servants were excluded from both the terminological umbrella of the working girl and the reformist organizations that emerged to support her suggests the easy equation people drew between working girls and the urban public sphere at the turn of the twentieth century: domestic workers labored in private homes, and their profession was neither recognizably new nor socially disruptive in the same way. As Vanessa May has shown, women's reform groups were active in writing labor legislation that limited the length of a female employee's workday, instituted a minimum wage, regulated working conditions, and helped ensure that these laws had been passed by the conclusion of the New Deal. However, domestics were not protected by these laws. See Vanessa H. May, *Unprotected Labor: Household Workers, Politics, and Middle-Class Reform in New York, 1870–1940* (Chapel Hill: University of North Carolina Press, 2011). For the linkage between the development of modern machinery in the turn-of-the-century urban workplace and the growth of women as

wage earners, see Kessler-Harris, *Out to Work,* and Meyerowitz, *Women Adrift.*

13. See Laura Hapke, *Tales of the Working Girl: Wage-Earning Women in American Literature, 1890–1925* (Boston: Twayne, 1992), 2. The movement's institutional literature only lightly touches on the issue of interracial friendship within the clubs. *Far and Near* celebrated the formation of a club for black women in Columbia, South Carolina, but made it clear that it and other such clubs would be segregated. Another article claimed that a teacher at the Carlisle Indian Industrial School in Pennsylvania hoped to start working girls' clubs among her Native American students; the writer anticipated that "these Indian girls will become interested in club life and versed in club methods, so that when they return to their homes in the far West, they will be able to introduce them among their kinsmen and friends. We may yet hear of clubs among the Apaches, Pueblos, or Sioux." See Grace A. Hubbard, "Massachusetts," *Far and Near,* no. 11 (September 1891): 210.

14. Club leaders did not hide their kinship with the management class. They were connected to the local businesses that employed their "sisters" through familial and social networks, a fact that forever constrained the potential for taking radical politics seriously within the association. In their efforts to grow the movement, leaders regularly reached out to employers, asking them to promote the benefits of club membership to their female employees.

15. On the emergence of protected civic spaces for women, see Mary P. Ryan, *Women in Public: Between Banners and Ballots, 1825–1880* (Baltimore: Johns Hopkins University Press, 1990), 78.

16. See Murolo, "Appendix 5: The NLWW Bureaucracy, 1900 and 1918," in *The Common Ground of Womanhood,* 172. These are extremely conservative numbers, as many clubs were not formally affiliated with the National League of Women Workers and would not have been counted in its numerical assessment. It is important to note that these numbers probably surpassed the number of women involved in trade unions in those same years. On "vernacular gentility," or the cultivation of upper-class speech, dress, and manners by "middling people . . . who aspired to simple respectability," see Richard L. Bushman, *The Refinement of America: Persons, Houses, Cities* (New York: Vintage, 1992), xiii.

17. See Kessler-Harris, *Out to Work,* 93. See also the Association of Working Girls' Societies, *The Discussions of the Convention Held in New York City, April 15th, 16th, and 17th, 1890* (New York: Trow's Printing and Bookbinding, 1890), 33.

18. Rheta Childe Dorr, *What Eight Million Women Want* (Boston: Small, Maynard, 1910), 247.

19. See Christopher Castiglia, *Interior States: Institutional Consciousness and the Inner Life of Democracy in the Antebellum United States* (Durham, N.C.: Duke University Press, 2008), 103, 11. On the interconnectedness and individualism of benevolence projects in the nineteenth-century United States, see Wendy Gamber, "Antebellum Reform: Salvation, Self-Control, and Social Transformation," in Friedman and McGarvie, *Charity, Philanthropy, and Civility in American History*, 129–54.

20. Association of Working Girls' Societies, *The Discussions of the Convention Held in New York City*, 116.

21. Association of Working Girls' Societies, *The Discussions of the Convention Held in New York City*, 12.

22. Association of Working Girls' Societies, *The Discussions of the Convention Held in New York City*, 12.

23. See Amy Schrager Lang, *The Syntax of Class: Writing Inequality in Nineteenth-Century America* (Princeton: Princeton University Press, 2003), 7, 12. Although most club sponsors hailed from the upper classes, their uplift work in the club movement was meant to educate wage earners in the cultural norms and practices of the middle class.

24. Grace H. Dodge, *A Bundle of Letters to Girls on Practical Matters* (New York: Funk and Wagnalls, 1887), vii, 11.

25. Grace H. Dodge, "The Responsibilities and Opportunities of a Society," *Far and Near*, no. 2 (December 1890): 20, 21.

26. Association of Working Girls' Societies, *The Discussions of the Convention Held in New York City*, 19.

27. Nellie R. Fairchild, "Club Democracy," *Club Worker* 9, no. 6 (1908): 743.

28. Augst, *A Clerk's Tale*, 7.

29. On the importance of language and slang in wage-earning women's culture, see Peiss, *Cheap Amusements*.

30. See Rose H. Phelps Stokes, "The Condition of Working Women, from the Working Woman's Viewpoint," *Annals of the American Academy of Political and Social Science* 27 (May 1906): 165–75, here 168.

31. In friendly visiting, charitable agencies sent employees on unsolicited visits to the homes of working-class and poor families "to provide a mixture of support, scrutiny, and advice" and distinguish the "worthy" from the "unworthy" poor. See William Damon, Richard M. Lerner, K. M. Renninger, and Irving E. Sigel, eds., *Handbook of Child Psychology: Child Psychology in Practice* (New York: John Wiley and Sons, 1996), 706.

32. Association of Working Girls' Societies, *The Discussions of the Convention Held in New York City*, 92.

33. "Opportunity," *Far and Near*, no. 1 (November 1890): 2.
34. See Rita Felski's introduction to a special issue on comparison, *New Literary History* 40, no. 3 (Summer 2009): v–ix.
35. Murolo, *The Common Ground of Womanhood*, 40.
36. Association of Working Girls' Societies, *The Discussions of the Convention Held in New York City*, 18.
37. On the process by which the human interior came to be seen as a microcosm of the social world in the nineteenth century, so that "citizens were encouraged to understand the incessant labor of vigilant self-scrutiny and self-management as effective democratic action," see Castiglia, *Interior States*, 2. On the institutionalization of aspirational consciousness within the field of social work, see Barbara Cruikshank, "The Liberal Arts of Governance," in *The Will to Empower*, 43–66.
38. Florence Lockwood, "The Women Who Do the Work: Working Girls' Clubs," *Century Illustrated Monthly Magazine* 41 (1891): 793–94, here 794.
39. Amy Kaplan makes a similar point, suggesting that Lily "depends on the mirror of the gaping mob to maintain her identity. When she loses this mirror, she loses a self." Kaplan, "Crowded Spaces in *The House of Mirth*," in *Edith Wharton's "The House of Mirth": A Casebook*, ed. Carol J. Singley (New York: Oxford University Press, 2003), 102.
40. Veblen, *The Theory of the Leisure Class*, 71, 27.
41. Lockwood, "The Women Who Do the Work," 794, and Wharton, *Mirth*, 153.
42. Veblen directly addresses turn-of-the-century charitable and uplift organizations. He concludes that "enterprises of amelioration" like the settlement house are materially useless, designed merely "to authenticate the pecuniary reputability of their members, as well as gratefully to keep them in mind of their superior status by pointing the contrast between themselves and the lower-lying humanity in whom the work of amelioration is to be wrought." Veblen, *The Theory of the Leisure Class*, 225, 221. Wharton criticism has acknowledged the relevance of Veblen's writing to *Mirth*, most notably Ruth Bernard Yeazell's "The Conspicuous Wasting of Lily Bart," *ELH* 59, no. 3 (Fall 1992): 713–34, and Nancy Bentley's *The Ethnography of Manners: Hawthorne, James, Wharton* (New York: Cambridge University Press, 1995).
43. Veblen, *The Theory of the Leisure Class*, 225, 221, 38.
44. "Multiplying Wants," editorial, *Far and Near*, no. 10 (August 1891): 172.
45. See Murolo, *The Common Ground of Womanhood*, 119.
46. See Susan Porter Benson, *Counter Cultures: Saleswomen, Managers, and Customers in American Department Stores, 1890–1940* (Urbana and Chicago: University of Illinois Press, 1987), and Sarah Deutsch, *Women and*

the City: Gender, Space, and Power in Boston, 1870–1940 (New York: Oxford University Press, 2000).

47. Theodore Dreiser, *Sister Carrie* (New York: Barnes and Noble Classics, 2005), 324. Rachel Bowlby reads this scene in *Just Looking: Consumer Culture in Dreiser, Gissing, and Zola* (New York: Routledge, 2009), 58–59. Bowlby notes too that turn-of-the-century concerns about women's consumption "readily fitted into the available ideological paradigm of a seduction of women by men, by which women would be addressed as yielding objects to the powerful male subject forming, and informing them of, their desires" (12). On Dreiser, see also Fleissner, *Women, Compulsion, Modernity*. On the emergence in the 1840s of fiction concerned with working women, see Lori Merish, "Story Papers," in *The Oxford History of Popular Print Culture*, vol. 6, ed. Christine Bold (New York: Oxford University Press, 2012), 43–62. On the turn-of-the-century working girl novel, see Cathy N. Davidson and Arnold E. Davidson, "Carrie's Sisters: The Popular Prototypes for Dreiser's Heroine," *Modern Fiction Studies* 23, no. 3 (Autumn 1977): 395–407, and Michael Denning, *Mechanic Accents: Dime Novels and Working-Class Culture in America* (New York: Verso, 1998).

48. Opportunities for working-class women to give voice to their own experiences grew in the early years of the twentieth century, often in the women's sections of newspapers. Beginning in 1907, the *Chicago Tribune* offered thirty-five dollars per week to women who sent in the best letters detailing "the working girl and her problems." And throughout 1908, *Harper's Bazaar* commissioned a series of articles on "The Girl Who Comes to the City," with many submissions devoted to women's employment. But both series published articles that confirmed the biases of reformers, offering a rich array of firsthand material that reformers could then use to reinforce or justify their projects. Print opportunities like these were much scarcer in the 1890s.

49. Fleissner, *Women, Compulsion, Modernity*, 166.

50. Lori Merish, "Representing the 'Deserving Poor': The 'Sentimental Seamstress' and the Feminization of Poverty in Antebellum America," in *Our Sisters' Keepers: Nineteenth-Century Benevolence Literature by American Women*, ed. Debra Bernardi and Jill Bergman (Tuscaloosa: University of Alabama Press, 2005): 35–51. Dickens recalled his visit to the Lowell mills in *American Notes*. He complimented the textile operatives' appearance, manners, and cultural acuity. Their proficiency at piano and patronage of libraries came in for particular praise, as did the high literary quality of the *Lowell Offering*. See Sylvia Jenkins Cook, *Working Women, Literary Ladies: The Industrial Revolution and Female Aspiration* (New York: Oxford University

Press, 2008), 58–59 and 43. Louisa May Alcott, *Work: A Story of Experience* (New York: Penguin, 1994), 23.

51. Helen Campbell, *Prisoners of Poverty: Women Wage-Workers, Their Trades and Their Lives* (New York: Little Brown, 1887), 182–83. As Margaret Finnegan notes, the notion of being a "public" (as opposed to a "private" or domestic) woman was synonymous with prostitution in the nineteenth century. See her *Selling Suffrage: Consumer Culture and Votes for Women* (New York: Columbia University Press, 1999), 48.

52. Michael Trask, *Cruising Modernism: Class and Sexuality in American Literature and Social Thought* (Ithaca, N.Y.: Cornell University Press, 2003), 11, 12, 168.

53. See Emma Goldman, "The Traffic in Women," in *Anarchism and Other Essays* (New York: Mother Earth, 1910).

54. Mary A. Lonergan, "True Womanhood," *Far and Near*, no. 18 (April 1892): 113.

55. See Abbie Graham, *Grace H. Dodge, Merchant of Dreams* (New York: Womans Press, 1926), 94–95.

56. Warner, "Publics and Counterpublics," 84.

57. Warner's explanation of a counterpublic's oppositional status is key here: "The subordinate status of a counterpublic does not simply reflect identities formed elsewhere; participation in such a public is one of the ways its members' identities are formed and transformed. A hierarchy or stigma is the assumed background of practice. One enters at one's own risk." See Warner, "Publics and Counterpublics," 87.

58. Edgar Fawcett, "The Woes of the New York Working-Girl," *Arena* 4 (1891): 26–35, here 26.

59. Laura Cate, "Correspondence Column," *Far and Near*, no. 20 (June 1892): 164. This language of "types" shows Cate and the working girls' club movement taking part in a broader fixation on systems of classification and taxonomy, which traversed intellectual, popular, and scientific spheres in the nineteenth and early twentieth centuries. See the discussion of "types" in Beer, Knights, and Nolan, *Edith Wharton's "The House of Mirth,"* 40.

60. Cate, "Correspondence Column," *Far and Near*, no. 20 (June 1892): 164.

61. Laura Cate, "Correspondence Column," *Far and Near*, no. 21 (July 1892): 187.

62. Laura Wexler, *Tender Violence: Domestic Visions in an Age of U.S. Imperialism* (Chapel Hill: University of North Carolina Press, 2000), 161–62. On the ethnographic conventions and moralizing bent of Edgar Fawcett's

slum fiction, see Keith Gandal, *The Virtues of the Vicious* (New York: Oxford University Press, 1997). Gandal argues that turn-of-the-century slum fiction represents urban women as being in greater peril than men, since women who "fell" could neither recover their chastity nor reconstitute their lives by moving to a better environment.

63. Clare de Graffenried, "The Condition of Wage-Earning Women," *Forum* 15, no. 68 (March 1893): 68–82, here 80.

64. Association of Working Girls' Societies, *The Discussions of the Convention Held in New York City*, 69.

65. Association of Working Girls' Societies, *The Discussions of the Convention Held in New York City*, 82.

66. See Hapke, *Tales of the Working Girl*, 16.

67. I am quoting here from an address delivered by M. E. Brady, a member of the Steadfast Club, at the movement's 1890 association meeting: "A large body is sometimes represented and estimated by one or a few associates; the world has not time to take into consideration each individual, and average the worth of the band; the army of working girls have no special privilege, whereby the good only impress. No; every working girl owes it to every co-worker to bear in mind that at any moment she may be used as a representative of the whole, and act as she would under notice of same." See Association of Working Girls' Societies, *The Discussions of the Convention Held in New York City*, 85.

68. See Levine, *Forms*, 2, 5.

69. Bruce Robbins, "Chomsky's Golden Rule: Comparison and Cosmopolitanism," in *Comparison: Theories, Approaches, Uses*, ed. Rita Felski and Susan Stanford Friedman (Baltimore: Johns Hopkins University Press, 2012), 191. On the imbrication of comparison and power, see also Ann Laura Stoler's contributions to *Haunted by Empire: Geographies of Intimacy in North American History*, ed. Ann Laura Stoler (Durham, N.C.: Duke University Press, 2006).

70. Wexler, *Tender Violence*, 105. See also Stoler's account of the "principles of comparison of historical actors themselves" in Stoler, *Haunted by Empire*, 6.

71. On Wharton's conservative politics, see Jennie Kassanoff, *Edith Wharton and the Politics of Race* (New York: Cambridge University Press, 2004).

72. See Katherine Joslin, *Edith Wharton and the Making of Fashion* (Lebanon: University of New Hampshire Press, 2011), 91.

73. Edith Wharton, *The Fruit of the Tree* (Boston: Northeastern University Press, 2000), 228.

74. Wharton, *The Fruit of the Tree*, 231.

75. Wharton framed the connection between *Mirth* and its immediate

successor in terms of the spatial reality of the urban neighborhood, writing to her editor that *The Fruit of the Tree* would explore "life in New York & in a manufacturing town, with the House of Mirth in the middle of the block, but a good many other houses adjoining." See Kassanoff, *Edith Wharton and the Politics of Race*, 60.

76. See Ammons, *Edith Wharton's Argument with America*, 45.

77. See Hermione Lee, *Edith Wharton* (New York: Vintage, 2007), 464. Wharton sought to pique her American readers' sympathies in her war writing, which includes articles in *Scribner's* and two book collections, and she was indefatigable in her efforts to cull donations from her wealthy New York City and Newport social circles. See Goodman, *Civil Wars*, 91. Dale M. Bauer notes that Wharton's participation in relief and welfare work lent a sharper edge to her postwar fiction. See Bauer, *Edith Wharton's Brave New Politics*, 26. On Wharton's wartime activities, see Alan Price, *The End of the Age of Innocence* (London: Palgrave Macmillan, 1996), and Julie Olin-Ammentorp, *Edith Wharton's Writings from the Great War* (Gainesville: Florida University Press, 2004).

78. See Wharton, *A Backward Glance*, in *Novellas and Other Writings* (New York: Library of America, 1990), 356–57. The expression "organized beneficence" turns up in Wharton's final, unfinished novel *The Buccaneers* as well.

79. Mary Cadwalader Jones, "Women's Opportunities in Town and Country," in *The Woman's Book Vol. II* (New York: Scribner's Sons, 1894), 181.

80. Jones, "Women's Opportunities in Town and Country," 192.

81. Jones, "Women's Opportunities in Town and Country," 190. See Joslin, *Edith Wharton and the Making of Fashion*, 94. Jones triangulated reform, philanthropy, and literature in another published work from the 1890s, contributing a chapter on the education of blind people to Goodale, *The Literature of Philanthropy*. She published under the name "Mrs. Frederick Rhinelander Jones." Jones sat on numerous reform and charity committees, including the New York Society for the Prevention of Cruelty to Children, and had a special interest in charity hospitals and training schools for nurses. I have found little evidence that Jones was particularly active in the working girls' club movement: she never wrote in the institutional periodicals or spoke at public events. An 1891 article in the *New York Times* notes Jones's affiliation with the New York Association of Working Girls' Societies, detailing how a campaign for cleaner streets began within the Association and was presented to Mayor Grant; Jones was one of the signees named in the article. She was also actively involved in mounting exhibitions on American women's work as part of the New York State pavilion at the 1893 Exhibition in Chicago. See Board of Women Managers of the State of New York, "Minutes of the Meeting of

the Executive Committee, Held at the Capitol, Albany, January 10, 1893, at 1 p.m.," *Minutes of the Meeting of the Board of Woman Managers of the State of New York*, 1892–94, Nineteenth Century Collections Online, 51–53, https://www.gale.com/primary-sources/nineteenth-century-collections-online.

82. In the 1911 story "Xingu," Wharton satirizes the married members of women's clubs as self-satisfied matrons and "indomitable huntresses of erudition." Reading "Xingu" alongside another Wharton short story, "The Pelican," which chronicles a lady lecturer who offers secondhand intellectual material by force of personality, one realizes why Wharton never championed women's culture clubs and why she poked fun at would-be reformers like Gerty, Carry, and Lady Cressida Raith in *The House of Mirth*. See her "Xingu," in *Edith Wharton: Collected Stories, 1911–1937* (New York: Library of America, 2001), 1–25, and "The Pelican," in *Edith Wharton: Collected Stories, 1891–1910* (New York: Library of America, 2001), 76–94.

83. Jill M. Kress, *The Figure of Consciousness: William James and Edith Wharton* (New York: Routledge, 2002), 131.

84. While Dale M. Bauer suggests that Wharton was not particularly interested in exploring "social problems" in her early work (*Edith Wharton's Brave New Politics*, xii), recent critics have explored social dynamics in *Mirth* that extend beyond an inquiry into the upper classes. Meredith Goldsmith argues that *Mirth* responds to the conventions of temperance discourse, suggesting that Lily identifies with other women across the class spectrum not through her experiences as a worker but through the shared act of female self-medication. Goldsmith's analysis puts the novel in dialogue with reform by means of the Pure Food and Drug Act of 1906. See her "Cigarettes, Tea, Cards, and Chloral: Addictive Habits and Consumer Culture in *The House of Mirth*," *American Literary Realism* 43, no. 2 (Spring 2011): 242–58. Gavin Jones examines how Wharton employs sociological and psychological theories of poverty in *American Hungers: The Problem of Poverty in U.S. Literature, 1840–1945* (Princeton: Princeton University Press, 2008).

85. Wharton, *Mirth*, 27. Amy Kaplan makes a similar point in her important chapter on *Mirth* in *The Social Construction of American Realism* (Chicago: University of Chicago Press, 1988), 88–103.

86. Wharton, *Mirth*, 122.

87. See Foote, *The Parvenu's Plot*. Foote charts the ways Lily's life is staged as a spectacle for the benefit of the novel's many parvenus (the Wellington Brys, Norma Hatch, the Gormers). I attend here to minor characters that do not find a place in Foote's analysis (Nettie Struther, Mrs. Haffen) because their status is so decisively outside the domain of the upper classes to which the novel's upwardly mobile characters aspire.

88. Wharton, *Mirth*, 119.

89. See Singley, "Introduction," in *Edith Wharton's "The House of Mirth,"* 9. Elsewhere, Singley makes the point that Wharton's novel distributes meaning through contrast, though her argument supports a reading of Lily Bart as a "dislocated spiritual pilgrim" navigating the divide between science and religion. See Singley, "Spiritual Homelessness" in *Edith Wharton: Matters of Mind and Spirit* (Cambridge: Cambridge University Press, 1998): 67–84, here 73.

90. Wharton, *Mirth*, 33, 136, 77, 186, 75, 256, 239.

91. Wharton, *Mirth*, 225.

92. Wharton, *Mirth*, 63, 75.

93. Wharton, *Mirth*, 189, 117. Mark McGurl makes an important and related point about the relation of class settings to Lily's identity in *The Novel Art* (Princeton: Princeton University Press, 2001), 91.

94. Wharton, *Mirth*, 206–7.

95. Wharton, *Mirth*, 222.

96. Wharton, *Mirth*, 25. On mass travel and modernity in Wharton's fiction, see Bentley, *Frantic Panoramas*.

97. Wharton, *Mirth*, 223.

98. Wharton, *Mirth*, 246–47.

99. Wharton, *Mirth*, 259, 258, 257, 140. Stephanie Foote reads Lily's social descent in concert with her growing association with the novel's "new people" like the Wellington Brys and Simon Rosedale. Whereas most novels represent their parvenu characters through a narrative of social ascent, Lily is instead constructed as a parvenu through her social decline. See Foote, *The Parvenu's Plot*, esp. 133–15.

100. Wharton, *Mirth*, 251, 296.

101. Wharton, *Mirth*, 264.

102. Gavin Jones explores the psychological modality of poverty in his persuasive analysis of *Mirth*. He argues that Lily's poverty is a mind-set that manifests in images of strain, drowning, and submersion in an abyss and that her "dread of worse horrors" forces her into protracted periods of passivity and dependency. See Jones, *American Hungers*, 95.

103. Wharton, *Mirth*, 268, 267.

104. Wharton, *Mirth*, 268.

105. Wharton, *Mirth*, 153, 291.

106. Wharton, *Mirth*, 292.

107. Wharton, *Mirth*, 289.

108. Wharton, *Mirth*, 291, 294, 297.

109. For more on the gift economy at work in *Mirth*, see Hildegard Hoeller,

Edith Wharton's Dialogue with Realism and Sentimental Fiction (Gainesville: Florida University Press, 2000), 115–16. Elaine Showalter sees the ending as "a vision of a new world of female solidarity" in "The Death of the Lady (Novelist)," *Representations* 9 (Winter 1985): 133–49, here 145, while Elizabeth Ammons reads the scene of Lily embracing the child of working-class parents as the birth of the New Woman in *Edith Wharton's Argument with America*, 42.

110. Edwin Wildman, "What Grace Dodge Has Done for the Working Girl," *World Today: A Monthly Record of Human Progress* 19 (1910): 1363–66, here 1364.

111. Kaplan, *The Social Construction of American Realism*, 102, 103.

112. Wharton, *Mirth*, 34.

113. Wharton, *Mirth*, 110, 34, 137.

114. Wharton, *Mirth*, 137.

115. Wharton, *Mirth*, 111.

116. On Progressive responses to the servant problem, see Lara Vapnek, *Breadwinners: Working Women and Economic Independence* (Urbana and Chicago: University of Illinois Press, 2009).

117. In an interesting account of Wharton's representation of servitude, Ann Mattis notes that servants often appear in fiction, particularly gothic fiction, as a doppelganger or surrogate for the protagonist. See her "Gothic Interiority and Servants in Wharton's *A Backward Glance* and 'The Lady Maid's Bell,'" *Twentieth-Century Literature* 58, no. 2 (Summer 2012): 213–38, here 217. Such is not the case in *Mirth*.

118. Wharton, *Mirth*, 153.

119. Wharton, *Mirth*, 162–63, 55. On Wharton's "detachable epigrams," see Lee, *Edith Wharton*, 180.

120. Wharton, *Mirth*, 129–30.

121. Wharton, *Mirth*, 40, 152, 281, 297.

122. See Roger Lathbury, Jerry Phillips, and Michael Anesko, *Realism and Regionalism: 1860–1910* (New York: Chelsea House, 2010), 70.

123. Critics who place *Mirth* within the tradition of literary naturalism have taken a variety of approaches. Eric Carl Link contends that "it is *theme*, rather than genre, methodology, convention, tone, or philosophy, that qualifies a text for inclusion in the 'school' of American *literary* naturalism"; see his *The Vast and Terrible Drama: American Literary Naturalism in the Late Nineteenth Century* (Tuscaloosa: University of Alabama Press, 2004), 18. Paul J. Ohler contends that Wharton applied Darwin's theories of the interrelations of different species to the context of class interrelationships in the city of New York; see his *Edith Wharton's Evolutionary Conceptions: Darwinian Allegory in Her Major Novels* (New York: Routledge, 2006), 48. Gavin Jones examines

Wharton's naturalism as a formal device in *American Hungers*, 63. Elaine Showalter argues for a view of the novel as a plot of decline in her "The Death of the Lady (Novelist)," and Jennie Kassanoff links the novel's naturalism to racialized discourse, arguing that Lily's survival "requires certain choice conditions" that no longer exist in a modernizing, diversifying United States and that her early death is testament to a "eugenic preservationism" that makes her "a site of racial elegy"; see her *Edith Wharton and the Politics of Race*, 320. In *Edith Wharton*, Singley argues that the novel combines deterministic elements clearly influenced by Darwinian thought with idealism. Jennifer Fleissner sees Lily's trajectory less as a path of decline than as a directionless but nonetheless committed form of seeking. Fleissner redefines naturalist determinism as a form of compulsion in *Women, Compulsion, Modernity*.

124. Wharton, *Mirth*, 29.

125. See Richard A. Kaye's "Textual Hermeneutics and Belated Male Heroism: Edith Wharton's Revisions of *The House of Mirth* and the Resistance to American Literary Naturism," *Arizona Quarterly* 51, no. 3 (Autumn 1995): 87–116, here 92.

126. See Ammons, *Edith Wharton's Argument with America*, 3.

127. Wharton, *Mirth*, 291. Donald Pizer makes the point that "Nettie's progress from 'victim' to 'victory' within her own category of social determinism is thus a clear gloss on a potential of a similar kind within the category represented by Lily." See his "The Naturalism of Edith Wharton's *The House of Mirth*," *Twentieth-Century Literature* 41, no. 2(Summer 1995): 244.

128. Financial markets were prone to collapse and upheaval during this era, with nationwide financial crises happening approximately every seven years between 1865 and 1910. The working girls' club movement's belief that wealth is a static condition is particularly telling—and willfully ahistorical—in this context. Thank you to Sheila Liming for pointing this out to me. On financial collapse in American literature, see David A. Zimmerman, *Panic! Markets, Crises, and Crowds in American Fiction* (Chapel Hill: University of North Carolina Press, 2006).

129. Foote, *The Parvenu's Plot*, 130.

130. Wharton, *Mirth*, 156.

3. CORRELATION AND CONFORMITY

1. Booker T. Washington, "The Atlanta Address," in *Civil Rights since 1787: A Reader on the Black Struggle*, ed. Jonathan Birnbaum and Clarence Taylor (New York: New York University Press, 2000): 222–26.

2. Booker T. Washington, *Working with the Hands* (New York: Doubleday, 1904), 162.

3. Carla Willard, "Timing Impossible Subjects: The Marketing Style of Booker T. Washington," *American Quarterly* 53, no. 4 (2001): 624–69, here 624.

4. Thanks to Patricia Crain for originally suggesting this turn of phrase to me.

5. Booker T. Washington, *The Booker T. Washington Papers: Volume 13, 1914–1915*, ed. Louis R. Harlan and Raymond W. Smock (Urbana and Chicago: University of Illinois Press, 1984), 350.

6. See Michael Hanchard, "Afro-Modernity: Temporality, Politics, and the African Diaspora," *Public Culture* 11, no. 1 (1999): 245–68, here 253. Hanchard defines "racial time" as the "inequalities of temporality that result from power relations between racially dominant and subordinate groups. Unequal relationships between dominant and subordinate groups produce unequal temporal access to institutions, goods, services, resources, power, and knowledge, which members of both groups recognize."

7. See Rayford Logan, *The Betrayal of the Negro, from Rutherford B. Hayes to Woodrow Wilson* (New York: Collier, 1965).

8. See Carby's *Reconstructing Womanhood*, 6.

9. Consider Du Bois's claim in *The Souls of Black Folk* (1903) that "the colleges [white abolitionists] founded were social settlements; homes where the best of the sons of freedmen came in close and sympathetic touch with the best traditions of New England. They lived and ate together, studied and worked, hoped and harkened in the dawning light." See Du Bois, *The Souls of Black Folk* (New York: Penguin, 1995), 84.

10. By ideology I mean "a world view readily found in the population, including sets of ideas and values that cohere, that are used publicly to justify political stances, and that shape and are shaped by society," as political theorist Michael C. Dawson has defined it; Dawson quoted in Gene Andrew Jarrett, *Representing the Race: A New Political History of African American Literature* (New York: New York University Press, 2011), 10.

11. Henry Morehouse, white executive secretary of the American Baptist Home Mission Society, coined the term "Talented Tenth" in 1896 as a way of distinguishing the aims of his society from those that catered to people of "average or mediocre intellect." The origin of the term among white northern missionaries has been superseded by its identifications with Du Bois, who famously wrote and spoke extensively about the Talented Tenth. See Evelyn Brooks Higginbotham, *Righteous Discontent: The Women's Movement in the Black Baptist Church, 1880–1920* (Cambridge, Mass.: Harvard University Press, 1994), 25. Even in its most progressive forms, racial uplift advocated

cross-racial equality within the context of a class-bound intraracial hierarchy, subscribing to the "ostensibly universal but deeply racialized ideological categories of Western progress and civilization" that associated progressively higher categories with "the accomplishments and class privileges of Anglo-Saxon whites." See Jarrett, *Representing the Race*, 77.

12. Higginbotham, *Righteous Discontent*, 40.

13. See Kimberley Johnson, *Reforming Jim Crow: Southern Politics and State in the Age before Brown* (New York: Oxford University Press, 2010), 117. As Washington's biographers have outlined, Washington secretly organized and financed lawsuits combating legal discrimination, disenfranchisement, and peonage. See Robert J. Norrell, *Up from History: The Life of Booker T. Washington* (Cambridge, Mass.: Harvard University Press, 2009).

14. While the formation of new sites of racial uplift reflected broader institution-building energies of the Progressive Era, racial self-help was a crucial ethos and organizing mechanism for black communal organizations. As Evelyn Brooks Higginbotham has shown, black communal organizations were forced to rely heavily on their own financial and human resources. Despite some limited interracial cooperation within large organizations such as the YMCA and YWCA, which maintained African American branches, the vast majority of smaller African American communal institutions thrived at a remove from white associations. See Higginbotham, *Righteous Discontent*.

15. The best book on the social, civic, and political meanings of racial uplift remains Kevin Gaines's *Uplifting the Race: Black Leadership, Politics, and Culture in the Twentieth Century* (Chapel Hill: University of North Carolina Press, 1996). Gaines nicely summarizes the tension implicit in the concept of racial uplift: "On the one hand, a broader vision of uplift signifying collective social aspiration, advancement, and struggle had been the legacy of the emancipation era. On the other hand, black elites made uplift the basis for a racialized elite identity claiming Negro improvement through class stratification as race progress, which entailed an attenuated conception of bourgeois qualifications for rights and citizenship" (xv).

16. Kelly Miller, "The Education of the Negro," in *U.S. Bureau of Education Annual Report* (Washington, D.C., 1902), 733–854, here 803; Barber, quoted in Gaines, *Uplifting the Race*, 33.

17. Morehouse, quoted in Higginbotham, *Righteous Discontent*, 40.

18. See Warren, *What Was African American Literature?*, 146.

19. Some important exceptions to this general rule exist. These include a brief but compelling discussion of how divergent definitions of "the literary" within black colleges institutionalized different relationships to books and reading in Richard Brodhead, *Cultures of Letters: Scenes of Reading and*

Writing in Nineteenth-Century America (Chicago: University of Chicago Press, 1995); Anne-Elizabeth Murdy, *Teach the Nation: Pedagogies of Racial Uplift in U.S. Women's Writing of the 1890s* (New York: Routledge, 2002), and a subset of Du Bois and Washington scholarship that approaches these thinkers as literary figures.

20. Thanks to Autumn Womack for helping me articulate this insight.

21. In 1880, 70 percent of the black population was illiterate, according to U.S. Census data, and by 1910 30 percent remained so. See Elizabeth McHenry, *Forgotten Readers: Recovering the Lost History of African American Literary Societies* (Durham, N.C.: Duke University Press, 2002), 4.

22. See Anderson, *The Education of Blacks in the South*, 239–40, 249.

23. On this point, see Higginbotham, *Righteous Discontent*, 29.

24. See Stuart Grayson Noble, *Forty Years of the Public Schools in Mississippi* (New York: Negro University Press, 1918), 110.

25. *New Orleans Times-Democrat* quoted in Susan Kates, *Activist Rhetorics and American Higher Education, 1885–1937* (Carbondale: Southern Illinois University Press, 2001), 6.

26. Black normal schools offered a curriculum lasting two or three years and did not grant a bachelor's degree. Students were admitted to such programs with an elementary school education and completed the normal school program with the equivalent of a tenth-grade education. Graduates were issued a common school teaching certificate. In contrast, teachers' colleges required a high school diploma for admission and offered a four-year curriculum leading to a bachelor's degree. See Anderson, *The Education of Blacks in the South*, 34–35.

27. The Second Morrill Act (1890) delegated federal funds to black public colleges and universities, but southern states granted those institutions an average of only 43 percent of the state funding they were entitled to. See Johnson, *Reforming Jim Crow*, 150.

28. "Little Tuskegees" refers to the small, rural industrial schools founded by former students of Booker T. Washington. These schools typically replicated the mission and curriculum of the larger institution and were rewarded with Washington's continued patronage and the philanthropic foundations' financial support. See Fairclough, *A Class of Their Own*, 205–8, and Anderson, *The Education of Blacks in the South*, 247, 71, 254.

29. Alice M. Bacon, "Reflex Action of the Carolina Troubles," *Southern Workman* 28 (1899): 90, 91.

30. Bacon, "Reflex Action of the Carolina Troubles," 91–92.

31. Miller, "The Education of the Negro," 809, 805, 802, 810.

32. Efforts to integrate education with life and learning with labor, as

articulated by European educational theorists Johann Pestalozzi, Friedrich Froebel, Maria Montessori, and Johann Friedrich Herbart and American Pragmatists Dewey, Addams, and William James, culminated in a definition of industrial training as "modern" and progressive. This definition encompassed African American vocational training and yet did not discern the important social and pedagogical differences inherent in the Tuskegee model.

33. My thanks to one of my anonymous manuscript readers for suggesting this turn of phrase.

34. The expression "Jim Crow realism" also appears in Ross's *Manning the Race.*

35. J. L. Whiting, *Shop and Class at Tuskegee: A Definitive Story of the Tuskegee Correlation Technique, 1910–1930* (Boston: Chapman and Grimes, 1940), 71.

36. Roscoe Conkling Bruce, "Tuskegee Institute," in *From Servitude to Service: Being the Old South Lectures on the History and Work of Southern Institutions for the Education of the Negro* (Boston: American Unitarian Association, 1905), 81–114, here 112–13.

37. H. B. Frissell, "Fortieth Annual Report of the Principal," *Southern Workman* 37 (1908): 291–305, here 292.

38. Richard Brodhead makes a related point in *Cultures of Letters,* 187.

39. For an interesting reading of the statue in relation to black cultural politics of the nadir, see James Smethurst, *The African American Roots of Modernism* (Chapel Hill: University of North Carolina Press, 2011), 40.

40. Washington, *Working with the Hands,* 21–22.

41. Booker T. Washington, *The Booker T. Washington Papers: Volume 10, 1909–1911,* ed. Louis R. Harlan and Raymond W. Smock (Urbana and Chicago: University of Illinois Press, 1981), 584–85.

42. Michael Scott Bieze and Marybeth Gasman, *Booker T. Washington Rediscovered* (Baltimore: The Johns Hopkins University Press, 2012), 15.

43. See Blair, *Reading Up,* 2–3.

44. The first public library serving African Americans opened in Birmingham in 1918 and was named after Booker T. Washington. The first public library serving white people in Alabama opened in 1904. See Toby Patterson Graham, *Right to Read: Segregation and Civil Rights in Alabama's Public Libraries, 1900–1965* (Tuscaloosa: Alabama University Press, 2006), 9.

45. Washington, *Working with the Hands,* 97.

46. Whiting, *Shop and Class at Tuskegee,* 15.

47. Booker T. Washington, *My Larger Education* (New York: Doubleday, 1911), 137.

48. Franklin E. Frazier, *Black Bourgeoisie* (Glencoe, Ill.: Free Press, 1957), 245.

49. Booker T. Washington, *The Booker T. Washington Papers: Volume 4, 1895–1898*, ed. Louis R. Harlan (Urbana and Chicago: University of Illinois Press, 1975), 146–47.

50. Louis R. Harlan, *Booker T. Washington: The Wizard of Tuskegee, 1901–1915* (New York: Oxford University Press, 1983), 149.

51. Booker T. Washington, "The Story of Tuskegee Institute," *Nautilus*, February 1912, 44–51, here 50–51.

52. See Washington, *Up from Slavery*, 71.

53. Harlan, *Booker T. Washington: The Wizard*, 163.

54. See Booker T. Washington, *The Booker T. Washington Papers: Volume 3, 1889–1895*, ed. Louis R. Harlan (Urbana and Chicago: University of Illinois Press, 1974), 279.

55. For two distinct accounts of the rise of English studies in the academy, see Renker, *The Origins of American Literary Studies*, and Graff, *Professing Literature*.

56. See Brodhead on "antiliterary prejudice" in *Cultures of Letters*, 187.

57. Washington, *Up from Slavery*, 129.

58. Washington, *Up from Slavery*, 32.

59. Washington, *Working with the Hands*, 136.

60. Washington, *My Larger Education*, 133, 142–43.

61. Charles W. Chesnutt, "The Negro in Books," in *The New Negro: Readings on Race, Representation, and African American Culture, 1892–1938*, ed. Henry Louis Gates Jr. and Gene Andrew Jarrett (Princeton: Princeton University Press, 2007), 174.

62. Washington, *My Larger Education*, 12, 13.

63. Notably, Washington's theory of the word and immediacy is directly opposed to the ideas of his contemporary, Memphis-based Baptist minister and novelist Sutton Griggs, who spoke of the need for greater black literacy and access to books—significantly, in the year after Washington's death. See Griggs, *Life's Demands, or According to Law* (Memphis: National Public Welfare League, 1916), 26, 51–52.

64. Washington, *My Larger Education*, 100.

65. Cathy N. Davidson, *Revolution and the Word: The Rise of the Novel in America* (New York: Oxford University Press, 2004).

66. Washington, *Up from Slavery*, 155.

67. Washington, *Up from Slavery*, 144. Washington was confident in his own books' social utility. The U.S. commissioner of education, William T. Harris, commended him on writing a book that might reform the nation: "Mrs.

Harriet Beecher Stowe wrote 'Uncle Tom's Cabin' and thereby produced a civil war in the Nation. You have written a book which I think will do more than anything else to guide us on the true road on which we may successfully solve the problems left us by that civil war." Quoted in Louis R. Harlan, *Booker T. Washington: The Making of a Black Leader, 1856-1901* (New York: Oxford University Press, 1972), 248. Moreover, Kelly Miller raised the wonderfully ironic point that Washington's prominence as a racial leader and educational figurehead came about as a result of his "intellect and oratory," and not by any means through his success in manual endeavors. "If Mr. Washington had been born with palsied hands, but endowed with the same intellectual gifts ... Tuskegee would not have suffered one iota by reason of his manual affliction." Miller, quoted in Ross Posnock, *Color and Culture: Black Writers and the Making of the Modern Intellectual* (Cambridge, Mass.: Harvard University Press, 1998), 59.

68. Harlan, *Booker T. Washington: The Wizard*, 151.

69. Susanna Ashton makes the important point that "imagination may have been more important to Washington than he admitted," since, to narrate his life experiences, he relied on ghostwriters who obviously lacked firsthand experience of that life. See her "Entitles: Booker T. Washington's Signs of Play," *Southern Literary Journal* 39, no. 2 (2007): 1-23, here 18.

70. Washington, *Up from Slavery*, 90.

71. Du Bois favored higher education that would train talented black students in modern culture and endorsed a curricular model that matched the curricula at majority-white universities, which in the early twentieth century meant the classics, modern languages, mathematics, philosophy, science, and English. See Fairclough, *A Class of Their Own*, 149. Beginning around the time of his 1933 address "The Field and Function of the Negro College," Du Bois would increasingly advocate an Afrocentric curriculum.

72. W. E. B. Du Bois, "The Negro College," *W. E. B. Du Bois: A Reader*, ed. Meyer Weinberg (New York: Harper and Row, 1970), 165-66.

73. See W. E. B. Du Bois, "Atlanta University," in *From Servitude to Service: Being the Old South Lectures on the History and Work of Southern Institutions for the Education of the Negro* (Boston: American Unitarian Association, 1905), 153-98, here 156, 157.

74. W. E. B. Du Bois, "Galileo Galilei," *The Education of Black People: Ten Critiques, 1906-1960*, ed. Herbert Aptheker (Amherst: University of Massachusetts Press, 1973), 17-30, here 30.

75. Du Bois, "Galileo Galilei," 29, 28.

76. Fairclough, *A Class of Their Own*, 149.

77. Fairclough, *A Class of Their Own*, 172.

78. Renker, *The Origins of American Literary Studies*, 75.

79. Renker, *The Origins of American Literary Studies*, 249.

80. The first shrill warning quoted here was issued by administrators of the Southern Education Board (the public relations wing of the General Education Board) in 1906, quoted in Fairclough, *A Class of Their Own*, 151. J. H. Phillips, educational reformer and superintendent of Birmingham schools, voiced the second in "Essential Requirements of Negro Education," in *Journal of Proceedings and Addresses of the Southern Education Association* (Atlanta: Southern Educational Association, 1908), 123–26, here 125.

81. Du Bois, "Galileo Galilei," 28.

82. In 1917, the U.S. Bureau of Education and the Phelps-Stokes Fund published a 724-page report on African American higher education that maligned the liberal arts colleges and endorsed vocational training for black students. Research for the report had been conducted several years earlier in preparation for the new era in black education that its writers knew would come with the passing of Booker T. Washington, which occurred in 1915.

83. W. E. B. Du Bois, quoted in David Levering Lewis, *W. E. B. Du Bois, 1919–1963: The Fight for Equality and the American Century* (New York: Henry Holt, 2000), 136.

84. See Claudrena Harold, "Reconfiguring the Roots and Routes of New Negro Activism," in *Escape from New York: The New Negro Renaissance beyond Harlem*, ed. Davarian Baldwin and Minkah Makalani (Minneapolis: University of Minnesota Press, 2013), 208.

85. Martin Anthony Summers, *Manliness and Its Discontents: The Black Middle Class and the Transformation of Masculinity, 1900–1930* (Chapel Hill: University of North Carolina Press, 2004), 275.

86. W. E. B. Du Bois, "Fisk," *Crisis* 29, no. 6 (April 1925): 247–51, here 250.

87. On the student uprisings, see Raymond Wolters, *The New Negro on Campus: Black College Rebellions of the 1920s* (Princeton: Princeton University Press, 1975); Summers, *Manliness and Its Discontents;* and Joe M. Richardson, *A History of Fisk University, 1865–1946* (Tuscaloosa: Alabama University Press, 2002). Arna Bontemps, a prize-winning novelist and poet associated with the Harlem Renaissance, thematizes the New Negro student protests in his story "Heathen at Home," published in a short story collection in 1973 but probably written during the 1930s. The story follows a student uprising at a fictionalized African American school, Mount Lebanon College. The grounds of student protest in this story match those of the New Negro uprisings — strict discipline, poor conditions, teachers' and benefactors' racism — and Bontemps pays special attention to the persistence of slave-master relations within the patron-client dynamics of philanthropic education. Bontemps was

a seasoned educator as well as an author; he taught at schools in Harlem, Chicago, and Huntsville, Alabama, and was forced out of his last position at Oakwood Junior College in 1934 in part owing to his literary aspirations. The story is collected in Bontemps's *The Old South* (New York: Dodd, Mead, 1973). See also Daniel Reagan, "Achieving Perspective: Arna Bontemps and the Shaping Force of Harlem Culture," in *Essays in Arts and Sciences* 25 (October 1996): 69–78.

88. See Davarian L. Baldwin's "Introduction: New Negroes Forging a New World," in Baldwin and Makalani, *Escape from New York*, 1–30, here 20.

89. See Hanchard's "Afro-Modernity," 256, 264.

90. Washington, *Working with the Hands*, 82.

91. See Henry Louis Gates Jr. and Gene Andrew Jarrett, "Introduction," in Gates and Jarrett, *The New Negro*, 4.

92. W. E. Sumlin, quoted in *New York Age*, February 21, 1925.

93. W. E. B. Du Bois, *Autobiography* (New York: International Publishers, 1968), 241. Du Bois's ideal educational system would operate vertically, "by founding the common school on the university, and the industrial school on the common school; and weaving thus a system, not a distortion, and bringing a birth, not an abortion." Du Bois, *The Souls of Black Folk*, 119.

94. Raymond Blaine Fosdick, *Adventures in Giving: The Story of the General Education Board* (New York: Harper and Row, 1962), 129.

95. Larsen, *"Quicksand" and "Passing,"* 4, 3.

96. Larsen, *"Quicksand" and "Passing,"* 4, 8, 7, 3, 12, 17, 4.

97. Larsen, *"Quicksand" and "Passing,"* 7.

98. Larsen, *"Quicksand" and "Passing,"* 4.

99. Larsen, *"Quicksand" and "Passing,"* 13.

100. Larsen, *"Quicksand" and "Passing,"* 45, 48–49, 38, 103.

101. Larsen, *"Quicksand" and "Passing,"* 3, 48.

102. George Hutchinson, *In Search of Nella Larsen: A Biography of the Color Line* (Cambridge, Mass.: Harvard University Press, 2006), 238.

103. Mary Helen Washington is credited with Larsen's "discovery." See her "Nella Larsen: Mystery Woman of the Harlem Renaissance," *Ms.*, December 1980, 45.

104. Carby, *Reconstructing Womanhood*, 171.

105. Hutchinson, *In Search of Nella Larsen*, 63.

106. Hutchinson, *In Search of Nella Larsen*, 222.

107. Washington, *Working with the Hands*, 105.

108. See, for example, Claudia Tate, "Desire and Death in *Quicksand*, by Nella Larsen," *American Literary History* 7, no. 2 (Summer 1995): 234–60; Hutchinson, *In Search of Nella Larsen;* Charles R. Larson, *Invisible Darkness:*

Jean Toomer and Nella Larsen (Iowa City: University of Iowa Press, 1993); and Thadious Davis, *Nella Larsen, Novelist of the Harlem Renaissance: A Woman's Life Unveiled* (Baton Rouge: Louisiana State University Press, 1996).

109. Larsen, *"Quicksand" and "Passing,"* 6.

110. Larsen, *"Quicksand" and "Passing,"* 1, 2.

111. See Larsen, *"Quicksand" and "Passing,"* 18, 69, 70, 20, 70, 89, 62. In this critical tradition, Helga's aestheticism operates metaphorically as a medium of displacement and surrogation. This metaphorical-allegorical critical model dominates scholarship on Larsen's *Passing* as well, epitomized most clearly in Deborah McDowell's influential reading of the novel as queer allegory. *Quicksand* has received critical interpretations as well: Mark McGurl names Helga "a belated fin-de-siècle aesthete," an avid beholder of beauty but not quite a producer of it. See McGurl, *The Program Era,* 106. Linda Dittmar reads Helga as a thwarted artist figure in her "When Privilege Is No Protection: The Woman Artist in *Quicksand* and *The House of Mirth,*" in *Writing the Woman Artist: Essays on Poetics, Politics, and Portraiture,* ed. Suzanne W. Jones (Philadelphia: University of Pennsylvania Press, 1991), 133–54. Cherene Sherrard-Johnson calls for a "painterly" reading of Larsen's work and analyzes the composition of Larsen's "visual tableaux" in her "A Plea for Color," *American Literature* 76, no. 4 (December 2004): 833–69. Pamela E. Barnett explores the visual modes of representation in the novel in "'My Picture of You Is, After All, the True Helga Crane': Portraiture and Identity in Nella Larsen's *Quicksand,*" *Signs* 20, no. 3 (Spring 1995): 575–600. Claudia Tate declares Helga's subjectivity imagistic rather than rhetorical in her "Desire and Death in *Quicksand,* by Nella Larsen."

112. W. E. B. Du Bois, "Diuturni Silenti," in Aptheker, *The Education of Black People,* 41–60, here 54.

113. Alain Locke, preface to *The New Negro,* ed. Alain Locke (New York: Touchstone, 1992), xxvii.

114. Locke, "The New Negro," in Locke, *The New Negro,* 6.

115. Larsen, *"Quicksand" and "Passing,"* 118, 111, 118, 119.

116. Larsen, *"Quicksand" and "Passing,"* 119, 134, 135.

117. Larsen, *"Quicksand" and "Passing,"* 5, 52, 133.

118. C. Ann McDonald summarizes the range of critical assessments of Larsen's endings in her entry on Nella Larsen in *American Women Writers, 1900–1945: A Bio-bibliographical Critical Sourcebook,* ed. Laurie Champion (Westport, Conn.: Greenwood Press, 2000), 188–89.

119. See Leela Gandhi, *Affective Communities: Anticolonial Thought, Fin-de-Siècle Radicalism, and the Politics of Friendship* (Durham, N.C.: Duke University Press, 2005), 25.

120. James Weldon Johnson, preface to *The Book of American Negro Poetry*, ed. James Weldon Johnson (New York: Harcourt, Brace, 1922), 9.

121. Larsen was the first black woman accepted to the New York City Public Library School. On Larsen's work as a librarian, see chapter 10 of Hutchinson, *In Search of Nella Larsen*, and Karin Roffman, "Nella Larsen: Librarian at 135th Street," *MFS: Modern Fiction Studies* 53, no. 4 (Winter 2007): 752–87.

122. Beginning in 1913, new accrediting agencies emerged and began issuing reports that would eventually standardize the definition of "high school," "normal school," "college," and "university," which put pressure on institutions of black higher learning to meet national educational standards or risk losing their accreditation. See Anderson, *The Education of Blacks in the South*, 250–51.

123. See David Levering Lewis, *W. E. B. Du Bois, 1868–1919: Biography of a Race* (New York: Henry Holt, 1994), 286.

124. W. E. B. Du Bois, "The Negro College," in *Du Bois on Education*, ed. Eugene F. Provenzo Jr. (Walnut Creek, Calif.: AltaMira, 2002), 247.

125. Miller, quoted in Wolters, *The New Negro on Campus*, 88.

126. Robert R. Moton, "Hampton-Tuskegee: Missioners of the Masses," in Locke, *The New Negro*, 323–32, here 328.

127. On McKay's trajectory, see Sonya Posmentier's "The Provision Ground in New York: Claude McKay and the Form of Memory," *American Literature* 84, no. 2 (June 2012): 273–300, especially 273. Higher education played a key role in literary texts written by white affiliates of the Harlem Renaissance as well. Annie Nathan Meyer, noted social reform writer and founder of Barnard College, wrote a short play, *Black Souls*, that wove together questions of educational method and the threat of racial violence. *Black Souls* is set entirely on the campus of Magnolia, a southern industrial college staffed by teachers and administrators who aspire to a liberal arts curriculum. Meyer began writing the play in 1924 and it finally debuted at the Provincetown Playhouse in 1932, with production notes penned by George Schuyler. Meyer, a New Yorker, undertook research for her play at Morehouse College in Atlanta, where she interviewed John Hope, the first black president of that institution. Though ostensibly a play about the nexus of interracial sex and lynching in the South, what is most striking about *Black Souls* is the way in which literature—writing it, reading it, teaching it to black people—is rhetorically aligned with the threat of racist violence from the beginning of the play. The alliance between literary intellection and racial violence is particularly visible in scenes featuring David Lewis, "Professor of Belles Lettres" and promising poet, who is the victim of a savage lynching

in the final scene of the play. *Black Souls* condemns the General Education Board, the Slater Fund, and other philanthropic bodies for "making the constitution of the United States the laughing stock of the whole world" (165). In a pivotal scene, the state governor comes to the Magnolia campus to deliver an address that mirrors the white preacher's speech at Naxos in the first chapter of *Quicksand:* "Without putting foolish ideas of equality or of false grandeur into the heads of his people, [the school, Magnolia] has, on the contrary, taught them to become better farmers, willing and able tillers of the soil, workingmen, self-respecting, God-fearing laborers, knowing their place and keeping it." See Annie Nathan Meyer's *Black Souls,* in *Strange Fruit: Plays on Lynching by American Women,* ed. Kathy A. Perkins and Judith L. Stephens (Bloomington and Indianapolis: Indiana University Press, 1998), 133–73, here 166. For the fullest existing scholarly account of *Black Souls,* see Carla Kaplan, "*Black Souls:* Annie Nathan Meyer Writes Black," in *Miss Anne in Harlem: The White Women of the Harlem Renaissance* (New York: HarperCollins, 2013), 169–92.

128. Scholars have thoroughly examined the institutional contours of the Harlem Renaissance. Both Cary D. Wintz and George Hutchinson have written important cultural histories of the Harlem Renaissance that emphasize the importance of social institutions and networks to the movement's development. Wintz has described the "group of black writers and poets, orbiting erratically around a group of black intellectuals positioned in the N.A.A.C.P., the Urban League, and other African American political and educational institutions" (see his "Series Introduction," in *The Politics and Aesthetics of "New Negro" Literature,* ed. Cary D. Wintz [New York: Routledge, 1996], x). Hutchinson's *The Harlem Renaissance in Black and White* (Cambridge, Mass.: Harvard University Press, 1997) chronicles the networks of cultural organizations as well as the intellectuals, reformers, and artists who together made up the movement.

129. Johnson, quoted in David Levering Lewis, *When Harlem Was in Vogue* (New York: Oxford University Press, 1981), 97.

130. W. E. B. Du Bois, "Negro Writers," *Crisis* 19, no. 6 (April 1920): 298–99, here 299.

131. Du Bois had also recently turned to writing fiction himself. Du Bois's novel, *Quest of the Silver Fleece,* was published in 1911—one year after he assumed editorship of the *Crisis* and between his two public addresses at Fisk. *Quest* fictionalizes contemporary debates over the content and methods of black education. ("You are planning to put our plough-hands all to studying Greek, and at the same time to corner the cotton crop—rot!" exclaims the

white Alabaman Harry Cresswell, invidiously referencing the liberal arts education being offered to black students in his state.) See Du Bois, *Quest of the Silver Fleece* (Mineola, N.Y.: Dover, 1974), 120.

132. W. E. B. Du Bois, "Criteria of Negro Art" *Crisis* 32, no. 6 (October 1926): 290–97, here 290.

133. It is also important to note that Du Bois constantly revised his own views on art and propaganda. His views changed mid-decade as the hoped-for sociopolitical changes were slow to arrive and had certainly changed by the early 1930s, when he bitterly dismissed the accomplishments of the 1920s.

134. James Weldon Johnson, "Race Prejudice and the American Negro," in Wintz, *The Politics and Aesthetics of "New Negro" Literature*, 281–90, here 283.

135. See Locke, "The New Negro," 13–14, 15, 15–16. For more on the dispute between Locke and Du Bois over the relationship between art and propaganda, see Gates and Jarrett, "Introduction"; see also Alain Locke's "Art of Propaganda?," in Gates and Jarrett, *The New Negro*, 260–61. The Harlem Renaissance's white patrons also spoke the pragmatic language of social utility. Speaking as a representative of the American literary mainstream at the March 21, 1924, Civic Club dinner, *Century* magazine editor Carl Van Doren referred to the "strategic" nature of the coming Renaissance: "The Negroes of the country are in a remarkable strategic position with reference to the new literary age which seems to be impending." Lewis, *When Harlem Was in Vogue*, 93. In this case, however, Van Doren's strategic interest is in the bright publishing prospects for new black writers, and not in collective social gains for the race.

136. Charles S. Johnson, "The Social Philosophy of Booker T. Washington," in Wintz, *The Politics and Aesthetics of "New Negro" Literature*, 372–76, here 372, 373, 375, 376.

137. Thurman, quoted in Martha Jane Nadell, *Enter the New Negroes* (Cambridge, Mass.: Harvard University Press, 2004), 72.

138. Larsen was recruited to write for *Fire!!* but declined to publish there. Du Bois famously praised *Quicksand* in a review that seemed, in fact, to misunderstand it. Of Harlem Renaissance figures, Larsen's primary social and artistic alliance was with Carl Van Vechten, for better or worse.

139. On this point, see Morgan, *Questionable Charity*, 102.

140. See Kelly Miller's "Howard: The National Negro University," in Locke, *The New Negro*, 312–22, here 316.

141. Addams, *Democracy and Social Ethics*, 92.

142. See Hutchinson, *The Harlem Renaissance in Black and White*, 53.

143. McGurl, *The Program Era*, 104.

4. FORMS OF MEDIATION

1. On this lecture's iconic status, see Victoria Bissell Brown, *The Education of Jane Addams* (Philadelphia: University of Pennsylvania Press, 2007), 263. The School of Applied Ethics was a summer program based on the Chautauqua model and was held annually from 1891 to 1895. The school was founded by Felix Adler of the Ethical Culture Society and focused on so-called practical sociology.

2. Addams, "The Subjective Necessity for Social Settlements," 11–12. Eric Schocket addresses this passage in his essay "Middle-Class Melancholy and Proletarian Pain: The Writer as Class Transvestite," in *Vanishing Moments: Class and American Literature* (Ann Arbor: Michigan University Press, 2006), 132–33, focusing on Addams's construction of the unidirectional visual link between rich and poor.

3. "The barbarities . . ." in Frank Lentricchia, *Modernist Quartet* (Cambridge: Cambridge University Press, 1994), 19. "The cult of experience" in Lears, *No Place of Grace,* xii. Of the turn of the century, Lears further writes, "Amid spiritual confusion, intense experience became an end in itself. Discontented Victorians embarked on a frustrating quest for authentic selfhood." Lears, *No Place of Grace,* 124.

4. Addams, "The Subjective Necessity for Social Settlements," 11.

5. Other scholars have assigned different names to these texts. Eric Schocket names them "class-transvestite narratives," but I reject this title for its mobilization of an outdated, derogatory term as an analogy. Mark Pittenger uses a variety of titles for this genre, including "down and outers," "class-passing narratives," "undercover investigations," and more. I use these latter terms relatively interchangeably with "undercover literature." See Pittenger, *Class Unknown: Undercover Investigations of American Work and Poverty from the Progressive Era to the Present* (New York: New York University Press, 2012), 4.

6. As critic Esther Romeyn has noted, "The active pursuit of reality through firsthand knowledge . . . was characteristic of turn-of-the-century middle-class culture." See Romeyn's *Street Scenes: Staging the Self in Immigrant New York, 1880–1924* (Minneapolis: University of Minnesota Press, 2008), 37.

7. Cornelia Stratton Parker, *Wanderer's Circle* (New York: Houghton Mifflin, 1934), 89; Parker, *Working with the Working Woman,* 4, hereafter referred to as *Working.*

8. I have found little evidence of undercover texts written by immigrants or people of color. Walter White's expeditions in the U.S. South on behalf of the NAACP, passing as a white man to investigate lynching, is one exception

to this rule. Because White's undercover texts were explicitly connected to the work of a governing institution, I do not include him in this chapter.

9. Parker, *Working*, 246.

10. Mrs. John Van Vorst and Marie Van Vorst, *The Woman Who Toils: Being the Experiences of Two Gentlewomen as Factory Girls* (New York: Biblio-Bazaar, 2006), 113, 18.

11. Walter A. Wyckoff, *The Workers: An Experiment in Reality. The East* (New York: Scribner's Sons, 1897), vii; Parker, *Working*, 2–3.

12. Wharton, *Mirth*, 152; Washington, *My Larger Education*, 133.

13. Here I draw on Jean Marie Lutes's useful account of late nineteenth-century sob-sister journalists. See her *Front-Page Girls: Women Journalists in American Culture and Fiction, 1880–1930* (Ithaca, N.Y.: Cornell University Press, 2007), 227.

14. Gandal, *The Virtues of the Vicious*, 62.

15. See the anonymously written *Four Years in the Underbrush: Adventures as a Working Woman in New York* (New York: Charles Scribner's Sons, 1921).

16. I am not the first to note the genre's bridging function. Eric Schocket identifies an important generic distinction: most texts produce knowledge about the poor through distancing rhetoric of the social spectacle: newspaper report, photo documentary, muckraking book. Class-passing narratives, by contrast, "reverse this process, producing authentic knowledge—and performing authenticity itself—through the act of embodiment." See Schocket, *Vanishing Moments*, 108.

17. In what follows, I switch between calling this collection of texts a "genre" and a "mode." I recognize that some conceptual inaccuracies may result from this slippage between terms that do in fact have distinct meanings, and perhaps "subgenre" would be the most accurate term to use—yet I find it too clunky to be useful.

18. Phillip Barish, *American Literary Realism, Critical Theory, and Intellectual Prestige, 1880–1995* (New York: Cambridge University Press, 2004), 10.

19. Longer nonfictional undercover narratives are a Progressive Era species of the nonfiction novel. Leonora Flis dates the birth of the American nonfiction novel (the "documentary novel") to Truman Capote's work in the 1960s; see her *Factual Fictions: Narrative Truth and the Contemporary American Documentary Novel* (Newcastle, U.K.: Cambridge Scholars Publishing, 2010), 4. Nonfictional undercover texts include Walter Wyckoff's two-volume study *The Workers* (*East*, 1897, and Wyckoff, *The Workers: An Experiment in Reality. The West* [New York: Scribner's Sons, 1898]); the Van Vorsts' *The Woman Who Toils* (1903); Lillian Pettengill's *Toilers of the Home* (1903); Maud Younger's "The Diary of an Amateur Waitress" (1907); Rheta

Childe Dorr's *What Eight Million Women Want* (1910); Edwin A. Brown's *"Broke": The Man without the Dime* (1913); Frances Donovan's *The Woman Who Waits* (1920); Whiting Williams's *What's on the Worker's Mind, by One Who Put on Overalls to Find Out* (1921); and Cornelia Stratton Parker's *Working with the Working Woman* (1922). According to Mark Pittenger's calculations, forty-nine nonfictional undercover narratives (nineteen by women, thirty by men) were published between 1877 and 1929; see Mark Pittenger, "A World of Difference: Constructing the 'Underclass' in Progressive America," *American Quarterly* 49, no. 1 (1997): 55. In both article and book, Pittenger's definition of an undercover narrative excludes fictional texts or texts with authors whose investigations down and out were not confirmed at the time his article was published in 1997. So while Pittenger does not count Dorothy Richardson's *The Long Day* within the corpus, Alice Fahs has since proven that Richardson performed undercover research for her book before burying that fact in a text she framed as the autobiography of a "real" working girl. See Fahs's *Out on Assignment: Newspaper Women and the Making of Modern Public Space* (Chapel Hill: University of North Carolina Press, 2011).

20. On the rise of corporate philanthropy in relation to the U.S. literary marketplace and the dependence of twentieth-century publishing companies on philanthropic models, see Sawaya, *The Difficult Art of Giving*.

21. See Charlotte Perkins Gilman, *What Diantha Did*, ed. Charlotte Rich (Durham, N.C.: Duke University Press, 2005), 88; "little body of adventurers..." in Stuart Pratt Sherman, "The Autobiography of Josiah Flynt," review of *My Life*, by Josiah Flynt, *Nation* 88 (February 25, 1909): 1988; O. Henry, "The Higher Pragmatism," in *Forty-One Stories*, ed. Burton Raffel (New York: Signet Classics, 1984). The Van Vorsts' *The Woman Who Toils* was a best seller, outselling Helen Keller's and Booker T. Washington's respective autobiographies for upwards of a year. See Brooke Kroeger, *Undercover Reporting: The Truth about Deception* (Evanston, Ill.: Northwestern University Press, 2012), 93. The undercover genre continued to develop beyond the historical parameters of this study. It slowed down in the 1920s, but the Depression breathed new life into the genre with such texts as James Agee and Walker Evans's *Let Us Now Praise Famous Men* (1941) and the motion picture comedy *Sullivan's Travels*, written and directed by Preston Sturges (1941), while the civil rights movement later inspired white authors like John Howard Griffin and Grace Halsell to artificially darken their skin and attempt cross-racial journeys into the heart of the racist South—and, of course, to write popular books telling their tales.

22. See Laura Hapke, *Labor's Text: The Worker in American Fiction* (New Brunswick, N.J.: Rutgers University Press, 2000), 6. Elsewhere, Hapke notes

that labor fiction focused increasingly on women workers by the 1890s; see Hapke, *Tales of the Working Girl*.

23. On Riis's deceptive practices, see Susan M. Ryan, "'Rough Ways and Rough Work': Jacob Riis, Social Reform, and the Rhetoric of Benevolent Violence," *American Transcendental Quarterly* 11, no. 3 (September 1997), 204.

24. See Mark Pittenger, "'What's on the Worker's Mind': Class Passing and the Study of the Industrial Workplace in the 1920s," *Journal of the History of the Behavioral Sciences* 39, no. 2 (Spring 2003): 143–61, here 150.

25. See Chad Heap, *Slumming: Sexual and Racial Encounters in American Nightlife, 1885–1940* (Chicago: University of Chicago Press, 2009), 13.

26. See Van Vorst and Van Vorst, *The Woman Who Toils*, 44. See also Jennifer Fronc, *New York Undercover: Private Surveillance in the Progressive Era* (Chicago: University of Chicago Press, 2009), 14.

27. Journalist James Greenwood wrote a series of articles collectively titled "A Night in a Workhouse" and published them in the British *Pall Mall Gazette* in 1866. He portrayed his investigation as a matter of class masquerade and performance. Writers concerned with the very poorest residents of the urban slums, such as Jack London, George Orwell, Stephen Crane, and Walter Wyckoff, followed patterns established by Greenwood. The best-known texts written in this mode are Jack London's 1902 *People of the Abyss* and George Orwell's 1933 *Down and Out in Paris and London*.

28. See Fronc, *New York Undercover*, 13. Banks distinguished her undercover journalism from the work of reform-minded contemporaries in her autobiography, published in 1902: "I did it for copy, to earn my living, you know. I knew it was a subject that would interest everybody.... I'm not a hypocrite and won't pose as a reformer." See Elizabeth Banks, *Autobiography of a Newspaper Girl* (London: Methuen, 1902), 92. On Bly, Banks, and their contemporaries, see Fahs, *Out on Assignment;* Lutes, *Front-Page Girls;* and Seth Koven, "The American Girl in London: Gender, Journalism, and Social Investigation in the Late Victorian Metropolis," in *Slumming: Sexual and Social Politics in Victorian London* (Princeton: Princeton University Press, 2004), 140–80.

29. The tide had turned away from stunt journalism and toward the more searching explorations of undercover literature by 1900. Laura Hapke credits the appearance of Margaret Sherwood's novel *Henry Worthington, Idealist* and Annie Marion MacLean's investigation of the waitress, both published in 1899, with initiating a shift away from the "adventuresome reportage" of Bly and her ilk to more serious undercover writing. See Hapke, *Tales of the Working Girl*, 48.

30. Schocket, *Vanishing Moments*, 134.

31. Van Vorst and Van Vorst, *The Woman Who Toils*, 20.
32. Van Vorst and Van Vorst, *The Woman Who Toils*, 118.
33. See Parker, *Working*, 4. On the down-and-outer's erotic investment in the poor, see Cathryn Halverson, "The Fascination of the Working Girl: Dorothy Richardson's *The Long Day*," *American Studies* 40, no. 1 (Spring 1999): 95–115, and Schocket, "Middle-Class Melancholy and Proletarian Pain."
34. Annie Marion MacLean, "The Sweat-Shop in Summer," *American Journal of Sociology* 9, no. 3 (November 1903): 289–309, here 294.
35. Michael A. Elliott, *The Culture Concept: Writing and Difference in the Age of Realism* (Minneapolis: University of Minnesota Press, 2002), xxvi, 53, 41.
36. Van Vorst and Van Vorst, *The Woman Who Toils*, 129, 195.
37. Kenneth W. Warren, *Black and White Strangers: Race and American Literary Realism* (Chicago: University of Chicago Press, 1993), 82.
38. See Pittenger, *Class Unknown*, 32–33, 35.
39. Parker, *Working*, 12, 11.
40. Frances R. Donovan, *The Woman Who Waits* (Boston: Richard G. Badger, 1920), 81.
41. See Annie Marion MacLean, "Two Weeks in Department Stores," *American Journal of Sociology* 40, no. 6 (May 1899): 721–41, here 730.
42. Parker, *Working*, 41.
43. See Dorothy Richardson, *The Long Day: The Story of a New York Working Girl* (Charlottesville: University of Virginia Press, 1990), 282, 184. On the analogy between linguistic and cultural degeneration, see Gavin Jones, *Strange Talk: The Politics of Dialect Literature in Gilded Age America* (Berkeley and Los Angeles: University of California Press, 1999), 68–69.
44. Richardson, *The Long Day*, 127.
45. Jones, *Strange Talk*, 7, 2.
46. Van Vorst and Van Vorst, *The Woman Who Toils*, 169, 170.
47. Jones, *Strange Talk*, 8, 9.
48. See Richardson, *The Long Day*, 26, 53.
49. Lamarckian views of evolution were beginning to fall out of favor by 1905. On Lamarck and undercover writing, see Pittenger, *Class Unknown*, 22.
50. Van Vorst and Van Vorst, *The Woman Who Toils*, 36, 127.
51. See Michael North, *The Dialect of Modernism: Race, Language, and Twentieth-Century Literature* (New York: Oxford University Press, 1994), 11.
52. North, *The Dialect of Modernism*, 18.
53. On identity becoming "envoiced" in relation to modernism, see Pamela L. Caughie, "Audible Identities: Passing and Sound Technologies," *Humanities Research* 16, no. 1 (2010): 91–109, here 94. Caughie discusses

the concept of auditory passing on 99. The scholarship connecting urban experience to observation and visuality is vast. See Georg Simmel, "The Metropolis and Mental Life," in *The Blackwell City Reader*, ed. Gary Bridge and Sophie Watson (Oxford: Wiley-Blackwell, 2002). Walter Benjamin's *Illuminations* (New York: Penguin Random House, 1969), and David Vincent's "Secrecy and the City, 1870–1939," *Urban History* 22, no. 3 (1995): 341–59 are both also excellent starting points. See also Dowling, *Slumming in New York;* Koven, *Slumming;* Schocket, *Vanishing Moments;* and Deborah Epstein Nord, "The Social Explorer as Anthropologist: Victorian Travellers among the Urban Poor," in *Visions of the Modern City*, ed. William Sharpe and Leonard Wallock (New York: Columbia University Press, 1983), 118–30. In "The Visible and Invisible City: Antebellum Writers and Urban Space," in *The Oxford Handbook of Nineteenth-Century American Literature*, ed. Ross Castronovo (New York: Oxford University Press, 2012), 187, 189, Jeffrey Steele argues against conflating urban experience with the visual field. Yet Steele doesn't talk about the sonic, nor does he attend to the class implications of voice.

54. See Ellen Ross, *Slum Travelers: Ladies and London Poverty, 1860–1920* (Berkeley and Los Angeles: University of California Press, 2007), 15.

55. See Van Vorst and Van Vorst, *The Woman Who Toils*, 89, and Parker, *Working*, 46.

56. Van Vorst and Van Vorst, *The Woman Who Toils*, 140.

57. Parker, *Working*, 127–28.

58. Parker, *Working*, 45.

59. Van Vorst and Van Vorst, *The Woman Who Toils*, 35.

60. See John L. Locke, *Eavesdropping: An Intimate History* (New York: Oxford University Press, 2010), 3.

61. Parker, *Wanderer's Circle*, 93.

62. See Ann Gaylin's *Eavesdropping in the Novel from Austen to Proust* (New York: Cambridge University Press, 2003).

63. Van Vorst and Van Vorst, *The Woman Who Toils*, 57.

64. Parker, *Wanderer's Circle*, 114.

65. Carolyn Betensky, *Feeling for the Poor: Bourgeois Compassion, Social Action, and the Victorian Novel* (Charlottesville: University of Virginia Press, 2010), 9.

66. Parker, *Working*, 242.

67. Richardson, *The Long Day*, 5. The plot of *The Long Day* is quite similar to that of Louisa May Alcott's 1873 novel *Work*. Alcott, however, devotes much of the novel to her heroine Christie's domestic redemption, whereas Richardson's narrative is limited to her heroine's period adrift in the city.

68. Throughout this chapter I rely on Alice Fahs's meticulous research on Dorothy Richardson.

69. Fahs, *Out on Assignment*, 215.

70. In an interview with Richardson published in the *New York Times Saturday Review* in 1907, the very first question the journalist asks her is whether she actually wrote *The Long Day*. "I have heard so many people say that Rose Pastor Stokes wrote the story," he explains. See Otis Notman, "Writers of Contemporaneous History," *New York Times Saturday Review*, May 25, 1907, 334.

71. Richardson, *The Long Day*, 117-18, 83, 144.

72. Richardson, *The Long Day*, 152, 153.

73. Richardson, *The Long Day*, 274.

74. "Not written by a masquerader..." in Izola Forrester, "One Working Girl's Struggles," *New York World*, October 15, 1905; "Who the author is..." in *American Monthly Review of Reviews* 32 (July-December 1905), 758.

75. Richardson, *The Long Day*, 130.

76. Richardson, *The Long Day*, 235, 236, 243.

77. Richardson, *The Long Day*, 276.

78. I am indebted to Amanda Anderson's formulation of Victorian detachment in *The Powers of Distance: Cosmopolitanism and the Cultivation of Detachment* (Princeton: Princeton University Press, 2001), esp. 9-12.

79. Richardson, *The Long Day*, 275-76, 71, 73.

80. See Cook, *Working Women, Literary Ladies*, 254.

81. Blair lists as examples of such manuals Noah Porter's *Books and Reading, or What Books Shall I Read and How Shall I Read Them?* (1881); George C. Lorimer's *What I Know about Books and How to Use Them*, (1892); Hamilton Wright Mabie's *Books and Culture* (1896); and J. N. Larned's *Books, Culture, and Character* (1906). See Blair, *Reading Up*, 4.

82. Richardson, *The Long Day*, 86.

83. Joyce Shaw Peterson argues that Libbey's romance formula offered a "success myth for women" in which working-class women transform into ladies. See her "Working Girls and Millionaires: The Melodramatic Romances of Laura Jean Libbey," *American Studies* 24, no. 1 (Spring 1983): 19-35. Barbara Sicherman makes a similar point in *Well-Read Lives*, 31. Influential accounts of Libbey's relation to working-class reading formations can also be found in Denning, *Mechanic Accents;* Hapke, *Tales of the Working Girl;* and Nan Enstad, *Ladies of Labor, Girls of Adventure: Working Women, Popular Culture, and Labor Politics at the Turn of the Twentieth Century* (New York: Columbia University Press, 1999).

84. Richardson, *The Long Day*, 300.
85. Richardson, *The Long Day*, 222, 224, 28.
86. Richardson, *The Long Day*, 30.
87. Richardson, *The Long Day*, 270, 272, 270.
88. See *The Habits of Good Society: A Handbook of Etiquette for Ladies and Gentlemen* (New York: G. W. Carleton, 1871), 50. On the history of women's reading and on constructions of reading as a leisure activity, see Kate Flint, *The Woman Reader 1837–1914* (New York: Oxford University Press, 1993), esp. 93–95.
89. Kathi Weeks, *The Problem with Work: Feminism, Marxism, Antiwork Politics, and Postwork Imaginaries* (Durham, N.C.: Duke University Press, 2011), 39.
90. Richardson, *The Long Day*, 278; emphasis in original.
91. Richardson, *The Long Day*, 270, 279.
92. Richardson, *The Long Day*, 273.
93. Blair, *Reading Up*, 2.
94. Quoted in Enstad, *Ladies of Labor*, 58.
95. Maud Younger, "The Diary of an Amateur Waitress: An Industrial Problem from the Worker's Point of View," *McClure's Magazine*, March 1907, 543–51, here 552.
96. Van Vorst and Van Vorst, *The Woman Who Toils*, 109.
97. Richardson, *The Long Day*, 283, xxvi.
98. Richardson, *The Long Day*, 289.
99. See Rose H. Phelps Stokes, "The Long Day: A Story of Real Life," *Independent* 59 (November 16, 1905): 1169–71, and Margaret Dreier Robins, "Review of *The Long Day*, by Dorothy Richardson," *Charities and the Commons* 17 (October 1906–April 1907): 484–85.
100. National League of Women Workers, *A Brief History of the First Decade of the National League of Women Workers, 1898–1908* (Philadelphia: Devine Printing, 1908), 13, 14. Reading *The Long Day* led to other investigations as well. Delia Lyman Porter was so inspired by Richardson's novel that she undertook doctoral research on female factory workers in Connecticut and helped pass the Woman Inspector Bill in that state. See Delia Lyman Porter, "How Connecticut Got Her Woman Factory Inspector," *Chautauqua* 50 (May 1908): 425–29.
101. O'Reilly's unpublished editorial is copied nearly in full in Meredith Tax, *The Rising of the Women: Feminist Solidarity and Class Conflict, 1880–1917* (Urbana and Chicago: University of Illinois Press, 2001), 117–18.
102. On this sequence of events, see Mary J. Bularzik, "The Bonds of

Belonging: Leonora O'Reilly and Social Reform," in *History of Women in the United States,* ed. Nancy F. Cott (Munich: Die Deutsche Bibliotek, 1994), 464–87.
103. See Wexler, *Tender Violence,* 101.
104. Richardson, *The Long Day,* 300–302.
105. Richardson, *The Long Day,* 289.

CODA

1. See "Our Favorite Lower East Side Books," *Tenement Museum,* http://www.tenement.org/research.html.
2. See "College Preparation," *Girls Write Now,* available at the Internet Archive's Wayback Machine, https://web.archive.org/web/20121029102326/www.girlswritenow.org/gwn/node/1175.
3. Scott McLemee, "Guerrilla Librarians in Our Midst," *Inside Higher Ed,* November 2, 2011, http://www.insidehighered.com/views/2011/11/02/essay-librarians-occupy-movement.
4. See, for example, William J. Maxwell's "Born-Again, Seen-Again James Baldwin: Post-Postracial Criticism and the Literary History of Black Lives Matter," *American Literary History* 28, no. 4 (Winter 2016): 812–27.
5. It should be noted that Tania Bruguera prefers the expression "behavior art" to "performance art" in descriptions of her work. See Stephanie Schwartz, "Tania Bruguera: Between Histories," *Oxford Art Journal* 35, no. 2 (June 2012): 215–32.
6. See "What Is Arte Útil?," *Museum of Arte Útil,* http://museumarteutil.net/about/.
7. See Michael Szalay, *New Deal Modernism: American Literature and the Invention of the Welfare State* (Durham, N.C.: Duke University Press, 2000).
8. See Randy Kennedy, "Tania Bruguera, an Artist in Havana, Has a Great New York Week," *New York Times,* July 13, 2015, http://www.nytimes.com/2015/07/14/arts/design/tania-bruguera-an-artist-in-havana-has-a-great-new-york-week.html.
9. Tracie McMillan, *The American Way of Eating: Undercover at Walmart, Applebee's, Farm Fields, and the Dinner Table* (New York: Scribner, 2012), 112.
10. Arianna Huffington, "Is *Undercover Boss* the Most Subversive Show on Television?" *Huffington Post,* May 8, 2010, http://www.huffingtonpost.com/arianna-huffington/is-iundercover-bossi-the_b_490989.html.

Index

abolitionist movement, 5–6, 67–68, 79, 270n9
abstraction, 127, 141, 147–49, 173, 209
accent, 40, 46, 79, 118, 196. *See also* dialect; speech
access (cultural), 3, 8, 23, 24, 26, 59, 80, 218; for black students, 16–17, 136, 156–57, 270n6, 274n63
acculturation, 35, 42, 53, 59, 229
activism, 24, 51, 52, 88, 95; and publication, 171
Adams, Dorothy. *See* Richardson, Dorothy
Addams, Jane, 51, 247n4, 248n12, 252n56; cross-class relation and, 17–18, 47–48, 50, 177–79; *Democracy and Social Ethics,* 175; pragmatism/vocational education and, 15, 137, 174–75, 273n32; "The Subjective Necessity for Social Settlements," 177–80. *See also* Jane Addams Hull-House Museum
aesthetics, 4, 12, 21–22, 37, 68, 72; comparison and, 76, 88–89, 100, 106, 111, 122; dovetailing and, 128; in *Quicksand* (Larsen), 159, 162–64, 166, 278n111; in *Salome of the Tenements* (Yezierska), 60; settlement house and, 32–33, 37, 41, 45, 49, 72–73; social justice and, 171; in undercover literature, 192, 195, 198–99, 201, 210, 215. *See also* beauty
African American communal institutions/organizations, 130, 148, 155, 271n14
African American education, 7, 16, 17, 125–76; liberal arts, 16–17, 132–34, 136–37, 151–53, 157, 241n16; vocational, 132, 149–50, 171, 175, 273n32, 276n82; wider African American community and, 153, 245n65. *See also* Du Bois, W. E. B.; Washington, Booker T.
African American educational institutions: colleges/institutions, 12, 24, 125–76; common schools, 132, 133, 277n93; funding, 134, 144–45, 151–53, 169, 241n16, 272n27; normal schools, 129, 133, 272n26; as social settlements, 270n9
African American literature and

culture, 17, 22, 127, 130–32, 137, 149, 152, 155, 170, 172. *See also* Harlem Renaissance; *individual authors*
Afro-modernity, 127–28, 154–56
Alcott, Louisa May, 40, 211; *Little Women*, 31, 211–12; *Work*, 93, 287n67
Alliance Review, 26–27, 40
American Hebrew, 39, 52, 58, 61
Americanization, 9, 36, 53, 62, 248n12, 251n41; via literature and culture, 8, 28, 31–32, 37, 39, 71; resistance to, 59, 73
American Way of Eating, The (McMillan), 232
Ammons, Elizabeth, 121, 257n5
anger, 17, 90, 91, 162; in *Quicksand* (Larsen), 157, 159, 161
antebellum reform writing, 21, 67, 81
antiliterary sentiment, 146, 148–49
antireform sentiment, 23, 58–59, 61
Arnold, Matthew, 22, 42–43
art, 22, 70, 231, 244n53; Harlem Renaissance and, 170–74; literature and, 39, 71; as propaganda, 171–72, 281n133, 281n135
arts, the, 59, 60, 85, 170–71, 174; education and, 137, 139, 170
aspiration, 13–14, 76, 146, 157, 271n15; aspirational consciousness, 87–88, 123, 261n2; aspirational reading, 142
assimilation, 248n12; African American, 161, 175; -by-culture, 42; and drama, 41; settlement house, 36, 41–43, 62, 72
Association of Working Girls' Societies, 1, 221, 258n11, 265n81

Atlanta University, 132, 134, 144, 150, 169, 170, 241n16
Augst, Thomas, 38–39, 84
aurality, 197–98. *See also* speech
authenticity, 50, 177, 282n3; assimilation vs., 50, 57, 60; inauthenticity and, 47, 178; undercover writing and, 192, 200, 208, 283n16
authority: of firsthand experience, 16, 176; institutional, 241n18; the settlement house and, 72, 247n7; undercover writing and, 184, 185, 188, 200, 207, 225; in working girls' clubs, 89, 90
autobiography, 205, 208, 215, 220, 284n19. *See also* memoir(s)
automation, 17, 110
autonomy, 9; Afro-modernist, 128; black university and, 150; individual, 128, 164, 167; modernist, 17, 28, 239n5; settlement house literature and, 33, 50, 72–73
avant-garde, 28, 72, 174

Bacon, Alice M., 134–37, 172
Baldwin, William H., Jr., 16, 134, 170
Banks, Elizabeth L., 189, 285n28
beauty, 12, 43; in *The House of Mirth* (Wharton), 107–8; in *Quicksand* (Larsen), 16–64, 165, 278n11; in *Salome of the Tenements* (Yezierska), 13, 59–60, 251n38. *See also* aesthetics
Beckley, Zoe: *A Chance to Live*, 45, 252n56
benefactor-beneficiary relation, 14, 33, 49–50, 59–60, 69, 113. *See also* comparison/comparatism;

INDEX   293

contact; friendship; exemplification
Benefactors of the East Side, The (Gordin), 23–24, 33, 54–58, 60–61, 63, 69
Besant, Walter, 97, 98
Betensky, Carolyn, 202–3
biraciality, 160, 161
black colleges/schools. *See* African American educational institutions
black communal organizations. *See* African American communal institutions/organizations
black culture. *See* African American literature and culture
black education. *See* African American education
black elite/bourgeoisie, 143, 271n15
black literacy. *See* literacy
black literature. *See* African American literature and culture
Black Lives Matter, 229–30
black middle class, 130
Black Souls (Meyer), 279n127
black writers, 22, 172, 173, 280n128, 281n135
Blair, Amy L., 142, 211, 218
Bly, Nellie, 189, 204–5
Bontemps, Arna, 276n87
book learning, 128, 153, 171, 175, 183
books: African American education and, 125–28, 131, 134–36, 137, 139–48, 150, 169, 271n19; as secondhand/mediated, 126, 147, 148, 183, 184, 203; settlement house and, 31, 32, 39–40, 47–48, 55
Bourdieu, Pierre, 10, 13–14, 73
bridging (of social gulfs), 13; contact and, 80, 178; costume and, 191; literary method and, 179, 184–85, 244n54, 283n16; reading and, 187, 201, 203, 217
Bruguera, Tania, 230–32, 290n5
business interests, 126, 133, 145, 259n14
busyness, 83–85, 90–91, 95, 98, 216
By Bread Alone (Friedman), 45–46, 50

Cahan, Abraham, 53, 58
Campbell, Helen, 68, 94, 98
capitalism, 5, 15, 96, 233; apartheid, 157; urban-industrial, 5, 9, 188, 223
Carnegie, Andrew, 8, 142, 240n12, 241n16, 252n52
Carnegie Corporation, 7, 153, 240n14
Cate, Laura, 96–97, 118, 263n59
categorization (social), 78, 85–86, 97 123, 194; racial, 40, 271n11. *See also* classification; differentiation; taxonomy
Chance to Live, A (Beckley), 45, 252n56
characterization, 25, 67, 187, 193
Chesnutt, Charles W., 20, 131, 147
Christodora House, 41, 43, 70; journal, 26; Loyalty Club, 38; Poets' Guild and Anthology, 256n91
citizenship, 16, 24, 46, 56, 130, 271n15
civic body, the, 68
civilization, 178, 179; determinism and, 121; the New Negro movement and, 172, 173; racial uplift and, 134–36, 140, 150, 153, 160, 271n11; settlement house and, 42, 56

Civil War, the, 6
class, 72, 83–85, 123, 239n2, 271n15; conflict/antagonism, 77, 84–85, 91; consciousness, 53, 111; disparity, 86, 91–92, 233; -passing narratives, 207, 215, 223, 282n5, 283n16; privilege, 183, 198, 222, 271n11; -related feelings, 17, 245n65
classics, 131, 135, 152, 275n71, 280n131
classification, 96, 99, 263n59. *See also* categorization; differentiation; taxonomy
clothing, 92, 107, 114–15, 163–65, 191–92, 199. *See also* costume; disguise; dress; fashion
Club Worker, 91, 92, 103, 221
Cohen, Rose, 63, 228; *Out of the Shadow,* 31–32, 33
College Settlement, 39, 43, 49, 52
colonial language, 35
"combination," 82, 85
commodification, 19, 75, 107, 165
comparison/comparatism (interpersonal), 85–90, 92, 95, 99–100, 103–4, 114, 123, 178, 180; in *The House of Mirth* (Wharton), 76–77, 99, 101, 107, 110–11, 113, 118, 120, 122–23, 183; invidious, 89–91, 99, 106, 108, 111, 118, 120
composition, 2, 139, 142–43, 149
condescension, 17, 49, 57, 184, 198, 218, 251n41
conformity, 17, 136, 154, 161, 164; anglo-, 36
conservatism, 4, 10, 174; African American education and, 154, 159, 162, 174, 176; settlement workers and, 219; undercover writing and, 211, 218, 224, 232; working girls' clubs and, 80, 81, 85, 88, 101, 123
consumerism/consumption, 13, 75, 92, 210, 262n47
contact (personal), 6, 11–12, 15–17, 19, 146, 229: settlement house and, 36, 41, 46–49, 51, 62, 251n41; undercover literature and, 178, 180–83, 195, 202, 206, 217, 233; working girls' clubs, 75, 86, 88
conversation, 44, 46, 198–200, 223
correlation. *See* dovetailing/correlation
costume, 94, 181, 191, 206. *See also* clothing; disguise; dress
counterpublic, 96, 263n57
Crane, Stephen, 181, 186, 285n27
Crisis, 150, 154, 171, 280n131
Cruikshank, Barbara, 10, 242n31
cultivation, 3, 22, 43, 49, 53, 55, 71; black intellectual, 141, 145, 146
culture, 11, 15, 21–23, 37; reform and, 55; socialization and, 41

dance halls, 29, 37, 42, 80, 85, 92, 93
décor, 43, 45, 159, 163. *See also* domesticity
democracy, 17–18, 36, 48, 62, 177
department stores, 79, 92, 93, 188, 190
dependency, 9, 25, 244n46
depersonalization of outsiders, 100–101
determinism, 98, 101, 121–23, 269n123, 269n127; economic, 93
Dewey, John, 15, 37, 137, 174–75, 178, 273n32

dialect, 116, 194–97, 212. *See also* accent; speech
Dickens, Charles, 45, 93, 262n50
differentiation (social), 85, 104, 109, 184. *See also* categorization; classification; taxonomy
dignity of labor, 132, 140, 146, 213
discipline, 10, 211; black education and, 132, 140, 154; self-, 27, 81, 213, 216–17
discrimination, 86, 197, 271n13
disenfranchisement, 129, 131, 147, 271n13
disguise, 179, 188–89, 191–93, 198, 206, 208; reality TV, 232; of speech, 196. *See also* costume
disobedience, 94
distance, 50, 68, 233; representational, 70, 127–28, 143, 203, 215; as self-protection, 63–64, 69, 95, 178; social, 2, 85, 106, 177, 179, 181–82, 195–96, 202–3, 206, 224, 233
Dodge, Grace Hoadley, 14, 78–79, 82–84, 113–14, 188
domesticity, 43–45, 193, 100, 250n33; domestic comfort, 105, 114; domestic virtues, 40, 83; training, 81, 211. *See also* décor
domestic servants/workers, 78, 257n9, 268n117; exclusion from club membership, 79, 99, 117–18, 258n12; in *The House of Mirth* (Wharton), 84, 95, 101, 114–18; the servant question/problem, 117–18
Donovan, Frances, 193, 219
Douglass, Frederick, 146, 160
dovetailing/correlation, 127–28, 137–52, 156–57, 159, 165, 168, 173–76, 183

downward mobility, 77, 191, 204; in *The House of Mirth* (Wharton), 101, 108, 110–11. *See also* mobility; social mobility; upward mobility
drama, 33, 41–42, 44, 70; Yiddish, 51–52, 58, 70. *See also* theater
Dreiser, Theodore: *Sister Carrie*, 92
dress, 5, 80, 114, 163–64, 197; dress code, 154, 162, 164. *See also* clothing; costume; disguise; fashion
Du Bois, W. E. B.: educational methods/philosophy, 149–51, 154–55, 157, 169, 275n71, 277n93, 280n131; Fisk addresses, 150–51, 153–54, 162, 164; the Harlem Renaissance and, 170–72; proximity and, 13; *Quest of the Silver Fleece*, 280n131; review of *Quicksand* (Larsen), 281n138; *The Souls of Black Folk*, 19, 154, 270n9; Talented Tenth, 129, 270n11; and Booker T. Washington, 16, 126, 128, 272n19

eavesdropping, 198, 199–201, 223
education. *See* African American education; African American educational institutions; dovetailing/correlation; Du Bois, W. E. B.; industrial education; vocational education; vocational realism; Washington, Booker T.
Educational Alliance, 37–38, 46, 52, 70–71, 247n7, 250n29; send-up of, 54
Educational League, the, 52–53, 54, 61
employers, 18, 259n14

English (language), 8, 31, 40, 60, 71, 136, 193; African American use of, 139–40; Jewish press, 39, 54, 72; nonstandard, 194–97
English (studies), 38–39, 71, 145, 249n20; and dovetailing method, 139, 143; 149; and liberal arts, 131, 135, 275n71
environment: as conditions, 16, 69, 136; environmental determinism, 96, 120–22; as explanation for social problems, 28, 65–66, 81; as setting, 42–43, 80–81, 158, 167; transcending, 193
environmentalism, 36–37, 69, 70, 255n88
envy, 17, 87, 92
equality, 135, 152, 271n11
equals (interact as), 111, 180
etiquette, 23–24, 81, 115, 165, 198, 200; guides/manuals, 23, 86, 211, 216, 245n58–59. *See also* manners
evolution/devolution, 120, 129, 134–36, 196, 286n49. *See also* naturalism
exclusion, 86, 98, 101, 118, 127
exemplification (role models), 46, 86–88, 90, 100, 217
exoticism, 163–64, 193
experience, firsthand, 15; in African American education, 16, 126, 147–48; cult of, 178; reading and, 203, 224; remoteness from, 141, 142; undercover writing and, 180, 182–85, 187, 192, 195, 199, 203, 214–15, 224

fallen women, 67, 93, 264n62
Far and Near, 1–3, 26–27, 90–91, 96, 117, 239n3, 259n13

fashion (clothes), 2, 81, 162, 164. *See also* clothing; dress
Fauset, Jessie Redmon, 156, 170
Fawcett, Edgar, 96–97, 98
Fire!!, 174, 281n138
Fisk University, 127, 132–34, 150–57, 161–65, 169, 176; funding, 151; student protests/uprising, 153–54, 156, 165; trustees, 152, 153
Foote, Stephanie, 21, 122, 266n87, 267n99
Foucault, Michel, 10
Friedman, Isaac Kahn: *By Bread Alone*, 45–46, 50
friendly visiting. *See* visiting
friendship (cross-class): 17–20, 85; in *The House of Mirth* (Wharton), 84, 99, 101, 109, 112, 113; in *The Long Day* (Richardson), 208, 209; settlement house, 19, 29, 49; in undercover literature, 196, 198, 199, 221; in working girls' clubs, 1–2, 12, 82, 84–85, 87, 91, 117, 123, 178, 211
friendship (interracial), 145, 259n13
Frissell, H. B., 139–40
Fruit of the Tree, The (Wharton), 101–2, 104, 265n75
"fullness," 11–12

Gandal, Keith, 184, 264n62
Gandhi, Leela, 167
gender, 4, 9, 13, 24, 26; authority and, 188; class and, 83; mixed socializing, 93–94; settlement work and, 38, 51, 247n7; socialization, 45; undercover writing and, 190, 198; ungendering, 115; working girls' clubs and, 77, 80, 83, 87, 90, 106–7

General Education Board, the, 133, 134, 145, 151–53, 157, 276n80, 280n127
generalism (cultural), 38–39, 249n20
gentility, 53, 85, 112; "vernacular —," 81, 259n16
ghetto, the, 25, 35–36, 53–55, 58, 66, 228
Gilded Age reform writing, 68
Gilman, Charlotte Perkins, 20, 48, 186
girl stunt reporters. *See* journalism
Goldman, Emma, 23, 51, 94
Gordin Jacob, 28, 52–54, 72; *The Benefactors of the East Side*, 23–24, 33, 54–58, 60–61, 63, 69
Graffenried, Clare de, 98
gratitude, 9, 17, 50, 65, 261n42
Greenwood, James, 189, 285n27
Griggs, Sutton, 131, 274n63

habitus, 13–14
Hampton Institute, 133–35, 137, 139, 149; funding, 153, 241n16; student uprisings, 155–56
Hapgood, Hutchins, 54, 57–58
Harlem Renaissance, 24, 168–74, 280n128; collective identity, 168; dovetailing/correlation and, 138, 149, 165, 168, 173–74; literary method and, 168, 171–72, 174; student protests, 27, 156, 276n87; white affiliates, 279n127, 281n135. *See also* New Negro movement
Harper and Brothers, 181, 186
Harper's Bazaar, 262n48
Harper's Magazine, 171, 201–2
Hazard of New Fortunes, A (Howell), 19–20

Hebrew Institute, the, 247n7. *See also* Educational Alliance
Henry Street Settlement, the, 31, 52, 63, 248n8, 250n29
hierarchy: class, 19, 84, 89, 90, 194, 218; class and race, 184, 263n57, 271n11; in *House of Mirth* (Wharton), 84, 101, 106, 109, 111; and immigrants, 33, 36; and race, 134, 136
Hirsch, Emil, 66
homogenization, 57, 59
House of Mirth, The (Wharton), 75–78, 80–81, 84, 89, 99–101, 103–23, 183, 257n5, 266n84, 267n102; beauty, 107–8; differentiation/comparison, 76–77, 99, 101, 105–13, 118–20, 122–23, 183; domestic servants (Mrs. Haffen), 84, 95, 101, 114–18, 268n117; friendship, 84, 99, 101, 109, 112, 113; hierarchy, 84, 101, 106, 109, 111; identity/selfhood, 101, 107–11, 114, 120, 261n39; naturalism, 120–22, 268n123; poverty, 75, 76, 183, 267n102; similes, 101, 118–20; Nettie Struther, 105, 112–13, 115, 122
House on Henry Street, The (Wald), 64–65
Howard University, 129, 130, 132–34, 136, 155, 169
Howell, William Dean: *A Hazard of New Fortunes*, 19–20
Howes, Edith M., 82
How the Other Half Lives (Riis), 187, 197, 256n88
Hull-House, 18, 36, 175, 227–28, 247n4; Charlotte Perkins Gilman and, 48; as queer, 18,

243n43; Bessie Van Vorst and, 219
humanitarianism: impulse/consciousness, 184, 203; organizations, 102; politics, 75, 77
Hutchinson, George, 161, 174, 280n128
hypocrisy, 160, 167, 252n56, 285n28

identity: black, 22, 168, 271n15; collective/communal, 42, 62, 168; environment and, 256n88; ethnic, 72; in *The House of Mirth* (Wharton), 101, 107–9, 111, 114, 261n39; Jewish, 62, 63; in *Quicksand* (Larsen), 160, 167, 168; undercover, 199, 205; voice and, 197; white, 248n8
immediate, the (in Jim Crow), 16, 150, 172, 274n63
Immigrant Movement International, 230–31
immigration, 4, 5, 34, 63, 68, 72; restriction, 69
imperialism: anti-imperialist friendship, 167; politics of, 100; rhetoric of, 35
indigent populations (in undercover literature), 190
individualism, 14, 28, 81, 84, 167, 261n37; as social reform, 82, 88, 99, 224
individuation, 95, 99, 110–12, 118
industrial education, 16, 127, 131, 133, 137, 144, 172. *See also* vocational education
industrialization, 5, 13, 17, 22, 93, 117
inequality: between beneficiary groups, 8; class/social, 49, 75–76, 100, 108, 119, 199, 220; race-based, 16, 129–30, 156–57, 270n6; of reformist friendship, 3, 8, 85, 254n68; urban, 35, 66; writing about, 3, 18, 24, 183
influence, 14, 34, 43, 73, 89; pedagogy of, 37, 41, 46, 50, 63
"institution(s)," 9–11, 241n18
investigative journalism. *See* journalism

Jackson, Shannon, 41, 43
James, Henry, 3, 52; "The Art of Fiction," 97; *Princess Casamassima,* 19
James, William, 20, 22, 178, 273
Jane Addams Hull-House Museum, 227–29
Jarrett, Gene Andrew, 131, 156
Jeanes Foundation, the, 133, 152
Jewish immigrants, 24, 36, 52, 54, 59, 66
Jewishness, 59–60
Jewish philanthropists, 18, 25, 57–59, 62
Jewish representation/public image, 56, 58, 61–65, 68–69; identity conflict and, 62–64
Jewish settlement: Christianity and, 40; culture, 18, 29, 42; self-preservation and, 36, 61–62; writing, 59, 63, 69
Jews, American/assimilated: 18, 42, 56, 62–63, 65, 69
Jim Crow: conventions of, 40; education and employment, 125, 130, 140, 157; education for present conditions of, 128, 135, 138, 145, 160, 175–76, 178; expression

and, 22, 164; identity and, 168; the immediate, 15–16; uplift and, 129, 167
Johnson, Charles S., 155, 170, 173
Johnson, James Weldon, 169–70, 171
Johnson, Kimberley, 129–30
Jones, Gavin, 195, 267n102
Jones, Mary "Minnie" Cadwalader, 88, 103–4
Jones, Mrs. Frederick Rhinelander, 265n81
journalism, 45–46; investigative, 179, 188, 189; photo-, 255n88; Dorothy Richardson (pseud. Adams), 204, 207; stunt, 189, 285n29; undercover, 285n28
journals, 26–27, 40, 69, 81, 90–92, 96–97, 209, 229. *See also* periodicals
Judaism, 55, 56, 62, 63
justice. *See* social justice

Kaplan, Amy, 106, 114–15, 261n39
knowledge, 47, 52, 142, 147, 199; firsthand, 184, 194, 203, 214, 215; social, 29, 121, 177, 183–84, 233

labor, 51, 83–84, 91, 220; activism/agitation, 50, 54, 209, 219; conditions/issues, 5, 35, 81, 85, 180, 193–94, 202, 220; critique, 223; culture and, 6; in *The House of Mirth* (Wharton), 101, 105, 110, 115–18; industrial, 24, 180, 183, 210; in *The Long Day* (Richardson), 214–17; morality and, 98; reading as, 216, 217; reform, 12; slave, 143; studies, 181; undercover, 181, 186–87, 193, 203–4, 214, 232–33; women's waged, 27, 83, 91. *See also* manual labor; unions; work
labor fiction, 187, 285n22
labor force (female), 5, 78–80, 94
Lamarck, Jean-Baptiste, 121
Lamarckian evolution. *See* evolution/devolution
language, 119; assimilation and, 8, 35; Jim Crow and, 140, 143, 153; marginalized, 182; undercover literature and, 193–97
Larsen, Nella, 13, 28, 161–63, 168, 174, 279n121, 281n138; *Quicksand*, 17, 128, 153, 157–68, 174, 175, 278n11, 280n127
leisure, 43, 47, 71; constructive, 81; reading as, 216
Levine, Caroline, 9, 12, 100
Libbey, Laura Jean, 211–12, 213, 214, 288n83
liberal arts, the, 71, 141. *See also* African American education
libraries, 15, 216; African American education, 132, 142, 146, 154; People's Library, the, 229–30; public, 7, 8, 142, 168, 273n44; settlement, 26, 35, 37, 39–40, 55; working girls' club, 81
Listener in Babel, A, (Scudder), 48–49
literacy, 26, 182, 230; black, 136, 137, 140, 142–44, 146, 148–49, 272n21, 274n63; settlement house and, 38, 44; working-class, 211
literary authority, 72, 184–85, 207
literary clubs and societies, 4, 26, 38, 40–41, 47, 70, 127
literary criticism, 97, 132, 186; labor critique and, 223

literary form: reform and, 9, 63, 73, 182; undercover writing and, 179–80, 184, 196, 201, 216; vocational realism and, 149
literary value, 23, 28; African American education and, 127–28, 149; the settlement house and, 32, 37, 45–46, 72–73; undercover writing and, 183
Little Women (Alcott), 31, 211–12
locality/the local, 125–26, 143, 172, 192, 195
Locke, Alain, 155, 170, 172, 281n135
Lockwood, Florence, 88, 89, 103
London, Jack, 181, 186, 190, 220; *People of the Abyss*, 51, 285n27
Long Day, The (Richardson), 28, 186, 194, 196, 203–22, 224–25, 284n19, 287n67; class-passing in, 206, 207–8; friendship in, 208, 209; language/speech in, 194, 196, 205–6, 222; racial difference in, 209, 217; reading in, 208–18, 224–25; reception of, 220–22, 289n100

machine metaphors, 17, 158, 169, 203, 217
MacLean, Annie Marion, 188, 193, 218, 285n29
magazines, 23, 27, 92, 186, 215
manners, 2, 23, 41, 79, 85, 87–88, 160; novel of, 23, 245n59. *See also* etiquette; gentility
manual labor: African American workforce and, 24, 133, 135; art/representation and, 173; domestic, 115, 118; literature and (vocational realism), 9, 24, 28, 127–28, 132–33, 137, 139–40, 146, 150, 159; undercover writing and, 186–87, 193, 204, 232–31
marriage, 4, 102, 108, 165, 212–13
massification, 63, 104, 110–12, 118, 159–60, 194; language of masses, 109; mass culture, 72; mass production, 17
Mayer, Hattie. *See* Yezierska, Anzia
McGurl, Mark, 9–10, 106, 175, 278n111
McKay, Claude, 17, 169
McKenzie, Fayette, 153, 154
McMillan, Tracie: *The American Way of Eating*, 232
memoir(s), 13, 32, 70. *See also* autobiography
Meyer, Annie Nathan: *Black Souls*, 279n127
Miller, Kelly, 130, 136–37, 169–70, 175, 275n67
minstrel shows, 40, 42
missionaries, 35, 132–33, 150, 270n11
mobility, 101, 109, 136, 139, 183. *See also* downward mobility; social mobility; upward mobility
modernism, 28, 72–73, 174, 197, 223, 239n5
modernity, 9, 15, 17, 77, 155, 174–77; Afro-modernity, 127–28, 154–56
Moore, Helen, 39–40
morality, 40, 81, 104, 193, 244n46; women's, 77, 80, 85–86, 99, 121
moralizing, 22, 66, 94, 194
Morehouse, Henry, 130, 270n11
mouthpiece (for working women), 181–82, 197
Murolo, Priscilla, 79, 258n12, 259n16

INDEX 301

National Association for the Advancement of Colored People (NAACP), 7, 154, 171, 282n8
National League of Women Workers, 221, 259n16. *See also* Association of Working Girls' Societies
Native American rights, 79
Native American students, 259n13
naturalism, 28, 66; *The House of Mirth* (Wharton) and, 120–22, 268n123; *The Long Day* (Richardson) and, 220. *See also* evolution/devolution
neurasthenia, 47–48, 179
New Negro, 169, 172
New Negro movement: college protests, 127–28, 154–56, 165, 168, 174, 176, 276n87; politics, 153, 174; Renaissance, 155, 161, 170, 172, 173; selfhood and, 155. *See also* Harlem Renaissance
newspapers, 69, 148, 189, 262n48, 283n16
nostalgia, 228–29
novel, the, 19–21, 23, 24

Oberlin College, 132, 144
objectification, 19, 93, 164
observation, 93, 106, 178, 192, 287n53; participant, 188
Occupy Wall Street, 229–30
optimism, 35, 121
O'Reilly, Leonora, 221–23, 289n101
Out of the Shadow (Cohen), 31–32, 33

Park, Connie. *See* Parker, Cornelia Stratton
Parker, Cornelia Stratton, 12, 180–83, 185–86, 188, 191–94, 196, 199–202, 205, 218; *Working with the Working Woman* (Parker), 181, 182, 201
parlor, the, 43–44, 49, 68, 112, 174, 220
participation (civic), 152, 172, 263n57
patronage, 18, 49, 129, 170, 251n41
pedagogy of influence. *See* influence
People of the Abyss (London), 51, 285n27
periodicals, 4, 11, 26–27, 56; settlement house, 61–62; and undercover writing, 186; and uplift, 131, 170; working girls' club, 1–2, 90–91, 127. *See also* journals; magazines
periodization, 19, 28
personhood, 68, 83
Pestalozzi, Johann, 175, 273n32
Phelps-Stokes Fund, the, 7, 133, 276n82
philanthropic foundations, 7–8, 133, 157, 272n28, 280n127
philanthropy: corporate, 6, 7, 143, 284n20; industrial, 134, 144
Phillips, J. H., 16, 276n80
photography (documentary), 187, 255n88
Pittenger, Mark, 188, 282n5, 284n19
pleasure, 37, 76, 89, 106, 200; of literature, 33, 39, 73, 139, 211
poverty, 51, 244n46; the black community and, 136, 160; in *The House of Mirth* (Wharton), 75, 76, 183, 267n102; the Jewish community and, 31, 58, 59, 60, 65; in

A Listener in Babel (Scudder), 48; in *The Long Day* (Richardson), 203–4, 206, 215, 225
pragmatism, 15, 17, 175, 178, 211, 220
prescriptive literature, 23, 83, 211, 216
print: circulation of, 27; culture, 2, 77, 93, 186; instrumentality of, 203; public sphere, 25, 95; venues, 69
privacy: of the lower class, 187, 200–202; of the wealthy, 80
profanity, 193, 223
professionalization, 4, 6, 19, 91; of literature, 71–72, 239n5
Progressivism, 5–6, 10, 18, 59, 65, 82, 123, 240n13, 251n41; Progressive reform writing, 64, 67–70
prostitution, 5, 94, 263n51; prostitutes, 67, 94, 205
Protestantism, 20, 36, 61, 216, 220; Protestants, 18, 80, 258n11
public health, 5, 64, 232
publicness, 25
public perception/opinion, 25, 85, 95, 98
publishers, 90, 186, 205, 239n5
publishing, 11, 24, 73, 171, 186, 284n20

queer/same-sex sociality, 18, 19, 243n43, 278n111
Quicksand (Larsen), 17, 128, 153, 157–68, 174, 175, 280n127, 281n138; aesthetics/expression, 162–64, 166, 174, 278n11; correlation, 157, 159, 165; critique of educational methods, 158–59, 167; mechanical metaphors, 17, 158, 159; New Negro politics, 153, 165, 174; racial uplift, 157, 160, 165, 166–67

"race feeling," 134
racial difference/divides, 57, 181, 209
racial pride, 148, 163
racial time, 127, 155–56, 270n6
racism, 68, 85, 157, 164, 167, 173, 197, 279n127; reform and, 40, 56, 99, 276n87; working around/against, 133, 136, 145–46, 173–74, 230. *See also* white supremacy
radicalism, 35, 49, 81, 239n2, 259n14; Jewish, 60, 62; radical texts, 52, 154; reform and, 6, 10, 102
readers, 26, 63, 67, 97, 180, 215, 230, 233; black, 135, 148; of black writers, 170, 172; immigrant, 26, 40; middle-class, 202–3, 210, 215, 218, 224; model, 208, 210; of undercover literature, 184, 187, 201–3, 212, 214, 217–20, 224–25; unintended, 98; white, 135, 170, 203, 217; women, 2, 212; working-class, 27, 40, 202, 210, 212–14, 218, 222, 288n83
reading for reform, 24, 26, 184, 203, 213, 217–18, 224–25
reading manuals, 23, 211, 216, 288n81
realism, 28, 53–54, 58, 60–61, 66, 97–98; moral, 256n88; realist syndrome, 69–70; undercover writing and, 192–93, 195, 197, 212, 220, 223; vocational and literary, 148
reality television, 234. See also *Undercover Boss*

Reconstruction, 5, 127, 129, 130, 156
redemption, 49, 214, 223
religion, 48, 61, 65, 167–68, 240n9. *See also* Judaism; Protestantism
reportage, 58, 214, 285n29. *See also* journalism
representation, 25, 67, 100, 172–73, 179, 203, 209–10; distance from experience/reality, 70, 143, 209, 214, 224; Jewish, 61; misrepresentation, 96–98; political, 131, 172; racial uplift and, 130–31; self-protective, 63, 69; theory of, 98, 149; of white women workers, 92, 96–97, 209, 223
resentment, 18, 157, 161, 91, 202
respectability, 45, 80, 98, 259n16
Richardson, Dorothy, 3, 28, 188, 196, 208, 220, 224–25, 288n70; as Dorothy Adams (pseud.), 204–5; authenticity, 208; *The Long Day*, 28, 186, 194, 196, 203–22, 224–25, 284n19, 287n67, 289n100
Riis, Jacob, 58, 68, 201, 255n88; *How the Other Half Lives*, 187, 197, 256n88
Robbins, Bruce, 14, 17, 100
role models. *See* exemplification
Rubin, Joan Shelley, 41, 256n94
Ruskin, John, 22, 51, 224
Russian (language), 52, 53, 253n62
Ryan, Susan M., 6, 61

Salome of the Tenements (Yezierska), 59–60, 251n38
same-sex intimacy, 19. *See also* queer/same-sex sociality
Schiff, Jacob, 18, 55, 56, 61, 63

Schuyler, George, 171, 279n127
Scudder, Vida, 12, 49, 247n4; *A Listener in Babel*, 48–49
secularism, 6, 31, 52–53, 63, 79, 247n7
segregation, 35, 99, 144, 157, 248n8, 259n13
self-construction/making/fashioning, 14, 25, 106, 108, 114, 197
self-determination, 9, 146, 148, 155
self-expression, 2, 73, 154, 155, 162–64, 172, 175
self-help, 82, 129–30, 148, 248n8, 271n14
selfhood, 15, 106, 108, 111, 113, 119–20, 155, 282n3
self-improvement, 6, 23, 82–83, 86–88, 100, 213, 216
self-preservation/protection (Jewish), 36, 61–63, 66, 69
self-reform, 81–82, 210, 224
sensationalism, 53, 189, 205, 213–14, 222–23
sentimentalism, 21, 28, 33, 66–68, 97, 100, 193, 209–10
servants. *See* domestic servants/workers
settlement house movement, the, 4, 7–9, 18, 31–73, 80, 127, 228; criticism of, 23, 219; literacy, 12, 26; queerness and, 19; social distance/proximity, 12, 15, 177–78, 181
sexual favors, 92, 105, 108
sexuality (of women), 68, 93–94, 98, 161, 213
sexual vulnerability (of women), 86, 93
sex work, 94. *See also* prostitution

Shakespeare, 8, 16, 31, 38, 45; as a bore, 224
shame, 31, 33, 63, 87, 147
Singley, Carol, 106-7, 267n89, 269n123
Sister Carrie (Dreiser), 92
slang, 85, 118, 193-94, 196, 223
Slater Fund, the, 133, 151, 153, 280n127
slavery, 131, 146
slum fiction, 58, 62, 97, 264n62
social control, 22, 35, 139, 184, 245n57
social disorder/crisis/breakdown, 184, 187, 244n53
social investigation/investigators, 180, 188-89, 203
social justice, 85, 171, 184, 219, 228, 230
social mobility, 14, 123, 136, 229; in *The Long Day* (Richardson), 213, 225; personal qualities and, 84, 90; phobia of, 94
social policies, 25, 35
social science, 4, 176, 179-80, 189, 256n88; departments of, 34, 155
social service(s), 19, 139, 227, 230-31, 241n18
social work, 26, 66, 69, 84, 197-98, 228, 244n46; of literature, 24, 43, 211, 216; social workers, 34, 50, 66, 69
sociology, 97, 188, 282n1; the sociological novel, 187
"solidarity of life," 113, 114
Souls of Black Folk, The (Du Bois), 19, 154, 270n9
space/spaciality, 11-13, 44, 37, 135, 184, 196, 229; private, 35, 163; public, 35, 80; settlement house, 37, 43-46, 73; urban/working-class, 35, 36, 121, 180, 229, 265n75; working girls' club, 80, 111, 114-15, 221
specialists, 39, 249n20
speech: defects, 196; and literary representation, 98; refined/refining, 2, 37, 40, 41, 84, 87, 116, 205; working-class vernacular, 193-97, 202, 206. *See also* accent; dialect; language; slang; vernacular
Spirit of the Ghetto, The (Hapgood), 57-58
Stansell, Christine, 251n41
Stokes, Rose Pastor/Phelps, 85, 220
Stowe, Harriet Beecher: *Uncle Tom's Cabin,* 21, 225, 275n67
structural problems, 48, 90, 219, 224
structural reform/change, 5-6, 18, 81, 85, 88, 102
student protests. *See under* New Negro movement
surveillance, 10, 200-201

Talented Tenth, the, 129, 174, 270n11
Tanner, Amy, 188, 218-19
taste, 14, 22-23, 39, 85, 163, 209, 211, 225
taxonomy (social), 77-78, 118, 263n59. *See also* categorization; classification; differentiation
Taylor, Charles, 11
temperance movement, the, 5, 7, 21, 79, 266n84
Tenement Museum, the, 228-29
theater, 41, 52, 250n29; Yiddish, 13, 37, 52-54, 58. *See also* drama

Theory of the Leisure Class, The (Veblen), 8, 51, 89–90, 261n42
Thirty-Eighth Street Working Girls' Society, the, 79, 83
Thurman, Wallace, 174
Tocqueville, Alexis de, 5
Toynbee Hall, 34, 246n4
trade unions. *See* unions
translators (of the poor), 181–82, 184, 195–97, 203, 225
Trask, Michael, 94
treating, 92. *See also* sexual favors
trustees, 7, 52, 144, 152–54,
Tuskegee Institute, 126, 133, 169; educational methods (vocational realism/dovetailing), 16, 126–27, 137–40, 142–46, 176; funding, 8, 133–34, 144, 146, 153, 241n16; Nella Larsen at, 162–63; library, 8, 142; Little Tuskegees, 133, 153, 272n28; model, 151, 219, 273n32; racial uplift and, 129; student uprisings, 155; "Tuskegee machine," 17

ugliness, 76, 164, 165
Uncle Tom's Cabin (Stowe), 21, 225, 275n67
Undercover Boss, 232–34
undercover writing/literature, 9, 12–13, 23, 25, 27–28, 51, 127, 177–225, 227, 232
unions, 7, 57, 81, 102, 188, 219–22, 232, 259n16; WTUL, 218, 222
University Settlement, 39, 50, 52, 58, 247n4
unworthy poor, the, 244n46, 260n31. *See also* worthy poor
Up from Slavery (Washington), 16, 26, 146, 149, 217, 274n67
upward mobility, 9, 14, 35–36, 83, 117, 160, 204; in *The House of Mirth* (Wharton), 101, 105, 122; in *The Long Day* (Richardson), 213, 216; marriage and, 212; reading and, 142. *See also* downward mobility; mobility; social mobility
urban-industrial life/conditions, 177, 180, 187, 188, 223
urbanization, 5, 13, 22, 197
urban space, 35, 36–37, 64–65, 121, 229, 265n75
U.S. Bureau of Education, 136, 276n82
utilitarianism, 22, 23, 218
utility (social — of literature), 5, 23, 28, 73, 214, 230; black education and, 22, 126–28, 148, 274n67; the Harlem Renaissance and, 169, 172, 174, 281n135; undercover writing and, 203, 217

Van Vorst, Bessie, 182, 186, 191, 196, 198; reform activity, 188, 219; *The Woman Who Toils*, 182, 199–201, 284n21
Van Vorst, Marie, 181, 186, 191, 196; characterization, 193, 195; reform activity, 188, 219; *The Woman Who Toils*, 182, 199, 284n21
Veblen, Thorstein, 180; *The Theory of the Leisure Class*, 8, 51, 89–90, 261n42
verisimilitude, 53, 97
vernacular, 85, 111, 143, 194–95, 202, 223; vernacular gentility, 81, 259n16
victimization (of working women), 93–94, 96, 121–22

violence, 10, 85, 100, 161, 209, 244n53; police, 230; racial, 279n127
virtue, 92, 104; domestic, 40, 83
visiting (charitable/friendly), 17, 86, 110, 201, 244n46, 260n31
vocational education (black), 132, 149–50, 171, 175, 273n32, 276n82. *See also* dovetailing/correlation
vocational realism, 127–28, 130, 141, 143, 146, 148–50, 153, 155–56, 176, 211
voice, 90, 131, 197, 223

Wald, Lillian, 61, 63–70, 188, 228, 248n12; *The House on Henry Street*, 64–65
Warner, Michael, 25, 71, 96, 263n57
Warren, Kenneth W., 22, 131, 193
Washington, Booker T., 14, 271n13, 273n44, 275n67, 275n69, 276n82; Atlanta Compromise/Cotton States address, 125, 132, 143, 146; educational philosophy (dovetailing/correlation/vocational realism), 127–30, 132, 133, 137–49, 174–75, 183; literature and books, role of, 16, 125–26, 137, 139, 141, 146–48, 274n67; *My Larger Education*, 147; the New Negro and Harlem Renaissance movement, 155–56, 172–75; Dorothy Richardson and, 183, 211, 217–18; style, 126; *Up from Slavery*, 16, 26, 146, 149, 217, 274n67; and white patronage, 16, 129, 133, 144, 152
wealthy women, 80, 90, 222
welfare work, 20, 85, 160, 265n77

Wexler, Laura, 98, 100, 224
Wharton, Edith, 13, 75, 85–86, 103, 121, 183; *The Fruit of the Tree*, 101–2, 104, 265n75; *The House of Mirth*, 75–78, 80–81, 84, 89, 95, 99–101, 103–23, 183; "The Pelican," 266n82; politics, 257n6; and social dynamics, 266n84; war charities, 102–3, 104; war writing/fundraising, 265n77; "Xingu," 266n82
white supremacy, 17, 128, 130, 133, 144, 152, 157; challenges to, 129, 155; racial uplift and, 128, 157. *See also* racism
Wilberforce University, 155, 169
Wildman, Edwin, 113–14
will to empower, the, 10
Wilmington massacre, 134
"Woes of the New York Working Girl, The" (Fawcett), 96–97
womanhood, 68, 82, 84, 115; models of, 86–97; white, 86, 95; working, 97, 99, 209
Woman Who Toils, The (Van Vorst and Van Vorst), 182, 199–201, 284n21
Women's Municipal League, 188, 220
Women's Trade Union League, 218, 222
work, 173, 220. *See also* labor
Work (Alcott), 93, 287n67
work ethic, 98, 216, 220
working class, the, 4, 46, 199, 201–2, 211
working girl problem, the, 75, 77, 86, 93, 95, 96, 98–99, 121
working girls, 79. *See also* working/working-class women

working girls' clubs, 1–2, 9, 12, 25, 75–123, 221, 227, 2246n65
Working with the Hands (Washington), 125–26, 140–41, 142, 162
Working with the Working Woman (Parker), 181, 182, 201
working/working-class women: African American, 78, 99, 118; categories of, 86, 95, 97, 99; as commodity, 223; comparison and, 90, 92; determinism and, 98, 121–22; immigrant, 99; morality and, 77, 99, 121; portrayal in print, 93, 96–98, 204, 209–10; readers, 212–13, 218, 288n83; stories of, 95, 200; voices of, 90, 262n48; white, 9, 77, 78, 85, 86, 100, 217; working girls' clubs and, 80, 87, 88, 91, 93, 122, 221
worthy poor, the, 5, 260n31. *See also* unworthy poor, the
writing, 24, 182, 185
Wyckoff, Walter, 183, 190, 285n27

Yezierska, Anzia, 13, 28, 50, 59–60, 72; "How I Found America," 254n69; *Hungry Hearts,* 59; *Salome of the Tenements,* 59–60, 251n38
Yiddish (language), 52, 62
Yiddish drama/theater, 13, 33, 37, 51–54, 58, 70
YMCA/YWCA, 7, 78–79, 166, 258n11, 271n14

Laura R. Fisher is associate professor of English at Ryerson University.

CPSIA information can be obtained
at www.ICGtesting.com
Printed in the USA
BVHW042237020519
547248BV00007B/40/P